C000054097

NONF

# Ghosts

## REALITY BEYOND BELIEF

INTERNATIONAL EDITION

**Also available as 'More Ghosts of St Andrews'**

A wealth of previously unpublished paranormal experiences
**134 New Haunted Locations** (200 total)
**262 New Ghosts** (over 300 in total)
**317 New Recorded Experiences**
(418 total + over 1000 at the Haunted Tower alone)

RICHARD FALCONER

**1st Edition 2021**

Published in association with

*St Andrews Ghost Tours*

# *Ghosts*

Copyright © 2021 Richard Falconer
First published 2021 by Obsidian Publishing

All rights reserved. No part of this book may be reproduced, utilised in any form or by any means, electronic, mechanical, photocopying or recording by any information or retrieval system, without the prior permission in writing from Obsidian Publishing.

The moral rights of the author have been asserted.
A catalogue record for this book is available from the British Library.

978-0-9927538-7-0

Cover design, content layout, formatting/non-sourced photographs by Richard Falconer

Back cover photo and photo on p.21 courtesy of D. C. Thomson & Co. Ltd, Dundee.
Photos p.146, p.574, published with permission of Historic Scotland, Edinburgh.
Photo from the Star Hotel, 1921, p.265, reproduced courtesy of the St Andrews Preservation Trust
Photos on p.546 to p.548 courtesy of Marysia Denyer.
All other photos credited throughout where appropriate and my grateful thanks for all submissions.

www.obsidianpublishing.com
enquiries@obsidianpublishing.co.uk

## Also available by Richard Falconer

Nonfiction / Paranormal / Educational

***More* Ghosts of St Andrews** (2021)

*Localised version of Ghosts*

Nonfiction / Paranormal / Educational

**Ghosts of St Andrews** (2013)

*Incorporating 65 St Andrews locations*

Nonfiction / Paranormal / Educational

**St Andrews Haunted Tower** UPDATED 2021

**(formerly A St Andrews Mystery, 2015)**

*An Investigation into the Chamber of Corpses and the White Lady Apparitions of St Andrews*

Nonfiction / Paranormal / Educational

**Ghosts of Fife** (2013)

The only book devoted to the paranormal in Fife

*Incorporating over 80 places throughout the Kingdom*

Fiction / Paranormal

**St Andrews Ghost Stories** (2021)

*William Thomas Linskill*

*Original 1911 version with extensive annotations*

## Coming soon

Nonfiction / Paranormal / Educational

**Pocket Guide to St Andrews Ghosts**

*A small compendium of 200 haunted locations*

Nonfiction / Local History / Educational

**History of St Andrews**

Focusing on the 6th to 17th Centuries AD

# A note from the author

The deeply historic and unique Scottish town of St Andrews is more than the home of golf, it is also the home of ghosts. Following initial experiences of myself and others in the 1970s, I began looking to find the extent in both St Andrews and Scotland, which then developed into international research to ascertain the true extent. This was for my own curiosity at the time. On a local level my research included the gathering of information from residents in St Andrews beginning in the 70s. Letter requests for information from the 1980s to present through local, national and especially the international press. I conducted lengthy research through the National Library for Scotland in Edinburgh, the University of St Andrews, and the David Hay Fleming Library (when it existed). I scoured most of the tomes in this Victorian historian's collection written about St Andrews and Scotland over the centuries to find the recorded historical extent. This amounts to approximately 13,000 books and manuscripts to date, including his personal notes in the margins of historical information he found out since their publication. I went through all the newspapers spanning back to their first publication (18th-19$^{th}$c. to current), plus many face to face interviews.

Since the publication of my initial books, many more have come forward with their experiences, either in person or via email. With shared commonalities through paranormal experience I found St Andrews is a direct microcosm of global phenomena.

In 2014, I created *St Andrews Ghost Tours* based on the volume of information gathered over the decades. These are educational nonfictional tours beyond contrivance or sensationalism that partly led to the publication of this volume. I have witnessed well over 1000 aspects of paranormal behaviour with a great many experiences having occurred on tours over the last 7 years to 2021.

My involvement also extends through many magical/esoteric organisations as a spiritual mystic. With insight through interaction I understand the deeply rooted mechanics of reality operating beyond the veil of the physical where the laws governing phenomena reside and with this I educate mediums to a deeper spiritual understanding.

# *The Complete Record of Haunted Locations in St Andrews, Scotland*

"A lot of people don't understand when you tell them you have seen things like a ghostly figure or heard weird sounds. People just laughed at me before when I was telling them. Thundering carriage wheels passing, and the ghostly figure of Archbishop Sharpe, but as I have said to myself over the years from childhood to the present day, I know I see things and I do believe that only certain people are able to see and hear things that others can't."

**Ronnie Howe, St Andrews**

Contrary to the gradual conditioning of the West since the 17th century, Ronnie was right, but like everyone else he was unaware of the extent.

St Andrews for its *size* is the most haunted location in the world. Consider this volume as the qualification for this statement, and if you are looking for 'proof' you will find the testament of it here in eye opening abundance.

**Richard Falconer, St Andrews**

The following list covers fifteen pages of phenomena I have recorded through my three nonfiction books for St Andrews, commencing with this present volume:

# *Testimony*

## *Ghosts* (G)

**Table of Contents**

## *Testimony*

# *Ghosts*

# *Ghosts*

## *Testimony*

# *Ghosts*

# *Ghosts*

# *Testimony*

## *Ghosts of St Andrews* (GOS)

Page numbers are for GOS

## *Ghosts*

## Haunted Tower (HT) Formerly: *A St Andrews Mystery* (STAM)

# *Ghosts*

**Apparitions along the East Scores Path and Castle**

18 White Lady East Scores Path
19 White Lady cliff side between the castle and turret
20 White Lady East Scores path above St Rules Cave
21 White Lady Shoreline by St Rules Cave towards Castle
22 White Lady Scores path above St Rules Cave
23 White Lady Courtyard of St Andrews Castle

**Two Apparitions along Kirk Hill**

26 Apparition between harbour turret & Haunted Tower
27 Green Lady on Kirkheugh or Kirk Hill

**White Lady Apparitions of the Pends**

28 White Lady Mill Port to the Pends
29 White Lady Pends Lane inside the Mill Port
30 White Lady on top of Hepburn's Wall by Haunted Tower
31 White Lady on the wall by the top of the Pends
32 White Lady by the 'Eye of the Needle' of the Pends entrance

**The Colourful Apparitions of Queen Mary's House**

Witnessed in different rooms and private garden

33 White Lady, Queen Mary's House
35 Green Lady, Queen Mary's House
36 Blue Lady, Queen Mary's House
37 Purple Lady, Queen Mary's House
38 Black Lady, Queen Mary's House

# *Preface*

Published as ***Ghosts*** – *Reality Beyond Belief*, for the international audience, the local title is ***More Ghosts of St Andrews*** (MGOS), as the sister volume to *Ghosts of St Andrews* (2013).

**Barnardo's charity book launch, St Andrews, 2013**[1]

This volume has more of the mechanics of phenomena, while MGOS has more detailed localised background history. The mechanics of this global phenomena is explained through experience, insight and understanding. It is all illustrated here through hundreds of testimonial experiences taking place in St Andrews over the years as examples for its universal nature. No theories, no speculation, nothing is alleged or purported and no myths, just plain facts. Extensively cross-referenced with all my books, this is also the most complete single volume of study and published record there has been for any location of a comparable size.

A lot has happened since *Ghosts of St Andrews* (2013), *Ghosts of Fife* (2013), and *A St Andrews Mystery* (2015) were published. My 2013 publications were the most complete list of haunted locations there has been for St Andrews and Fife. *Ghosts of St Andrews* was and still is an eye-opener for St Andrews, and has been a local bestseller since publication. With the addition of this current volume, believe me, there is nowhere to hide!

References where appropriate for experiences published in my other nonfiction books are abbreviated as follows:

| | |
|---|---|
| **GOS** | *Ghosts of St Andrews,* 2013 |
| **GOF** | *Ghosts of Fife,* 2013 |
| **STAM** | *A St Andrews Mystery,* 2015 (now updated for 2021 as HT) |
| **HT** | *St Andrews Haunted Tower,* 2021 |
| **(G)** | *Ghosts* 2021 (current volume) |
| **HoS** | *History of St Andrews* (2022) |

In 2014, I created *St Andrews Ghost Tours,* initially based on my research and experiences spanning five decades at that time as published in GOS. Always kept current, these are nonfiction educational paranormal tours with no theatrics, contrivance, scares or fictional stories. Conducted by myself they are now one of only four walking tours in Scotland with five stars through the Scottish Tourist Board and are considered by many as one of the most unique 'must do' ghost tours in the world.

This volume includes a great many experiences from these tours spanning 2014 to 2021. I have also included contextual reports of St Andrews most famous and prolific ghost the 'White Lady' from STAM (HT) along with all the paranormal material I gathered for St Andrews between 2013 and 2021, plus inclusions from GOS where appropriate including many updates. I recommend the other volumes as they contain a vast amount of experiential material not featured here. Most of the accounts in this volume are recent, they are still taking place and are presented here for the first time alongside explanations of paranormal behaviour and type, leading to the recognition of set patterns none were unaware of.

Experience is generally looked at in isolation, and any physical explanation or potential for a physical replication is given in the abstract. Essentially, the paranormal is a breeding ground for western preconceived ideas and assumptions, regardless of, or to the negation of any surrounding circumstantial evidence. It is also typically determined to the negation of previous anomalies occurring independently in the same location. If these were included a conclusion may be ascertained with a more educated base away from speculative arbitrary preconceptions. This is an additional complex area of involvement where patterns are formed to give further insight into both the nature of phenomena and its inextricable link with the psychology of determination. Indeed, the gamut of psychology for those experiencing phenomena, and equally those looking to determine the same carry no little importance. The mechanics of both are also recorded throughout, and with all this in mind I have devised two reference checklists:

**CAI** – Categories for Anomalous Images
**PERL** – Paranormal Experience Reference List

By analysing the background information of experiences (where known), further important insights may be gleaned into their nature that will more often otherwise be missed.

**CAI** is for determining additional information for a photographic image displaying anomalies. This reference list will be found as part of the introduction to **Photos** on p.517.

**PERL** is for determining additional information from experiential phenomena. It will be found as **Appendix 1** (p.579) and is worth a peak to give an idea of the level of paranormal involvement to be found throughout.

PERL can also be used in conjunction with CAI when background details of a photo are known.

# INTRODUCTION
# *Reality Beyond Belief*

There are many books about ghosts as a subject, from fictional stories to A to Z anthologies of haunted locations.

I received an email from a travel writer. She has several books under her belt on a host of random subjects, but nothing on the paranormal. So, her publisher thought it a good idea if she wrote one about the paranormal in Scotland. She contacted me for any information I could give her about the paranormal in St Andrews, so I sent a brief reply inviting her to come on one of my tours. At that point I had two nonfiction books on the subject for St Andrews and one for Fife, a tour would give her material for her book and serve as a good grounding for the extent of the paranormal here. She replied that she was based in England and had no plans to come to Scotland. This was well before Covid. I found this quite incredulous. All she was doing was emailing anyone she thought might have information she could use, like ghost tours, and write her book without leaving the comforts of her computer chair. This kind of armchair research really annoys me. I have no doubt anyone reading whatever she ends up churning out will deem her an 'authority' on the subject, otherwise why would any buy her book.

The fact she calls herself a 'travel writer' would have put the cherry on the cake – had there been one. A travel writer with a debatable knowledge of the paranormal, who won't come to Scotland to conduct any research about the place she is being commissioned to write about… I think you get the picture.

I have always found it difficult and frustrating to read anything written by those who don't know what they are writing about. Unfortunately, most of the books on the paranormal fall into this genre. There is the odd book on the paranormal which is refreshing, but the majority are writing about a subject they have never experienced, so they follow the same old stereotypical 'spooky story' line with a vocabulary to match, serving no other purpose than to feed our naivety regarding the subject. It sums up the way the industry has been for many years, and why there is so much rehashed pulp in our stores. Maybe that is what sells, maybe that is what people want, but it does nothing to further our understanding for what you will find is a very complex subject. If that is what you are looking for, prepare to be disappointed, I have no desire to follow this age-old pattern.

I have on my ghost tours website that my tours are 'nonfiction, educational tours with no theatrics or contrivance and my only 'jumper ooters' are the real ones.' I also don't try to scare anybody and I have no fictional stories. Collectively, these admissions usually keep those looking for 'spooky entertainment' at bay and I have taken over 40,000 people on tours, but I do get the odd one slipping through the net. Usually they see the words 'Ghost Tour' and don't bother reading what it actually involves. They just assume my tours will follow the same stereotypical formula of fictional entertainment to be found strewn across most towns and cities around the world through a few thousand ghost tours. They all have their place of course, but feeding expectations is a populist exercise that contorts reality through entertainment, it does nothing by way of education as to its reality, so I quite happily break the mould.

One such person slipping through the net and expecting to be 'entertained', gave me what she thought I guess was a bad review following her tour in 2018:

'My boyfriend and I attended the ghost tour on a particularly spooky night in November. But no amount of spooky atmosphere could have prepared us for the horror show that was this ghost tour. It is fair to say that we were amongst the 20% of people who are "sceptical" about the existence of ghosts, and this tour did little to convince us. Richard promised to separate the fact from the myth but then proceeded to talk to us about ghosties as if they are real. We were hoping for a night of spooky tales and actors jumping out at us etc but instead received this "factual" tour except not factual at all as ghosts obviously aren't real. All this being said, if you are delusional and believe in ghosties then this could be for you!'

Without knowing, she did me a great favour in highlighting to a wider audience what my tours do *not* involve. She also serves to suitably highlight a very real lacking in understanding as to the nature and reality of paranormal phenomena. Another family on a tour didn't make it past the first ten minutes. They booked through my website and also failed to read it. I could see the expression on one of them changing as I spoke of the reality of the paranormal. They then stopped me and said "I obviously heavily believed in ghosts, and can see where this is going, but we were expecting theatrics and fictional stories." I could see the kids were both enthusiastic and disappointed at their reaction, but for the adults it was as though I was about to mention something apocryphal. Far from giving the kids nightmares, it was as though the mere suggestion of its reality would give them the wrong impression.

The fabrication of fiction has partly served to condition the West to a distortion of its reality, and through a reluctance to accept it as being anything other than fiction, little to no attention has been given to its understanding and even less to the terminology surrounding it. Our limited vocabulary has become a barrier to our understanding. For example, we casually insert words and mixed synonyms as taglines attached to testimony of paranormal experiences that only reinforce our prejudice as stereotypes. Words like alleged, claimed or believed. Supposedly, apparently, seemingly and purportedly etc. We readily accept these terms when it comes to the paranormal as they sit quite comfortably with our expectations, but they are words more appropriate for our lacking in historical understanding that we would never use for our own experiences. Their casual acceptance advertently qualifies a belief that it is fiction, while inadvertently reinforcing a systemic ignorance for its reality in measured detriment to the recipient of an experience by way of scepticism. When was the last time you heard someone tell you about an experience they allegedly had? and how often do you then disbelieve what they are telling you? The bottom line is it doesn't matter at all whether you 'think' you are sceptical or 'think' you believe. I tar both of those words with the same brush. Scepticism? Belief? Is there a difference? Nope! You will find these two words are called opinions and they have absolutely no bearing on reality. Experiencing phenomena has no dependency on what we think, not least on our opinions, and spirits have absolutely no reliance on what we think for their existence.

It hasn't always been this way. The term paranormal was coined c.1920, before this time it was called 'supernatural' and until the 19th century it was simply an accepted aspect of reality, so how did it come to this? The following is the short answer. A more in-depth analysis will be found in Appendix 2.

In the early middle ages through the Roman Church, the quest by scholars for an enlightened understanding of reality encompassed intellectual and spiritual knowledge. They promoted an embodiment of the physical, the philosophical, the spiritual and the supernatural. This was directly reflected through the ancient sciences coming to us primarily through Greece, Egypt and Babylon around the 2nd or 3rd century AD. The oldest science being astrology/astronomy, originating in Mesopotamia nearly 5000 years ago. Although these terminologies did not exist at that time, the principles did. They were exploring the heavens and the patterns of their configurations as correlating with events that led also to a future determination. Scholars were recognising how everything is related, and through a greater exploration of the ancient sciences, a greater understanding could be gained of the self and the universe, one being reflected in the other. All can be summed up in the Christian axiom, 'On earth as it is in heaven', borrowed from the ancient Greek Hermetic axiom, 'As above so below', the esoteric unification of man with the universe.

The spiritual forms the basis of belief systems, but there is no dependency on these for its reality, nor for its reality to be known. The spiritual and all it encompasses has been an accepted part of reality since the dawn of mankind. So too has the supernatural as a physical expression. The Asian continent for example, covering billions of people through the majority of what is now 48 countries, including China, India and Japan do not think of ghosts in the abstract as we do today in the West, and they certainly do not laugh at their expense or dismiss them as fiction. Their relationship is a mix of love, fear and respect, as they know these are spirits of the deceased, that these are our relatives, our elders, and they pay homage to them through ancestor worship. It is why Japan has at least 27 classifications for ghosts alone, China 20, Indonesia 11 etc, whereas technically we have 1 – 'ghost', with any others we have being perceived as substitutions for the same. They also have respect for spirit-mediums who relay information back and forth between those of the living and those now deceased. The West was of a like mind, but with universal physical discoveries being met with heresy, the 17th century would see a gradual split away from the spiritual/esoteric sciences with an emerging scientific model that would be devoted purely to a physical quantification of a physical universe. It came in the form of an idea by Sir Francis Bacon who you may know as Shakespeare in one of his more noted of guises. Known as the Baconian method it formulated empiricism through inductive methodology of facts as a means of studying and interpreting *natural* physical phenomena. Scholars didn't break away from the spiritual/esoteric sciences or disciplines because of any lacking in their integrity, noted scientists and academics of the day including Paracelsus, Isaac Newton, Johannes Kepler and Robert Fludd were employing both. As a model, the physical sciences partly gave more freedom for scholars in their pursuits away from church control which was now running concurrently with these other scholarly disciplines. Through its physical innovations during the scientific revolution, it became a very fashionable new science that would develop into the methodology of the empirical sciences we know today.

As a separate model it was never designed to encroach on the spiritual/esoteric sciences, or the supernatural - and that was the point, the idea, and the key for where the populist mindset finds itself today. They were never part of its quantitative remit, so logically, they do not, and have never existed within its physical model. Through the emergence of new generations of scholars as the West embraced this new physical science as their focus, the spiritual/esoteric dynamic would eventually become virtually unknown to them outside religious and esoterically minded circles. Move forward to the late 19th century and empirical science had become the dominant science of the West. With this, it became easier for the layman to assume that because spirituality and the supernatural does not exist in 'scientific' terms, it does not exist in general terms, not that they just do not exist within the remit of the empirical scientific model. With this premise being encouraged through fiction as fiction, it is the reason why the populist Western assumption for it not existing has stuck as a conditioned misconception, a misguided belief to this day. It is also why in the East and through various longstanding organisations in the West, spiritual/esoteric disciplines are recognised and accepted, not necessarily because of any religious or philosophical affiliation, but as a tangible and undisputed factor of reality. I have expanded on all of this considerably in Appendix 2.

# Ghosts

Despite the populous accepting the conventions of reality, the bottom line is we all live in our heads. I guarantee that whatever you think reality is, it will not be quite the same as anyone else reading this volume.

**Everything you will read herein happened.**
**Nothing alleged, nothing purported, it all just happened.**

**Do you believe in ghosts?**

I am often asked this question. My reply is always the same, "Of course not!" This brings about a smile in those thinking I have just qualified their prejudice and a smile to my face when I observe their reaction. If I don't then qualify my reply with a follow-up explanation (which few expect me to do), it seems to reassure them. My qualification for saying this is very simple, we don't use the word belief for our experiences.

The paranormal in the West is one of those rare subjects where everyone becomes an instant expert through opinion about a subject they know absolutely nothing about.

For its reality to be known, the main problem is explaining its mechanics in a way that meets with comprehension. For this to happen there must be an association, and for that to happen there must be familiarity, and that is where you come in.

**Take everything you think you know about the paranormal, turn it on its head and you will find the opposite is true . . .**

Common myths about the paranormal include it must be dark, stormy, or a full moon to experience something. It doesn't, they can occur at any point day or night right through the year, and across the board over 50% of occurrences happen during daylight hours as you can see more. The stormy night is a fiction to give a false sense of atmosphere, and the full moon can increase our awareness but has no bearing at all on when or if phenomena will happen. Halloween is another myth. With so much chaos at Halloween, you will find that is the one day you will be least likely to experience anything of a paranormal nature. The name Halloween comes from All Hallows' Eve, (Hallows' being Saints') followed by All Saints' day where all Saints are remembered. It was borrowed from the Celtic fire festival Samhuinn or Samhain which marks the transition from summer to winter and is celebrated in particular circles as the Celtic New Year. A time when reflection on the year before includes those no longer with us, which is why it was adopted by the Catholic Church as a time to reflect and celebrate the Saints. It then transitioned to the dark hours with spirits roaming and All Hallows' Eve became Hallowe'en.

Phenomena is not 'appear on demand' and 100% happen when least expected, that is guaranteed. It is all about being at the right place, at the right time, and for the visual - looking in the right direction. Yet, unless something defies the laws of physics, chances are you will not realise what you are looking at or experiencing is out of sorts with convention. We all experience more than we are aware of. Unless it is obvious, there may be a niggling feeling that something isn't right, that something is out of place, but our fast paced lives are rarely given to dwelling on such matters and phenomena is *always* the last thing you will expect to experience. Even if you want to or think you are looking for it to happen it is easy to miss their subtlety, especially if you are looking for a stereotypically dramatic display. Equally, playing hardball with your own perception by being dismissive and attributing occurrences to your imagination or some tenuous implausible explanation will do you no favours in this regard.

You can think of the cause of phenomena as being good, bad, evil or with an indifference, that is your prerogative, although the latter is rare and they are not trying to kill you, they are not even trying to scare you – what would be the point? we do that suitably ourselves as we overlay our prejudices and assumptions on their reality. With this, it is easy for us to over think our own importance for what is generally incidental impersonal contact. Spirits who are aware of you are primarily neutral and are rarely trying to communicate with you, in fact, they more often have nothing more dramatic to offer than to notify they are there. You must remember it is us who have wandered into their environment, and for a time we are sharing a space they have occupied for a lot longer. Although rare, if they are looking to communicate with you it tends to be by someone drifting in with a connection to you, a deceased relative is the most common. I move into the details and further explanations of everything I have just mentioned shortly.

**Ghost Classifications**

Mr G. N. M. Tyrell, President of the Society for Psychical Research from 1945-6 divided ghosts into four categories, which was somewhat limited, although they do serve important distinctions. It will be noted his emphasis is more on Crisis or Post Mortem Ghosts. This makes sense as we were just realising the true extent of the devastation to human life caused by the Second World War and the grief that came with it:

**Experimental Ghosts:** Astral Projection.
These are the appearances of people still alive, caused by astral projection and crisis phenomenon:

**Crisis Ghosts:** Appearing around the time of great crisis such as severe illness or death.

**Post-Mortem Ghosts:** Appearing after death to somebody known. One of the most common post-mortem sightings is when a close member of the family having just passed away comes back to comfort loved ones and deliver a message of reassurance that they are ok. These are similar to Crisis Apparitions but rather than just appearing, they tend to warn or impart something and can appear long after they have died. Unlike Crisis the recipient knows they are no longer alive. They are only seen once they are dead, whereas Crisis can appear during near-death experiences such as the time of a serious illness.

There are also a few additional categories:

**Recurrent Ghosts**
These appear at the same place and time at certain times of the years, perhaps on the anniversary of their death.

**Ghosts of the Living**
The living persons double is also known as a doppelganger. There are many cases of people observing, sometimes even speaking with somebody they know or are familiar with that was physically elsewhere at the time, although they appear real in every detail. Unlike Experimental Ghosts, no explanation is ever forthcoming as to why they are appearing, other than historical associations correlating with their appearance as portents of death or conversely as a sign of longevity.

**The Mirage Effect**
The mirage effect is caused when the difference in temperature between layers of air cause differences in density, and these in turn cause light rays to travel in curved paths. The light rays reach the eye as if they have travelled in straight lines – and as the mirage appears above or below the true image, it frequently appears magnified and with great clarity.

Cases have been known for whole towns to appear in this way, often many miles from where they actually are. People have also been seen and battles re-enacted in the sky. The latter phenomenon may have occurred many years previously.

I saw a cottage by Crail in Fife at the end of a track one hot summer's day when it was actually sited some 150 feet down a steep slope beyond the end of the track by the sea.

For the mainstay of ghosts, Tyrell has **Ghosts: Habitual Hauntings.** For this classification I have two main types which I shall be referring to throughout as follows:

**Group A: Impressionistic Phenomena**

**Group B: Spirits of the deceased**

There is also: **Group C: Empathic residue**
This is both a category of natural ambiance, and a subcategory of A. & B., where every action and emotion leaves behind an energetic residue. If the conditions are met, they are both symptomatic of unaccountable empathic feelings. This is the most common and easily misattributed form of paranormal manifestation which I shall delve into in the next section.

Once you understand their traits you will begin to distinguish which grouping the enclosed testimonies fall into, and given the parameters of these anomalies, what can and cannot occur in that locality as there is nothing random about the paranormal.

Beginning with **Group A: Impressionistic Phenomena**

This is the brief merger with an earlier time as a snapshot, and can be accompanied by the whole scene being transformed to an earlier state. It is like looking through a corridor or window through time, what you are observing is still taking place, so ghosts in this category are not aware of you. There is no interaction so there is never any poltergeist activity when this is the only phenomena associated with a location. If the same transformation or sequence is subsequently observed by others, it is not a segment of time in a loop per se, rather it becomes the activated observance of a passive looping memory imbued on the energetic field of that locality.

**Group B: Spirits of the deceased**

**These are either Progressed Spirits or Stasis Spirits**

In many ways Group A. is more complex to understand, while this grouping is more complex to explain. It is typified by:

1. The manifestation or partial manifestation of the spirit of a deceased person.

2. **Poltergeist activity** (German word for noisy ghost or spirit). Caused by a spirit looking to make itself known by utilising the energy in the locality to cause a physical anomaly.

**Group B. Attributes**

1. They are intelligent and are aware of us. Like the rest of us, they have an inquisitive nature – they silently observe us.

2. They are ever present, but they are not always active.

3. They defy the laws of physics and defy any assumptions we may have about the nature of death.

4. They are aware of physical space but are not confined by it.

5. They have no sense of time, or at least not in the way we observe time. What appears to be a few years to us can be moments to them. It is more a state of being.

6. They don't like change. They tend to become more active, perhaps unsettled and agitated when their environment changes: Structural changes, moving furniture or redecorating. Moving in or out of a place can do it.

7. The only physical harm is localised to bite marks, wheel marks, scratches, slaps, bumps or taps. On brushing past, they can cause rashes to appear, as can Group A. Both can cause mild psychological disturbances, but nothing to match the malign potential created by the naivety of our mind.
8. Contrary to mistaken belief, when an object is flung across the room it is very rare they will intentionally hit anyone. If anything, they could aim to miss in looking to attract your attention. However, not all poltergeist activity is caused by spirits of the deceased. There are two other sources or forces to note: Psychokinesis and intelligences. Their reality is manifest through mischievous forces. These have been known to cause objects to hit those present, although incidents of the latter are rare, they are the headline grabbers, giving the impression that all activity, especially poltergeist activity is synonymous with evil spirits causing violent outbursts.

**Group B. continued: Why are ghosts here?**
This is the most common question I am asked. Oddly, no one ever asks why we are here?

### The Answer to the Riddle of Life and Death

There are those who say we arrived in this world with nothing and we leave with the same. This is not true. To give a riddle in a similar vein as the Sphinx – there is one thing we each arrive with when we are born, and one thing we leave with when we die. What is it?

The answer is our spirit. The spirit drives an awareness partially recognised by our subconscious and far more profound than physical consciousness can comprehend. Following death our awareness is imbued with the culmination of everything experienced whilst alive. Unless our death is premature at birth we will always leave with more than we arrive with.

**Spirits of the deceased**

We are intelligent (apparently), and like the meditative state, awareness in death is without thought, it is a knowing, but it is not gnosis. As with our arrival in this world and contrary to the belief of some, there is no immediate enlightenment following death. The existentialist questions dwelt upon in life are not met with anything other than our awareness of a seamless continuation in death. This is a juxtaposition as natural and automotive as breathing.

**Progressed Spirits**

When we die the spirit naturally progresses to the next stage of our existence. Under given circumstances it is possible for the progressed spirit to return to the physical by merging through the vibratory planes, resulting in personal visitations to subtly notify continuation to loved ones, to watch over, to protect, or for unfinished business etc.

**Stasis Spirits**

This is a very rare anomaly in terms of progression but it is far more prevalent than progressed spirits. In stasis, continuation or progression of the spirit following death has been suspended 'between worlds' so to speak. Those in this state have slipped through the net of the dynamics dictating this natural progression experienced by the majority. A jarring of the spirit has occurred, where 1/ the energetic impact of death on the spirit, 2/ reinforced by a mix of energetic mental stimuli, perhaps generated through circumstance, and 3/ often coupled with the natural energy already present in the physicality, 4/ have all transpired to hold the energies of the spirit in a form of vibratory stasis, 5/ a suspension of our state of being in what could be deemed an flux of intelligent vibratory energy held in the physical, 6/ and thus preventing its immediate progression.

There is no telling who it might happen to, and we are not given a choice per se as to whether we are going to remain in the world we inhabited when living. If we find ourselves held by such a circumstance, we are tied to the environmental location or specific area that has a personal association for us. This is our sphere of involvement, and is generally where we met our end or lived out our days. We can also flit to a favourite location where our energies are impactfully imbued, but again there is no choice in the matter. This sphere can cover quite an area and its scope is very involved, albeit restricted. Like the examples of Lady Kinkell who roams her former estate, or the ghosts of Kingask (Fairmont) I shall speak of later for the same.

Operating through laws unimpeded by illusory physical constructs, there is no dependency on any currently known laws of physics. They are no longer part of the same physical vibratory frequency, which is why they do not share in the same physical space. The only physical quantification of their existence is through our observance of their influence. They interact with physical reality by altering the vibratory nature of the physical in conformity with their will – rather than thought. This is instantaneous, but there is little control once initiated.

A peaceful death and weak spirit can be held energetically just as readily as the violent energies of a fatal situation; a sudden death typified by suicide, murder or accident for example. The former is subtle, the latter more stereotypical when it comes to mundane attempts at explaining their nature.

When experiencing phenomena, an energetic link is created and any attempt at understanding their nature through the physical or psychological state alone is futile.

### The Ouija and Poltergeist Activity

Nothing is random with the paranormal. For poltergeist activity to occur there is always a trigger and we can inadvertently be that trigger as we call upon forces without realising. The Ouija board is a classic example which uses your subconscious as a conduit. It is why the Ouija tends to bring your own worst fears to the forefront, making it very personal and direct. It also opens a channel like a magnet for spirits to merge through to the physical. The Enfield poltergeist beginning in 1977 was after 12 year old Janet messed with the Ouija. The word poltergeist would soon become a household name through subsequent well publicised events. There appears to have been a few spirits, which is why Joe Wilkins, a previous occupant who died in the house came through, but he wasn't the source of the disturbances. Janet and her sister Margaret (13) admitted to consciously creating about 2% of mischief, but it would have been more. As more investigators became involved and the publicity grew, the need to perform was accentuated. Some believe it was all consciously produced, however, I believe there was a mix. I would attribute the poltergeist activity to Janet through a mix of trickery and psychokinesis. The latter generally stems from the spent up energies of an adolescent who is unaware of their involvement. A clue was a piece of Lego hitting a photographer on the forehead. The disturbances they consciously caused were matched or accentuated by disturbances caused through her subconscious, manifesting as psychokinesis and witnessed by many, including a policewoman. In using the Ouija, she had opened the door for her subconscious energies to manifest as child-like antics. The subconscious utilises the same energy as spirits for the manifestation of poltergeist activity. This is why when suggestive elements like "poltergeists start fires" were introduced to her, small fires would then occur – be it by conscious or subconscious means. Its most famous and debated event involved the sisters being thrown about the bedroom. It is in-keeping with horror films but the display is replicable and somewhat out of sorts with general phenomena. For genuine phenomena, in 2010, recordings of the banging on walls and the movement of furniture were analysed and their sound wave patterns were found to be 'abnormal' by comparison to scientific recreation. Enfield is complex. There were noted researchers, global media with their customary embellishment and sensationalism, all hyped up through suggestion producing expectation, excitement and fear through placebo. Add in a family with a broken marriage which added to Janet's anxiety and the volatile mix created one of the most publicised and controversial poltergeist episodes in recorded history. Others coming close for attention were Pitmilly and Borley Rectory.

### The Imagination

Confronted with an incident defying the laws of physics such as a coffee cup moving from A to B for example, we can use our imagination as a scapegoat to deny it happened, or conversely, we can read too much into it and once again call upon our favourite horror films as a qualification for what could happen next. In this regard it must be understood, the paranormal and the imagination have never gone hand in hand.

For all the imagination we think we have, we need this trigger to activate it, otherwise it is not your imagination at play. Therefore, during or after a paranormal experience, the imagination can go wild, but never the other way around (placebo is different). Once phenomenon has occurred it becomes fair game and we can conjure things far more disturbing, violent and damaging than spirits of the deceased could ever wish for or conceive of causing.

### Imaginary friends

The depiction of an invisible friend has been featured in several films, including: *The Shining*, *Drop Dead Fred*, *Sixth Sense* and the 2013 film *Imaginary Friend*. The one that tops them all however is the 1959 classic – *Harvey*, starring James Stewart and a wonderfully poignant portrayal of his invisible friend, a Pooka, a benevolent spirit of Celtic mythology. This particular variety tends to take the form of an animal hence in the film it was a large white invisible rabbit with a height of six foot three and one half inches to be precise.

There are so many correlations within the film *Harvey* to invisible friends. Stewart's character - Elwood P. Dowd on recounting when he first met Harvey said: "You have the advantage on me. You know my name and I don't know yours." And right back at me he said, "What name do you like?" Well, I didn't even have to think twice about that. Harvey's always been my favourite name. So, I said to him, I said, "Harvey," and, this - this is the interesting thing about the whole thing. He said, "What a coincidence. My name happens to be Harvey."

Elwood stays with his sister and niece, or rather they stay with him and his large invisible rabbit. On becoming desperately concerned for his welfare they can't make up their mind if Harvey is caused through drink or mental illness, so they look to have him committed, whereupon he temporarily ends up in a sanatorium at their behest. Of the many wonderful classic quotes in the film, Elwood says: "I've wrestled with reality for 35 years, Doctor, and I'm happy to state I finally won out over it." The psychiatrist releases Elwood when he starts seeing Harvey himself!

There is an innocence to the film that comes through Elwood's outlook for those around him. He sees the best in everyone which is insightful and refreshing, and being a social outcast himself he helps others he can relate to. Elwood also describes Harvey as being especially fond of social outcasts and during the film Elwood's sister Veta is asked by her daughter how someone possibly could imagine a rabbit. Veta says to her: "Myrtle Mae, you have a lot to learn and I hope you never learn it." The film doesn't explore the specifics of Elwood's background other than he regularly drinks in the local bar with Harvey and invites new acquaintances back for dinner. "Harvey and I have things to do... we sit in the bars... have a drink or two... play the juke box. Very soon the faces of all the other people turn towards me and they smile. They say: "We don't know your name, mister, but you're a very nice fellow." Harvey and I warm ourselves in these golden moments. We came as strangers - soon we have friends. They come over. They sit with us. They drink with us. They talk to us. They tell us about the great big terrible things they've done and the great big wonderful things they're going to do. Their hopes, their regrets. Their loves, their hates. All very large, because nobody ever brings anything small into a bar. Then I introduce them to Harvey, and he's bigger and grander than anything they can offer me. And when they leave, they leave impressed. The same people seldom come back, but that's – that's envy, my dear. There's a little bit of envy in the best of us. That's too bad, isn't it?"

We have all heard of imaginary friends. There is quite a high chance you had one yourself when you were young, perhaps you still do? Ask your parents if they are still alive. A report published of a survey in the USA showed around 65% of young children from the age of 3 years to 7 years have imaginary friends. 3 years of age is a very magical time for the developing child and is also around the time when speech and the recognition of language become more advanced, so communication and interaction become more pronounced.

We easily dismiss children who have imaginary friends as exactly that, imaginary friends, but there is a muddle with this. The imagination tends to involve the conscious inventions of mind bringing to life a doll, an action figure or a teddy bear for example. They are exceptionally inventive and they interact with everything in their environment as though they are communicating with humans. They put their toys through scenarios, often mimicking situations they have been involved in themselves, or recreating situations they have seen playing out around them. This is all part of their early learning development and is always very revealing in itself.

Imaginary friends as opposed to inanimate dolls and toys is a very different matter. They are not imaginary and strictly speaking they are not all friends. It is an interaction with spirits of the deceased. We could also call them guardian angels. These tend to be a mix of progressed spirits and those in stasis.

A guy on a tour said when he was young, he always wanted an imaginary friend, but no matter how he tried he never had one. This struck me as being very poignant. If it was his imagination he could have had a room full of them!

They fulfil a particular purpose in the development of life. They are trust worthy, children feel safe with them, they share secrets with them, they protect them, and generally they are there for them through good and bad times. Importantly children don't question their reality, they just accept them. They can have imaginary friends because they are lonely or suffering from trauma. Equally, many are not lonely, they have physical friends and call upon their imaginary friends when their physical friends are not around. A survey in the UK showed how 46% of children also have imaginary friends, and 9% at 12 years of age. The global figure though has been put at between 70% and 80% for those who have or have had imaginary friends. It is actually higher than this. The ratio between the sexes is more in favour of girls than boys as they tend to be more naturally sensitive with a greater intuition. Other than this there are no obvious differences or additional signs between those who do have them and those who don't.

A person on a tour said he used to talk to someone. His parents said he described his dead great grandfather, complete with all the expletives. Particular traits, likes and dislikes, mannerisms etc are all hallmarks, and the imagination doesn't work that way, remember the imagination needs a trigger. I am sure many parents reading this have set an extra place for a child's imaginary friend at the dinner table. On saying this though, a young boy said "I have an imaginary friend! He appears when I am feeling lonely." His mother was standing behind him and had never heard him come out with this before. She was quite taken aback. He just came out with it as we were talking about them. For them it is a new friend to play with, to share time with and who they can call on. They can give them names of fictional characters from books, cartoon characters from the television or they can be based on real people as archetypes they look up to, but more often the spirit will give them their own name and the name given to them will become a nickname. They young boy had no name for his friend.

A girl on a tour told me about her imaginary friends. She said when she was young two angels would visit her. They would take her arms and the three of them would fly around the room. Her mother said she couldn't remember the names her daughter gave them at the time but they were not in English. She said they sounded Arabic!

I received an email from Karen Cark. She came on the 7:30pm tour in July 2021 and had a few experiences on the tour which I mention later. She also gave me details of other experiences she has had. I have laced these throughout where appropriate. The following is about an imaginary friend she had when she was young: "I had a rather mischievous 'imaginary friend' as a wee girl called Mary. She was so naughty that she encouraged me (age 3) to cut the sleeves out of my dad's pyjama jacket. My Granda Stewart (a fantastic storyteller and poet) wrote a wee poem about it. The last few lines went as so...

Poor Daddy saw his sleeves had gone,
But said she meant no harm.
Wee Mary said "Had you had it on -
You would have lost your arm!"

A professor and his family staying in Priorsgate in St Andrews I give details for later, heard his son talking to someone in the bedroom. He knew there was no one else in the apartment and went through to his room. He asked who he had been speaking to. His son said, "With my grown-up friend." So, the professor believed he had an imaginary friend. A while later, the family were invited to a reception at Holyrood Palace in Edinburgh. They were walking along one of the corridors when their son pointed to a painting and said, "That's my friend from home!" It was a portrait of Lord Darnley, Mary Queen of Scots second husband, and he was too young to make any historical connection (refer to **Priorsgate**).

As the child develops and the impact of the physical world becomes more apparent, they invariably disappear. It tends to only be your parents who remember them. It is not to say they are lost forever. It is possible for progressed spirits to come back and aid in times of need through a myriad of almost imperceptible ways when the general impositions of life become too much, and when they do, something at the back of your mind will remind you of a friend you once had that you cannot quite place.

**The ultimate answers we seek – Vibratory Frequencies**

Comprehension and the answers we look for can come to us in several ways, but a realisation of the mechanics behind reality can only be fully answered by those who also experience its reality while in the spirit. With this it can only then be communicated through a spiritual perspective, and not as a faith, belief or conviction, as these would be little more than theoretical constructs without confirmation through experience of the latter, otherwise, any attempt at understanding will invariably result in eternal speculation.

**Are ghosts scared of humans?**

Children tend to come out with far more thought provoking questions than their adult counterparts. Adults tend to ask stupid questions or questions they could answer themselves if they could bring themselves to apply a modicum of thought. I was once asked on a tour by a small boy, "Are ghost scared of humans?" What a good question. The answer is no, but I had to think about it for a second before answering. They are never scared of humans but humans can annoy them, and when this is the case they will make it apparent.

**Can you see a ghost throwing something?**
I thought this was an interesting question. Ghosts don't throw anything. They use energy linking the object through awareness to either move them from A to B or make them simply disappear from the physical by altering their vibratory frequency.

**Can ghosts can see other ghosts?**
It is these seemingly simple questions I am occasionally asked that are often the most complex to answer, as they can only be answered by explaining a few fundamental mechanics. Group A. impressions are fixed in their own time with no interaction with the here and now, so this question only applies to Group B. ghosts – Spirits of the deceased. There are potentially a great many variables here involving the vibratory realms including the physical, time, subtle spiritual energetic dynamics, the connections between the vibratory realms of spirit and the nature of those realms, plus the role and energetic advancement of the individual spirits involved. Many examples will be found throughout this volume, such as the girl and the nun who share the same locality but are not aware of each other as they are from different times. The girl in the Cathedral you will read about who is aware of the energetic residue exuding from the graves of children despite their spirits not being present, and the ghosts of Fairmont who are aware of each other as they appear to have died at the same time and in the same location.

All frequencies have the potential to merge with the frequencies of this time - being the physical here and now. Stasis spirits who are between these realms or planes of existence are in this state of vibratory stasis I briefly touched upon earlier.

They can interact with others who died at the same time in the same locality as they are of the same vibratory frequency rooting through from the moment of death. Otherwise their temporary merger with the physical means they will only be able to interact with those in the realm of the physical here and now, as they each comprise of different frequencies and so will not be aware of each other. It is why a ghost from the 19th century for example will not be aware of a ghost sharing in the same locality from the 20th century.

With most spirits progressing to where they should be following death, each merge with the realm attuned to their level of comprehension, dictated and determined by the level of spiritual ambiance amassed to that point, so it is not possible to progress to a plane beyond your natural state. There are countless spirits interacting with each other in each realm.

**Spiritual realms**

The vibratory plane where they find themselves can be likened to the physical in the lower realms and more abstract and subtle in the higher realms. The majority in the physical realm are unaware of the underlying mechanics of the reality they inhabit. Physics for example can be thought of as an attempt to scrape its surface. The underlying mechanics of reality involve processes they are not able to detect, so there is no comprehension, let alone any attempt at deciphering it. Like those in the physical, the spirits of the deceased and most mediums are unaware of the underlying principles governing the spiritual realms. It is however a major aspect or preoccupation of various philosophical/religious/arcane bodies that have their base in what is known as high magic, which I speak of in Appendix 2 with regards to a shift in understanding through the natural philosopher and magician with a deep spiritual understanding of the underlying motivation of reality, as compared to their more modern counterpart – the scientist who has a mundane understanding of reality through a physical quantification alone. Everything in the physical has its initial motivation and reality in the spiritual. With this in mind, through an understanding of the dynamics of the spiritual nature and how it affects the physical, it is thus possible to influence the physical through the spiritual. Its importance and the true understanding of its extent is only known by a few in any age. The mystic as magician utilises these dynamics through an inherent understanding of the ancient sacred art and science of Magic which bridges the gap between the dynamics of the physical and the spiritual.

In the same way the physical has its own set of fundamental natural laws, each spiritual plane of existence also has its own unique set of spiritual laws. The more advanced the realm, the subtler and more refined their energetic vibratory frequencies become, and likewise the scope of their operations through degrees of purity. It is only possible to comprehend these higher planes or subtle realms through the harmonisation of these laws utilising the energies within spirit coupled with experience.

This spirit is the dynamic vehicle, the subtle body that survives death. The physical body is the shell the spirit inhabits and the two are inextricably but only temporarily linked. Through experience in the spirit, a 'knowing' or gnosis is obtained. Unlike the cognitive mental concepts of knowing and understanding, gnosis shares in a reality beyond mind that becomes an inherent part of what we call self, (being the awareness aspect of spirit). It is possible through astral projection to leave the physical body and travel in the spirit. A cord, sometimes called a silver cord, or life force links the two. If this were severed, there would also be a severing between the physical body and the awareness in spirit, the result is a physical death and a continuation of spirit. The cord will always be present, but I have to say in all my travels I have yet to see it. The vibratory frequency of the present physical realm is transcended as the spirit rises through the subtle vibratory realms of existence. Also known as 'rising on the planes' it requires the subtle harmonisation of the vibratory frequency of self – the spirit with those of each subtle realm traversed by magical/spiritual means. The harmonisation could be thought of as a process of acclimatisation, achieved through a process of understanding and equating the energies of each plane of existence by natural/induced assimilation as experience. This resultant assimilation is one of becoming those energies as the self becomes an integral aspect of each realm or plane.

This progression by the spirit to each plane is through a hierarchy of subtlety often resulting in an interaction with a corresponding hierarchy of spirits and intelligences governing the inherent motivating forces of each plane or realm. There are also intelligent spiritual energies or intelligent agencies operating through various vibratory realms of existence. All are personified or embodied with classical esoteric associations such as gods, angels, spirits and demons. The personification of their energetic associations influences our everyday lives and their classical representations are accurate for the scope of their remit, translating then to the attributes they then display.

They can only pervade through from their natural realm of operation to the lesser advanced, lower or base realms, including that of the physical realm. This law applies to all agencies through all realms including the physical, and is why the higher realms can perceive the lower including the physical, but rarely the other way around.

**Energy and EEM**

To give it a more localised explanation for the physical, their effects can be perceived but not their cause. Occasionally there are crossovers where the boundaries between realms or planes are energetically more compatible and so more conducive to energetic interaction. These are the energy centres and ley lines resulting in brief glimpses of ghosts for example as the heightened pronunciations of energy represent the temporal merger or conduit between worlds as great vibratory seas. It is important to understand that all the planes of existence operating through to the physical are here all the time. They are not higher or lower in a literal sense which is why they can merge through to the physical so readily.

Ley lines are energy lines linking energy centres together. The vibratory frequency of electromagnetic energy can also expose paranormal manifestation through an overlapping of physical vibratory frequencies to that of the spiritual.

Heightened energies at these localities enhance and recharge our own energies like a battery, especially at certain auspicious times when the energetic fluctuations are at a peak. The attraction is immediate to our spirit and is then partially recognised by our subconscious. Spirits are amongst us all the time and phenomena can happen anywhere, but these centres are more conducive to our glimpsing of phenomena. Spirits utilise the energy of these localities more readily for the same reason. The heightened energies cause distortions in our reality through poltergeist activity. By this mutuality, a greater opportunity is afforded to experiencing what are always rare and generally brief encounters for the majority.

**Intelligent energy and the dynamics of energetic motivation**

Stasis spirits are looking to notify they are still here. If you acknowledge them by saying something like: "Hi, I know you are there," they usually stop. This can allay disturbances for a few hours, days or even years. If they are more persistent, it tends to be for unfinished business, and like a jigsaw, given their generally abstract nature, it can take years to put together the clues they leave in place – if we are able to do this at all.

I call this EEM, the 'essence of energetic motivation' and it will be as hard to grasp as it is to explain. It is a spiritual essence equivalent to the essence or encapsulation of a physical scenario. As an analogy, it is the same as how a particular smell can pull together a whole set of memories or a sequence of events as if it had just taken place, or is still taking place (the spiritual essence). The 'energetic' is then the embodiment, and the 'motivation' is for a just conclusion.

Energy is a holding ground of reality, a conveyor of memory of sorts for those able to pick it up, but unlike the memory we possess and are accustomed to, its intelligence on a locality will contain everything that has ever occurred in that locality. This is not the same as what it is able to inherently incorporate within itself as an energetic intelligence. It does not extend itself to any further attributes we would normally associate with the human mind such as evaluation, reasoning, analysis and judgement for example. Energy is intrinsically neutral and singular in its purity. Being then subject to influence from its environment there can be positive or negative attributions we would recognise in part as emotion. With absolutely everything being composite of energy, it follows that absolutely everything stores progression as a permanent record of information. When applied to our species, in one sense everything you do through your life is recorded. This is an attribute of the physical evolving through the spiritual realms, thus it also extends to everything, inanimate as well as animate in the physical.

To explain this further; in the spiritual, everything is dynamic, we could in one sense say everything is alive because energy is intelligent, and everything is retained within energy as this memory, so everything conveys its own essence. By way of a particular sympathy, everything becomes its own observance. This last sentence is easily missed in the overall thread of these words, but it contains a truth about the spiritual realms reflective in spirits that is an important one to note. Everything, whether animate or inanimate has a particular energy field associated with it. This is a unique energetic blueprint that individually distinguishes it from everything else. As subtle as it may be, and as difficult as it may be to discern, an example is when two objects are produced from the same production line, they can look the same and have an identical composition, but they will share three initial distinctions as differences. Firstly, for the production line model, the energetic blueprint includes the exact moment the object was produced. Secondly no two physical objects share the identical same space in the same time. Thirdly, following their production they will both have their own journey in and through reality. The influx of energy they receive from their surroundings and their usage etc, add to, and can modify their own especial energetic composition as the energies merge and interact with an ever evolving environment. If we were to communicate with an object it would tell us the unique story of the journey it has been exposed to as its own unique history, but its scope is very limited. So, beyond appearances and physical composition, no two objects in the physical universe can be the same – and that applies to everything – including atoms etc.

Whether they have come off the same production line or have been naturally formed, everything, whether it is animate or inanimate through physical observance is marked by these differentiations. We may not be able to pick up these energies if we are not attuned to them, but we can *physically* observe the effects the energies have had on them by their spiritual and physical phenotypes as distinctions or characteristics. A phenotype is the observation of characteristics in relation to environmental factors and genetic or chemical composition. For humans, we could observe phenotype characteristics in many different ways. How we physically change as we adapt to living in certain locations or to certain jobs, hair and skin changing colour depending exposure to temperature, differences between life expectancy in certain socially poor or affluent environments etc. Observances of how culture and belief can manifest differentiation in our psychological temperament etc. Translated into spiritual terms we can look at how it can all affect our level of understanding, how we feel about what we are observing in the mundane, and moving deeper to the reasons behind this, even if we cannot explain why something appeals to us or not, we are picking up on, and in this sense connecting with these spiritual dynamics all the time.

We can look at how it all affects our level of tolerance to spiritual understanding, and the comparisons to be made between how a trouble-free, or conversely how a stressful environment impacting as energies will cause positive or negative sociological and biochemical changes to occur in the locality. Every scenario has its distinctive energetic makeup and every scenario affects our spiritual, mental and physical health and wellbeing accordingly. This is all further expanded through **Group C. emotional residue creating empathic feelings** in the following section.

It all moves directly into the butterfly effect through cause and effect and our glimpse into these mechanics through synchronicity which I delve into later. By virtue of these interlinked dynamics as observed on the mundane, the potential exploration of this is vast as these energetic combinations produce unique fingerprints correlating with the complexities of destiny which everything energetically conspires towards - everything is linked, and no matter how insignificant our whims or decisions might appear to be, everything is both important, impartial and predetermined and ultimately correlate with the predetermined blueprint of existence.

The key to both spiritual and physical existence is through the root mechanics of energy and time, but, the time I refer to is not linear. That is just a restriction for those in the physical here and now. You will get closer if you ask "which here and now?" The balance between energy and the nature of 'all' time I speak of holds the key for physicists looking to bridge the gap between Einstein's outmoded theory and what quantum theorists are beginning to understand, but it will require a change in methodology through a change in mindset if this is to be achieved. It will come down to a progressive evolutionary scientific perspective, one not hampered by the restrictive boundaries of an equally outmoded scientific doctrine.

# Perceiving Paranormal Phenomena

## Introducing your perception to Groups A. B. & sub C

Opening the mind to new possibilities is not easy as it immediately reopens many questions we thought we already had answers for, but to do otherwise is to prevent the reality of an experience from becoming apparent by allowing doubt to override its integrity and thus as a bitter irony, serve as its own unwitting injustice on the self.

Paranormal phenomena can be experienced:

1. Through all the senses, although taste is rare.

2. As a sense, an intuition, a knowing, a feeling, a thought, vision or an impression through the mind's eye of what is or has taken place, both partially or as a more complete picture. This can then move into psychometry or Group A. future events through precognition. The list is potentially long.

3. Through communication with Group B. requiring an awareness attuned to this aspect (mediumship), and/or by a diverse array of occult/spiritual extensions.

Aside being in the right place, right time, there can be a great many subtleties requiring a degree of experience if we are to distinguish between independent phenomena and a physical/psychological cause. The following is the simplified energetic flow/process of perceiving independent paranormal phenomena, be it on an individual or group basis aside placebo:

### Group A. Impressions

1. The level of energetic impact of the cause itself.
2. Coupled with the level of the energetic field of the locality.
3. The degree of energetic perceptibility of the individual dictated by awareness.

The impact of (1.) always needs to be pronounced if it is to be picked up as an energetic residue later. It is then between a mix of (2.) and (3.) for it to then be picked up. Essentially, the heightened level in one can supplement a lower level in the other. On being picked up, be it by the observance of a ghost, the complete shift in time, or empathy, it causes us to react in ways comparable to our own level of understanding and experience in such matters, or more the point, the lack of.

**Group B. Spirits**

1. An active spirit of the deceased.
2. The level of energy at a locality.

The emphasis has changed here from the energetic impact of the cause to an active spirit. You will also note here that the energetic perceptibility of the individual (3.) is not present for Group B. There are exceptions where (3.) can communicate/determine the presence of spirts (The girl in the Nun's Walk you shall read about for example), but it is not generally required. That is why even the most diehard sceptics or believers on my tours from all walks of life have experienced phenomena. Personal persuasions have nothing to do with paranormal phenomena and spirits have no interest in such matters, if the conditions are right, you will experience.

**Group C.** Emotional residue creating empathic feelings as a subcategory of A. and B.

A brief recap of **A.** and **B.** with the addition of **Group C.**:

**Group A.** Impressions

1. A complete window to an earlier time.
2. A glimpse of impressionistic ghosts.
3. **Emotional residue creating empathic feelings.**

**Group B.** Spirits

1. **Emotional residue creating empathic feelings.**
2. The manifestation of spirit/s as ghosts.
3. An interaction of spirit/s through poltergeist activity.
4. A direct interaction/communication with the deceased.

As a subcategory of Groups A. and B., if the conditions are met, Group C. is symptomatic of unaccountable empathic feelings and sensations, that can also apply to physiological symptoms as we have with the Haunted Tower you shall read about later.

This is the most common aspect of paranormal phenomenon, and is unknown to the majority unable to make any distinction between the more obvious, or telling signs of Group A. or B.

Every thought, every action, every feeling, conveys an energetic vibration that combines with existing energies in the locality. This opens their involvement in many directions, adding to the general air of an environment as an ever evolving and ever shifting energetic residue. Every location has an air in-keeping with its environmental setting, and everyone is continually picking up these dynamics subconsciously. The principle being, the greater the energetic charge, the greater the vibratory impact, which accordingly increases the level of the existing energies in the locality. The sustained energetic ambience of a theatre for example, continually being filled with an air of excitement and expectancy. Aside the psychological expectation when arriving for a performance, this general ambience can easily be felt when it is empty. It subtly filters through to consciousness as an empathic spectrum of influence, producing unaccountable and often overwhelming feelings and moods. Location and circumstance dictates anything from elation, joy and peace, to feelings of being tense or on edge, depression, and I guess poignantly for present considerations, fear or even terror for no apparent reason.

Individual circumstance rarely has any marked degree of influence as actions and emotions tend to merge into the collective fairly quickly. For an individual circumstance to become apparent when entering that same vicinity it takes a hard hitting circumstance where the impact jars the neutral ambiance with a focus of intense energy. It can be especially telling when a murder or suicide has taken place, but it is far from dependent on these extremes as being the only cause.

When picked up, our empathic display mirrors that of its cause in positive or negative ways and by degrees of intensity.

Aside more obvious atmospheric settings, when they happen, a prolonged or traumatic incident having previously occurred in that locality will not be our first thought. It then follows, the more pronounced the symptoms, the more noticeable and inexplicable they will appear to be. It requires our awareness to be finely tuned, and a degree of experience to recognise what has previously taken place for us to understand why we feel the way we do.

The ability to determine these attributes when applied to physical objects we call psychometry. It is possible to hold an item and from it gain both the historical information and emotional framework surrounding it. This premise or rule is the same by extension for buildings, locations, spaces and people.

Activity and empathic feelings are further accentuated at energy centres or on those ley lines I spoke of, where this vibratory signature of the spiritual and the physical are merging more readily. This is apparent at Kellie Castle near Anstruther, where a growing number over the years have been overwhelmed at the entrance by intense negative feelings, and a very 'heavy air' as it has been described. All with no apparent cause and with enough impact to stop them from entering the building (GOF p.43). Conversely, despite Balgonie Castle near Markinch having at least 14 ghosts, it has a very pleasant, harmonious and light air (GOF p.68). Alongside their lengthy histories, they are both on ley lines.

There are many examples through this volume of Group C., with the dynamics of hotels and accommodation providers being prime examples amongst them.

Specific and uniform patterns of paranormal behaviour are achieved in the physical through the following…

**Testimony**

Those looking for phenomena are usually disappointed when nothing happens, and often wish they hadn't when it does.

Whenever someone asks is this or that true regarding the paranormal, once you understand its reality it becomes very easy to dispel the myths about the subject. Likewise, it becomes easy to know when someone tells you about an experience that it is genuine, although contrary to popular belief, people do not tend to make up their experiences regards the paranormal. Why would any bother when ridicule is the first conditioned reaction of those it is imparted to? Interestingly, the recipient is generally the first to be dismissive of their own experience.

Due to its subtlety and the eternal unexpectedness of phenomena, its presentation does one of two things:

The first is opposite to what you might suppose. There are many who do not realise what they have experienced, as it doesn't match with their sensationalistic expectations, so it can be easy to misattribute an experience to a more mundane cause, however implausible.

Everybody knows somebody who has experienced something they are unable to explain. Phenomenon is far more common place than people realise. In fact, I guarantee you have. Everybody experiences phenomena but an isolated incident may not register or be retained. It is to these slight, almost unassuming experiences where the majority of experiences reside, and although they are often deemed as being relatively insignificant, they are all very important. To realise you have take's thought and trust in yourself of what you have experienced. What you are looking for is something unusual you dismissed because you couldn't place it. Perhaps something you attributed to your imagination. A few of you reading this volume will read about experiences you can relate to and realise for the first time how others have experienced what you have.

Secondly, it changes those who realise what they have experienced, as it challenges prior conceptions. Not least because the framework under which your expectations and your casual familiarity operates through reality has just been challenged, and that survival of death is not an exercise in blind faith or wishful thinking. Or that your experience had absolutely no dependency on belief or faith. It is doubtful you will understand the nature of your experience, and an analysis of the same will keep you occupied for a long time to come, but you cannot deny the reality of what you have just experienced.

All your preconceived ideas almost immediately crumble to dust, not least the parameters of the laws of physics. So too does the conviction or persuasion that it is all the work of fiction or hearsay. The realisation brings deep changes within the psyche of the sceptic and believer alike. The word belief disappears as its reality has now been experienced, and equally, it banishes the concept of scepticism as it challenges your prior conceptions to the point where life will never be the same again.

The unexpectedness of phenomena is always displayed through the reaction of the recipient. Everyone handles phenomena in their own way but a commonality for the initial stage is very much one of disbelief and confusion as the mind tries to make sense of what just happened. It is always the last thing we would expect to encounter, especially if we do not believe it exists. Audibly repeating the incident over several times to try and work it out is a commonality as the mind tries desperately to move to the comprehension stage. The fact it cannot come to terms with it is when we get scared. That is universal. There is always this delay and as I say, no one is quite the same again. You will find many examples of this laced throughout the enclosed experiences.

People's knowledge in general about the reality of the paranormal is at best misguided and dramatic. When they don't know what is happening, it can be terrifying to experience. As I mentioned, spirits of the deceased are primarily neutral, but when that coffee cup moves from A to B and it shouldn't move from A to B, we think the next thing that will happen is the walls will be dripping in blood and we are going to be murdered in our beds. A completely understandable premise when the only point of reference we have in our mind for what could happen next is a back catalogue of our favourite bloodbath horror films to call upon. We overlay our prejudices and assumptions on *everything*. It is why the cause of phenomena can be perceived as good, bad, evil or even demonic, depending on outlook or tradition regardless of its source, intrinsic inherent nature or true motivation. So, you will find every report across the world is a mix of two important factors, the experience itself, and the mind trying to make sense of it.

We tend to think of ghosts in the abstract, where dark scenarios are played out, but the reality is far more subtle and its motivation is invariably far more innocuous than we have been led to believe. Most testimony is not dramatic, and it is rare you will ever know who the ghost you have encountered is. It then follows that if we do not know who it is, there will be no history, so although we are accustomed to backstories there usually isn't any. Most backstories are fictional.

Many come on my tours specifically to share with me their experiences in St Andrews and often from around the world. Some experiences happened too long ago for them to recollect the kind of details I am sure you would like to hear more of, while others are able to recollect almost every detail. It depends on the nature and subtlety of the incident, the impact it had at the time and the nature of the person. When looking in the eyes of those who recollect every detail you can see it is as if they are currently experiencing what they are describing.

There are around 6,500 residents and 10,000 students in St Andrews. With there being such a large academic body, accommodation here tends to revolve around the university. A lot of students are staying in different residences in different terms. Not long after they move in some start to notice odd things happening. They then come on my tours to tell me what they are currently experiencing, or what they have experienced. A common expression is; "We have someone in our flat!"

It has got to the point in most cases where they will tell me their experiences and I will tell them their address. That is how specific it can be. There tends to be something unique, something characteristic that is localised to each. There are still surprises of previously unreported locations, and the occasional experience I have not heard about before in locations with a history of activity, but most of the time, if I am unfamiliar with what they are talking about it is because they are communicating their experiences in an unfamiliar way. They are rarely aware of the history of the locality or know anything about the experiences of previous occupants, and this is also one of the commonalities. It is not something you will find on a lease, although accommodation in St Andrews is at a premium so I guess they are getting their money's worth.

The disclosure of prior phenomena in a residence by estate agents would make for interesting statistics and is not as outlandish as it may sound. In the USA it is known as *Stigmatized Properties*. Those from the States may be familiar with what I am speaking of here. A seller has a duty to disclose the history of a property that is unrelated to its physical conditions or features. Stigmas vary between local jurisdictions, but the types that must be disclosed include criminal, debt, murder, suicide, phenomenon and public. Yep, you heard that right, phenomenon. *Phenomenon Stigma* is the official term for the disclosure of a house renowned for being haunted, be it poltergeist activity or sightings of ghosts. While 'Public Stigma' involves properties that often become unwanted public attractions. A famous and regularly cited case spanning both is the house featured in *The Amityville Horror*, where they changed the name of the house and even the road name as an attempt to retain some privacy. It didn't work! The film itself was very loosely based on real events, but it was given the full Hollywood treatment and has become an attraction ever since.

**Corroboration**

There is a very defined and tangible logic to paranormal activity that can only be discerned through correlating the testimony of first-hand experiences. Additional testimonies give further insight into the phenomena of a locality no one was aware of. It opens the scope to the understanding of a bigger picture both in terms of localised disturbances and its nature. Scaled up to a global level, when phenomena are correlated together they give universal patterns of paranormal phenomena.

**Patterns**

The quantification of phenomena gives insight into the mechanics of phenomena and goes some way to the disclosure of set laws for the behaviour of activity amid the many potential variables residing within them. Patterns of testimony appear through a mix of shared commonality, corroboration, persistence/regularity and volume. These can give additional insights into the nature of individual incidents including the short and long term psychology surrounding the same involving reaction, comprehension and attribution etc.

You shall see quite a number of patterns as you progress through this volume. They are not something any were aware of. For that matter, most experiences involve people who had never heard anything about what they have experienced in a location before their mention of it to me.

# William Thomas Linskill
## 1855 to 1929
## The Fiction – The Truth

A name you will see cropping up throughout this volume for his early paranormal contributions in St Andrews is William Linskill. In 1911 he published a short fictional booklet: *St Andrews Ghost Stories.* His stories made quite an impact in St Andrews, more so than he would realise. Gaining momentum, they soon became engrained as legends resonating through the town as quickly as Dracula's exploits through a Transylvanian village. As a flamboyant Victorian gentleman with a keen sense of humour and an equally keen eye for golf and ghosts, he would have quite a chuckle at the thought of his fictional stories having such a marked influence over 100 years after their publication.

Fictional stories in themselves, like myths and legends, rarely hold up to historical scrutiny, although elements of truth often reside at their heart. Like most works of fiction his booklet was nine parts fiction and one part fact, problem is, which is which? Through my researches I have found the more prominent ghosts in his stories have a reality, the background stories are fiction.

I republished it in GOS (2013), and again with further additions in 2021 as the first hand-transcribed standalone. Heavily annotated his publication is twice the length it was. I reference Linskill in places to either dispel his myths or by linking some of the ghosts he mentions to further attributions.

## Synchronicity

One of many running themes throughout this volume is the nature of coincidence, or more poignantly, synchronicity. The *St Andrews Citizen*, September, 1926, posted a short article featuring the musings of Victorian antiquarian William Linskill taking an evening stroll around some of the more auspicious haunted sites of St Andrews.

In 2013, the Special Units Collection Department for the University were looking to conduct a private ghost tour based on William Linskill's fictional booklet *St Andrews Ghost Stories* for Halloween 2013.

On writing about their adventure, Maia Sheridan, Manuscripts Archivist, recorded:

'...most spooky of all, and you will find this hard to believe but it really is true, although we had the stories we didn't know the route of the ghost tours which Linskill took [he didn't conduct ghost tours]. I was in one of our strong rooms looking at another collection, when my eye was drawn to the shelf below. There were some volumes labelled 'newspaper cuttings,' which I had never looked at before. I don't usually have time to explore curious looking archives but this time felt I had to look in them – they turned out to be 5 scrapbooks of the St Andrews Antiquarian Society, compiled by Linskill himself! And the very first article I read, which wasn't even in the first book I opened, was the one featured here of Linskill's moonlight walk through haunted St Andrews, giving us the perfect ghost tour route to follow in his footsteps. Was Linskill in there with me guiding me to the right place? Who knows. But out of 13km of material housed in Special Collections, it's quite a coincidence to randomly open a volume at exactly the right page. I like to believe I had a little help in finding those scrapbooks.'[2] Maia certainly did and other examples present themselves throughout this volume where the spirit of the deceased compels conscious action by influencing your subconscious through your spirit with no conscious reason or suggestion.

Like Maia's experience, Clark and myself experienced something similar up at Fairmont (refer to **Hotels**). The odds against what happened were at least 1.76 billion to 1. For Maia's experience the odds against would be increased to the power of something far greater.

I do not adhere to coincidences per se, but I do adhere to the reality of synchronicities. Starting with coincidence, the dictionary definition is 'a remarkable concurrence of events or circumstances without apparent causal connection.' We know coincidences occur regardless of, and independent of our reasoning, but could there be an *apparent* cause underlying the perceived random factor of chance?

Analytical psychologist Carl Jung explored this avenue at great length and in great detail over many years. In 1931 he introduced a principle called synchronicity. The dictionary definition being 'the simultaneous occurrence of events which appear significantly related but have no discernible causal connection,' which is getting closer the mark but the true definition of synchronicity is from Jung himself. He stated a synchronicity is 'a meaningful coincidence of two or more events where something other than the probability of chance is involved,'[3] and that is where we find ourselves here.

At its simplest, a synchronicity is a streamlined aspect of existence where seemingly disparate elements in reality are falling into place. They are a sure sign of the spiritual influencing physical events in ways leading to something special, something that is meant to be. The operations of synchronicity only make sense at the time to those who recognise them. They are the only ones who can make the connections and appreciate the odds against something meaningful for them occurring, and the only conscious involvement is one of recognition leading to a greater understanding of a moment. It is always personal and it always astonishes those it happens to.

Moving deeper into the mechanics of synchronicity, they are not the origin of an event, they are correspondences operating through complex spiritual energetic dynamics. We could think of it as the universe willing a favorable progression for a specific outcome, but it is doing this *all* the time, it is called life, we just don't tend to recognize the telling signs of how everything links together unless there is a more obvious connection to give us an associative meaning. When these rare moments of recognition happen, we are given a brief glimpse into underlying principles of reality in the physical as marker points. They represent the merging of destiny with time as either a physical event, or a series of physical events that go way beyond the remit of chance.

Synchronicities can be instigated through the energetic fingerprint of a spirit close to the recipient. Their localised poltergeist activity has a particular familiarity whereby only the recipient will be able to make the connection as to its source. Perhaps a distinctive associative smell as a reminder, a sense of a presence often coupled with distinctive feelings, a thought or a mental impression of who is now present. When this happens, you can be sure they are looking to directly let you know they are close. However, the signs can be subtle, so they can be easily missed and all too often dismissed.

On the following page is another example of those subtle interconnected synchronicities where it is possible to know where the influence has come from. Refer also to Harry Houdini, **Appendix 2.**

September 7, 2016 Evening Telegraph 19

# New twists in soldier's heroic story a century on

**DUNDEE soldier Frank Grant was killed in action 98 years ago – but continues to be the subject of some very unlikely coincidences.**

Events began when his great-great grandson Jan Tero, 9, of St Andrews wanted to be dressed as a "hero" for Children and Need.

He made a cardboard medal just like the one Frank won during the war and wore it to school – on November 13.

The Evening Telegraph looked into the heart-warming tale and discovered Frank had actually won his medal for saving a life on November 13 1916.

"It was the day Jan went to school with his cardboard medal," said his mum Jennifer Low.

"Honestly, you could have knocked me down with a feather."

A photographer was sent to take a

Dundee soldier Frank Grant.

BY STEWART ROSS

picture of young Jan to illustrate the tale and called on November 15, which it turns out was Frank's birthday.

"When I was about 12 I was taken to Edinburgh Castle," recalls Jennifer.

"There was a book of Remembrance listing all the Scottish soldiers who died in the Great War.

"I opened it at random and right there in front of me on the first page I looked at was Private Frank Grant, Royal Scots.

"I know this sounds incredible but the same thing happened to my sister when she went – she opened the book at the page with Frank's name."

And now there's been a new twist.

Jennifer revealed: "I decided to order a Somme commemorative poppy made out of the shell cases from the battlefield.

"It's for my husband's birthday as he likes this sort of thing!

"Each one comes with a certificate commemorating the life of a soldier who died in the battle and is chosen at random.

"The one I have received just happens to commemorate the life of a Pte R Thomson."

Thomson could have been from anywhere but he wasn't – he was Black Watch, his folks lived just up the road in Alyth.

And Robert Thomson died in 1916 on . . . November 13.

Jennifer was amazed. She said: "Spooky or what?

"Could it be just a little reminder that Frank is my spirit guide? I'm joking . . . I think!"

Frank Grant has been lying in France for nearly 100 years but, in a funny way, he's still in touch.

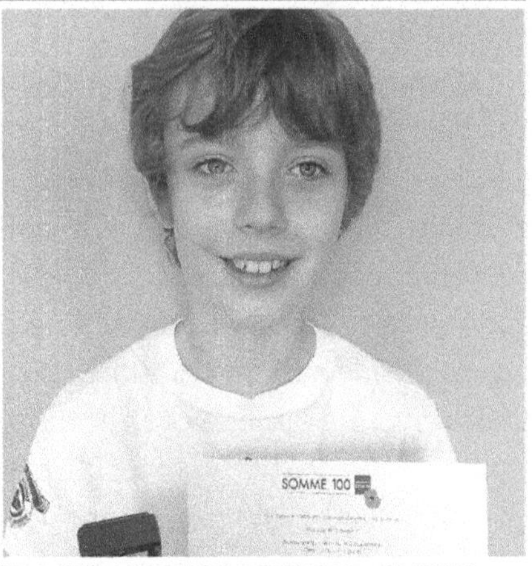


Nine-year-old Jan Tero with the certificate in memory of Private R Thomson of The Black Watch.

Evening Telegraph, September 7, 2016. The article reads:

**DUNDEE soldier Frank Grant was killed in action 98 years ago – but continues to be the subject of some very unlikely coincidences.**

'Events began when his great-great grandson Jan Tero, 9, of St Andrews wanted to be dressed as a "hero" for Children in Need.

He made a cardboard medal just like the one Frank won during the war and wore it to school – on November 13.

The Evening Telegraph looked into the heart-warming tale and discovered Frank had actually won his medal for saving a life on November 13 1916.

"It was the day Jan went to school with his cardboard medal," said his mum Jennifer Low.

"Honestly, you could have knocked me down with a feather."

A photographer was sent to take a picture of young Jan to illustrate the tale and called on November 15, which it turns out was Frank's birthday.

"When I was about 12 I was taken to Edinburgh Castle," recalls Jennifer.

"There was a book of Remembrance listing all the Scottish soldiers who died in the Great War.

"I opened it at random and right there in front of me on the first page I looked at was Private Frank Grant, Royal Scots.

"I know this sounds incredible but the same thing happened to my sister when she went – she opened the book at the page with Frank's name."

And now there's been a new twist.

Jennifer revealed: "I decided to order a Somme commemorative poppy made out of the shell cases from the battlefield.

"It's for my husband's birthday as he likes this sort of thing!

"Each one comes with a certificate commemorating the life of a soldier who died in the battle and is chosen at random.

"The one I have received just happens to commemorate the life of Pte R Thomson."

Thomson could have been from anywhere but he wasn't – he was Black Watch, his folks lived just up the road at Alyth.

And Robert Thomson died in 1916 on . . . November 13.

Jennifer was amazed. She said: "Spooky or what?

"Could it be just a little reminder that Frank is my spirit guide? I'm joking . . . I think!"

Frank Grant has been lying in France for nearly 100 years but, in a funny way, he's still in touch.'

For the present circumstance, the connection with Frank is an input of energetic connections rather than any conscious act on behalf of Frank in the spirit. The subtle short bursts of synchronicity are through energetic correspondences marked by the medal and the Book of Remembrance linking Frank in the physical through the trauma of war with the energetic field of family members. Associative energetic connections can also be denoted by circumstance, or time for example, which we also have here by way of correspondence through the connecting date of November 13th. The energetic displays are subtle and as I mentioned could only ever be made by those who would recognize the connections. The energetic attributes or influences were not great enough for Frank to be the soldier whose life was commemorated, but the surrounding information of another soldier including the date was nonetheless enough for there to be a connection that was picked up as a link to Frank.

There is a house in St Andrews on the route of the tour with the ghost of a woman. She is in the attic room but causes activity throughout the house which is now two apartments. The premises can be like a vacuum. Always like an icebox with objects disappearing and reappearing in different locations and the feeling of being watched. I have a few reports of the those going to bed in the attic room to find the imprint of someone lying in it. A woman after a tour in August 2021 sent me an email. She was in the attic room adjoining the room the woman was in. A woman came through the wall into her room.

On Monday 16th August 2021, the ground floor lights were on, but we saw no one in the rooms. When we were walking away from the house along the road, I was facing backwards talking to the group and all the lights in the house came on, went off, then on, then off three times, with a short pause each time. After the tour I was walking to the car, which was parked just along the road from the house when the car lights of the car parked in front of mine flashed on and the beeper went as though someone just unlocked their car. There was no one around. The following day I received a phone call from an old friend that Malcolm Mackie had died in Thurso the morning before. He was someone I considered a brother, so I was quite shocked. That evening I wondered if the lights could have been Malcolm sending me a sign as the two incidents the night before were just very odd. It then dawned on me. He stayed in that house when he was at university here and was one of those who saw the imprint in the bed – there was my connection.

A background introduction to

# *St Andrews*

St Andrews is a small beautiful historic town of note. With its Great Cathedral it is also a city. Set on the east coast of Scotland overlooking the North Sea in the Kingdom of Fife, it now only has a population of some 6,500 people and around 10,000 transitional students. As I stated, for its size it is the most haunted location in the world. A big bold statement, but then with many world firsts, St Andrews is full of big bold statements.

St Andrews has many precedents, including the home of golf (c.1400) and Scotland's oldest university (1413). This was also the greatest seat of Catholic power outside Rome in Europe. It was one of the early pioneers of photography, and is now one of the top tourist destinations in Europe.

Its history spans back to 500 BC with the arrival of the Celts from Ireland. It then became a seat of the Pictish Kings with Druidry as the main spiritual discipline until the 6th century and the arrival of the Celtic Church through the Céilí Dé from Ireland. Six bones or relics of St Andrew were then brought here in c.736 AD. St Andrew was the first apostle of Christ and the

Céilí Dé were their entrusted keepers. The arrival of the relics saw the advent of tourism, with pilgrims arriving mostly from Europe for the healing powers of the saint. The arrival of the Catholic Church through the Augustinians in the 12th century saw a marketing machine that led to a name change to St Andrews c.1144 from Kilrymont (with many etymological associations). It then became a major centre for the Cult of St Andrew that saw over 20 million pilgrims arriving at its door from Europe over the next four centuries alone. This was Rome II. In 1559, through John Knox, Protestant reformers overthrew the Catholic Church and St Andrews would be virtually desolate for the next three centuries.

The university has some of the finest research facilities to be found, and the golf now attracts millions of pilgrims, including astronauts, Hollywood stars, American presidents, sports personalities and rock stars. St Andrews is very informal and with its intimate nature you meet everyone, either in the street, cafes, bars, restaurants or by the golf courses.

**Why is there so much paranormal activity in St Andrews?**

There is a unique quality here that is felt by many. It is partly due to it being off the beaten track which is why it is known as a bubble. A subtlety rarely picked up is the emotional intensity through the sheer volume of pilgrims arriving from Europe over a core period of 400 years. This has created a lasting energetic footprint contributing to its magnetic flair and raising the inherent level of natural energy that saw St Andrews as a major spiritual centre for well over 1000 years. Plagues wiped out between 30% and 60% of Europe so the healing powers of the saint were a big draw. Like the traveller of today, it was the pilgrim who spread the disease. The result saw a great many dying here. Energy fluctuates, and if all the conditions are met, an in-between the worlds feel leads to the observance of Group A. phenomena here. A quality noted at times when the haar comes rolling through its older quarters . . .

# The Mysterious St Andrews Haar

There is something eerie about the haar as it drifts in from the North Sea and the familiar landmarks of St Andrews begin to disappear. It seems to bring with it something of the past, or perhaps for a moment it has the power to transform St Andrews to an earlier time. Seeing it coming in always reminds me of John Carpenter's film 'The Fog' with Clint Eastwood. A mysterious fog comes in from the sea and on sweeping over the town, deceased mariners begin to emerge. The film is fiction though it carries interesting parallels with experiences here. As an opener for the great many paranormal anomalies to be found in St Andrews as examples of universal phenomena, along with explanations where appropriate, the following comprises a few experiences taking place when the haar comes rolling in.

**East Sands Monks**

Cathy Buchanan, a dear school friend from Kilrymont days came on one of my tours with her son Ross while she was recovering from cancer. She has wanted to come on a tour for a while and it was a privilege to take her and Ross around St Andrews. With beating cancer, Cathy was still weak, but equally determined to complete the tour, which she did with great strength, and has now been on my tour three times!

At the end of the tour we were in the Central, where Cathy relayed a story her grandfather told her when she was young that she has always been in two minds about. Her grandfather, John Souttar, was a fisherman in St Andrews and was in his boat not far offshore. He was moving parallel to the East Sands travelling toward the harbour. The haar started coming in easterly from the sea, and with it, in front of him, he saw what looked like monks walking from the sea onto the beach. A few minutes later the haar began clearing and the monks disappeared.

After Cathy told me this she said she never knew whether to believe him or not and wanted to see if I could shed more light on it. I was quite taken aback, and with a smile relayed to her the following: A woman I met was walking her dog early one morning along the East Sands toward the harbour end of the beach. It was clear to start with, then as she continued walking the haar started coming in from the sea. All the usual landmarks of the pier, the harbour buildings, and Cathedral ruins started disappearing. She then saw some people walking toward her on the sands at the head of the haar as it rolled along the beach.

The haar soon became lighter and cleared, and as it did so, the figures she was observing disappeared with it. There was nowhere for them to go, and for that matter, there was nowhere they could have come from.

Cathy was so excited when I told her this, as she realised after all these years her grandfather's story was true.

**The West Port and Archbishop Sharpe**

I was having a few drinks with Ronnie Howe in the Blue Stane just after New Year 2016. We got onto the subject of ghosts and he told me about a few of his own experiences in St Andrews that you will find recorded throughout this volume. There is a consistency in what he relates that hasn't wavered over the years. By this I mean there has never been any unnecessary embellishment whenever he mentions them and the conviction is always the same.

On this occasion, he was standing outside the Whey Pat on Bridge Street. The haar was coming in fast as a figure appeared standing by the left side of the West Port in the regalia of a bishop. Ronnie said Archbishop Sharpe was the one that kept coming to mind. The mist then cleared as quickly as it came and the figure disappeared. "That bugger Sharpe," he would say, "he keeps following me around St Andrews!"

When Ronnie was young he heard the coach in Market Street (p.248), which has an association with Sharpe through Linskill. We always attribute what we see to the first thought that comes to mind, and for Ronnie, like the town, Linskill's stories are as fresh as they were in 1911. They are stories we all grew up with, but they don't detract in any way from the reality of the experiences themselves. Ronnie's experience of hearing the coach and horses was also when it was like, "pea soup" as Ronnie put it, with the haar well into the town. Refer also to p.248 and p.261, for Ronnie's other experiences. What Ronnie saw by the West Port was also seen in Abbey Street in 1952. Refer to p.315.

### The Cathedral Ghost Photo

Francis Quinn and her partner came on one of my tours. The following morning, they were wandering around the Cathedral grounds. The haar was present and thick throughout the grounds and the town. It was a cold day and crucially they were the only ones in the grounds at that time. Francis took a photo from the right-hand cloister archway of the graveyard looking toward the Square Tower. In the photo there is a figure standing looking at a cross-shaped grave.... Full details along with the photo can be found on p.553.

### The Square Tower

Michael Alexander, Lead News Feature Writer for the Dundee Courier has three experiences of St Andrews. One was a head leaning out of the upper window of the Square Tower lit by an unknown source as the haar was settling across the Cathedral grounds. (p.100, p.161, p.180)

### Pends, Mint Security Wall

We used to print our own money in St Andrews. I have another photo taken when the haar was closing in of what appears to be a white figure of light on the security wall of the former mint. (p.552)

### South Street/West Burn Lane

Along South Street a few years ago, a man was walking eastwards by the Town Hall. The skyline began disappearing through a wave of haar coming in from the sea. Rapidly enveloping the buildings his attention was diverted by the sound of someone coming up behind him, someone wearing what he thought were segs on their shoes making a loud noise on the pavement as they walked... (p.303).

# *Cathedral Precincts*

Taking 158 years to build (consecrated 1318), and with a history spanning hundreds of years, there is a mass of phenomena taking place in the Great Cathedral precincts of St Andrews.

This first report for the Cathedral occurs in the former (new) Chapter House of the Cathedral and involves four separate sightings by Kyle Stewart.

**Report 1.**

Kyle started working for Historic Scotland back in 2015. Kyle has had visual experiences in both the Cathedral and the Palace (Castle) precincts recorded later p.218. On four occasions in the Cathedral precincts he has seen the same hooded figure in black standing by the stone cist graves of monks in the former Chapter House. It is always when he is about to lock up St Rule's Tower for the night. He turns to see if anyone is around, and catches a glimpse of a figure standing just to the west of the burial cists. The figure appears to be looking down at the information plaque. Once the tower is locked he turns again and no one is there. The black cowl covers the face so he hasn't been able to tell if it is a man or woman.

His first sighting was during the winter of 2017. From what he mentioned it is an Augustinian monk. Known as black canons from their black habits, they extended St Rule's, built the Great Cathedral and ran the precincts for 415 years.

The location is reminiscent of the murder of Robert De Montrose, a Lord of Parliament who had precedence over all other Priors and Abbots in Scotland. He was murdered by an unruly monk by the name of Thomas Platter in 1394.

The proceedings were popularised in a fictional story by Linskill attributing Robert De Montrose as the ghostly monk of St Rule's Tower, but his attribution is incorrect, the monk seen in the tower is a Franciscan as he is wearing brown not black (p.87). A contender for the ghost here could be Thomas Platter, but his bones were finally interred on holy ground on the 15th July 1898, and he appears to be finally at peace. There are intriguing circumstances surrounding the aftermath of this fourteenth century murder, and especially circumstances surrounding how Platter's bones came to be laid to rest some five centuries after his death. In brief: It was recorded by the town council that a hotel employee had two visionary experiences which led to the exhumation and reburial of his bones by town officials in 1898. Lord Bute was one of those present at his funeral. Refer to GOS p.126.

The stone cists in the Chapter House were each fashioned from single large stones and were individually shaped to the bodies of their occupants. One weighs over two tons!

**Note the stone coped lid on the top left cist. The information sign stands just behind.**

I am never sure why, but it is common for people on my tours to try them for size. Sometimes it takes the whole family to then get them out, especially if they have just had their lunch!

With the ghost still being seen here I would wager the ghost seen by Kyle is Robert De Montrose. There are a few reasons for this. He was an Augustinian monk and where Kyle has seen him is only yards from where he was murdered to the right. The stone cists currently exposed in the Chapter House are of monks. There is a reference to Montrose being interred here and the dates of the cists match the period of the fourteenth century. A skeleton is still present under the stone coped lid, just by where Kyle has seen him. The figure Kyle has observed is not looking down at the information sign, he is looking down at his own grave just beyond the sign. I believe the skeleton you are looking at is Montrose himself.

This photo was taken in 1904 and appeared in the local press as one of William Linskill's many finds during his 'howkings' in the precincts of that time. The bones were not forensically examined, if they were to be examined at some point in the future the telling sign would be for evidence of stab wounds.

If I mention about the skeleton still being present on tours I am not sure some believe me, while others comment how easily someone could lift the lid and steal the bones! Aside the lid being of an optimal weight for a hernia, the simple answer to this is Linskill cemented the lid in place in 1904. The graves were then surrounded by a black four foot high iron railing fence which was removed for the war effort.

**Report 2.**

Alistair and his partner came on the 7:30pm tour, Saturday 4th October, 2020. We were standing on the rise of the Scores Path between the Haunted Tower and the Palace overlooking the sea and the Cathedral precincts. The location where Kyle is standing in the photo. Alistair mentioned seeing two people walking along the high ruins of a wall in the Cathedral grounds. It was dark, and both the figures and wall were silhouetted by the lights of St Leonards Ollerenshaw dormitory shining in the distance from behind.

He saw them for a few moments, turned to mention them to me, and when we all looked they had gone. I said there was no reason for anyone being up there at that time, or at any time for that matter. It isn't a wall where you need to climb over to get to anywhere. It is just a ruined part of the precincts. He then put a short piece about his experience on my tripadvisor page:

**Tripadvisor 4th October**

"Thoroughly enjoyed this. First time going on a ghost tour and would highly recommend this to anyone interested in the history of St Andrews and paranormal activity. Richard's knowledge was spot on, could have listened to the guy all night. I'm very sceptical about this but seen 2 silhouettes travelling across a high wall. Even went back and checked the area once the tour was finished. Don't know why anyone would be up such a high wall at that time of night and the direction they were going led to nowhere except to a large drop. Highly recommended."

Old habits are hard to break, but I know he is not nearly as sceptical as he was before the start of the tour.

**A link between the observer and the observed**

Ghosts can and do disappear in front of us, either just vanishing or fading into nothing. This is partly through the dissipation of energy in the locality. One of the common global patterns, and displayed through this volume is seeing something, then looking or glancing away and on looking back it has gone. That is when they realise it was a ghost.

The importance is they always disappear at that exact instant. The same with sound, which I explore later for coach/horse phenomena, where an energetic connection, an energetic link is temporarily created between the observer and the phenomena that is broken the moment we acknowledge the direction of sound. For ghosts it is very similar, we look away, we are distracted or blink etc, and looking back they are gone.

The link can be sustained more readily when it involves the spirit of a deceased person rather than an impression as there is more of a focus where they are utilising the energy in the locality, so the energy tends to be stronger. There is never an 'either or' with the paranormal, instead there are many variables. It all depends on the circumstance, and within this, again there are also many variables, and as I state often it is all very subtle, with varying degrees of complexity. It is through the emerging patterns forming through the wealth of corroborated evidence that these patterns of behaviour or what I sometimes refer to as 'ghost law' can be fathomed.

The energy inherent in our recognition of phenomenon is a good disperser of the energy surrounding phenomenon. This is spiritual energy, the underlying source of reality. Its behaviour and manifestation as with all paranormal activity share particular attributes with physical energy but its scope is far more profound and cannot be physically quantified in the same way.

These are shared commonalities of both groups A. and B. and symptomatic of what I spoke of in Group A about the nature of energy operating on and through subtle levels.

# *St Rule's Tower*

## Energy Centre 2.[i]

As a preliminary note this was the first Cathedral in St Andrews. The tower is generally called St Rule's Tower or the Square Tower as it is known locally. This was the bell tower and was adorned with a spire. Originally this was the Reliquary Church of Regulus or St Regulus, then the Church of St Andrew or St Andrew's Church. As Spottiswood in 1655 stated, 'the church of Regulus, now called St Andrews.'[4]

I lace many historical aspects of St Andrews throughout this volume where appropriate to give additional background to phenomena. The history is complex, not least due to conflicting accounts and dates.

Despite accepted authorities over the centuries promoting their findings as fact or more often being taken as such, we appear to have five definitive dates and a loose decade depending on the historian or commentator you fancy for its original construction. I don't consider myself to be a collector of dates as such, but we appear to have: 1070, 1127, 1138, 1144, 1145 and the 1160s. There will be more equally definitive dates out there. Refer to HoS.

---

[i] There are six energy centres in the older quarter of St Andrews. Refer to p.120.

I favour it being built by the Céilí Dé, as James Taylor intimated in 1859, and would put the date at c.1070 with Fothad II as Bishop. Bishop Robert then enlarged it in 1144, but proving too small for the pilgrims now arriving they set about building the Great Cathedral, 1160-1318 (not 1158!). Bishop Robert died 1159/60 and was buried in St Rule's.

There were a series of wooden floors in the tower accessed by wooden ladders giving access to the floors, bells and the top of the tower. Following the Reformation in St Andrews these fell into disrepair. Fleming says the remnants of branders "which were probably the joists for carrying the floors, seem to have been taken down by the magistrates, in or shortly before 1765, under the pretext that children were in danger of losing their lives by climbing upon them, as there were no shut doors to keep them out."[ii5] He says 'pretext' because they would no doubt serve a more useful purpose elsewhere. The council were fashionably corrupt so this doesn't surprise. What does surprise is that around 1779 they built a newel stone stair up the south-east internal corner of the tower. Fleming in his handbook regarding the minutes of this time, says, 'the cost for the initial repairs to the tower in 1779 before the newel stair was put in was £111 11s 5d sterling.'

The addition of the newel stair was an unusual move for two reasons, the council were bordering on bankruptcy and the Cathedral precincts were being used as quarry stone for the town. The only reason I can fathom for them repairing the structure and constructively building the stair, was that at 108 feet high, the tower made an ideal vantage point for any looming trouble. Created from grey sandstone ashlar it was also of far better quality and construction than the Cathedral, and had stood the test of time up to that point for just over 700 years.

---

[ii] Fleming, Dr. Hay, St Andrews Standard Guide, first published 1881, republished 1949, p.66.

# *St Rule's Tower Phenomena*

13 Aspects of Phenomena (A)
19 Reports (R)

## In 3 Parts

**13 Aspects of Phenomena**
This is then followed by details of each experience:

| | |
|---|---|
| **Part 1.** | **Tower Reports: Ghosts of Franciscan Monks** |
| A1. R.1. | Figure peering over the top of the tower when closed |
| A2. R.2. | Figures at the top of the tower when closed |
| A3. R.3. | Monk at the foot of the tower pointing up |
| A4. R.4 & 5. | Monk helping people to the top |
| A5. R.6 & 7. | Passing a monk on the newel stair |
| A6. R.8. | Monks seen on one of the former floors |
| A7. R.9. | Door slamming and a monk seated in the tower |

**Part 2.** **Tower Reports: Further anomalous activity in the tower**

A8. R.10-11. Something brushing past on the stair

A9. R.12. Sound of footsteps (Linskill's experience)

A10. R.13. Flickering lights in window of tower

**Part 3.** **Tower Reports: Ghost of a White Lady or Céilí Dé Monk?**

A11. R.14 Lights and a figure in white

A12. R.15. Light coming out of the top window and a head peering out

A13. R.16-19. Bright figure in white being seen in the top window

## Tower Reports Part 1.

# Ghosts of Franciscan Monks

(A) Anomalies
(R) Example Reports

One of the main colours of the Franciscan monk's habit is brown. They travelled here over the centuries following their 1209 formation in Italy, and had an established seat here from 1458. Sited on what was the far western fringe of St Andrews it was known as Greyfriars Franciscan Friary or Monastery. Appropriately named after their greyish brown attire, p.490. The Student's Union now occupies the site.

R1. Figure at the top of the tower when closed (Woman)
R2. Figures at the top of the tower when closed (Marini. J)
R3. Monk at the foot of the tower pointing up (Simpson)
R4. Monk helping people to the top (Various)
R5. Monk helping people to the top (Elder)
R6. Passing a monk on the newel stair (Visitors)
R7. Passing a monk on the newel stair (Boyd)
R8. Monks seen on one of the former floors (Visitors)
R9. Door slamming and a monk seated in the tower (Girl)

**1/ A1. Local woman – Tower Report 1. (Group A or B)**
**Figure peering over the top of the tower when closed**

A local woman saw a figure peering over the top of the tower silhouetted against the night sky when it was all closed-up. She was making her way to the east end of Lamond Drive and was walking along the East Scores Path towards the harbour when she saw it. She thought it was a monk but the figure was too far away for her to be more specific. Her observation was from the same location as where Michael Alexander observed something unusual in the tower. (p.101)

**2/ A2. John's Tower Report 2. (Group A or B)**
**Figures at the top of the tower when closed**

Others have seen a few figures wandering around the top of the tower when closed to the public, including John Marini who saw someone one morning at 7:30 am. He was standing outside the New Inn on St Mary Street. It was long before the tower was due to open to the public.

**3/ A3. Dave's Tower Report 3. (Group B)**
**Dave (*KISS Army*) Simpson! – Monk at foot of the tower stair**

One afternoon in 1970, David Simpson, a six-year-old boy, was scouring the East Sands for empty bottles of pop – as you do. Irn Bru, Cherryade, it didn't matter the flavour. In 1915, Barr's, the global soft drinks company hailing from Glasgow offered a small recompense if bottles were returned to an outlet that sold them. He had never been up the Square Tower and needed money to do so.

After trading in his bottles, he went to the Cathedral grounds and paid his money to the custodian. On entering the tower, he was greeted by another man standing against the wall by the stair pointing upwards. There are 158 steps to the top. This is one of the tightest and steepest stairs in Scotland and a dizzying trek for anyone let alone a six-year-old boy. He must have thought he was climbing to the moon.

He eventually made it to the top and excitedly admired the view. When he came back down, the custodian seated in the booth by the entrance asked, "Did you find your way to the top ok?"

In reply to the custodian, he said, "Sure, a man showed me the way up."

"What man?" the custodian replied, "You were the only one in the tower." That is when both Dave and the custodian realised he had seen the famed ghost of the monk.

Much to his disappointment, this is the only experience Dave has had in all the years of being in St Andrews, although this is still one noted experience more than most, and it did feature the appearance of one of the most famous ghosts in St Andrews, so not all bad.

He didn't take any notice of what the figure was wearing apart from to say he didn't look like the custodian who was more official-looking and wearing a cap, but he believes he was bald on top with longish hair either side of his face.

We rarely question our experiences, especially when it is in-keeping with the setting, when it doesn't defy the laws of physics, and more especially when we are young.

**4/ A4. (Various) Tower Report 4. (Group B)**
**Monk helping people to the top**

Peter Underwood – one of the foremost authorities on ghosts who sadly passed away in 2014, wrote in his book *Gazetteer of Scottish Ghosts,* published in 1973: 'The monk appears at the time of the full moon, he is friendly and helpful, frequently appearing on the treacherous dark and twisting stairway of St. Rule's tower to help a visitor who is in danger of slipping. He is reported to have helped people in this way on occasions in 1948, 1952 and 1970.'[6] GOS p.129.

The appearance of the monk on a full moon is a myth, he can appear at any time but the tower is now only open during the day. So, if you are looking to see him inside the tower during the hours of darkness and during the full moon, you're efforts will be in vein, the tower is locked. I could say, with Underwood being old school that he liked to slip in these embellishments to generate a bit of atmosphere, but this was probably his publisher. Far from being old school, it is now unfortunately the western normal to include such elements.

Underwood remains one of the few who understood the nature of ghosts as a reality. He devoted his life to researching locations and phenomena, and is certainly missed, not least because he did so much for the SPR, the Ghost Club, and the furtherment of ghosts as a subject for the public in general.

**5/ A4. Michael Elder's Tower Report 5. (Group B)**
**Monk guiding him to the top of the tower**

Dave's early experience is reminiscent of an experience I reproduce in GOS p.127. This is the 1948 incident Underwood refers to and published by Stewart Lamont, 1980:

'Michael Elder a young actor from the Byre Theatre had a peculiar experience within the tower one summer's day in 1948: 'I paid my three pence and was climbing the wooden stairs near the bottom when I noticed the legs of a man standing above me clad in a sort of cassock. I didn't think of the strangeness of the dress at the time and when he asked if I was going up I said yes. "You can follow me up," he said, but when I got to the top and looked around, there was no one in sight. There was no way that I could have squeezed past him on the narrow stairs, I got a cold shiver, panicked and ran down the stairs as fast as I could.

When I got into the sunshine, the custodian was standing watching two men mowing the grass. I asked him if he had seen anyone come out of the tower. "There has been no one in or out since yourself," he replied.'[7]

**6/ A5. Visitors – Tower Report 6. (Group B)**
**Passing the monk on the newel stair**

One afternoon in the middle of November 2014, visitors were climbing the stairs of the tower and halfway up they passed what they thought was a woman wearing a brown dress and sandals. It wasn't until they got to the top they realised the stair was too narrow for two to comfortably pass on the stair at the same time. That is when they realised it was a monk they had passed, not a woman.

**7/ A5. Greta's Tower Report 7. (Group B)**
**Passing the monk on the newel stair**

In the late 1980s I had the great pleasure of meeting Greta Boyd when conducting research for the first book – GOS. As a local medium, there are a number of experiences she related to me for St Andrews.

The following is from GOS p.128: 'When 14 years of age, Greta Boyd visited St Regulus Tower with some friends. The old worn steps tightly and steeply spiralling within the tower were precarious and dark, so her concentration had been directed toward them. When nearing the top, a figure wearing a brown skirt appeared from around the corner above her, before carrying on she moved to one side to let the woman pass. Once at the top, her friends asked what had taken her so long. After explaining about the woman, they looked at her astonished and informed her there had been no one else on the stair at all. What Greta had assumed to be a woman wearing a brown skirt had in fact been the habit of the famed monk of St Rule! It was only then she realised it wasn't possible for the figure to have squeezed past her on the narrow stair, and there had been no physical contact.'

Refer to p.484 for Greta's experience at Kinburn and to GOS for more of her experiences around St Andrews.

**Delayed reaction and the complexities of perception**

We each have what is known as 'selective perception' whereby we automatically accept that which has a familiar frame of reference for us, one favouring our interpretation and our interests more readily. Lucas says it is 'a form of bias because we interpret information in a way that is congruent with our existing values and beliefs.'[8] With this we also have, as Griffin states, a 'tendency to either not notice or more quickly forget stimuli that causes emotional discomfort and contradicts our prior beliefs.'[9] This applies across the board and in present context when passing someone on the stair wearing a brown dress and sandals, the last thing witnesses think of is a monk. The delay in our comprehension is a uniform pattern across those having seen the monk whilst within the tower. It is also uniform across most experiences in general. Michael Elder saying, he, "didn't think of the strangeness of the dress at the time."

Our conscious mind is programmed to focus on what is important at any given moment in time. Everything else is present but it all just sits happily on the peripheries attracting no conscious thought or attention.

Even when we are looking for ghosts it is still the last thing we expect to see as they are so rare to observe, and in one respect we don't think we will be so 'lucky' to see something so elusive. This gives away the difference between their reality and how we perceive them to be, so when we do experience them, as I recorded in the first section we more often don't realise we are.

It tends to be the unusual that attracts our attention after the event, when the mind, often through a niggling feeling that something wasn't right, has had time to digest what has just happened. Like the visitors and Greta, who only realised after their experience that the stair was too narrow for two to pass without any physical contact. This leads to an important observation I make later.

It could be asked, why does no one see their face? Well, they do, the subconscious retains every detail, but they are visually observed as whole – as a person. Unimportant detail does not register in the conscious mind, so they are not absorbed, which is why there is rarely any conscious recollection.

There is also more than one monk in the tower. There is a spirit (Group B.), and two separate Group A's. There are also various additional reports where the grouping cannot be determined. For the following two reports, one is Group A, the other is a double whammy, Group A and B:

**8/ A6. Tower Report 8. (Group A.)**
**Monks seen on one of the former floors**

I was chatting away with Bill, one of the custodians in the Historic Scotland Visitors Centre at the Palace. He related to me that visitors told him they had seen monks seated around a table on one of the former wooden floors of the tower.

**9/ A7. Visitor Tower Report 9. (Group A. and B.)**
**Door slamming and a monk seated in the tower**

Independent of this and uncannily similar, a woman I had on a tour told me when she was young she was with a school trip to the Cathedral. She was the last one to enter the tower and was about to start climbing the stairs when the heavy wooden entrance door slammed shut behind her. She opened the door and looked out but no one was around. It is a big heavy door and it opens from the inside, so whoever did it, was in there with her – not outside. [iii]

She started up the stairs and the same thing happened again. This time she ran up some of the stairs. On her way to the top she looked through one of the portal windows and saw a chamber with a wooden floor and a table, seated at which was a monk. She carried on up to the top, then on her way down she looked again through the same window and saw the same thing. It was her first visit up the tower and she has never experienced anything of the sort since.

Seeing monks on former floors in the tower were unpublished experiences until now, so it was not possible for each to know they were not alone in their experience.

As I mentioned earlier with Fleming, there are no wooden floors in the tower anymore. Aside the enclosed spiral stone stair in the south east corner and the roof walkway the tower is hollow, which has its own relevancy on p.104.

---

[iii] This was before Historic Scotland took over the grounds from the council and put turnstile barriers just beyond the heavy wooden door.

## Tower Reports Part 2.

# Further anomalous activity in the tower

R10. Something brushing past on the stair (Woman)
R11. Something brushing past on the stair (Taylor)
R12. Sound of footsteps (Linskill)
R13. Flickering lights in window of tower (Various)

**1/ A8. Tower Report 10.**
**Feeling of something passing on the stair**

A local woman working in Barnardo's in Bell Street was telling me when she was 14 they put metal steps in the lower section of the Square Tower (the lower section was originally made of wood). She was climbing to the top and without seeing anything she felt something pass her on the stair.

**2/ A8. Allan's Tower Report 11.**
**Something brushing past on the stair**

One afternoon I met Allan Taylor of Westburn Court Bed and Breakfast in West Burn Lane. He told me about his unusual experiences around St Andrews. He felt something brush past him when he began climbing the stairs of the tower. This is the monk Dave Simpson saw standing at the bottom of the stair, and the same one who slammed the door shut. Refer to p.228 and p.304 for Allan's other experiences.

**3/ A9. Linskill's Tower Report 12.**
**This is Linskill's only recorded paranormal experience**
William Linskill made the ghost of the monk famous through his fictional story, 'The Monk of St Rules Tower' originally published in his *St Andrews Ghost Stories* booklet of 1911, and reproduced in full in GOS p.303. His story was a stylisation of events leading to the murder of Montrose I briefly relayed earlier that occurred in fourteenth century, GOS p.127.

Linskill knew the reality of the ghosts, and even though he said he never experienced anything himself, he did have at least one experience. It shortened his life by at least the two hours he spent at the top of the Square Tower one night on his own in the hope of observing the monk for himself.

From HT p.21: 'Linskill ended up in St Rules Tower one Halloween night as the result of a wager by one of his fellow roommates that one of them wouldn't spend a couple of hours alone at its top. Not that they were all looking at Linskill of course, but he was first to rise to the challenge. With his necessary supplies of brandy and cigars to see him through his impending ordeal he boldly went to the tower. As he climbed the steep spiralling stairs his bravado began to lack the eagerness witnessed by his friends back in the comfort of their brightly lit and warm lodgings. On reaching the top he complied with the terms of the wager and remained there for exactly two hours. From his report, the experience terrified him! Despite there being no one else in the tower and locking the door to the tower behind him, he knew he was not alone. Whilst at the top he heard the footsteps of someone walking up the tower, he called out a few times, but no one replied and no one ever arrived at the top. When his two hours were up, and with a sigh of relief, he began making his way down the spiral stone steps. As he did so, he again heard the same footsteps, but this time they were coming from above. Something was now behind him, following him down the stair. He stopped and could still hear the footsteps but again no one arrived. When he returned to the ground, he locked the door and made his way to the Cathedral's keeper of the keys where he gladly received a very stiff whisky.

**4/ A10. Various Tower Report 13.**
**Flickering lights in the tower windows**

Like Pete Marini's experience (p.99), 'Lights like the flickering of candles have been seen in recent times shining through the windows of the tower late at night when all is silent and locked.' (GOS p.129).

As an observation, there is only the sensation of physical contact in the tower when nothing is seen. When the monk is seen on the stair there is no physical contact despite the stair being so narrow which is what alerts them to it being a ghost. The monk at the foot of the stair is a spirit, who is also the cause of the physical sensations on the stair. The monk seen on the stair and not felt is an impression, which makes sense as the monk does not acknowledge those it passes, but it poses a bit of a problem, a conundrum. Impressions are observed on the original level of ground of a building etc from when they were alive but the newel stair was not there when the monks were here, so how can there be an impression of a monk on the stair from an earlier time? The only explanation I can give, is the point at which the monk passes corresponds with a former floor or former stair at those sections where the monk appeared to pass them.

There is also another ghost in the tower. Always in white and always very brightly lit...

## Tower Reports Part 3.
## Ghost of a White Lady or Céilí Dé Monk?

### 6 Reports

St Cainnech (St Kenneth) founded the first church here between 563 AD and 565 AD on land called the Lady Craig and sited off what is now the end of the pier. This was *the Church of our Lady on the Rock*. Run by the Céilí Dé (Culdee), a monastic order from Ireland who administered the Celtic Christian faith here. The Celtic Church was a blend of Paganism, Druidism and early Christianity, as part of what the Roman Church called Insular Christianity. Céilí Dé priests could marry and there were a lot of women in their Order. They also all wore white in-keeping with their Druidic origins which gives an indication for the provinence of the White Lady.

The journey for her identity through the Céilí Dé is in HT, as an update to all the interconnecting material.

The Céilí Dé were the natural entrusted keepers of the relics of St Andrew since their arrival at Kilrymont[iv] in c.736 AD (Skene, 1860) not 732 AD. The relics were housed in various Céilí Dé churches including Lady Craig, then to the Reliquary Church of Regulus c.1070, which was built by the Céilí Dé and where they continued as they had before through the Cult of St Andrew. They were not housed in St Mary on the Rock as they didn't built that church until 1123. Once the Augustinians built the Great Cathedral, the relics were moved to there.

There is a lot of mystery surrounding the Céilí Dé. Conjecturally, I believe their role in whole or in part remained with them until 1559, despite the recorded bias of the Roman Church naturally promoting the Augustinians and an eventual Céilí Dé incorporation (disappearance). Refer to HoS.

---

[iv] The name of this locality before being renamed St Andrews in 1144.

**St Rules Tower**

R14. Lights and figure in white (Marini. P) early 90s
R15. Light and head upper window north side (Alexander) 1995
R16. Figure in white top window west side (Falconer +9) 2015
R17. Figure in white top window west side (McGillivray) 1990s
R18. Figure in white top window west side (Student) 2018
R19. Figure in white top window west side (Student) 2019
R20. Figure in white 2nd window west side (Clark/Falconer) 2021

Along with Group B. Franciscan monks on the former floors, there is also a figure dressed in white, in the top windows. Most reports also describe an accompanying bright light. I saw the figure myself for 10 minutes with a party of Austrians in 2015 which I record later. With the Céilí Dé wearing white, and given their historical associations, it could be a Céilí Dé monk. However, it is always too far away when observed to make out the detail. My thoughts, and those of others who have seen it, think it is the White Lady. Admittedly, our initial conclusion is due the white attire, but through other reports you will read, of it being bathed in light I believe it is her.

**1/ A11. Pete's Tower Report 14.**
**Lights and figure in white**

I recorded the following in HT p.227:

'In the early 1990s, a light was seen one night in the lowest window of the tower by Pete Marini and a few others. It then disappeared and reappeared in the next window up and then up to the next. The light then disappeared once more and a figure in white appeared peering over the top of the tower. The figure then disappeared and the lights were again seen lighting up each window in succession down the tower. The heavy wooden door is locked at night so no one could have gained entry and certainly, nobody ever appeared at ground level.'

**Michael Alexander's Experiences**

I was interviewed in December 2015 by Michael Alexander, Lead News Feature Writer for the Dundee Courier. He read my book STAM (HT) and wanted to do an editorial about it.

A few things were happening on tours around that period which I didn't have time to mention, and as it turned out, Michael had a few he didn't have time to mention to myself!

Not long after our meeting I received an email from Michael about his own experiences of St Rule's Tower and the Haunted Tower. I have reproduced part of his email below about St Rule's Tower, his experiences at the Haunted Tower are reproduced in that section on p.161 and p.180. Each part is followed by my reply to Michael, together with other subsequent accounts received since that time and relating to the same. Michael's first report concerns the haar I mentioned in the opening section of this volume:

**Michael Alexander Email Part 1.**

Thursday, 24 December 2015

Hi Richard,

'Good to meet you yesterday and thanks very much for the fascinating overview and mini-tour regarding the White Lady.

A piece has been written and hopefully, something will appear in print in The Courier over the festive period. Will also look to get a piece online after it's been in print.

I didn't mention yesterday that I had several unexplained experiences of my own around the Cathedral in the 1990s...

**2/ A12. Michael's Tower Report 15.**
**Light and head? In the upper window of the tower**

One of these experiences involved St Rule's Tower in October 1995, not long after I started work in Dundee with DC Thomson and The Courier/Evening Telegraph.

I had been back through visiting St Andrews and saw what I can only describe as a light in the upper window of St Rule's Tower on the north side (where the two slits are). The motionless light appeared to be tucked partially inside the tower but partially outside. It did not illuminate any other part of the tower's innards. To be fair it was a dark foggy night – the haar was well in – but it was an odd thing and I know there's nothing up there that can reflect light. It also resulted in a case of the 'heebie-jeebies'!

In fact, so perplexed was I at the time, I penned a letter to the Evening Telegraph about it (sanctioned by the then letters editor Alan Proctor) and asked Historic Scotland whether they had left a light on in the tower. They confirmed "there is no night light deliberately put on in the square tower. If someone saw it then it is likely to have been because the staircase lights were left on by accident." I have attached a copy of my letter that appeared in the Tele on October 5, 1995, from my scrapbook. To avoid conflict with being a Tele reporter, the letter was written under the alter ego Archie Sharpe! (As a youngish reporter at that time I used to keep everything!)

I was therefore interested to read on page 227 of your book [*A St Andrews Mystery*] (which I finished the last 50 pages of tonight) about Pete Marini's description of the light in St Rule's Tower in the early 1990s. Whilst the light I saw didn't move, it sounds like a very similar experience with a similarly eerie ambience.'

**The Dundee Evening Telegraph, 5 October 1995**

*The square St Rules Tower in the centre of the St Andrews Cathedral ruins.*

**Ghostly light shock**

As a resident of St Andrews I was walking home alone along the clifftop path at Kirkhill, beside the cathedral, well after midnight on Friday night/Saturday morning (September 29).

It was very dark and very quiet with a slight haar swirling in from the sea, but to my surprise when I looked in the direction of St Rules Tower I saw a steady, but not very bright, light shining from one of the slit windows near the top on the North side of the square tower.

I have heard reports of this light before. With the mist swirling around the tower it looked very much like a head protruding from the tower.

I am aware of the ghost stories associated with the cathedral and as a result got the "heebie-jeebies" and made a fast exit from the vicinity of Kirkhill.

Can anyone tell me the reason for the night light?—**Archie Sharpe, Lamond Drive, St Andrews.**

*[A spokeswoman for the St Andrews Cathedral visitors centre said, "There is no night light deliberately put on in the square tower.*

*"If someone saw it then it is likely to have been because the staircase lights were left on by accident.*

*Alternatively, it may have been the ghost of the monk who supposedly haunts that tower, if you believe in that sort of thing..."]*

**Ghostly light shock**

Text: 'As a resident of St Andrews, I was walking home alone along the clifftop path at Kirkhill, beside the Cathedral, well after midnight on Friday night/Saturday morning (September 29).

It was very dark and very quiet with a slight haar swirling in from the sea, but to my surprise when I looked in the direction of St Rules Tower I saw a steady, but not very bright light shining from one of the slit windows near the top on the North side of the square tower.

I have heard reports of this light before. With the mist swirling around the tower it looked very much like a head protruding from the tower.

I am aware of the ghost stories associated with the Cathedral and as a result got the "heebie-jeebies" and made a fast exit from the vicinity of Kirkhill.

Can anyone tell me the reason for the night light? –

**Archie Sharpe, Lamond Drive, St Andrews**

(A spokeswoman for the St Andrews Cathedral visitors centre said, "There is no night light deliberately put on in the square tower. If someone saw it then it is likely to have been because the staircase lights were left on by accident. Alternatively, it may have been the ghost of the monk who supposedly haunts that tower. If you believe in that sort of thing…")'

The second part of Michael's email is on p.161.

In the above tele article, the staff member of Historic Scotland stated, "If someone saw it then it is likely to have been because the staircase lights were left on by accident." It would appear she hadn't seen what the tower looked like at night when the lights are left on.

With doing the tours a few times pretty much every night I have seen what the tower looks like when the lights are left on overnight (three or four times now). The only visible light is one shining quite brightly out of the first-floor western window above the entrance door. No other visible light can be seen coming from any of the other windows up the tower, and this was before the tower and Cathedral were lit at night so everything was a lot darker.

I always find the dismissive for the nature of the paranormal as intriguing as the phenomena itself. The tagline, "If you believe in that sort of thing" is the same as inserting the word 'purported' or 'alleged' (as per first section) into a witness statement involving a paranormal experience. Uncompromisingly predictable they are not words used for general everyday experiences yet they fit comfortably when it comes to the paranormal as conditioned western responses in believing it to be the stuff of fiction.

**My Email reply to Michael pt. 1**

31 December 2015

Hi Mike,
Many thanks for your reports, the newspaper cutting and the update for the appearance of the article. Most of all, many thanks for finding time to come through and spend some time with myself…

**3/ A13. Richard's Tower Report 16.**
**Figure in white top window west – December 2015**
Something happened on one of my tours only a couple of weeks ago. Things have been happening fairly regularly on the tours. This particular incident is in-keeping with what you mentioned about the light in the window of St Rules Tower. There were 10 of us on the tour and it was just after 8 pm. We had just reached the front of the Cathedral ruins and I was talking about the history and ghosts of St Rule's Tower when a woman on the tour pointed and said there is something white in the top window (western side). It was a figure in white moving across the window from side to side but not consistently. As you know there are no floors in the tower. We all saw it and observed it for about 10 minutes before we moved on. We tried taking photos of it but it was too dark and grainy for the camera phones to make it out.

It is interesting how all it takes is time for the corroboration of seemingly isolated incidents to start forming more substantial patterns.

Part 2 of my email reply can be found on p.164.

There are a few things I didn't have a chance to mention in my email to Michael. This was such a rare observance on several levels…

**In the Light of the Cold Full Moon**

This was an elderly party of nine in number from Austria who were more interested in history than ghosts. The Austrians viewed this figure as an observation, nothing more. They thought it was a woman in a white dress highlighted and vibrant with the moon standing in the top window. We all saw it. I said "You do realise there is no floor behind that window – it's a 100-foot drop!" They didn't believe me.

I had to try and convince them that what they were looking at really shouldn't be there. I am used to people being quick to call a trick of light cast on a distant stone a ghost, this bunch were the complete opposite.

I said "If you come here tomorrow, go through the entrance and look up, you will see it is hollow, there are no floors." After a pause and a brief silence as they observed the figure, I continued, "I would try and take photos of this because what you are looking at is so rare." That is when it sunk in for a few of them and the camera phones came out, but what we all observed with the naked eye was far too distant for the camera phones to pick it up with any clarity. What we did see in the photos was little more than a blur. Everyone saw the figure, and indeed, some were mentioning it to their partners if they could see it as well, their replies were an assertive, "Of course!" as a rebuttal to their husbands for the suggestion because what they were looking at was so obviously a person.

I don't know how long we could have observed the figure for. Ten minutes later we had to carry on with the tour, it was still there when we moved on. Some of them still thought I was pulling their leg about there being no floor, which I found quite amusing. Had the group been more interested in ghosts, they would have quite happily foregone the rest of the tour and continued their observation until it disappeared – however long it might have taken.

If they did go in the tower the next day and looked up, it would have changed their lives. They would have realised that for 10 minutes the night before they were trying to take a photo of something they didn't believe existed!

This is the view they would have seen when entering the tower. The floors in the tower either disintegrated following the start of the ransacking of the precincts in 1559, or they were removed and used elsewhere – I wager the latter.

Ghosts can be fleeting or persistent. As far as it goes this was certainly persistent. Looking back, I find it kind of ironic how we needed to carry on the tour in the face of experiencing something so rare. If inserted into a casual conversation few would believe it. Coupled of course with the double whammy of being the ultimate reason many come on my tours, and I had the one group who expressed no interest in the subject!

Back then the Cathedral was in general darkness at night. I remember when it was lit many years ago. It has been lit now since St Andrews Day, 30th November 2018. On the night of our experience, a large and very bright halfmoon lit the Cathedral ruins, highlighting the vibrancy of the white attire we were looking at. The ruins were brighter and lit with a more uniform light than the artificial light of the spotlights we now have. It so happened this moon would develop into the first full moon on Christmas Day (2015) for 38 years. The next time it does this won't be until 2034. Being the last full moon of the year, this is called the 'Cold Full Moon,' as it occurs at the beginning of winter. Quite an appropriate term given the context of what we all experienced.

**4/ A13. Craig's Tower Report 17.**
**Figure in white top window west – early 1990s**

One evening in the early part of 2017, I had just finished a tour outside the Central Bar at the top of College Street. I was chatting with Craig McGillivray, a chef at the Central Bar. He was on his break and asked how the tours were going. He then mentioned an experience he had one night as a young boy in St Andrews. He said he had seen the White Lady when he was either 8 or 9 years old, so early 90s. He had just come back from Dundee with his parents and what he saw gave him a scare. I asked where this was. He said, "It was in the tower." I smiled and asked, "Which one?" He said it was, "In the top window of the Square Tower."

This is the first time Craig had spoken to me about this which kind of took me by surprise, not only because it is rare to see. I have mentioned aspects of the paranormal to Craig before, but he had not spoken about the figure in white in St Rule's Tower and he was unaware of the other reports.

Craig also had another experience in St Andrews. He was up at Pipeland Woods at the back of St Andrews with a few friends in the late 90s, when they all saw the figure of a man in blue dungarees hanging from a tree. He was a few feet above the ground. They heard later there had been a suicide there.

**5/ A13. Student Tower Report 18.**
**Figure in white top window west – 2018**
A student in St Andrews in 2018 also saw the figure in white illuminated in the top window on the western side of the tower. The report was from a few students on one of my tours in 2019, who knew the student that saw the figure. Remember until now, most of this is unpublished material. They would not have known about the other sightings of the same.

**6/ A13. Student Tower Report 19.**
**Figure in white top window west – 2019**
Another student on a different tour saw the same in the tower in 2019. She was walking back to her residence after visiting a friend in North Street. When she was passing the front of the Cathedral precincts she saw a figure in white in the top middle window of the tower. The same window and same figure Craig saw in the early 90s, where myself and the 9 Austrians observed it in 2015, and where the other student saw it in 2018.

Michael's experience of 1995 was not that long after both Pete and Craig's experiences. The three of them had no notion at the time of the other experiences in the same location, and relatively speaking in the same time-period.

Sometimes I will have those on my tours, who, on being dragged along by their partners are unable to get past the stage that the paranormal "is all nonsense created by a gust of wind, the rattling of pipes, or the imagination." There is also the odd remark of 'how much had they had to drink'." Really! If only they would read this, they would see how futile and how far removed their barren assumptions are in the face of circumstance and corroborated testimony. Like a mirror, it reveals a lot more about their own psychological base than it does the phenomena they look to frivolously decry.

Everyone knows of the monk of St Rule's as wearing a brown habit through Linskill's perpetual story, and confirmed by the experiences of those I recorded above having seen him inside the tower. So, a figure in white in the tower is off base, which should make them all the more compelling for those who may have any lingering doubts.

**7/ A14. Karen/Richard Tower Report 20.**
**Figure in white second window west – 2021**

Karen Clark, I spoke of earlier with regards to her imaginary friend, experienced the following on my tour on 13th July 2021. She said: "I am convinced I saw the White Lady in the 2nd window of the tall tower. You were telling us at the time about the group of Austrian tourists who did not believe in paranormal activity but were simply interested in the history of St Andrews. I saw a petite, slender figure at the 2nd window. As others have said, the figure glowed brightly. I tried to convince myself that it was the sun reflecting off the glass. Is there glass in those windows?! I also noted that there was no light shining through the first window and no real explanation as to where the light was coming from. The White Lady simply faded away. I went back round the next day at around the same time to see if I could see the same thing but I did not."

There is no glass and I saw her as well on this tour, but with taking the tour it wasn't until Karen emailed that I realised I had. It was broad daylight and warm. I can still visualise it and it was white, slender and bright. At the time I didn't think anything of it. You could suppose the light of the eastern window was shining through as it was very bright. It didn't occur to me the light from the other windows don't shine through from where we were standing – and how many tours have I done!!

# The Famed *White Lady*

**Introduction**

I deliberately didn't include very much at all about the White Lady in GOS, there was so much I soon realised I was writing another book – STAM (HT), rather than a chapter. I had the publication date of STAM referenced in GOS as 2014, but I delayed it by a year to 2015 as new information presented itself I needed to investigate. It turned into a 266 page historical investigation into the White Lady phenomenon.

Female ghosts tend to have names attributed to them through the colour of their attire. You will be introduced later to ghosts covering some of the rainbow spectrum, especially in Queen Mary's House with its resident white, green, blue, purple and black female ghosts.

The most famous ghost in St Andrews is the White Lady. Due to her attire it is easy to attribute her to other sightings with a similar description, and to other aspects of phenomena in the vicinity of the Cathedral precincts. This may not be wholly unfounded, as there are patterns of association linking together the figure in the Square Tower, South Transept arch and the Haunted Tower. The latter location being where she is traditionally associated as being seen through Linskill's two fictional stories and early Victorian reports. Before I give the transept arch sightings in the Cathedral precincts, lying due west of St Rule's Tower, I start here with a list of the White Lady ghosts sharing similar descriptions in other locations.

# *White Lady of the Cathedral Precincts*

## *Other White Lady Ghosts*

**White Lady sightings, South Transept Arch** – Next page

**White Lady sightings, Haunted Tower,** starts on p.149

**G – Queen Mary's House** – Mary Queen of Scots

p.335 White lady – two locations

**G – Apparitions on Old Harbour Road**

p.124 White Lady walking across path of Gregory Place end into bushes by the East Scores Path west of the Haunted Tower (visitor) 2015

**G – White Lady Illusions – Palace**

p.535 White Lady illusion in the Palace (Various tours) 2014-2020

**G – Lady Buchan**

p.213 White Lady cliffside between the castle and turret (Linskill) 1911

p.213 White Lady walking along the East Scores path above St Rules Cave

p.213 White Lady walking along the shoreline by St Rules Cave

p.213 White Lady walking 10 feet straight out to sea from Scores path above St Rules Cave before disappearing

**G – White Lady Apparitions of the Pends Hall**

p.162 White Lady on the wall by the top of the Pends (Dobson) 2010

p.382 White Lady by the Pends entrance (visitor) 2015

p.382 Woman in grey/white dress by the Pends entrance (American woman) c.1970s

**HT – Bishop's Palace – Marion Ogilvy**

p.241 White Lady in the courtyard of Palace (Historical)

**HT – White Lady Apparitions of the Pends**

p.229 White Lady standing by the Mill Port to the Pends (Historical)

p.230 White Lady on the Pends Lane just inside the Mill Port, (McIntosh) late 1970s

# *The South Transept Arch Sightings*

**South Transept Arch – (HT)**

1 White Lady in the ruins (Stevenson) Pre-1973

2 White Lady by the transept arches (Falconer +5) 1978

3 White Lady by the transept arches (Falconer +2) 1981

**South Transept Arch – (G)**

4 White Lady by the transept arches (Girl Guides) 2017

5 White Lady by the transept arches (Student) 2018

**White Lady Report 1.**
**White Lady sighting pre 1973** from HT p.216
Peter Underwood in his *Scottish Ghosts*, 1973, writes, 'when she was fourteen years of age Mrs Stevenson of Elgin saw the 'White Lady.' She was standing in the ruined abbey with her brother on a bright moonlit night when they both saw the figure, all in white, with a veil hiding the features.'[10]

This account is the same as the following reports. Given the description, it must be the same locality.

I have now seen the White Lady in four locations. Once in St Rule's Tower, twice in the south transept arch, twice looking out of the top window of the Haunted Tower, and numerous times standing by the Haunted Tower. The following are my two archway sightings I recorded in HT p.204.

**White Lady Report 2.**
**White Lady in the South Transept Arch**
'I have always been fascinated with anything associated with the supernatural. From the age of thirteen, I would often go to the Cathedral ruins in the dead of night, and with a deep breath jump over the low western wall and wander the grounds. Many have done the same over the years and experienced how the expansive blackness of this quarter soon diffuses the glare of the street lighting. The effect gives a defined sense of removal from the rest of the town.

From well within the precincts, sounds of laughter and shouting occasionally filter through the night air, and I would see the odd stray party come over the entrance wall in the distance, no doubt as a dare or bet. They would laugh and joke, but with all their bravado, they would not stay long or stray far from the comfort of the nearby street lighting and the familiarity of their friends.

Whilst wandering the grounds I would think of William Linskill and his ghostly tales and wonder what was hiding in the cold dead of night. My slow pace through the ruins matched those of my wandering thoughts of how the Cathedral must have looked before the Reformation took hold. Attracting thousands of pilgrims a year, this was a great seat of power and a deeply holy and peaceful place for hundreds of years.

As with so many spiritual places, there is always something very calming about being within the grounds, it brings to mind feelings that this is indeed a haven in which to contemplate matters of other realms. I would often go there when I was young with a question in mind and walk out with an answer.

Over the years, I spent a great many nights wandering its precincts, and occasionally others dared to cross the threshold into this quiet sanctuary with me. It was on such a night in 1978, I persuaded six of my classmates to accompany me on a night time visit in the hope of catching a glimpse of the Phantom Monk, the White Lady, or some other famed apparition described in the pages of Linskill's famous work. On this occasion, we assembled outside the main entrance to the Cathedral grounds around 9:30 pm one cold October evening. For a bunch of thirteen-year-olds, this was unknown territory.

On this particular night, a cold bitter sea breeze whirled around the graveyard so we were not up for staying there all night. After wandering around for a couple of hours, we sat for a time on the grassy slope just to the right of the main entrance for a rest. By this time, we were so engrossed in swapping ghostly tales it never bothered us the grass was slightly damp. There was nothing quite like a few stories in an idyllic setting to get into the right frame of mind. Not that we needed any encouragement of course, every faint sound created its own air of expectancy. Eventually, we decided to call it a night, but as we began to get up, one of the party suddenly called out. "What's that over there?" Startled by his tone, we all looked to where he was pointing and standing out distinctly from the fading grey of a pillar was a figure.

It was by the right-hand arch of the south transept just behind the cloisters. It was in this area Thomas Platter murdered Robert De Montrose, the Prior haunting St Rules Tower [which I dispelled earlier]. The figure was a slim human form, not very tall and adorning what appeared to be a white dress, with a white veil obscuring the face. We looked hard and saw it was not a dress and veil but a full-length shroud. It was almost luminescent and appeared to glow very slightly against the black background. It made no gesture and had no movement. I would say it was unnaturally still. We moved toward it, and I can only describe it as fading into the stone pillar behind as we did so.

We all became scared when we realised what we had seen and as we climbed over the entrance wall, a police car came around the corner from North Street. On seeing us it stopped. The police officer in the passenger seat wound his window down and asked what we had been doing in the ruins. I must have been as white as a sheet as I leant into the window and told him we had just seen a ghost! He said something to the driver, wound up his window and before we knew it, they were off down South Street. All of us were left in no doubt that what we had witnessed that night was the famed White Lady.

**White Lady Report 3. The White Lady Appears Again**

HT p.207. 'Under similar conditions to the above visit, in September 1981, three of us went there with one aim in mind – to see a ghost. It was a dry still night and as we wandered the precincts, the only sounds came from the occasional passing car and the waves from the sea crashing against the nearby cliffs.

There was something different about this night to pretty much all previous occasions. I can only describe it as having an atmosphere of its own. After about an hour of aimlessly wandering clockwise around a mix of grass and the occasional stretch of dark gravel path, we walked through the archways. When we reached the grassy slope by the main entrance, we

turned, and standing in the same spot as where myself and a few others had seen her a few years before, was this slim ghostly white figure. Once again, she appeared to shimmer or glow very slightly. We all saw her and after a moment she was gone.'

**White Lady Report 4.**
**Another Sighting of the White Lady in the Arches**

I had a party of girl guides on a tour in 2017. We were at the top of the Pends and were making our way through the narrow security entrance known as the 'eye of the needle.' It took a while for them all to get through as I spoke of a very old St Andrews tradition – spinning around etc (p.378).

I was standing in the middle of the Pends Lane to make sure no traffic was going to come down the Pends from Gregory's Green or South Street while they were filtering through and crossing the road. Once through, they were collecting along the perimeter wall of the Cathedral by the Pends entrance. After the last one had gone through, the first ones to arrive at the wall then came up to me, excitedly a girl said they had just seen someone in white standing in the archways. As she said this, the others were nodding and pointing in the direction of where they saw it. One of the others said "It just dissolved," as another said "it was all lit up," the heads of the others were again nodding up and down in agreement. The teachers didn't know what to make of it and just smiled at me as if to dismiss it as childhood enthusiasm. My jaw just dropped. I knew what they had seen. The word *dissolved* struck me as much as their genuineness. People rarely use that word in terms of their experiences, but a very apt word it was, and one I have adopted for three specific experiences I have had with groups on tours I speak of later. It is at this point on my tours I give mention to the experiences of myself and others at this location in 1978 and 1981, when we saw the White Lady in the arch. They beat me to it! There was no way they would have been aware of this. The rest of the children were disappointed they didn't see it, but they were still making their way through the Pends entrance at the time, and I didn't see it on this occasion as I was standing in the middle of the road waiting for them all to cross the road.

**White Lady Report 5.**

She was seen again in 2018 by a student, standing in the same arch. She came on the tour to tell me and thought it was a light to start with. When she looked closer it was a figure.

**Odd feeling (Group C.)**

In Report 2. I stated 'As with so many spiritual places, there is always something very calming about being within the grounds.' It is very noticeable. I had a young woman in her late teens on a tour, who, at the end of the tour, said she felt very odd in the Cathedral ruins earlier that day, and wasn't herself at all until they walked out the North Gate. From her tone I could tell she had experienced something that seems to have shaken her. Thinking it was something oppressive, on asking what it was she experienced, she said it was a sense of peace. I then realised that was the first time she had experienced a sense of peace, which I hadn't thought about before. Many people spend hours in meditation trying to achieve what happened to her by default of being in the ruins. It can change you as much as seeing a ghost. It had an impact she didn't understand and was pretty confused by, so I had to explain to her it was a good thing and although rare to experience in the grounds it is a common state of being through various spiritual disciplines.

Refer also to p.120, foot of p.192 and to HT, where I give details of the energetic significance of this area as having a marked influence on the spiritual seat existing here for thousands of years.

Detracting slightly, a guy from St Andrews on a tour was talking about a club he was involved in. Part of the initiation was to be taken to the door of the Square Tower in the dark, and told to stay at the tower entrance for an hour. Meanwhile, unknown to the candidate, someone else was around the back by the roofless chapel area. When it got to the stage where they were becoming suitably self-spooked, one of them would appear around the corner dressed as the White Lady and scare the life out of them. If they ran away they failed their initiation. I don't imagine his club had many members, and by this same token, with them hiding in the darkness of the ruined chapel mistakenly thinking they were alone, I have to wonder how many costumed White Ladies they went through!

# Old Harbour Road

**A stroll with the unseen**
Exploring the ghosts from Gregory's to Kirkheugh...

**53 reports – 16 ghosts – Three sections**
1. Gregory's to Haunted Tower
2. Haunted Tower – 5 parts
3. Kirkheugh

I have given details here of 53 reports along this often lonely stretch of path from Gregory's to Kirkheugh, running along the precinct wall and cliffs. A few of these reports also include further cluster reports as a collective of anomalies, so these 53 reports do not comprise the totality along here. There is a lot more. If I included all the lower chamber experiences at the Haunted Tower, the figure would be well over 1000.

The pathway from North Street to the harbour was called the Old Harbour Road. The singular stretch of path where the divergent paths meet from the North Gate to the Haunted

Tower is Dane's Wark or Walk. A name shared with the cliffside along that stretch. According to the Ordnance survey book of names it was so called from a Dane employed to construct an embankment. On receiving money in advance, he left the contract unfinished and returned to his own country, but that sounds more like a fanciful tale than a historical event.

**6 Energy Centres**

I spoke of energy in the first section. As a fundamental universal factor of existence, everything is energy and energy is everywhere, but it is not uniform everywhere in its intensity, and as I mentioned, energy does fluctuate. There are certain areas where the concentration of natural energy is more intense. Deemed as energy centres or energy fields, these are conduits between vibratory planes of existence and are localised centres of concentration for the manifestation of paranormal activity.

We have already explored St Rule's Tower **Energy Centre 2.** Along the Old Harbour Road is North Gate **Energy Centre 4.**, Haunted Tower **Energy Centre 3.**, and Kirkheugh **Energy Centre 1.** Energy attracts energy and it links up like a grid (ley lines), so there are also pockets of energy along its length.

The other areas around St Andrews where the same energetic fields are displayed with the same degree of intensity are the pedestrian security entrance to the Pends **Energy Centre 5.**, and Queen Mary's House **Energy Centre 6.** Then slightly further afield is the Fairmont Hotel, and its neighbouring Clubhouse/Restaurant by the cliffs, which have volcanic inclusions.

It is the energies of this quarter that also give a significant clue as to the reason for its spiritual significance through Pagans, Druids, Pictish Kings, Céilí Dé and the early Roman Church who all recognised the energies here, and they each utilised its properties in their favour for spiritual development and worship.

## Old Harbour Road Part 1.

# *Phenomena*

Gregory's to the Haunted Tower
Incorporating Energy Centre 3. and 4.

**Old Harbour Road Reports (OHR)**

1/ Footsteps in the snow at Gregory's
2/ Figure walking south to north by Gregory's
3/ Figure walking north to south by Gregory's
4/ Figure walking north to south by Gregory's
5/ North Gate – A collective of subtle incidents
6/ North Gate – Whirlwind
7/ Something brushing hair
8/ Odd unaccountable feelings
9/ Feeling of being prodded
10/ Figure walking west, vanishing by the North Gate
11/ Orb – Report Part 1. (Pends Hall)
11/ Two Visual Orbs – Report Part 2. North Gate
12/ Figure walking east, vanishing by North Gate
13/ White Lady – North Gate to Haunted Tower
14/ Report 1. Ghost of a student opposite the Haunted Tower
15/ Report 2. Ghost of a student opposite the Haunted Tower
16/ Report 3. Ghost of a student opposite the Haunted Tower

This includes North Gate **Energy Centre 4.** and is followed by the Haunted Tower phenomena **Energy Centre 3.** with 31 reports alone (plus over 1000 experiences for one aspect) in 5 sections, and Kirkheugh **Energy Centre 1.** with a further 6 reports.

**Gregory's (Fisher's School)**

Until 1957, part of Gregory's was called Fisher's School and Fishers' District School. It was Gregory Cottage before this. The name Gregory comes from James Gregory, the 17th century mathematician and astronomer at the University who had a residence in the north wing of Dean's Court.[v]

Fisher's School was an infant school, originally for the children of the fisherfolk in this area. There were some 145 fisherfolk living along here in the 1880s alone. Back then it was called Ladyhead, a term originally denoted for the area around the crossroads of North Street with North and South Castle Street. A few centuries later it would become known as Fishergate, after the Port that stood by North Gate I also give mention to later.

**Fisher's School, location of reports 1-4**

[v] The wide expanse of road at the top of North Street in front of the Cathedral was called Gregory's Green. It was a grass area the fisherfolk here used as a drying green for their nets. The name also applies to the stretch of road bridging North Street with South Street in front of the Cathedral.

**A stern warning**

The teachers of the school used to warn the pupils not to play along the stretch of path from the school to the Haunted Tower because of the White Lady, and there are those in St Andrews, who, in still taking heed, will not walk this way after night fall. This was also recorded in the Victorian age. Despite the reassurance of a thriving fishing community here, two public houses down the Shore and a functioning fixed beam lighthouse shining out to sea, many still avoided this stretch after dark if possible. To visualise what it was like back then, everything east of the lighthouse was very brightly lit, including the Haunted Tower and Kirkheugh. These factors were still not enough to reassure those wary of the unseen. Rumours of the occupants of the tower were even rife during the Reformation in St Andrews of 1559, with the Protestants leaving the Haunted Tower well alone. This was all compounded in 1893, when an article appeared of eyewitness accounts from the 1826 and 1868 openings of the Haunted Tower. The revelations still influence the deeper psyche of St Andrews to this day.

**Fear of the unknown**

Ghost are not here to harm or scare you. After I have told people this they ask, "Then why do people get scared?" It is the same as when some ask me, "If ghosts cannot harm you, why would the teachers warn the pupils not to play along here?"

The answer to both is simple, nobody is ever told they cannot harm you, what I have just told you is not common knowledge. The reason we get scared is through the fear of the unknown, mixed with the fiction we have become accustomed to believing for what we think might happen. The majority, then and now, are completely unaware the only real harm they can do is psychological, not physical. Despite not knowing this, the teachers knew the last thing they wanted was a bunch of kids scared out of their wits by the apparition of something they knew to be very real, that was very unpredictable, and that they knew absolutely nothing about.

During or following an experience we look to logic to try and make sense of our experience. Once all possibilities have been exhausted (which usually takes longer than the experience itself to process), that is when potential feelings of being scared can come to the fore as the great unknown takes a hold of our imagination.

**OHR Report 1.**

**Footsteps in the snow at Gregory's.**

While the children were told not to play along by the Haunted Tower there were a few things lurking closer to home. An interesting report for here is from a member of a boy's club that once took place at Gregory's. Walking through thick snow he was making his way to the building. As he approached, he saw footsteps in the snow heading in the same direction. The footsteps led up to the main door. He tried the door but it was locked. He unlocked the door and called out but there was no reply. He searched the building for whoever had entered and the building was empty, but there were no footsteps of anyone leaving.

**OHR Report 2.**

**Figure walking south to north by Gregory's**

At the beginning of 2015 there was a large group of us standing in front of the Haunted Tower. I was facing the sea and they were facing me and the tower. When we were walking toward the Bishop's Palace, one of the guys on the tour stopped me by the brae of the East Scores Path. He said, "Richard! I didn't want to stop you at the tower because you were on a roll, but I've just seen her." He said I was describing her as he was observing her. While I was speaking he glanced down the pavement toward the former Fisher's School and saw a figure crossing the path south to north and disappearing by the bushes. He saw her for a few seconds. His wife punched him on the arm and said "What! and you didn't tell us!" but we are not that quick when it comes to these things. It takes a while for the mind to process what we are observing. It isn't until we've exhausted all feasible possibilities that we're left with no other conclusion. Even though I was describing her at the same time, it still took a while for him to register what he was observing.

Eddie McGlinchey a local resident, has the wee famous dog Millie (photo on p.215), who Eddie has observed displaying odd behaviour along here I relate later. Eddie believed what the man saw was one of the residents in her night attire. He had a chuckle when I told him. There is a small gate between the building and bushes for access to the residences here. I cannot deny that as being a possibility, however, there have been two other occasions since then when we have seen a figure, but the figure is not walking north into the bushes/gate, it is walking south through the wall. Here are my accounts:

**OHR Report 3.**
**Figure walking north to south by Gregory's**

On one of my tours in the winter of 2017, we had just started walking up the brae towards the Palace when we saw a fleeting figure walk across the pavement north to south and disappear. That part of wall was in darkness but either side of it is lit. It was only for a moment that we saw it and there was nowhere for it to go other than through the Precinct wall.

**OHR Report 4.**
**Figure walking north to south by Gregory's**

The other time was on the 9pm tour in the spring of 2018. We were walking towards the corner of the Old Harbour Road from North Street, there were six of us on that tour and someone walked across the pavement about twenty feet in front of us, again north to south just after the bollards at the bend in the pavement. I didn't think anything of it until we got to the corner and there was no one on the path in front of us, and nowhere for them to go. I asked if anyone saw a person walk across the pavement just now. It was just one woman who piped up and said she saw it as well. On each occasion it has been dark when it happened.

This stretch of wall from North Gate to North Street was eventually rebuilt as a windbreak for the cemetery following the collapse of the 200-foot-high Cathedral Bell Tower c.1584. That is why the wall along this stretch is half the height to the rest (barring the western wall along the main entrance to the Cathedral which was remodelled by the Edwardians in the early 1900s). The Precinct wall, Hepburn's wall, or Abbey wall as it is known now, has thirteen turrets or towers around its near mile length. Originally it had sixteen. Three of these were along this stretch of the wall. One of them was at this corner. On Geddy's map of c.1580 there was an entrance at this same location (marked with a circle) where we have seen the figures. Beyond it, a thoroughfare track is marked on the map like a short cut from here, through the Cathedral grounds to the main gates. This then makes sense of the figures waking across this section of path, or road as it was then and through the wall.

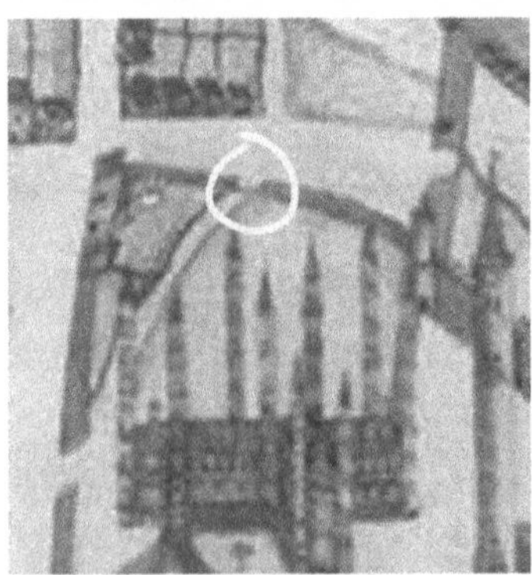

Part of John Geddy's plan of St Andrews c.1580
with the opening in the wall

## Old Harbour Road – Energy Centre 4.
### The North Gate Anomalies

Around the North Gate, between the fork in the path and the lighthouse turret there is a bubble of energy covering the diameter of the pavement space.

**OHR Report 5.**
**A collective of subtle incidents**
From HT p. 203: 'The stretch of wide pathway between the fork in the path to the front of the side gate by the Lighthouse Tower has a very unusual feel at times. Covering an area of only around 20 to 30 feet, it can be likened to walking into a freezer. I have experienced this on a few occasions and generally there will be a very heavy oppressive feeling accompanying the cold, one completely different to anywhere else along this stretch.

This phenomenon has been noticed and mentioned by numerous people on tours and only then have I mentioned what myself and others have experienced. Some have a sense of fear when they reach this location, while others have a sense of foreboding. This can be especially pronounced, and a few on reaching this spot have been reluctant to venture any further towards the Haunted Tower.' Like the feelings at the entrance of Kellie Castle I spoke of in the first section.

The boundary is like a wall. It can be so defined you can just put your hand into it and feel the difference in the sudden drop in temperature. When people have done this on my tours, it is to their complete disbelief. They cannot explain it and always find it so unusual. It then becomes the talking point for the rest of the tour.

**OHR Report 6.**
**Whirlwind**

The wind at this spot can also be very unusual. A gale will blow in this small area when all around is completely still. One evening in July 2015, a few of us experienced this on two back-to-back tours when coming along here. The first of the two tours was with John Marini. We dwelt here for a while and could find no reasoning as to why it should feel so different. Thus far, it has always been dark when a change has occurred.

It is like a whirlwind or mini vortex, the same that happened out the back of the flat at Jannettas p.311. This can of course be dismissed as natural phenomenon, and any qualification for a paranormal suggestion as wishful thinking, but it is not so much the specific nature of how it can occur, as to why it occurs where it does, as you will find in the following reports, which is far from natural in the physical sense. If it were of a physical *origin* it would not find a mention here.

**OHR Report 7.**
**Something brushing past**
There have also been a few times when something has either brushed past my hair or the hair of others.

**OHR Report 8.**
**Odd unaccountable feelings**
Like other aspects of phenomena on locations of the tour, the anomalies here rarely find space for a mention. I had a couple on a tour in November 2020. The young woman said she felt very odd as we were walking through this spot and felt so cold. Unlike the girl earlier, her odd feeling wasn't a sense of peace. She couldn't explain it but knew something wasn't right and couldn't place what it was.

**OHR Report 9.**
**Feeling of being prodded**
I was walking toward the Haunted Tower with a young couple on a tour in December 2019. It was a very cold night. On reaching this spot the woman grabbed her partner's arm very tightly. I gave her a sympathetic smile thinking she was cold. She later said something had prodded her on her shoulder and she was scared stiff, which is why she grabbed his arm.

Something brushing past the hair or body should be more believable because it is not inflated or dramatic. There is no joking or fooling around, just confusion and often a degree of worry. I always take a mental note to jot everything down later, including location and anything I feel may have a bearing or influence, such as the general nature of the person, demeanour, temperament, susceptibility, etc. All of which tends to be more obvious than any are aware. When the same things then happen at the same specific locations, they again create patterns, but the reasons for their occurrence can be illusive. The only random factor is in not knowing when it will happen and to whom.

That is why every tour is unique. They are never weather or more precisely wind dependent. The wind flows and messes with our hair, it doesn't physically brush through it just the once, and it doesn't tap you on the shoulder.

There are seven locations where these subtle aspects of brushing past or prodding etc occur with a noted regularity and four of them are along the East Scores Path being: North Gate Energy Centre 4., the Haunted Tower Energy Centre 3., the brae just up from North Gate, and the stretch of East Scores Path along from here above the former cave of St Rule or Lady Buchan. The other locations are the Square Tower Energy Centre 2., the Nuns Walk, and the Eye of the Needle at the Pends Security Hall Energy Centre 5.

For each location people have no idea of any previous experiences.

**OHR Report 10.**

**Figure walking east, vanishing by the North Gate**

I had a couple on the 7:30pm tour, 13th September, 2020. We were making our way to the Haunted Tower, and had just turned the corner of Gregory's by the southern end of the former school. The path was empty apart from a person walking toward us in the distance. I had started talking about the experience of an elderly gentleman from Aberdeen, which I record later, when the figure walking toward us just disappeared. It was one of those double take moments where you are not sure if what you just saw really happened.

Steven Flynn turned to me and said, "That person just vanished." We then spoke about what just happened. His partner didn't see it. It was just the two of us and left Steven pretty "gobsmacked" as he described it. The figure was walking toward us from the harbour direction along the south side of the path, there was no sound, and the figure vanished by the area of the North Gate. Steven put it on my tripadvisor page:

## *Old Harbour Road*

Tripadvisor review
September 2020

Outstanding. This tour is a must for anyone going to St Andrews, or indeed if you study there or live there. Richard is incredibly knowledgeable about both his subject, the town, and its history. It was a pleasure to listen to him. We even experienced a paranormal event around the side of the Cathedral. A man was walking along the path towards us and he never made it to us. He just vanished. And there was nowhere for him to go other than back the way, and if he had we would have been able to see him. Yet it didn't feel spooky or frightening. Just strange. I certainly see St Andrews in a totally different light now. It's a fascinating place. As is this tour. 5 stars all the way!! Thank you Richard!

**A psychological analysis of the moment**

This is a good example of the fragility of our perception. I was looking into the distance as we walked, so I saw a figure walking toward us, and I was looking at the figure when it disappeared, but because I was talking on a tour, and the figure was visual, it was secondary to what I was doing at that moment. So, when the figure disappeared there was no initial thought regarding what I had seen. It was there, then it just wasn't.

It takes a few moments for the mind to question what the eyes have seen – if it does at all as we are accustomed to accepting what we expect to see. When a subtle quark in reality occurs, the mind easily ignores it. It does this with more regularity than you may think. I had to make a mental effort to consciously question what I had just seen. Otherwise I could have carried on the tour and the moment may easily have been lost amid the continual distractions and preoccupations vying for my attention. We see everything around us, everything is absorbed into our subconscious, but our subconscious is selective in what it then feeds of this reality to conscious perception. Everything is secondary to our present preoccupations. If our subconscious were to download everything it takes in to our conscious mind, we would be instantly overloaded, in the same way a computer blows a chip. Focus, concentration, being engrossed in thought or action are example of this. Each are reasons enough for the subconscious to blot out the peripheral elements of reality deemed as superfluous to the requirements at hand. I carried on talking, but the thought 'did that happen?' came to mind, just as Steven said, "That person just vanished." Both Steven and myself experienced a short delay in comprehending what just happened. I saw a figure, Steven saw a man, and his partner didn't see anyone at all. So, there are many complex variables involved in one of the many aspects we take for granted – our perception, and it can all happen in a matter of moments. There is always a difference between the whims of the mind and genuine experience. If it is a purely visual experience there tends to be this delay before either someone mentions something they think is or was out of the ordinary, and likewise for group experiences, for how people, including myself, react. There is no placebo effect here – there is no ripple effect or suggestion.

These are brief impacting glimpses of merging realms. Those experiencing phenomena on a tour tend to share in the same reaction at the same time, and describe the same thing in the same way, with no prior suggestion of anything untoward. The only imaginative folly at work is on the part of a third party, who, on being told about it after the event, may attempt to dismiss it out of hand as anything I have just noted as not taking place. On almost every occasion where there is a visual paranormal experience, it confuses rather than scares, as the mind tries to work out the logic of what is or has just taken place. The majority will not be able to explain what they are experiencing, but none can deny their own observations. This leads us to another example of this same phenomenon, and the same difficulty of mind in trying to accept what it has observed.

**OHR Report 11.**

**Figure walking west, vanishing by the North Gate**

In January 2019, I had a family reunion from Aberdeen on a tour. We were standing by the Haunted Tower and I was talking about the formerly sealed middle chamber (p.143), when an elderly gentleman on the tour stopped me midsentence and said, "Richard! Is there an entrance down there in the wall?" as he pointed along the pavement towards Gregory's. "Yes," I replied, "there is a locked iron gate (North Gate) in the wall just behind the turret." As soon as I said this he quick marched himself down to the gate. His wife turned to me and said, "I think he's seen something?" which with hindsight was an unusual thing for her to say.

He checked the gate, which is always locked at night, and was looking around as if he had lost something. I could see he was confused, so I knew he had experienced something. He came back to us all at the tower and said, "Richard, I'm not pulling your leg, and I am traditionally sceptical with these things, but while you were talking, someone was walking along the path towards us. They then turned to their right and didn't reappear. They went through that gate, but it's locked!"

There are streetlights along the path, but they are fairly spread out, and those walking along here at night are just dark shadowy figures until they come into view under one of the lights.

For the next part of the tour he was annoying his large family as he repeated a few times what he had seen. Eventually, they said, "Yeah dad we believe you!" but he wasn't trying to convince us, he was vocalising what he had seen a few times to try and convince himself, he was trying to get to the comprehension stage of what he had just experienced which is what we do. Myself and Steven had seen a figure walking west then disappearing at North Gate, he had seen a figure walking east and disappearing at the same location. Refer also to the Northgate Shadow p.166.

**OHR Report 12.**
**Orb – Report Part 1 of 2**
I took Hayley Drysdale and Mick Morris from St Andrews on the 7:30pm tour, 13th December, 2020. There were two related experiences on this tour. The first involves the Pends Hall Energy Centre 5., and ties with the second experience on the same tour at North Gate Energy Centre 4. which I shall mention in a moment.

We were standing in the middle of the ruined Pends Hall. It all happened in the space of around 10 seconds, so the experience was a lot quicker than the time it will take for you to read about what happened.

I had just been speaking about one of the ghosts here and describing the Pends building, when Hayley looked up behind me. I thought she was just perhaps visualising what it once looked like, which many do. As she did so, the wall of the hall behind them was bathed in a slightly lighter blue-white light than the usual white light of the bright LED light above the South Street entrance. It was nothing dramatic and nothing I would have ordinarily paid any attention to. Mick then looked up as well for a few moments. They hadn't looked at each other. They were both focused on something high on the wall behind me. Knowing now what you are about to find out, there expression of awe was like a close encounter's moment.

The blue white light disappeared just as they both looked at me and said there had been a flash and there was something on top of the wall behind me. The flash was the appearance of light. I said I saw the flash. It wasn't until after the tour I started dwelling on what had happened. It was another of those instances where it happens too quick for the mind to process at the time.

Hayley emailed me later and said, "It was a ball of solid white light on top of the wall about the size of a tennis ball or a little larger. It then shot straight up and fizzled out."

Mick also emailed me and said, “It happened whilst we were standing at the pends and not long after you finished discussing ‘the white lady.’ It appeared right above the wall where you were standing. It was a single white light that raised pretty much vertically straight for just a few seconds and then completely disappeared as if it was a light and someone had literally just flicked a switch.

When I first saw it I actually thought it may have been a firework but there was no fizzle [different usage of terminology to Hayley] and then no noise to follow like you’d expect from a firework. So as soon as you finished speaking I had to ask Hayley if she saw it too and she did. It was certainly not something I can easily explain.”

We all had an experience from two perspectives. I was facing them and saw the reflected light of what they were looking at – which was an orb.

Being in the middle of a tour I didn’t dwell on the wall being slightly brighter. The lighting of an environment subtly changes at night as the moon appears from behind the clouds for example. It didn’t occur to me at the time there was no moon, and on looking at the records, it was a waning crescent with only a 2% brightness and it had set by mid-afternoon.

**Two Visual Orbs – Report Part 2 of 2.**

The second experience with Hayley and Mick happened when we were approaching the North Gate on the same tour. I saw a large shooting star in the sky and mentioned it to them as a possibility, but as I found later through email correspondence, what they saw in the Pends wasn’t fleeting across the sky, it was on the top of the wall and everything suddenly got slightly brighter. They both looked at me with a confused expression when I said that, but not for the Pends experience. What I also didn’t know at the time was that as I was looking at the star, they were observing something only a few feet away. They both saw two balls of solid bright white light. Similar in nature to the Pends Hall ball of light only 15 minutes earlier. Hailey said, "The lights were smaller than the one at the Pends, about the size of golf balls just above the height of the wall. They floated to the right and just disappeared." When the second one disappeared, Hayley said, "I could still see something moving, something still floating along."

In the email from Mick he mentioned the same, "The second was when we were outside the graveyard/cathedral. Once that light had vanished I saw something dark in the air floating along as if following the path that the light would have continued to take. Being from the town and being down that area a lot I have never ever witnessed anything like that. Especially not something that I just can't easily explain, it's left me completely baffled."

Hayley also had an experience of a similar nature when at Kirkheugh, p.198, and so too have a group of Germans, p.199.

Continuing with the subject of light for a moment, not all events at this particular location have a paranormal origin. On the 9pm tour, August 1st, 2020, myself and a family of four were standing here, and while I was mentioning the bubble of energy and some of the things that have happened here, there was a flash of bright white light just next to us. It was only for a split second. It was as bright as a lightning bolt and faster than a blink. One of the girls standing by me jerked back and excitedly said she just saw a flash. We were the only ones to see it and it happened right next to us. It was still daylight and really spooked her. The same thing happened on a tour the next day while in the Nun's Walk. Same flash of light. I then realised what it was. It was summer, so being warm I was just in a T-shirt and my iPhone was in my back pocked. With the phone being on silent, the torch flashes once when a new message comes through. That was the flash we had seen. Unless they read this book, those who experienced the flash on these two tours will go through their lives thinking it was a paranormal experience. Oops!

**Orbs – A brief analysis**

The experiences of the orbs on the night with Hayley and Mick occurred at The Pends – Energy Centre 5. And North Gate – Energy Centre 4.

An orb is the physical observance of the energetic essence and encapsulation of a spirit. Usually captured by digital cameras, they can very rarely be observed with the naked eye as we have here.

The energies in both locations are often quite apparent. The energies of that night were conducive to energetic manifestation. It is these heightened energies infusing the energy of the spirit that produces this concentration of spiritual energy we know in the physical as orbs. The orb in the Pends was larger than at the North Gate. It is apparent this was the energies of two spirits, with the core light of their spirits being close enough to emit a light bright enough to give the appearance of one larger orb. These were then seen as two smaller orbs of light by the North Gate.

We could think of them as flitting to this location directly through the precincts from the Pends, taking the shortest route, but they do not physically traverse the precincts as we would. They simply just snap from one energetic location to the other. From our perspective they are occupying physical space, but there is no in-between. They are not restricted by any physical limitation so there are no restrictions of time.[vi] As I intimated in the first section for energy and time, there is more than a passing connection.

All time is happening all the time. Few in their lifetime will appreciate what this means. You will know if you manage to fathom it, as everything – and I do mean everything, will fall into place for you as this riddle unravels the secrets of existence.

---

[vi] This then opens the nature of time to what you may think as 'time travel,' but not as a hypothetical construct and only as an observer.

The sphere of involvement for these spirits are restricted to the energetic parameters of the Cathedral precincts. Whoever they were in life, they are aware, intelligent, and are confined to the precincts in death. This is the same with the ghosts of Fairmont, p.438 and Lady Kinkell, p.505.

Hayley and Mick were looking at the orb directly, so they saw an intensity of bright white light, and that is generally what is seen. It is rare to be in a space close enough for their true light to become apparent. When reflected it is a blue-white light which is what I saw. Blue-white light is the colour of spiritual energy and that leads us to the following:

**A Key for the White Lady**

I used to think the white attire of the White Lady reflected under the light of the moon was the reason for her being so bright. When I have seen her, I describe her as being the same as if you took the full moon and cut out a human figure. That is how vibrant she is, and in the darkness, there is no mistaking, but I realised the moon is a red herring and would not cause her to be as bright as she can sometimes appear. The bright white light of the ghosts here, only applies to the figure in white in St Rule's, on the precinct wall, and in the south transept arch. I believe they are the same person, lit by the light of her own spiritual energy through which she manifests – the same as orbs. She does not require the external light of the moon or streetlighting for her illumination to be apparent, which then makes sense. Not all sightings are under a bright moonlight. Michael's experience of the light in St Rule's Tower was when the haar was in and it was "very dark." The same with the photo on p.552. When it was taken there was no moon and the street light wasn't enough to highlight the haar the way it did. Also, the bright white figure witnessed by myself and Karen in the Square Tower was at about 8:30pm in July 2021, when it is still daylight.

There is something sentinel about her. Note, she is not brightly lit or glowing when seen outside the precincts. Refer also to p.573, for a photo of orbs inside the Haunted Tower.

**What is the reason for the activity at this location?**

The figure/s, the subtle physical prodding or brushing past, the orbs and the extreme cold etc, can occur anywhere, but there is a greater propensity for their occurrence at energy centres where the boundary between worlds are more tenuous. These are spirit/s of the deceased notifying of their presence. At this location it is possibly caused by the man that Steven, myself and the gentleman from Aberdeen have each glimpsed.

They utilise the atoms in the atmosphere. As the vibratory rate of the atoms slow, the kinetic energy decreases causing the extreme cold to occur. It is common for there to be this noticeable dramatic difference in temperature without the accompaniment of any further phenomena.

There is also always a connection between phenomena and the recipient, so as well as being conducive for the manifestation of phenomena, they also accelerate the energies of the individual to perceive phenomena more readily. An example is at Kirkheugh with Hayley and the Germans, pp.198-199.

As to the reason to why they would be here, there were many centuries of active history at this location. The land along this stretch in Geddy's iconic map of c.1580, extended further north than it does now. Although the map is an artist's impression from a bird's eye sixteenth century perspective, it is clear some of the land and road to the north has been lost to the sea. This is the area of the 'Dane's Wark' I referred to earlier.

The arched wall by the North Gate, adjoining the eastern gable of the Cathedral to the precinct wall marks the former entrance to the grounds of Holy Trinity Church. It also spanned the Old Harbour Road from the western side of the Lighthouse Tower to where the cliffside stood. This was the

Harbour Hill Port, Shore Gait/Port or Fisher Gate (Gait or Port).

Historically, this was a major hub of activity between the harbour and town. In the port wall there appears to have been two entrances, one a large arched gate, like that of the Holy Trinity entrance cross the road, the other smaller, closer the cliffs. So, one access for carts and one for pedestrians.

This was one of nine ports or gaits into the town. As the town continued westwards, ports were created across its main thoroughfares. The most famous being the West Port (1587). These were not defensive constructions, far from it. 'Fences and gates at the end of the rigs on North Street and South Street [were all that] marked the boundary of the town [westwards].'[11] They were a civilised measure to control access, especially during the busy periods of summer and annual festivals and feasts.

The Turret Lighthouse was operated by wood and coal and used by the Catholic church until 1559 for shipping. In the 19th century it was again in use as a lighthouse right up to the mid 1940s.

## Old Harbour Road – Energy Centre 3.
### The Haunted Tower Anomalies

**OHR Report 13.**
**Ghost of a figure opposite the Haunted Tower**
Most are aware of the White Lady along here but there are also another 15 ghosts. I wrote about the following in HT p.202. 'On a night time tour in July 2015, I was with quite a large group. We were walking along the path towards the Haunted Tower.

The only other person on this stretch of pavement was someone standing against the wall behind the bench opposite the Haunted Tower looking out to sea.

We had just reached the North Gate when the figure up ahead walked toward the street light and promptly vanished. We all saw the figure, and we all saw it disappear. This caused a lot of confusion and disbelief amongst those on the tour as to what just happened.

**OHR Report 14.**
**Ghost of a figure opposite the Haunted Tower**
Two weeks later, the same thing happened again with another party of people. It was a 9pm tour, August 2015. A figure standing at the same spot looking out to sea did the same thing. Of all the tours these are the only two occasions this has thus far happened opposite the Haunted Tower' until 2017. . .

**OHR Report 15.**
**. . . Ghost of a student opposite the Haunted Tower – 2017**
A party of students were on a tour one night. When we were at the Haunted Tower, one of the guys said they saw a ghost here in 2017. A few students had been walking back into town from a University Ball up at Kinkell. As they were walking toward

the Haunted Tower along the coastal path, they saw a student wearing a red gown standing in front of the Haunted Tower, just by the sea wall looking out to sea. They couldn't tell if it was a man or woman but as they drew closer, the student just vanished. This was the same figure we saw twice standing at the same spot by the bench opposite the Haunted Tower.

From our perspective when we were walking along the path the street light was behind the figure, so it was silhouetted like a shadow. From the student's perspective, the figure was behind the light so they could see more detail and recognised the red gown of a student.

There is also the ghost of the White Lady standing by the Haunted Tower. Refer to p.130.

**OHR Report 16.**
**White Lady – North Gate to Haunted Tower**

The White Lady been seen coming out of the North Gate and walking along to the Haunted Tower. She is a small young woman, slim, with long black hair and wearing a long white dress. When she gets to the tower she stops, turns and disappears. Refer also to an addendum on p.188.

Old Harbour Road Part 2.

**Haunted Tower – Energy Centre 3. In 5 parts**
Sightings and Anomalous Phenomena (in abundance)
**31 Reports + over 1000 reports for the lower chamber**

# *Haunted Tower Part 1.*

## Introduction

Lair of the Tower Lady or White Lady

If you look closely at this photo[12], you will note the entrance to the middle chamber is still sealed with stone – a thin layer of stone as it turns out, only nine inches thick.

# Ghosts

### A Backdrop to the Haunted Tower Phenomena

Taken before 1868 there were still ten preserved bodies hidden within the middle chamber at that time. Nine males and one female – the White Lady.

There was a great deal of correspondence in the local and national press about the White Lady between 1893 and 1925. I republished most of the press articles in HT.

The tower was known as the Virgin Tower and Mary's Tower. The Victorians also knew it as the Lady's Tower, the Ghost Tower and the Haunted Tower. Although the latter was known before Linskill, it was adopted for his stories and correspondence, which is mainly why it is the one that has stuck with the town.

This is the lair of St Andrews most famous and compelling ghost – the White Lady. The Victorians also knew her as the Tower Lady. By comparing the detail in the 19th century reports of her corpse being seen, it would appear there are two White Lady corpses, and one is still here. Refer to HoS.

### The Chamber of Corpses – 1826

At the beginning of the first chapter of HT p.18, I record the following from a National Weekly Newspaper called the *Saturday Review* dated November 1893. I have reproduced it here as it gives a good synopsis of why the White Lady haunts the grounds of the Haunted Tower.

The newspaper reported on the opening of the middle chamber in 1826. 'A few explorers, who, on desiring to see what lay beyond the sealed chamber of the Haunted Tower, apprehensively gathered in secret early one morning to open it. A Professor of the United College in North Street headed the exploration. When they went in, they were amazed at what they found. It appears the chamber was the hiding place of up to 10 coffins dating from different centuries. There were nine males and one female. Some were wrapped head to toe in white wax cloth, including that of a slim corpse, four and a half feet long.

Under the wax cloth wrappings was the corpse of a woman, young and beautiful. She wore a long white silk dress, and it was as if she had fallen asleep that very hour. [She was also wearing long white leather calf-skin gloves and had long black hair.] Both she and the other corpses were in a perfect state of preservation. There was no obvious indication as to their identities, or why they should be entombed within the tower. Following a cursory examination, the Professor went to the Lord Advocate and told him of their discovery. He immediately ordered them to leave the bodies alone in their tomb and reseal the chamber.'

**The 1868 and 1888 openings**

The chamber was also opened in 1868, and resealed with corpses intact, but the lower chamber was also opened, it was literally full of bones which were removed and thrown over the cliffs by the workmen. These were town's people (HoS). The chamber was then left open. In the previous photo there is no sign of the lower chamber entrance the workmen made, which is how I know the photo was taken sometime before 1868.

In 1888 the middle chamber was opened again. This time Linskill was present and wanted to see her. To his disappointment, hay and straw lay on the ground and the body of the White Lady had gone.

**Investigation**

In STAM (HT), I unravel this and many other complex mysteries involving her, and incorporate most of the documentation recorded in the press about her from 1893[vii] when she first appeared in print to 1925, along with all the first-hand sightings of her I have been able to amass up to 2015.

---

[vii] Some of this comes from private letters of correspondence and reports written before this date and given to those who wrote the articles.

The bulk of the information was mostly newspaper articles and letters of correspondence detailing an extraordinary series of incidents and discoveries within the Haunted Tower. This period gripped the imagination of the Scottish public, and to an extent the British public, especially scholars in London. Everyone was fascinated by the disclosure of reports about her, all of which were primarily lost to the town before my republication of the original press articles.

When I published STAM, the *Citizen* described it as "Richard's latest fictional book." They never read my brief, and I guess they were not expecting a nonfiction work to come out about the White Lady. Of course it was fiction, how could it not be? Unfortunately, their mistake was a grave error that would prove contrary to the motivation of most who would buy it. In one respect it is a pity it wasn't fiction, I could have saved myself over 30 years of research.

I took this photo in 2015 when I was granted rare access into the Haunted Tower courtesy of Historic Scotland, who also granted kind permission for me to publish what I had taken. This is the long L of the middle chamber. From the outside, this is in the western wall beside the tower. It is where the White Lady and other corpses were found. I took a lot of photos of the chambers. There is another photo you will find in the section on Photos, p.573, taken from the same position and only a second or two later which has a few orbs. If it were dust they would also be in this photo – they are not.

**The Ghost**

From my initial first-hand experiences of the White Lady, it would be another 32 years whilst researching STAM before I would realise important observations about her.

She has two distinct forms. One is with long dark hair and wearing a long white dress. When seen in this form she is generally moving. This is the figure of her in life. It is her spirit, and she is aware of you. Her appearance is often accompanied by the feeling of being watched. The reports of her being seen in this form have her in the vicinity of the Haunted Tower and in the upper windows of the Square Tower.

The other form is of her head to toe all in white and seen either in the grounds by the Haunted Tower, or in the south transept arch I recorded earlier. This is the figure of her in death, an impression of her shrouded in white wax cloth entombed in the tower. Unlike the other form, she tends to be completely motionless, static, almost unnaturally so. There is no detectable wavering or motion at all which you generally find with someone just standing still. In this form she is not aware of you – Group A.

In all descriptions she is slim and between four and five feet tall, which complies with the reports of the White Lady entombed in the tower. Always silent, she is too far away when seen for there to be any potential communication. In fact, in the history of St Andrews there are no reports of her attempting to communicate with anyone at all, or vice versa. This has never been one of her attributes, so the reason for her still being present is not because of unfinished business, as intimated I believe it is because her body is still here (HT).

She is also benevolent. Spirits are generally neutral anyway, despite the assumptions of our mind misinterpreting the reasons for their behaviour. They can get as annoyed as any can, but they will cause no intentional harm.

# *Ghosts*

# *Haunted Tower Part 2.*

## The White Lady Ghost

**White Lady – Reports – HT p.195**

1 White Lady seen by three fishermen (early Linskill, 19th C)
2 White Lady cliffside – near Haunted Tower (Linskill) 1911
3 White Lady disappearing into Haunted Tower (Linskill) 1911
4 White Lady on top of Hepburn's Wall (early Linskill, 19th C)
5 White Lady on the cliffside – at the Haunted Tower (local woman) 1940s

**Reports 1-5 (OHR 17-21) above have little to no information, so we start here from OHR 22. Haunted Tower Report 6.**

6 White Lady in the ruins by the Haunted Tower (Grant/Hodges) 1968
7 White Lady walking in the ruins by the Haunted Tower (MacDonald) 1975

**White Lady – Reports – (G)**

8 White Lady – Haunted Tower (Citizen report) 1917
9 White Lady standing in grounds by the Haunted Tower c.1980
10 White Lady standing by the Haunted Tower (Falconer) Various
11 Middle window, feeling of being watched (various tours)
12 Middle window, woman's face peering out of the window (tour) 2016
13 Middle window, woman's face peering out of the window (tour) 2019
14 Hepburn's wall, ill-defined light Haunted Tower (Alexander) 1992

**OHR 22. Haunted Tower Report 6. (HT p.222)**
Peter Underwood in 1973, wrote: "In May 1968, she was reported to have been seen near the Round Tower by an arts student, Miss Alison Grant, and by a medical student Mark Hodges.[13]

The Round Tower is the Lighthouse Tower, but he was meaning the Haunted Tower. As was Andrews Green in the following report:

**OHR 23. Haunted Tower Report 7. (HT p.223)**
There is a report of the White Lady being seen during the day by two people in 1975 wearing a light grey dress... Andrew Green wrote, "Having been told on numerous occasions of the ghost that frequents the Round or Abbey Tower of St Andrews it was with considerable interest and pleasure that I met Ian MacDonald and his wife in June 1979, for they had both actually seen the apparition. They were on a visit to the golfing centre in 1975 and decided to spend some time looking round the ruins of the Cathedral. On nearing the tower in the Abbey Wall, they noticed the figure of a woman in 'a light grey dress' moving towards them… wearing a light veil. "You don't see that these days" Ian said to his wife. At that moment the ghost vanished leaving the couple open-mouthed with astonishment."[14]

This is either a confusing account or a very rare account. The light grey dress and moving is from the couple. The light veil is either an editorial addition based on Linskill as it doesn't fit with the other reports for her being seen here, or, that is what they saw. It points to the latter as there is no mention of her long black hair – hence the veil. Moving is her in life.

**OHR 24. Haunted Tower Report 8.**
A report I missed in STAM when publishing all the historical reports was the following from the St Andrews Citizen –

Saturday 19 May 1917

**Reappearance of the White Lady**

'The beautiful White Lady of the Haunted Tower has again appeared to several citizens. These citizens have informed him [Linskill] that they have seen this strange apparition, and, curiously enough, their descriptions of it agree with that of citizens of a former generation who were privileged to see it. The lady is robed in spotless white garments, she has a pale face of great beauty and long black hair. She has always been seen in the vicinity of the Haunted Tower and vanishes into it.'

**OHR 25. Haunted Tower Report 9.**
**White Lady in the grounds by Haunted Tower c.1980**

A lovely lady I had on one of the evening tours in 2018 was telling me when she was eight years old (c.1980) she was in the Cathedral grounds as part of a school trip. She saw a woman all in white standing next to the Haunted Tower. She was distracted by her friends and when she looked back the figure had disappeared. She mentioned this to them and far from believing her, they typically put her down and made fun of her.

Although she knows what she saw and has never forgotten it, when she mentioned it to anyone through her life they were always dismissive to her about it. So much so she sometimes doubted her own experience as to what she saw. I told her that others have experienced the same as her in the same location. She became quite emotional and apologised for her outburst.

This was the first time after nearly forty years someone believed her. She described it as a "weight being lifted." This might not seem like a big deal but when there is talk of ghosts, opinion born of ignorance outweighs the integrity of those experiencing it. This is especially true of the herd mentality, where for the sake of appearances the desire to 'fit in' precludes any individual thought, and ironically, everyone likes to think they are individual! Get each person on their own and the tables soon turn.

**OHR 26. Haunted Tower Report 10.**
**White Lady standing by the Haunted Tower – Introduction**
I mention often that we have all experienced phenomena whether we realise it or not. If you don't think you have, has it never struck you how you always turn to look in the right direction when you know someone is watching you? Seeing something out the corner of your eye that you dismiss as your imagination? Unaccountable feelings. Animals and babies following something with their eyes across a room. Our subconscious is good at masking the true nature of experience as a mechanism of self-protection. Our conscious mind is then left to deal with what it can by calling upon our imagination as the fall guy. Bear in mind the imagination needs a trigger, so dwell for a moment on what caused you to think something was your imagination before a casual dismissal completely denies you of all your sensibilities. If a ghost appears on a tour, everyone experiences the same. Although, as you will find a few times, there are exceptions. Not looking in the right direction being the main one. However, it is true the subtleties are more readily picked up by those with a more acute awareness. Mediums for example do the opposite to the casual observer, they take in more, so they observe these signs more readily as their consciousness can cope with an additional influx of reality.

There is always a marked difference in the behavioural characteristics of people when genuine phenomena are experienced, compared perhaps to those who insist on chasing shadows, scrabbling desperately in the dark through expectation for something to occur. Fortunately, I don't get many of the latter on my tours, which may surprise. I leave that attraction to so called 'paranormal investigations,' charging a fortune for twenty strangers to sit in a hotel room with the light off after being told it is haunted. Phenomena are not 'appear on demand,' and expectation is a magnet for the imagination. Water running through a pipe from a flushed toilet on the next floor, is, I am sure justification enough for the organisers to take their hard earned cash for all the effect it then has on those present. However, other than a crash course in psychology, the placebo effect has absolutely nothing to do with the reality of paranormal phenomena. Aside those looking to convince themselves of its reality, no matter what happens, nothing will ever constitute as proof to anyone outside that environment, the same with video or photos. So much for the 'investigation.' Aside the novelty of doing something 'different' or a moment of escapism, is there any point? So, a bit of a spoiler for you. At least 95% of programmes involving paranormal investigations are contrived. It can be years between things occurring depending on the circumstance, and nothing happening is not going to sell a programme. A producer throwing a pebble down a close, feeds the placebo for those present and the expectations of the west, but does the reality no favours.

I do get people coming on my tours with this conditioned expectancy in mind to see a ghost. All the while at the back of their mind they are thinking it is not going to happen, so when it does, they rarely realise it is, or has, until the impossibility of what they have just experienced is pointed out, or it finally sinks in after the delay I spoke of earlier.

**Reaction and placebo**

How many know how they would react if they were presented with a ghost? During a ghost hunt, there are too many expectations, collectively heightened through a mindset primed in anticipation of being part of a paranormal experience. The build-up of anticipation through the placebo effect or self hype causes fear and apprehension as the adrenaline builds.

We interpret by association. After watching a horror film, talking about ghosts or reading a book such as this we become super alert and sensitive to the slightest noise as our imagination hones into thoughts of a 'what if' scenario for what we are hearing. Everything suddenly has a paranormal potential, and we can be quick to attribute the paranormal to everything we would otherwise not even think about or even be aware of. The imagination is a powerful tool and easily runs riot as every little incident drives the mind to believe the wind has nothing to do with the rattling of windows for example. Or the way our mind tries to give recognition and form to the way light casts shadows on a wall. "Was that my imagination or is there something there?" we might say to ourselves.

**Examples of hype – hiding in the shadows**

Dabbling with the Ouija board is a classic example of how hyped we can become, and how easy it is to then give the natural a supernatural origin. When the paranormal is mentioned as taking place, the preconceived ideas of what we believe can happen is accentuated in our psyche. We then associate every little creek or knock as a manifestation of the paranormal when otherwise we wouldn't think anything of it because we are familiar with the knocking of water pipes or wood creaking as it cools and settles down. Our mind gives an association by suggestion. Such is the way our mind processes subject matter in line with its preoccupations. The subtle way it then impacts as an influence upon our state of mind can often have surprising consequences of itself.

Our level of awareness towards the paranormal has increased, although we might apply experience to our imagination there is something deeper at work here. By bringing the paranormal to the forefront of our mind we become closer to the hidden nature of reality. You think nothing of going upstairs to bed every night, other than the brief respite you are about to receive from the affairs of the day. However, after watching a creepy film you go up the stairs wondering if anything there will be up there when you arrive. All the lights are switched on as you go, not just to see your way anymore, it is just in case something is up there lurking in the shadows, and turning all the lights on is a warning to whatever it might be to flee before your arrival. This gives reassurance to your fears of the unknown which has been generated by this heightened state of mind focused in a singular direction. It is why in horror films when a sound has been heard and on looking for its source have you never wondered why the lights are never turned on. This feeds your anxiety of what could have caused it, even though it goes against the grain of what you would naturally do if you were in that same circumstance.

With this thought, it is important to understand there might well be something upstairs, just as there is a likelihood of something sitting next to you when watching that scary movie, or for that matter sitting next to you now, or standing in the corner watching you as you read this book. The world of the unseen is with us all the time. We are just unaware most of the time to this greater potential. But whatever is lurking in the recesses is unlikely to cause any harm.

**Silently being observed – Haunted Tower**

Through synchronicities, everything has a reason. Sometimes it is something happening when it does, as well as where it does that can give the reason. There is a ghost of a woman I have seen a few times now standing by the Haunted Tower. She started appearing shortly after I started researching the locality of a secret chamber where I believe the second White Lady corpse is still entombed.

The first time she appeared was January 2019. It is when I am talking about her that she sometimes appears. I catch her fleetingly out the corner of my eye. She is between 4 and 5 feet tall and always completely silent. She always stands in the shadow of the right-hand corner of the tower (west side). Being in the darkness there is little sense of depth and it is far too dark to make out any detail. Even though I am generally only around 10 feet away from her, I only know it is a small woman wearing a light dress. Given where she is standing it can only be the White Lady, but she is not glowing or as bright as a light. This appears to be reserved for when she is seen on the precinct wall or in the grounds. Her dress is dulled with being in the shadows. Her whole figure is greyed out. The same grey as her face which myself and others have seen in the Haunted Tower window I shall give mention to in a moment.

It can become very dark down here at the best of times. The pavement light across from the tower does not cut through the darkness that well. I took this photo January 2017 when we had a rare layer of snow. By morning it had gone. It is an opportunity to see the path looking a lot lighter than it normally does at night, and makes the area look a lot brighter, but as you can see in the photo, the corner ever remains in darkness.

Just before I see her, I always have that feeling of being watched, which is what sometimes attracts my attention. Sometimes I get that feeling then I look and see her fleetingly before she disappears. It can be quite unnerving, and always catches me off guard as she is always unexpected, and always distracting, but nonetheless always very special and very rare to observe.

When I first started seeing her, it wasn't easy to concentrate and continue speaking. I now say on the tours, "If I stop speaking midsentence during the tour it is for one of two reasons, there is something loud going on like traffic, or I have seen something."

To start with I had a couple of comments on different tours of people saying, "Are you ok?" when I stopped speaking midsentence, or paused for no apparent reason at the tower. That is when I told them we were not alone. We never are anyway, but when something is visually present it is all the more immediate.

Like the Half Moon Girl in the Nun's Walk also mentioned later, I just keep a lookout to see if anyone else notices. To date, no one ever has, even though she is always standing literally a few feet away, silently observing them, and me for that matter from the shadows.

I don't generally mention her because if I did, I know she would have disappeared by the time I had, and that could just put a dampener on the tour. It would also fuel the flame of a few who would think I am just saying it to embellish the tour.

**OHR 27. Haunted Tower Report 11.**
**The Haunted Tower upper window**

The feeling of being watched here can get overwhelming. There are several deceased spirits in this immediate locality, and when there is nothing to see, the instinctual direction you turn to gives an idea of where it is coming from, which can then narrow down which one it is watching us.

There have been several times on tours where we know it is something watching us from the window in the top chamber of the tower, but on looking up, there is not usually anything to see, however, on two occasions however, there was…

**OHR 28. Haunted Tower Report 12.**
**Woman's face upper window – Experience 1.**

There have been a couple of occasions where we have seen someone in the top chamber window of the tower looking down at us. The first time was in 2016. The face was mostly in darkness, half peering at us over the ledge of the window. The eyes had a red tinge from the pavement light opposite. My companion on this tour was a small American woman from the Bronx. I always remember her saying, "Should that happen?" She was fixed on us for about ten seconds, I had stopped speaking at that point while we observed her.

With so much information to mention on the tours, I am speaking all the way around, so ten seconds of me saying nothing is a long time in tour mode. My guest from New York queried what we were looking at, or rather, what was looking at us, but I think it was my silence that got her a little scared, as she then said, "Oh!" as she realised who was looking down at us. When the face disappeared back into the darkness of the tower I turned to the woman, and in reply to her comment said, "No, it shouldn't!"

From this you will gather she is more persistent than most ghosts. Not always disappearing the moment you spot her.

**OHR 29. Haunted Tower Report 13.**
**Woman's face upper window – Experience 2.**

The second experience was near the beginning of 2019. I was again talking about the tower and a grey face half peered out the middle window and disappeared again. It was dark and cold. Like the previous experience there was no sound at all. We were there for a while and nothing reappeared. There was nobody physically up there, and as I say, no sound. The White Lady has also been described by others as having a face 'as grey as stone.'

It was reminiscent of when I saw the ghost of 'Green Jeanie' at Balgonie Castle near Markinch in 2013. She also had a grey face, 'the face of the moon' is how I describe her in GOF p.70.

Green Jeanie is the most famous ghost at Balgonie and in all the years of her appearing, I am the only person to have seen her face.

The grey face is important and crops up a number of times to describe the face of apparitions. There is also another ghost at Balgonie with a grey face. Refer to GOF p.68.

**Observing another time**

When I experience something like this, I know straight away when it is not a physical person or a trick of light. It is as if something in the back of the mind is notifying that what I am looking at is out of place – that it is not of our time and should not be there. Along with what I mentioned earlier about the fragility of our perception and the mind questioning our own perception, I always find these experiences create feelings of being slightly out of sync with reality. A sidestepping of physical reality perhaps. I still get these feelings when I see something I know is not of the physical. The uniqueness of the moment is ever replicated, there is never any complacency when it presents itself, despite knowing how it operates, and no matter how many experiences you may have had, nothing prepares you, each experience is unique and always surprising.

Mike D. of St Andrews who you shall read about later, had an experience in Ninewells Hospital. It is what he wrote at the end of his email that has a poignancy in this regard. He said:

'I have also encountered a white lady at Ninewells Hospital [Dundee]. I could find no accounts of such sightings there. She was walking fairly quickly with respect to others between the double doors of the corridor to the chapel (I thought there was a morgue in that direction but no?) the hot snack shop and the middle ground. Medium height, slim/medium build, long white hair, age late forties or early fifties, wearing a white gown or hospital night-dress. Her right eye (left-hand side as viewed) was covered by skin or a patch. I think it was missing. She saw me and paused then carried on milling around. My impression was this was going on in parallel to "normal" time. Somehow, I was encountering both. Neither my friend or my uncle noticed her.' Refer also to p.216 and p.506.

It is the recognition of this sense of a parallel time to relative time that rightly gives one of the keys to their nature. The subconscious is the bridge between the awareness inherent in our spiritual nature and physical consciousness. A conduit where impressions and feelings including those of Group C. and etc, come from. Your subconscious knows exactly what it is you are looking at, or more the point, it is recognised through spirit and translated to the subconscious. It just takes a while for part of that recognition to then seep through to the conscious mind, which then attempts to work through the process. However, unless this understanding of the nature of spirit and how the paranormal operates is present, the conscious mind tends to just fumble around. It is trying to make sense of an experience that has just shattered the laws of physics into a million questions, hence part of the reason for the inherent confusion most experience. Attempts at a satisfactory explanation are made through a logic rooted in the physical and based on understanding through fiction, which inevitably just generates a distorted logic through its own contrivance.

Moments of clarity beyond this confusion are representative of this deeper recognition. The spirit temporally and partially, merges into consciousness and a greater reality impacts our psyche. It can cause a slight shift in the awareness as it adjusts to a different mode of consciousness. In this sense, consciousness is now open to a duality of realms, one overlaying the other.

This is deeper than general observance and there are varying stages involved in its merger. A partial merger is an indication of potential. A full merger is a lot rarer. When I started experiencing a full merger, everything in my vision tilted to 45 degrees and back as it was happening. I was in Greece at the time and it caused immediate dizziness and a feeling of nausea. It only lasted a few seconds and was like that experienced when waking into a wall of energy, but this was caused by the momentary shift in vision. It took a while to get used to it. A full merger is the spirit operating through and overriding consciousness, there is no requirement for thought, and analysis is not present or required when clarity is experienced in that state. Once adept, one can switch at will.

**OHR 30. Michael's Haunted Tower Report 14.**

**Michael Alexander email of experiences part 2.**

Thursday, 24 December 2015

**Strange light on wall – east side of the tower**

'In another incident in October 1992 (on the Saturday night of the Dunhill golf tournament I recall), my sister Caroline and I were walking along Kirk Hill past the Haunted Tower in the evening having been at the golf. No one else was around. After passing the Haunted Tower, and as we approached the top of the brae leading down to the harbour, I happened to look back at the Haunted Tower and can only say we both then saw a strange white smudged / ill-defined light towards the left-hand top corner of the tower. It stopped us in our tracks and a strange feeling came over us like we were being watched. It then appeared to fade into the tower and disappeared. Needless to say, we got what is commonly known as the 'heebie-jeebies' and I remember we ran about as far as Woodburn Park as we headed up the road! I cannot explain what we saw, but having passed their hundreds of times over the years, it was out of the ordinary and I've never seen it again.'

Refer to p.100 for the first part of Michael's email about St Rule's Tower and p.180 for the third part.

**The corroboration of testimony**

In HT I speak of Neil Dobson, a marine archaeologist from St Andrews who I mention later as seeing the figure of a woman on the high wall just beyond the Pends southern archway. He described her as being very bright like a light, moving slowly along the high Cathedral precinct wall.

I have reproduced a photo on p.552 that I received from a woman of something she captured on one of my tours. It was on the Pend's wall and is very similar to both Neil's experience and Michael experience at the Haunted Tower.

Linskill was aware of a White Lady roaming that stretch of the Pends. He also wrote about the White Lady being seen on Hepburn's wall by the Haunted Tower. I had never heard of any aside Linskill mentioning her being seen on the wall by the tower, so I assumed this to be a Linskill embellishment. Switching her location from the Pends to the precinct wall on the eastern side of the Haunted Tower to tie in various elements of her at that location. With now having reports of her being seen on Hepburn's wall it qualifies Linskill's suggestion, and it is always to the east of the tower where she is seen, never the west. This is further corroborated by the behaviour of dogs at the start of the following section.

# *Haunted Tower Part 3.*

## Additional Phenomena

### 2 Parts

### Part 1.
### Related to the White Lady

3 Anomalies (A)
4 Example Haunted Tower Reports (HTR)

| | |
|---|---|
| A1. (HTR15) | Hepburn's wall, dogs howling at something on wall (Barlow) 2015 |
| A2. (HTR16) | Millie the dog seeing/sensing something at the Haunted Tower (Eddie) 2015 |
| A2. (HTR17) | Millie the dog reacting – Haunted Tower (Eddie) 2016 |
| A3. (HTR18) | Japanese Akita petrified – Haunted Tower (Vanbeck) 2016 |

# *Ghosts*

# *Reports Part 1.*

## Odd behaviour of animals

**The second part of my email reply to Michael Alexander:**
31 December 2015

**1/ A1. OHR 31. Haunted Tower Report 15.**
**The odd behaviour of animals at the tower**

Did I mention the experience of a school teacher from St Leonards I had on a tour a few weeks ago? Dan Barlow walks his dogs along this stretch and I had seen him on a few occasions whilst on tour. He came on one of my tours a couple of weeks before Christmas with three Russian pupils and gave me the account of an incident only a few months before. It is in keeping with what you mentioned and what Linskill stated. He was walking along the Scores Path from the harbour with his dogs. He said he walked them along this stretch a lot and they always sniff their way along the ground as they walk, never looking up, but on this occasion when nearing the Haunted Tower, the dogs stopped and started barking frantically and whining like mad at something on top of Hepburn's wall to the left side of the Tower. They were making the kind of sounds only heard when dogs are scared. He couldn't see anything but they either saw or sensed something that was scaring them.

This is the same spot as where you saw the ill-defined light and the same spot Linskill mentions as being one of the locations of where the White Lady has been seen…

**Email continued:**

**2/ A2. OHR 32. Haunted Tower Report 16.**

**Millie – the wee dog**

I mention in HT p.198 about a lovely wee Yorkshire terrier called Millie that sometimes stops at the Haunted Tower, growls, sits down and puts out her paw. She only does this when someone is there. But those in her care never see anything, and it only happens when they are passing the Haunted Tower.

The third part of Michael's email and the last part of my reply can be found on p.180.

**3/ A2. OHR 33. Haunted Tower Report 17.**

**Millie – the wee dog**

Another experience Eddie observed for Millie was during the summer of 2016. Millie was standing by the tower facing east and was fixated by something on the path. There was nothing to be seen but she didn't move at all, then she held up her paw as she has done before at this spot. She didn't growl or sit this time but it was as though someone approached her and held out their hand. With her not growling points to her now being familiar with whatever it was she was seeing. Her unusual behaviour hadn't happened anywhere else around St Andrews up to that point, only around the tower. Since then there is also another location, refer also to p.214.

**4/ A3. OHR 34. Haunted Tower Report 18.**

**The Japanese Akita**

I was looking on Jo Woolf's Hazel Tree blog and read a brief post from Thomas Vanbeck about the strange behaviour of his dog:

Feb 8th 2016

'I was up the hill where the cannon sits [Kirkheugh] I had my Japanese Akita with me and it was petrified at the tower and I have never seen my dog being scared of anything.'[15]

On the 4th March 2016, Thomas commented on his earlier post: 'It was the haunted tower and the hair was standing up on the back of my neck what puzzles me is the archery window was full of earth but does a ghost still stand in that soil or is it still the way it was when the ghost was alive'

A reply to Thomas from Jo Wolf:

5th March 2016

'I don't think anyone knows the answer to that! But I would say – theoretically! – if you were picking up energy from another time, it doesn't matter what the window looks like today. Very spooky!'

Jo wrote 'I don't think anyone knows the answer to that!' then answered the question correctly, but used the word 'theoretical' as its preface, as most unfortunately do. However, clarification is required as I know the answer and it is not theoretical. A spirit of the deceased (Group B) will appear on the current level, whereas an impressionistic ghost (Group A) will appear on the original level. It is why the monk on the newel stair of St Rule's is Group B. and the monk/s seen on the original floors are Group A.

**The Northgate Shadow**

Hugh McCann posted the following in St Andrews Photo Corner 2nd September 2021: 'My uncle was out walking his dog late one night while he was staying at my grandas, he stayed in Gregory place. He was walking past the cathedral and the dog started going nuts, barking and growing. When he turned round he saw a shadow of someone but couldn't see a person so he kept waking. When he passed the cathedral gate [North Gate] he turned to see if anyone was there and he saw the shadow disappear through the gate.'

This was the same figure seen by the gentleman from Aberdeen.

# *Haunted Tower Part 4.*

## Additional Phenomena

Tactile Sense

## Part 2.
## The Lower Chamber

5 Anomalies (A)

**Lower Chamber Experiences – G**

A1. HTR 19 Physical contact: Over 1000 experiences 2014-2020
A2. HTR 20 Rare delay in physical contact (tour) 2017
A3. HTR 21 Arm being pulled into the tower (school pupil) 2015
A4. HTR 22 Prodding of hand (tour) 2019
A5. HTR 23 Static shock on hand (tour) 2014-2021

# Reports Part 2.

## Tactile Sense

**5/ A1. OHR 35. Haunted Tower Report 19.**

By far the most common aspects of paranormal phenomena happening in St Andrews concerns the lower chamber of the Haunted Tower, followed by events on the pavement side of the tower. With over 1000 people having lower chamber experiences on my tours over the last 7 years alone.

A local legend has it that if you throw money in the lower chamber the White Lady will grant you a wish. Well, don't waste your money, why would she! This isn't an old legend in St Andrews. A few years ago, someone threw a coin in and others followed suit. That individual thing again!

During the summer of 2018 someone threw a coin into one of the open archbishop's graves by the high altar of the Cathedral, before long there was a collection. That was a new one!

Most visitors passing the tower are unaware of the White Lady, but if they look through the loophole they will see money in the chamber, throw money in, and make a wish as they do with a wishing well. The money can build up pretty quickly, especially through the summer months. Pound coins, dollars, euros and children throw in chocolate money. At the moment I don't know which is worth the most! Historic Scotland now clear it out fairly regularly and give the money to charity. The same with the money that builds up in the former fresh water wells in the Cathedral grounds.

The entrance to the middle chamber has wire mesh across the iron railings to stop birds and rodents going in, but they still find a way in. There is nothing across the locked entrance gate of the lower chamber or loopholes. Even though it would take no effort for a rodent to saunter in at ground level from the precinct side and cosy up on a cold night, they don't. No birds, rodents or cats and there are bats in the precincts. If they did it would be full of mess and be more difficult for the staff to clear the money out and clean it before giving it to charity. Nothing going in there is important to know, as there is a longstanding legend in the town: *If you put your arm into the lower chamber you can shake hands with the White Lady.*

The main-focus is always on this middle loophole of the lower chamber. I always invite people on the tours to put their arm in. I never mention what actually happens until all those who are going to do it have, and we are then walking away from the tower.

I also never try and persuade any into doing it as I know what happens when it does and the psychological affect it can have.

**Apprehension**

I had the pleasure of taking comedians Rosie Jones and Harriet Kemsley on a tour September 2020. It was part of a Channel 4 short production they filmed with me called *Mission: Accessible | Ghosts and gliders in bonnie Scotland with Rosie Jones.* When we were at the Haunted Tower, Harriet said, "You do your job very well!" as she was genuinely reluctant to put her arm into the chamber. They both did it though, and so too did all the film crew – including the cameraman. They didn't experience anything on this occasion which is maybe just as well, especially the cameraman, his equipment looked expensive. I was wondering if any extras were going to appear! They all let themselves go a bit on the tour which was great to see and they all survived to record their time here.

I always say before inviting people to put their arm in, "There is no instruction manual, but it has never happened when anyone is wearing gloves." In the winter I add the caveat, "Don't kneel on the ground, you will get a wet knee!" I never used to mention this, but I do now as most would get a wet knee, even though they knew the ground was wet!

I am sometimes asked, "What do I do?" as they near the tower in anticipation of putting their arm in. There is not a lot to remember, rather than forgetting what to do I always know their question is a sign of nervousness as they prepare themselves. So, I just reaffirm, "There is no instruction manual."

When presented with surreal moments like this, the mind seems to become disorientated – that confusion thing again. It can become overwhelmed as the natural state of mind is confronted with something difficult or challenging. We don't like the unexpected unless it is a pleasant surprise. "You've got someone in there!" the odd one will laughingly say just before they do it to give themselves the reassurance that should something happen, in a bid to regain control of their own mind from its overwhelmed state, they have now pre-empted who they think it might be. Although they are completely unaware of what I have just told you as to the reason for them saying it. Some can get very professional, rolling up their sleeve before putting their whole arm in.

**What happens when you put your arm in?**

There can be a very visible sigh of relief when nothing happens, especially at night. Others kick themselves that they didn't do it. Often, they don't know why they didn't do it, or more the point for some, why they couldn't do it. There are many who can't bring themselves to put their arm in, even during daylight and after being told by their friends there is nothing in there, and often after having had a look inside themselves. Whether it happens or not, all are genuinely surprised at their own reaction. Karen Clark following a tour said "There was no way I was putting my hand down the hole to shake hands with her when you suggested it! A young boy did and I was panicking a bit as to what he might feel. I already felt that she was there and didn't really want the confirmation!" When it does happen, it doesn't try and shake your hand like the legend states. Barring a very few variations which I shall mention in a moment, the second the arm is put into the chamber there is the sensation of something forcefully brushing past either the palm or the back of the hand. When we are walking away from the tower and it hasn't happened, I demonstrate the same. It is physical, quick and very firm. No one has ever suggested it has tried to shake their hand, so it is not like the legend. When it does happen, they eventually demonstrate it themselves.

There is no sensation of heat or cold, it is not a draft from the wind blowing through the side loopholes or the back locked gate facing the Cathedral grounds, and as I mentioned, there is never anything in the lower chamber such as birds, bats, rodents or cats. It happens in all weathers, any time of year, day or night. Those experiencing it cover all nationalities, vocations and ages, and like all phenomena, it doesn't discriminate. It happens in equal measure to those of a 'sceptical' mind, as it does to those who 'believe,' or have experienced phenomena.

**Frequency**

The reality of what happens in the lower chamber of the tower is never what any would suppose it to be. No one has genuinely tried to fake what occurs as they don't know what happens, and all soon realise it is not that kind of a ghost tour. In over 4000 tours, no one has ever put their arm in and said it shook their hand, not even jokingly, which you would suppose could happen a lot. There is the odd one mucking around as they do, and theatrics or exaggerated melodramatics are always obvious to spot. They think everyone will be mucking around. In the same way when someone is late for a tour they say, "I imagine everyone is late!" Well, trains don't wait, and neither do I anymore!

They have no idea the ratio of those mucking around on my tours is around 1 in a 1000, which is negligible compared to brushing past the hand which works out at around 1 in 40.

It doesn't matter if it is day or night, although it happens a lot more during daylight hours. This is only because at night it is pitch black, and few will put their arm into the great unknown after dark.

**The reaction when it happens**

I always keep an eye on what is going on and most of the time I know straight away when it happens. Easier to spot when it is a small group. Although, I can have a large group on a tour where everyone is excitedly laughing, joking and deliberating on who shall go next to see if something will happen, and as this almost chaotic scene of jovial fear plays out, the person with their hand in the chamber and myself, are the only ones who know something already has.

Each incident of the paranormal holds its own when it comes to reactions. Visual phenomena in open spaces can often go unnoticed by many, or there is a delayed reaction for what is being observed. Visual phenomena/poltergeist activity in enclosed spaces where you know there is no one else present, especially the familiarity of your own home is completely different. It is a lot more personal and is perceived as a violation of your private space. Your reactions are a lot more immediate and the great unknown mixed with not knowing what will happen next, makes it a lot scarier. The same applies to physical contact in any setting. When something is tactile it is affecting you directly, so there is a direct reflex reaction.

When putting the arm in and it happens, it is not something any could fake. The reaction is anything from a yelp or a scream, to jerking back, running away or generally becoming upset. It is always overlaid by this same confusion and disbelief.

Needless to say, it deeply affects all who experience it. Their reaction matches their level of surprise, and I have witnessed every incident. It can take a few moments for others in the group to realise. You would never think something seemingly so simple could cause such dramatic reactions. Believe me, it does – always. The symptoms of trauma are a common indicator it has happened.

When you look in their eyes there is no one home. It can take a few moments for them to come around to themselves again. It is part of our inbuilt instinct for self-preservation, we like to think we are in control. That we know ourselves pretty well, but we don't know ourselves as well as we think we might, or how we would react to a given situation until it happens to us. There is nothing more dramatic than experiencing something we doubted the existence of. We can have all the bravado and boldness in the world when the sun is bright and others are around, but when we experience, our bravado rarely matches the reality of our behaviour. If you doubt its existence, and find yourself alone in the dark passing the tower, put your arm into the chamber.

Everyone is always fine after the event and not 'physically' harmed in any way, but it does leave its mark on their psyche as something they will never forget. As I say, it becomes very personal, and it does change those who experience it. They also realise everything I speak about on the tour is true. That is why I never try and persuade any to do it. Not because it brushes past their hand, but because there is a good chance they will go into shock.

Most ghost tours around the world try and scare you. I am one of the few that doesn't. Possibly the only one, and no hype. Some have aids called 'jumper ooters' to help with this task resulting in a scare, swiftly followed by hysterical laughter. Not one person who has experienced lower chamber phenomenon has laughed afterwards, and when others in the party realise something has happened, the tone for the rest of the tour changes. It becomes very serious for them. This is especially noticeable when there are 50+ people on the tour as they realise I wasn't joking. From then on, everyone hangs onto every word, and the stragglers at the back now stick to me like glue.

**Variations**

**6/ A2. OHR 36. Haunted Tower Report 20.**
***One minute later...***
In 2017, on a 4 pm daylight tour, a boy put his arm into the chamber. I thought it was stuck. His arm was in there for a good minute (so he currently has the tour record). I then realised he was playing up to two other children on the tour. They wanted a shot and he wasn't letting them. He wouldn't have gone near it in the dark, and he wished he hadn't gone near it in daylight. His bravado turned into a yelp as he ran from the tower down the path toward North Gate. His mother was standing just in front of me. He ran off and we looked at each other. Her demeanour quickly changed from one of, I guess playful intrigue to one of concern. He was fooling around before it happened, but not when it did – you can always tell. When we caught up with him at North Gate he was visibly shaken. Following a few moments, he came around to himself, held out his arm, and said something brushed past the top of his hand as he demonstrated the same with his left hand brushing past his right. Exactly how I always demonstrate it when it doesn't

happen and we are walking away from the tower. This has been the only incident that has deviated from the pattern of it happening the moment the arm is placed in the tower. I guess, if you do it and it doesn't happen straight away, try keeping it in there for a minute and see if that works!

It is not the only variant though of what can happen when your arm is in there. The following are examples of two other things that can happen, but they are not nearly as prevalent. . .

**7/ A3. OHR 37. Haunted Tower Report 21.**
**Being pulled in**

On Easter Saturday, 2015, I had 43 people on an evening tour including 30 school pupils aged between 10 and 12. All of them were very eager to put their arm through the loophole, which is uncharacteristic, as contrary to popular assumptions, most school children won't go anywhere near this tower once I have spoken to them about the ghost here, but this was a fearless bunch from Motherwell!

It only happened to one of them and what she experienced won't easily be forgotten by her or those present. When she put her arm into the chamber she burst into tears. It took three teachers to console her. It didn't brush past her hand or try and shake it as the legend suggests, it tried to pull her into the chamber. This is very rare indeed. It is also rare for phenomena in general to be so dramatic.

In April 2017, I had 10 adults and a small boy on a tour. I had barely finished mentioning about putting the arm into the chamber when he shot like a bullet to the tower and wedged his arm through the hole. I found that hilarious. The usual reaction when I mention putting the arm into the chamber is everyone taking a backward step in case I single any out for the task, which I never do. It is customarily followed by a tangible silence to what I have just suggested, as the almost audible cogs in their mind run on overtime in a bid to work out the prospects of their surviving such an escapade.

If the boy could have fitted his body into the chamber, it would have happened, but he wasn't trying to be cheeky. I find no humour in any showing off or trying to be smart. It was rare to see one move so fast. None of the adults would do it. When we were walking towards the Bishop's Palace, I was speaking about the girl's experience from Motherwell. A woman laughed, pointed to the wee boy and said, "He's from Motherwell you know!" I knew they were fearless! I always get a good bunch from Motherwell. Interestingly, their place name comes from a well dedicated to the Virgin Mary, which is also one of the dedications of the Haunted Tower as denoted by the sculpting of the pot of lilies on the middle chamber outer wall.

**8/ A4. OHR 38. Haunted Tower Report 22.**
**Prodding**

There was a party of University alumni on a tour one hot afternoon. They had gathered back in St Andrews for the birthday of a fellow graduate and surprised her with a tour. As it transpired she was the only sceptic amongst them, and surprised them with her brash sarcastic comments as we developed the tour. When I spoke about putting your hand into the chamber she became particularly dismissive. I could see the others were becoming a little embarrassed and annoyed at her behaviour. They were enjoying the tour and birthday girl wasn't going down to well.

There is a particular trait that is easy to spot, where a very select minority are immediately, and personally affronted I have the audacity to speak of the paranormal as if it is real. The tripadvisor review at the beginning of this volume is an example that saved me the job of describing what my tours are not. There is a difference though between conditioned conviction which that was, and bigotry, which this was. It is a funny thing that no one likes to be called a bigot, arrogant or ignorant, yet if they did not exist amongst us, neither would the words to describe them.

While everyone else was deliberating on whether to put their hand into the chamber or not, she tutted and said, "Oh let me have a go!" She duly thrust in her arm, paused, then pulled it out and said, "See!" in a dismissive tone as she waved her arm around displaying it was all obviously nonsense. This was followed by general chat amongst the group as a few others tentatively put their arm in before we carried on the tour. We then stopped on the nearby brae towards the Bishop's Palace. I demonstrated what sometimes happens when people put their arm into the chamber by customarily brushing one hand past the other. The same as the boy demonstrated earlier. She then piped up and said, "I felt nothing like that. All I felt was this" – as she stabbed the palm of her right hand with the index finger of her left. I gave her a reassuring smile and said "Apart from the money, there was nothing else in there, was there?"

"No" she replied.

"So, what do you think it was that just did that?"

She was a lot quieter for the rest of the tour as she dwelt on what she had just demonstrated to me and to all her friends. Because it did not do what the legend stated it would, she paid no immediate attention to what actually did happen.

The most recent incident of this was 12th September 2021. Deborah Broomfield on a daylight tour experienced the same. It wasn't until I was speaking about what happened as we were walking toward the Bishops Palace that she said she felt a light prod on the palm of her hand and demonstrated the same as the woman in the previous account. It left her feeling confused.

### 9/ A5. OHR 39. Haunted Tower Report 23. Static Shock – 2014 to 2021

There have been occasions where some have had a mild static shock on the palm of their hand or a tingling sensation, which are telling signs of a heightened energy in the chamber.

The last time was on a tour in 2021 with a slight tingling feeling on the palm of the hand.

# *Haunted Tower Part 5.*

## Further Anomalous Activity in and around the Lower Chamber

## Part 3a & b.
## Electronics and physiological anomalies

# *Tower Reports Part 3a.*

Additional Phenomena Examples
## Electronics

**10/ A1. OHR 40. Haunted Tower Report 24.**
**Michael Alexander email of experiences part 3.**

Thursday, 24 December 2015

Back in the early 1990s I was a student (in Dundee but living in St Andrews where I grew up). At that time, I had a part-time job as a projectionist at the New Picture House and often used to cycle home via Kirk Hill and the harbour around 10.30 pm / 11 pm. On several occasions, my personal stereo Walkman cut out as I was passing the Haunted Tower. May have been a coincidence, but it never happened anywhere else. Power would always return as I approached the slope at the top of the harbour.

I mention these incidents for your interest. I'm not suggesting these were ghosts but I'm an open-minded person and I cannot explain them. They were certainly out of the ordinary and left a mark at the time. And they still do.

Have a great Christmas, and keep in touch.

Regards

Michael Alexander
Lead News Feature Writer
The Courier

**This is the third part of my email reply to Michael:**

31 December 2015

The incident of your Walkman cutting out at that spot is very in-keeping indeed with those on my tours whose digital cameras and camera phones shut down when they try to take photos in the lower chamber of the Haunted Tower. As spirits try to utilise energy to manifest, the failure of electrical equipment is a commonality of the paranormal shared across the world.

I hope you have a great evening tonight and a very prosperous New Year.

Kind regards
Richard

**Anomaly 2. Cameras and Mobiles**
**OHR 41-43. Haunted Tower Reports 25-27. Introduction**

In Michael's report he said his Walkman stopped working a few times when passing the tower and thought it could be a coincidence, but it never happened anywhere else. He is not alone. I have had people on tours from the town since Michael's report, who, back in the day had Walkman's and said the same thing happened to them. They were either walking, running or cycling past the tower when it shut off. It is a moment of recollection for them when I mention it on tours, and not really something they had thought about, and they were certainly unaware of others experiencing the same.

With the advent of mobile phones, the same started happening – a lot. On the path outside the tower they can either completely switch off or a message might be displayed from an obscure app. When the camera or mobile is put through the loophole into the Haunted Tower the same can happen.

Whilst trying to take a photo it is so common for the flash not to work. Sometimes the flash won't work for the first photo, or it won't work at all, or the flash will work but the photos don't come out. All the permutations happen here. It can and does also change the settings on your mobile – so be warned!

The same with the torch on mobile phones. People look to put the torch on to see into the tower better, especially at night to make sure there is nothing, or rather no one in there before they will put their arm in. They just can't get the phone torch to work at all, it just won't switch on.

My phone is always playing up. It took a while to work out what it was to start with. At the end of a tour I couldn't figure out why it was off when there should have been plenty of battery, or why a message would be displayed from an obscure app, or how the torchlight would be on while it was in my pocket. It then dawned on me, I had been to the Haunted Tower. It made sense after that. None of these things have happened out with tours. There is nothing random happening here. With us now being 182 pages into this volume we are well beyond that point, and that was around the number of times it happened to people's mobiles on tours in the first two years alone.

**11/ A2. OHR 41. Haunted Tower Report 25.**

In HT p.202, I wrote: 'An American woman on a tour in 2014, put her digital camera through into the chamber. She was laughing and joking as most do. We then heard her zoom lens extend and withdraw and her camera completely shut down. Her camera has never done that before. She stopped laughing then and couldn't believe what had just happened.'

**12/ A2. OHR 42. Haunted Tower Report 26.**

Pete Rankin of St Andrews was a great example of what can happen here with mobiles. He was on a tour in 2014 and thought he would have a go. Not thinking anything would happen, he put his mobile through the loophole to take a photo. As he did, something completely shut down his phone, as if whatever it was didn't want him to photograph it. Ordinarily a mobile can only be completely switched down if authorisation is given, but with the rest of us watching, it had completely bypassed this procedure. It then took a few minutes to fire it up again before having another go, which then resulted in the same thing happening.

He tried three times and each time it did the same. We were there for a while! For the fourth time he fired up his mobile and showed us all it was on. He purposefully held the phone low down so they were not near any buttons and only put it in for a second or two. When he brought it out it had done it again, it had completely shut down.

**Pete Rankin and Mel Edwards with respective families from St Andrews checking their mobiles outside the Haunted Tower**

Everyone checks their mobile but there is never anything wrong. The others then got out their phones but it was only Pete's phone that was affected.

This was the first time something like this had happened to Pete's phone, and like Ronnie, it wasn't the first time things have happened to Pete. Refer also to p.311, p.388, p.503.

**13/ A2. OHR 43. Haunted Tower Report 27.**

In May 2016, I had three golfers from Houston, Texas on a late night tour. With a jovial air, two of them were urging the third to try it himself with his phone. He put his phone through and could take photos fine, but his flash wouldn't work at all. He checked his settings, and took a few test photos of us which blinded us all with the flash, he then tried again in the chamber. "It's the darndest thing," he said. "It's not having any of it." The joviality was still present for the rest of the tour but it was accompanied by a more pensive air as they listened far more intently to everything I said.

I have a great many accounts of this happening on the tours. It is only when the mobile or camera is in the chamber that the flash hasn't always worked. It never happens when the camera is level with the hole or on the path side. If you are going to try this, whatever you do, don't drop your phone.... Dear Historic Scotland!

Again, like so many aspects on tours there is so much to fit in I rarely mention about the malfunctioning of electronics anymore unless it happens, which then adds to the mass of testimony for the phenomenon.

One of the funniest moments on a tour was one night when a particular woman put her mobile through into the chamber to take a photo. The flash never worked for her, which didn't surprise me at all. None of it does anymore. Sometimes I am actually more surprised when something doesn't happen it is that common. The flash not working gave her a bit of a start. Then when she looked at her photo she gave out a gasp and said, "There's a face in the photo, and I can see the shape of a dark figure behind it!" I looked carefully at her photo, the image was very dark, but I soon realised what had happened. She had taken a selfie! The face in the photo was hers and the figure standing behind her was me. I always was known as the Dark Lord!

There has never been one recorded incident of anyone consciously taking a selfie with a ghost, although there are plenty of photos where ghosts have appeared behind them in photos, but they have not been aware of this until looking a little closer, and realise they have also captured something they were not expecting. Mumler being the first to do this. p.514.

# Tower Reports Part 3b.

## Additional Phenomena Examples
## **Physiological Sensations**

**Part 3b.**



### 14/ A3. OHR 44. Haunted Tower Report 28.
**A gentle reminder**

Like the example above where people have felt something tapping the palm of their hand when it is in the lower chamber, or a tap on the shoulder by North Gate, there has also been the same when standing near the tower with no one close enough to do it. One of the current experiences was following a 9pm tour in August 2020. I received a short poignant email from Chris Farquhar who came on a tour with his family.

5th August 2020

Thank you for the brilliant tour ... loved it. And near the handshake area ... I felt a small gentle dig in the ribs ... thought it was Fiona but nope ☺

Cheers Chris

**15/ A4. OHR 45. Haunted Tower Report 29.**
**Paralysis**
People on my tours have also felt a tightening of the chest like stomach cramps or partial paralysis of the arm at the Haunted Tower. The minute they are away from the tower the symptoms cease.

**16/ A5. OHR 46. Haunted Tower Report 30.**
**Tightening of the arms**
In HT (p.201) I wrote the following:

**'A Delayed Realisation**
This particular experience was on a tour in the autumn of 2014…

Hi Richard,
My wife and I took one of your tours on Monday, and thoroughly enjoyed it. I'm afraid the pictures I took through the hole at the side of the Cathedral are bog standard. If you ever want to know the numbering on the pipes there, I'm the man to consult.

There was, however, oddness that we didn't consider until later. When Lynn put her hand through the hole she felt something brushing against it. As you'd said people often felt grabbed, she didn't think about it at the time, but later felt it was strange. My experience was while standing upright by the hole. Even before I bent down to take photographs, I felt a tightness in both of my upper arms. I've not had this feeling before or since, and to start with ascribed it to hanging a rucksack off my shoulders for four straight days. The feeling was as if I was being gripped internally and the arm muscles were being squashed against the bone, rather than any sensation of the arms being gripped around the surface. This wore off fairly rapidly in my right arm, but continued for longer in my left. I remember still feeling it when we were talking outside the house Mary Queen of Scots used.

I appreciate e-mailing you now when neither of us mentioned anything at the time may appear odd. In my case, this was because I attributed it to muscle fatigue. It wasn't until the feeling disappeared and I realised it wasn't due to carrying a bag around that I began to ponder what else it might be.

If you consider this all to be fabricated after the fact of nonsense, I quite understand. I'd be suspicious myself under the circumstances, but better to let you know in case others later experience something similar.

All the best,
Frank Plowright

Again, this typifies the nature of experience. It can be so subtle we either dismiss it or attribute its cause to other possibilities. It is often when these possibilities don't fit, that a niggling feeling of their being something out of sorts alerts the mind to a possibility not previously considered.

There is also the innocuous nature of what has occurred compared to what we assume constitutes paranormal activity. Because of this we almost trivialise our experience to the point where it isn't worth mentioning. There are so many reports that go by the way side for this reason, and not wanting to bother anyone, i.e. me, about something so trivial is a shame. This volume would be a lot larger if more were as frank as Frank (apologies for the pun) and came forward.

Frank's experience is rare, but it is not unique. Others have had similar symptoms at the tower on tours and on moving away it disappears. How many more there are, and this applies to the paranormal in general who just don't mention anything we will never know. I refer to this again in the section on Hotels.

**17/ A6. OHR 47. Haunted Tower Report 31.**
**Tightening of the chest**

A woman on a tour in 2018 experienced a tightening of her chest. When we were away from the tower the feeling disappeared. She said "Maybe the White Lady suffered from a form of paralysis or tightening of the chest herself, maybe that is how she somehow died?"

These are Group C. empathic symptoms that are being displayed here, so by association it is more than possible there is a connection. At present, I do not know how the White Lady died, apart from to say she was a young woman.

As an addendum to the White Lady sightings there is the following from Vida Brown for St Andrews Photo Corner 2nd September 2021: 'In the mid 1950's I was walking home from the cinema with my boyfriend and we decided to take the long way home and go round the outside of the cathedral walls and down by the harbour. Walking past the cathedral walls we were overtaken by a lady in a long white coat- they were fashionable at that time! Walked further on and the path had collapsed into the sea and it was fenced off so had to turn back. The white lady didn't turn back so where did she go? Many years later we learned of the sightings of a lady in white who had been walled up in the cathedral walls. Did we see the white lady ghost?'

The Grey Lady mentioned later is also described as wearing a coat as the mind is looking to make sense of its observation.

There is a great wealth of additional information about the Haunted Tower and the White Lady Mystery in HT with complex historical associations for this area relating to the White Lady as an analysis. It unravels the potential identities of the tower occupants, gives architectural secrets of the Haunted Tower, and details of a second White Lady corpse who I believe could still be present and hidden within a secret chamber in the Haunted Tower.

## Old Harbour Road Part 3.

# *Kirkheugh*

## Kirk Hill

### Energy Centre 1.
6 Ghosts

**Introduction**

As you will have read, there is a lot taking place along the Old Harbour Road. There are also up to 6 ghosts at Kirkheugh. By familiarising yourself with the following you will begin to understand why.

Set high on the cliffside overlooking the harbour and the bay, this is an ideal beauty spot to spend time admiring the unobstructed views across the coastline of Fife. Other than the area being marked by low level ruins and an embarrassing mock gun emplacement, it will hold little or no importance to most compared to the impressive looming towers of the once imposing Cathedral precincts. Yet there are secrets here of great historical significance involving a diversity of cultures spanning back to 500 BC.

Two prominent excavations have been carried out at Kirkheugh. The dig of 1860 was probably the most destructive, and the excavation of 1980 the most revealing. In 1860, when levelling the ground for a gun emplacement (that they never built) they discovered the foundations of the church we see today along with a few graves. In 1919 a 32 ton tank (called Jo), and a war trophy – a German artillery gun, arrived as unwanted gifts to the town. Kirkheugh had become a dumping ground for scrap war munitions. Linskill devoted a great deal of time for their removal as they were undermining the cliffside. In 1929 they were scrapped. Ironic then that in more recent times another mock gun emplacement has appeared as a replacement. A large sandstone Celtic cross would have been far more appropriate.

The present low lying foundational ruins cutting through the grounds is all that remains of the *last* Church of the Céilí Dé at Kirkheugh. The first phase of this structure was built c.1123, as St Mary of the Culdees. It then became the Church of St Mary of Kilrymont, the Church of the Blessed Mary of the Rock, St Mary's *Collegiate* Church and St Mary on the Rock. It wasn't until the excavations of 1980 when any realised the surprising extent of what lay beneath this area. Along with the foundations, silently dwelling under the surface were not just a few graves as they found in 1860, some 300 graves were discovered, spread right across the area of Kirkheugh, and there are a lot more besides. It is believed as many as '500 people still remain not far under the surface of Kirkheugh.'[16]

The earliest archaeological burial remains discovered thus far date from around 500 BC. They are the oldest found in this area, meaning the evolution of Kirkheugh is the evolution of St Andrews (Hallow Hill is circa sixth century, refer to p.479). Its beginnings were an Iron Age settlement of Celts believed to have come from Ireland, so Kirkheugh and by extension St Andrews, has been inhabited for around 2,500 years with deep Irish roots through a Celtic, then Catholic connection right up to 1559. Wordsworth in 1982 wrote: 'There appears to be no evidence for a structure predating the present structure [church] and we know there were other structures here, monastery/abbey/church. While some had been there since 500

BC the majority are from the 3rd, 6th to 8th century and none of the graves had any suggestion of earlier building material. There was a settlement here but around the burial site.'[17]

This ancient burial ground was flanked by these progressive settlements shaped through Celts and Picts to the west, south and east. Burials and possibly dwellings would have continued to the north but have long been lost to landslides.

The first evidence for leprosy (Hansen's disease) in early Mediaeval Scotland was in St Andrews. An example was discovered at Kirkheugh, the other at Hallow Hill, both dating to the 8th century. The period marking the last burials at Kirkheugh. Refer also to Lunt.[18]

Kirkheugh holds the key to the development of the ecclesiastical seat of Scotland in St Andrews, with a progression through the foundations of: Kirkheugh, Kilrymont, the Cult of St Andrew, the foundations of the St Regulus legend, and St Andrews as a City. It all stems from the energetic prevalence here, recognised through the successive spiritual disciplines, and is why there is such a high degree of paranormal activity.

Kirkheugh is Energy Centre 1. These boundaries between the spiritual and the physical realms were often marked by stone circles or standing stones, so placed as to physically focus and enhance the spiritual energy of these localities. For those with an acute awareness, energy can be tangible, and those with eyes to see, can observe energy ever spiralling clockwise up standing stones with the same bluish white vibrant light I recorded earlier regarding orbs. While a lot of natural energy can be generated at each of these locations, it is not tangible all the time, energy fluctuates. Sometimes you know there is nothing of any consequence, while at other times the energies almost surprise with its degree of manifest intensity. Under such conditions, phenomena are more likely to occur, and, like the cell phones playing up, they can also surprise to an extent when they don't. Although to be fair, energy is one of many factors to be considered in how potential phenomena inherent in a locale can impact upon our psyche. Energy can focus the mind and equally confuse and overwhelm, which may give a deeper understanding into what can take place alongside the obvious psychology of individual reaction when experiencing paranormal phenomena in coming to terms with what they have witnessed.

The academic line which you will find on National Trust plaques across Britain is the mantra 'they were possibly used for religious or ceremonial purposes.' That one sentence is the sum collective of many years of academic research and holds absolutely no value to anybody whatsoever. Of course they were, there is no possibly. In magickal and ritualistic practice through ceremonial magic, Druidic, Celtic/Catholic practice for example, the energies are harnessed for a specific end. There are several techniques to achieve this and different names employed in its application. Once the space is purified, consecrated and charged, the influx of energy through the spiritual dynamic is then focused and utilised for specific spiritual and physical purposes. The consecration of objects, deeper spiritual understanding and physical or spiritual healing. They are each representative, regardless of tradition here. The symbology may differ, but the ceremonial procedure and intent is very similar. Remember Christian ceremonial technique has older roots.

This is the reason for there being such a long spiritual tradition at Kirkheugh. Beginning with the Celts and their eventual initiation into the Druidic culture, flowing through to the Picts and Pictish Kings as a Royal Centre. A merger with the monastic Céilí Dé (Culdee) community from c.563-5 AD, which saw a seam of spiritual devotion unifying paganism and druidry with christianity through the Celtic Church. Then overshadowed in 1144 by the powerful Roman Church, and all overthrown by Knox in 1559, thus marking the end of a *Christian* spiritual centre alone spanning over 1000 years.

# The Kirkheugh Ghosts

❖

When relaxing and lounging on the bright green grass, perhaps studying or enjoying a picnic of a summer's day amid the ruins, spare a thought for over 500 people lying beneath your feet as a legacy of Kirkheugh's remarkable historical lineage. When added to the intensity of spiritual energy merging with the physical here, it shouldn't surprise you are being watched, or more the point observed.

# *Ghosts*

**In brief:**
In the main the ghosts here tend to be shadowy figures that will observe and follow you…

1/ Green Lady following Jane Kilpatrick. (Refer also to GOS p.87 & HT p.131) Between the bench and the precinct wall.

2/ Figure standing on Hepburn's wall looking down, near to where the Green Lady was observed.

3/ Figure walking east to west along the precinct wall between the two round towers.

4/ A dark figure walking along Hepburn's wall, same location as 1 & 2.

5/ Figure following people up the steep Shore Path.

6/ Shadow of a small adult following from Kirkheugh (South) to the Harbour.

# *Kirkheugh*

The ghosts here are reminiscent of the figures following those walking along the Pends Lane p.391. I call these the Kirkheugh Followers. Report 1. Doesn't venture beyond Kirkheugh. Reports 2-4 could well be the same spirit. Report 5. is on the other side of Kirkheugh, and report 6. follows to the sea wall. So, between 3 and 6 ghosts and all are Group B. spirits.

**In detail:**

**OHR 48. Report 1.**

There is the ghost of the Green Lady who stands between the bench and the precinct wall. In 1989 the figure followed Jane Kilpatrick, a fourth year student at the time as she was walking to her residence down at the Gatty. She was standing between the bench and the precinct wall, and it followed her to the top of the steps leading to the harbour. Her right eye and face were distorted with what appeared to be a natural disfigurement. Refer to GOS, p.87 for the full report.

**OHR 49. Report 2.**

A dark figure was seen walking along part of Hepburn's north wall one night in 2000. A party were walking up the steep Shore Path from the harbour. As they neared Kirkheugh one of them heard a noise and looked across to the precinct wall where he saw the figure. As they walked a few feet further forward it disappeared. He thought it may have been someone mucking around up there, but there is no longer any walkway along the wall and the figure wasn't walking as if they needed to take any care. Again, it disappeared almost as abruptly as it appeared.

**OHR 50. Report 3.**

From HT p.234. There is also another ghost along here sharing similar characteristics with the Green Lady. It walks along Hepburn's Wall from the Harbour Tower westwards towards the next Round Tower. Interestingly it covers the same ground as the Green Lady and is possibly the same ghost. This figure has been seen at night by different groups of people. It was last witnessed by students in 2013.

On each occasion, it has been when they have reached Kirkheugh from the steep pathway by the sea, leading up from the north end of the harbour. It is also slim and appears silhouetted against the skyline. It too keeps pace with those walking along the cliff side path, following along the wall westwards for a few seconds before disappearing.

**OHR 51. Report 4.**

The shadow of a figure stands motionless on the precinct wall looking down. Same location as Report 1 and 2.

**OHR 52. Report 5.**

There is a shadowy figure who follows people up the Shore Path to Kirkheugh where it then disappears.

**OHR 53. Report 6.**

Simon Tough and his daughter from Aberdeen came on a tour in 2018. The following is his tripadvisor review on my ghost tours listing, followed by an email he sent to me a month later.

Tripadvisor review

# *Kirkheugh*

12th April 2018

Great Tour – Essential if in town – 5 Stars
Was only myself and my 8 year old daughter on the tour at 4pm (she wanted daylight for it). Despite this and freezing wind we got Richard to ourselves and it was a pleasure to hear him talk about the history of the town. I've been holidaying here for over 20 years and learnt some new things. Reminds me I was followed in '95 late at night from the haunted tower down to the beach where the shadow wouldn't step down from wall onto the beach.... I quickly got back to the caravan.

I definitely recommend this tour and keep an open mind, who knows what you will see.

Well done Richard.

3rd May 2018

Good day Richard
I have just finished reading your St Andrews Mystery book which was absolutely fascinating and will be seeking out your other books on Amazon.

I have been coming to St Andrews for many years, firstly holidaying with my parents from around 1988 until 1998 – I've also been taking my daughter regular since then several times a year, I know the town like the back of my hand.

There was one particular part of your book that stuck out to me and I recalled something I had encountered way back in 1995.

I had been in the Golf Inn at the time having several drinks and avoiding my parents as a 19 year old teenager does. Upon closing time, I made the long walk through the town up over the scores and past the Cathedral wall down Kirkheugh to the harbour and it was around this time I started to notice a shadow behind that was tracking me.

As I made my way over the harbour bridge and towards the beach it was still behind me – I jumped down onto the beach and down to the waterline – it was bright moonlight so I could see perfectly well. The shadow stopped atop of the seawall and wouldn't come further to my relief – I can recall standing facing it from a distance thinking why stop now.

I carried on back to the Kinkell braes caravan park and thought no more of it.

I certainly didn't know of all the supernatural tales of the town at this time or I'd have taken a different route that night.

I can only describe the shadow as being of a small adult possibly male I never felt threatened in anyway more that it was curious what I was up to.

I've never told this to anyone before as it's easy to discount with the fact I'd had several drinks but having had several other brushes with supernatural events since I now believe this to have been a genuine sighting.

Best Regards
Simon Tough

**The Pier Orb**

Hayley Drysdale featured earlier with the orbs (p.134), also saw an orb a few years ago at the pier.

"One night I was sitting at one of the benches at the cannons overlooking the pier with a friend and there was a ball of white light on the pier. This white light was moving really erratically. One minute it would be at the end of the pier, the next it would be closer to our end. We could see it going from the top bit of the pier to the bottom. I don't see how it could have been a person? We watched it for quite some time trying to work out what it was but eventually we got too spooked out and left. That's the only "paranormal" experience I have had apart from the other night with you.

The night at the pier has really stuck with me as I really can't explain it. Any ideas? It was so strange. I remember feeling terrified but I didn't want to stop watching it."

Hayley was on Kirkheugh Energy Centre 1. when she was observing the orb at the Pier. There is an energetic link between the recipient and phenomena which I mentioned earlier. The greater the energy level, the greater the scope for observing phenomena. Ley lines and especially the crossing of ley lines, electricity pylons, underground streams and fault lines etc. These are all receptivity conduits. Energy attracts energy, and while spiritual energy should not be, and cannot be thought of in the same way as physical energy, it can display similar traits in the way it operates through the physical as it is operating in the physical with the appearance and dynamics of ghosts.

I am not going to go into details here, but to give an idea, the Great Glen Fault in the Highlands has a direct bearing on the manifestation of what we know as the Loch Ness Monster (Group A.), but again, not in the physical sense. The same with UFOs (Group B.), not in the physical sense, which should give an insight into their energetic nature. Do they all exist? Yes. Are they of our time? No. It is for no reason the orbs witnessed by Hayley and Mick share behavioural characteristics to UFO sightings. While UFO's are obviously not orbs, they share in the same fundamental mechanics. The way they manifest and disappear is no different: the speed, the light, the temporal merger of worlds operating by their own set of energetic vibratory frequencies merging through different times. Chasing them is like chasing shadows - they will find you.

**German Paranormal Research Group**

There is never any shortage of unusual sights in St Andrews. A few years ago, whilst talking about the Haunted Tower one night with a group, we all became aware of a few people coming toward us from Kirkheugh with camera equipment, tripods and a couple of spotlights. This odd display turned out to be a layman's Gothic German paranormal research group. They were visiting Scotland to 'investigate' paranormal activity. As they were passing us, one of them stopped and told me they had been at the ruins (St Mary on the Rock) and had just seen mysterious lights, and he had been attacked by something malevolent, causing him to fall over. As it transpired, none of this had been captured by the mountain of equipment they had brought with them. Although that doesn't surprise when the paranormal is notorious in thwarting attempts to take or recover photos, videos etc. Mobiles playing up being one of many examples through this volume. So, in some ways it gives it more credence, which might sound contrary or as an excuse to the sceptical mind, but it is a little explored and little known quark of phenomena.

I received no additional details about the lights, but given the location it has the hallmark of what Hayley experienced, and there are no other reports around St Andrews of the same apart from here, which again holds its own significance.

For the record, no one has ever been attacked along at the Kirkheugh, at least not by any supernatural entity, and it is not in-keeping with how phenomena operate. Tripping over part of the ruins as a reaction to seeing the lights is not a malicious attack, it is called not looking where you are going!

We didn't chat very long, I had a tour to run and his friends were suitably blending into the distance. I asked him just before he left, "Did you pick up anything at the Haunted Tower?" as I pointed to the looming edifice directly in front of us. He turned and said, "No, I haven't heard of that one," then sped off to catch up with his friends. It was an interesting encounter.

The Germans were an odd, yet typically enthusiastic bunch in their late teens. I have to say 'investigations' of this nature are usually an exercise in futility, but I cannot knock their enthusiasm and they did see the lights – orbs.

❖

A woman mentioned when she was young hearing the sounds of what she thought was a circus outside coming closer to her house. The noise of trumpets, drums, and the sound of people creating a general excitement. She got excited herself, and as it approached, she looked out of her bedroom window to take a look. The sounds were getting louder as they were nearing the house, but there was nothing to see. She said it was like they were there and you just couldn't see them. She has never forgotten the experience and indeed, it is still as fresh in her mind now as then. She went down and told her father, who said "that's the pilgrims." The house was built by an old pilgrim way. He had heard the sounds himself a few times.

# East Scores Path

The coastal path up from the harbour towards the Palace is the East Scores Path. It then joins Sea Street, the road now known as the Scores running west to the Old Course.

**The Phantom Ship**

There have been rumours in St Andrews for many years about phantom ships being seen in St Andrews Bay. Not surprising with a great many lives having been lost over the centuries to the sea through ships floundering in storms here.

Marine archaeologist Neil Dobson was interviewed by Michael Alexander for the Courier, on speaking about St Andrew Bay he said "…between 1800 and the present day, there were 233 shipping losses alone between the River Eden and Anstruther. They range from the iron paddle steamer Windsor Castle grounded on rocks east of Crail in 1844 and the whaler Horn that became stuck hard and fast on the Babbert Stane rock in 1848. "But go even further back, and there must have been plenty of Viking ships wrecked on the

Fife coast. The Romans used to sail from the Forth to the Tay, and it was the Roman geographer Ptolemy who used to warn Romans not to sail up the River Eden by mistake!"[19]

A late 19th century newspaper article stated: 'A phantom ship has been seen in St Andrews Bay. Moving silently with sails full of the North Sea wind it heads for St Rules Cave from North Berwick and Earlsferry in Fife. These were prime guesthouse locations for pilgrims stopping off before making the last leg of their journey to St Andrews and the relics of St Andrew. Roads in Fife were few and difficult to traverse at the time, so the sea was the main highway to and from the City.'

A phantom ship in the bay is one thing, assuming it was heading for St Rules Cave is a romantic fancy aligned with Church propaganda through the legend of St Regulus. He was reputedly shipwrecked in the bay with the relics of St Andrew and spent his first few months on the Fife coast in the cave by the Palace which I shall mention again in a few pages.

The sea being the main highway is correct. Looking back at the moth eaten scraps of history, the early pilgrim routes were *to* Fife, not through it. Hopping on and off at different points along the coast and the May Island where there were dedications of saints. It is why the early dedications are mainly on or by the coast. Pilgrims began coming here in the 8th century following the arrival of the relics of St Andrew. Routes *through* Fife were not a one route fits all scenario, but a process of evolution from sea to land over subsequent centuries. Fife was heavily wooded and full of wild boar and wolves. The 'pilgrim way' as they are calling it, created in 2019 from Culross to St Andrews, is a contrivance of a *later* pilgrim development as it was hijacked with politically correct 'diversions' that were never part of any pilgrim route in a bid to boost the local economy in certain areas... good luck with that one! The *early* Pilgrim Way by name was a four mile stretch from Guardbride to St Andrews.

Most pilgrims and merchants came from Europe, so post Reformation arrival by sea was no longer the industry it once commanded. When they stopped coming from Europe the industry effectively dried up. It was replaced primarily by walking or travelling by horseback, as the few roads were still not suited to carriages. Mary Queen of Scots between 1561 and 1567 conducted herself and her retinue across Scotland by horseback for this reason. She did attempt to use a carriage in 1562. The futility was soon made apparent as it found its way to the coachworks in St Leonards grounds behind her holiday residence, and probably remained there.

**The Bells of the Cathedral**

Following the collapse northwards of the 200 foot high Cathedral Bell Tower c.1584, the bells of the Cathedral were said to have been taken aboard a ship for Europe. The collapse of the tower was the catalysed for the Cathedral to then become a quarry for the town until 1826.

In GOS p.132, I recorded: 'It was often stated by Martine, Archbishop Sharpe's secretary in the 17th century that the turrets were 'furnished with many fair, great, and excellent bells, which, at the razing of the church (during the Reformation), were taken down and put aboard of a ship, to be transported and sold. But it is reported, and certainly believed in this place, that the ship which carried off the bells sunk in the bay on a fair day, within sight of the place where the bells formerly hung.'[20]

'In an article to the local newspaper, *The St Andrews Citizen* [Jan 1927] Linskill wrote that 'some greatly favoured mortals have been able to hear the once beautiful bells of St. Andrews Cathedral.'[21] Linskill also incorporated the sound of the bells of the Cathedral into his ghost story *The Beckoning Monk*, GOS p.303, which contains a plethora of famed spectral visitations for the Cathedral area (GOS p.132). This is reminiscent of the family from Saudi Arabia hearing bells, p.268.

# The Grave Children of the Cathedral Precincts

When I was young, there is something I would see in the Cathedral grounds that I never really paid much attention to until a family came on a tour in 2016…

**The Grave Children of the Cathedral Precincts**
*The Saturday Review, 1893*
"There is a certain soil or a certain atmosphere which preserves dead bodies from decay. It exists in Milan, and it is now known to exist nearer home. And at a certain point from St Regulus Tower all the dead that sleep beneath its shadow are lying now as they lay on their death-bed."[viii]

The following is one of the more unusual and thought-provoking reports, and one that struck me personally. I had a couple from Glasgow on a tour in May 2016. They have been visiting St Andrews with their family every summer for many years. They were staying at Kinkell Caravan Park with their 14-year-old son who wasn't on the tour. They were saying when he was 4 years old they were walking around the Cathedral precincts one sunny summer afternoon (2006). He ran up to a gravestone with a big smile on his face and started laughing and playing. He then ran up to another and did the same thing,

---

[viii] *The Saturday Review*, November 25, 1893. Written at the end of an important epilogue about the opening of the Haunted Tower.

then to a third and a fourth. The parents read the inscriptions on the gravestones he'd been playing around and they were all the graves of children. The chances of running up to four random graves in the precincts and them all being the graves of children are very slim.

When the mother was speaking about this a feeling crept over me as it started dawning on me I have also seen them.

**My Experiences of the Ghost Children**

When I was young I followed Linskill's lead and believed Halloween or the full moon were the times to see ghosts. So, for a boy growing up in St Andrews with Linskill as my invisible guide and early mentor, it was easy to dismiss any casual encounters out with the stereotypical ghosts Linskill presented.

My early youth is in the graveyard. Almost every evening in the winter months I would take myself down to the precincts with the sole purpose of seeing a ghost. In the area to the right of the high altar facing west, just by where Linskill's grave is situated, I would see what appeared to be the dark shadow of a small figure, always completely silent, always fleeting, and always seeming to peer at me from behind a gravestone. Sometimes it would pop up from behind one, or peer around the side of one. The distant lights of the street hid the detail of the form as a silhouette.

These observations were always very brief, with just enough time for me to catch a glimpse of whoever it was. I was never scared by this, if anything it was because I never questioned what I had seen, that it never really stuck in my mind until the family above spoke in 2016 of their son's experience. There was a particular regularity with it, and my impression was always one of something being inquisitive, that whoever it was, wanted to see who was visiting them at this dark hour. I must admit it was more unusual to see the living in the grounds than it was the deceased, and if I did, it would just be someone fooling around up by the main road and they never ventured very far into the darkness if they came over the wall. Apart from that, of all the occasions I was in there, I never encountered the living once. I always found this surprising. Why was I the only one in the grounds every night when there was so much to explore? Not many in the recent history of St Andrews can say they have been in there after dark, and less before then, and certainly none as often as myself.

It makes sense that what I saw was the same as the 4-year-old boy, they are the ghost children of the Cathedral precincts but why would they still be there?

**The grave of an 8 year old girl**

I am well versed in the Cathedral grounds and its many graves, or at least I thought I was. In the last section of this volume on photos I have a rare photo of an adult figure taken by Francis Quinn in the Cathedral grounds on the 24th February 2019. I went to the Cathedral soon after and read the inscription of the grave the figure appeared to be looking at. I also looked at the surrounding graves in the area to see if there were any clues as to who the figure might be, or why it might be standing where it was. One of the nearby gravestones presenting itself was for an 8-year-old girl who was drowned in St Andrews Bay in the 1890s which I shall come back to in a moment.

**Report 1. A collective of subtle incidents**

After visiting the Haunted Tower on my tours, it is a scenic walk along the East Scores coastal path as we start making our way back into town via the Bishop's Palace.

When we are on the brae of the clifftop overlooking the bay and Cathedral precincts, we stop and I speak about the 4-year-old boy in the Cathedral grounds. If there is time I link it in with the children I saw in the grounds when I was young. While we are here, some have become slightly panicky and short of breath when I am mentioning this – including myself, and it doesn't happen anywhere else with the same degree.

Other aspects include having the coat or jacket tugged from the bottom. Something brushing past the leg. One woman on a tour in August 2020 nearly fell over sideways just after we started to walking towards the Palace. I asked if she was ok. She said she thought someone was coming up quickly from behind and lost her balance trying to move out the way. When I turned she was nearly in the bushes. This was an automatic reaction with social distancing in place due to Covid-19 at the time, but there was no one there, so she got quite confused.

Occasionally, some have experienced an overwhelming sense of fear here. They can't explain why and typically apologise for being silly, a bit like apologising for being ill. The fear, shortness of breath etc, is all Group C. and brings into play the nature of synchronicity again. There is always something meaningful in seemingly random events that form an associative pattern binding event's together. It is possible the girl whose grave I found, was drowned below the cliffs here. That would explain the slight feeling of panic, shortness of breath and the fear people experience here. It is all symptomatic of her fate, and would explain the tugging of the coats and jackets, something low brushing past the leg, and the sense of someone coming up close. The physical aspect out with Group C., is also reminiscent of the phenomena displayed by the Half Moon Girl in the Nun's Walk I speak of later.

It is easy to become cut off by the incoming tide around this part of the coastline, and takes many unawares. I have unfortunately been to too many funerals of friends caught out by the swirling tides and currents of St Andrews Bay. At low tide it is possible to walk right around the rocks at the base of the cliffs from the harbour to the sands by the Step Rock (Aquarium). As the tide comes in it appears as a trickle, but it rises very quickly around you without realising. As soon as the seaweed gets wet, it gets very slippery. It is then very easy to find yourself cut off, stranded on the rocks with nowhere to go. It happened to me when I was 10. On that occasion, I gave a few people the wrong kind of scare – including myself.

**Patterns**

While re-reading what I had written I realised something I had overlooked. I had assumed the 4-year-old boy was playing with four different spirits of children, each corresponding to the four children's graves he was playing around. Every time I retold the account I was always niggled by the thought of how rare it is for there to be four spirits of children (as opposed to impressions) in the same confined area, and to still have a localised awareness. This is generally reserved for those who may have died in some way at the same time, especially in a violent or sudden way. While there are graves of those dying of various diseases, there are no graves matching the same en masse nature for the same date. So, for the children here to die independently of each other, in different ways, different time periods, and still to be active, can and does happen but it is so rare in the general scheme of the paranormal, and that is when I realised it is not four children, it is just one:

**Realisation – Energy Residue**

I spoke in the first section of how everything in the locality, however brief it may be, is picked up and retained or stored in the locality like a memory. All graves have a residue of energy emitting from those buried beneath them. This residue resonates as an aura of energy specific to each, and while it is as distinctive and unique as our DNA, it conveys far more information, but the energetic residue weakens as time passes.

The energy spirals up the gravestones in the same way energy spirals up standing stones. The nature of a standing stone or stone circle serves a different purpose, they are so placed as to harness and focus existing energies already present at these locations. Next time you visit a graveyard, think of a headstone as being the person or persons lying beneath. I mean this in a literal sense, not figuratively through their inscriptions.

If you are able to utilise the technique of psychometry, you will understand this. Touching a grave stone can be a difficult experience. Along with an impression of the essence of who lies beneath, it is possible to experience personal hardship, suffering, illness etc., and the manner with which the person died, including any emotional accompaniment (all Group C.), which is what we have on the brae of the Scores Path.

The auric energy field itself can be perceptible and even seen as this bright blue-white light I spoke of earlier with regards to orbs, but it can only be fully interpreted by those sensitive to reading energy, be they children, adults or spirits of the deceased who can utilise these energy fields and know the associated characteristics they portray. In this instance, the energy fields of the children. There are different techniques for how this is achieved which can determine the level of the outcome.

The realisation I had, was the energy residue of the children is still present, but it does not have to be four children at all. It could just be the one child – the little girl who drowned in the bay and is still present in spirit after suffering a sudden death.

The boy in the Cathedral grounds wasn't running up to the four graves in turn because there was a child at each one, that never made any sense as it doesn't fit with the nature of their behaviour. He ran up to the first one because a girl was standing by it. The girl has an empathy with the energetic residue of the others. She was standing by her own grave when the boy saw her. They were playing together in the sun as she then ran around the other three graves and the boy followed.

His parents were going up to the graves he had been playing around and on reading they were the graves of children assumed he was playing with all their ghosts, as I also assumed when she told me this. One ghost would be far more logical. Apart from the little girl, the other three are no longer present, their spirits are long gone but their energy residue remains.

I also realised I only ever saw one figure at a time in the Cathedral grounds when I was young, a small figure, yet I had assumed there was more because what I saw wasn't always appearing in the same place. I didn't realise at that age that some ghosts can move around, so I hadn't thought about the figure I saw on different occasions as being the same person, the same spirit, which of course again would make far more sense.

**St Rule's Cave/Lady Buchan's Cave**

Further along the East Scores Path toward the Palace is a cave half way up the cliff face opposite the entrance to Gregory's Lane. This is the cave of the St Rule's legend and carries the same name. It is also called Lady Buchan's Cave and is sealed at this present time by landslides.

I cover the cave and Lady Buchan at some length in my other volumes, including a very detailed description of what it looked like inside (refer to GOS p.86 and HT pp.240-241), so I will just give brief details here along with new information about the activity.

**This rare photo of St Rule's Cave was taken in 1908.**[22]
Photo courtesy of the University of St Andrews Libraries and Museums

The cave comprised of two apartments, had a door, a stone altar and a niche for a statue. In this photo the frontage has all disappeared. In its day, this was a place of pilgrimage with hundreds, maybe thousands collecting over the rocky expanse at low tide for service and communion. The two main pilgrimage centres in St Andrews from a period after c.1144, were here, following the promotion of the myth of St Rule being shipwrecked here, and wherever the relics of St Andrew were housed. By this time, they were in the Reliquary Church of St Regulus or St Andrews Church – as it had been renamed (the first Cathedral).

From 1760 to 1765, Lady Buchan, a woman of apparent eccentric means, used the cave for relaxation and tea parties.

She decked it out accordingly with a linen table cloth adorning the altar. It was also 'said to have been elegantly fitted up with shell-work by Lady Buchan.'[23] These last words were written by John Leighton in 1811, I hadn't discovered this when I wrote STAM (HT). It was written only a few decades after she was resident here, so the shells had disappeared by the time of his writing, but recent enough for him to know about them. They had actually disappeared by 1807, when James Grierson wrote in wonderful detail about the interior of the cave. Had he been aware of the shell-work he would certainly have given them a mention.

**Lady Buchan's Ghost Revisited**

As I recorded earlier there are seven locations in St Andrews where people have felt something brushing by them on various occasions. This is one of the four locations on the East Scores Path.

In HT p.239, I wrote: 'Wearing a white summer dress, she wanders the area of the cliff tops and the shoreline between the Castle and the Haunted Tower.

Her apparition was seen from the Castle Sands standing on the pathway above the cave entrance. Leaving the path, she walks in mid-air about 10 feet seaward before vanishing. There have been many landslides in this area over the years, and in the 18th century the land at that part extended further out than it does now.' Straight out and vertically down the cliff face rather than sloping down and out as it does now.

**Report 2.**

A few people on seeing Lady Buchan say she is accompanied by the scent of a very sweet smelling perfume they do not recognise. It is not like anything they have come across before. A young Chinese student on a tour experienced it a few months before. She briefly saw a woman in white walking along the base of the cliffs. She said she knew her perfumes and this was very pleasant, but it was unusual.

**Report 3.**
Something brushing past a woman's hair on a tour on the path here.

**Report 4.**
An American woman on a tour yelped and spun around. She said "something just brushed past my butt!" No one was near her and I think her husband was more shocked than she was about what happened. It took a while for them both to come around from the confusion of that one.

**Report 5.**
**Millie – odd behaviour**
In the summer of 2017, Millie the wee dog was on the East Scores Path at this same location. Her behaviour here wasn't the same as at the Haunted Tower.

Her greeting there was for someone familiar to her, her behaviour here was for someone unfamiliar as she started growling and barking at something on the cliffside.

Known for their developed senses, animals are a lot more aware than we are, and they certainly see and sense the unseen residing around us a lot more readily.

**Millie taking Eddie for a stroll along the East Scores Path**

These are not random acts by Millie, it is only here and the Haunted tower where they happen.

**Report 6.**
A man on a tour had something brush past his right shoulder at this same spot. He was kind of joking about it, but I could see he was also a little bemused by it.

**Report 7.**

Mike D. I recorded briefly earlier about his experience at Ninewells, p.159, also wrote the following in his 2017 email as one of his other experiences tagged onto information he gave to me about Kinkell Castle. 'I have since encountered physical brushing of my head by what felt like a fine cloth, not wind, somewhere between the castle and the haunted tower after midnight.'

Until he reads this, he will be completely unaware that he is not alone in his experience along here. He doesn't give the exact location, but I would be very surprised if it were somewhere other than at the cliff top opposite Gregory' Lane, as further east on the brae, the activity doesn't seem to occur above hip level, never the head.

Refer also to Kinkell p.506, for another of Mike D's experiences.

Again, it is the location that gives the importance through patterns of otherwise easily dismissed behaviour, pointing once more to there being an intelligent spirit here – Lady Buchan.

**Report 8.**

**Pigs!**

An old local legend tells of ghostly pigs that run from below the cave entrance into the sea. The spectacle is always preceded by a gust of icy wind, which sends a chill through the spine. There is a long, now extinct history of wild boar in this area, so this is an unusual one, but it is in-keeping with historical associations here.

# The Scores

## (Sea Street/Swallowgate)

Originally the Scores was called Sea Street, in-keeping with North Street, Market Street and South Street. The stretch from the Russell Hotel to the Old Course was West Scores Walk.

**Bishop's Palace/Castle**

Built in the fourteenth century on the foundation of an earlier structure (c.1200), from the deeds this was specifically built as the Bishop's Palace that was later fortified – not as a castle per se. It could accommodate up to 1,600 people within its walls at its height. Hard to believe when looking at the fragmentary remains. One of the more unusual records state, 'in 1541 payment was made to men for carrying to the Castle [from the harbour] the head and tail of a great whale killed near Byrehills.'[24]

Following the Reformation, the Palace was occupied by Protestant Archbishops and the Sheriffs of Fife. It was abandoned in the 17th century when they ran out of money for its upkeep, and like the Cathedral it too became a quarry. Stone from both was used for the construction of a new pier at the harbour in 1656. The whole structure was a lot more sprawling than we see today. Through erosion the Great Hall on the eastern side collapsed into the sea in 1801. In 1888, the Victorians built a wall in-keeping with the stone of the structure to shore up the cliff face and prevent further collapse.

There are at least 7 different ghosts here, plus poltergeist activity. I give details here of a new account of a ghost by Kyle, refer to GOS for the others. It is followed by new accounts of activity in the siege tunnel.

**Ghost of a man**

Kyle Stewart, I mentioned earlier in connection with seeing the apparition of a monk in the Cathedral grounds (p.77), has also had an experience in the Palace.

He was closing the Palace one summer's evening in 2017. Walking across the courtyard thinking everyone had left the ruins, he then saw a man standing on the first floor walkway above the main entrance. He called out that the castle was now closed. The figure walked west and was gone from sight behind a wall as he neared the stair sweeping to ground level. Kyle waited for him to appear but he never came, so he walked up the stair to find him and there was no one around. He conducted a search, but the man had vanished.

**The Siege Tunnel**

In 1879, stonemasons demolished the Keeper's Cottage for the Palace that stood on the east corner of North Castle Street and the Scores. They were making way for a new building to be named Castlegate House. During the demolition a workman with a wheelbarrow full of rubble fell through the ground and ended up in a tunnel. Remarkably, the fear of evil spirits prevented the builders from exploring the passage any further than they needed. Bailie Hall, the local representative of the Palace and Cathedral, 'built a wall blocking up the castle passage preventing further exploration!'[25]

**Siege Tunnel Experiences**

In 1546, the Protestants took over the Palace. The tunnel was created by the Catholic church to breach the Palace and get them out. The Protestants fourth time lucky found where they were doing this and dug a counter tunnel. They met underground and the Protestants having higher ground thwarted the underground Catholic siege. The loss of life in the ensuing clashes is unknown, but the proceedings would have potentially been particularly gruesome at the point where the two passage met, marked now by a fixed metal ladder.

I had two separate parties of women on the same tour from the States vacationing in St Andrews in 2014. The two parties had never met each other before the tour. When we went to the Palace I spoke of its history and the siege tunnel. After this, we were moving further along the Scores and both parties started chatting to each other about the passage. They all said they had visited the 'castle' and had been down the mine. One party had visited earlier that day, the other party had visited two days before. The party that had been there in the morning began recounting how they had heard the chanting of monks when they were in the passage. They said it was a very strange feeling. There was no one else in there at the time and there was nothing that could have caused this unusual sound to occur. The other party were quite aghast. They said they heard exactly the same thing only two days before when they too visited the 'mine.' Again, there was no explanation, but the sounds were unmistakable for what they were.

Another party of 12 ladies I had on a tour in May 2015 had gone down in 2013. When they were at the ladder where the Protestants and Catholics met underground, the area became extremely cold and all the lights went out. They all screamed, and in their panic scrambled their way to the entrance, which wasn't easy. The roof is low, ground uneven and in near pitch black conditions they found it disorientating. When they neared the entrance, the lights came back on. Historic Scotland who maintain the property ensure the lights are working fine for strict health and safety reasons. There is no switch by the entrance, and no accounting for why they would have gone out when they did.

**The Castlegate House Experience**

36 The Scores

One evening in the late 1950s, Anne Morris a lovely warm hearted lady and a former director of the Preservation Trust, was babysitting here for a family she knew. During what was a peaceful evening, the baby started crying in the bedroom and the family dog ran to the living room door making a strange noise.

As soon as Anne opened the door, the dog with hair standing bolt upright ran into the hall making an unearthly sound, then ran around and around in circles on the spot in the middle of the hallway. Anne checked on the baby who was fine and had to drag the dog by the collar back into the sitting room.

A couple of years later the family were relocating to Cambridge. When they moved out, they rolled up the hall carpet to take it away and found underneath an old iron grate, like the one outside by the front door to the house. Whatever it was that disturbed the dog had come from the abandoned sealed part of the passage.

This is like an experience in the 17th century Skaill House by Skara Brae on Orkney, which has at least two ghosts. 'Visitors to the house explained how on one occasion their dog went berserk in the early hours of the morning. It barked, growled and "howled like it had never howled before." When a bedroom door was opened, the terrified animal fled into the room and lay cowering under a bed.'[26]

Anne lives in Buckie House in Anstruther. A very famous dwelling in the East Neuk, and one of the most photographed. Famed for its façade being covered in shells, I have the following from GOF p.119:

'Just along the road from the Dreel Tavern is Buckie House, famous for its decoration of sea shells or 'Buckies' that cover its outer walls. The house also retains some of its ancient interior as an old fisher's abode. One of the upper rooms has a small old wooden box bed set into a corner and an ornate shell covered ceiling set in much the same fashion as the exterior. It was here in the 1980s that the ghostly figure of an old man was seen by a couple not long after buying the property. It was believed the figure was of a fisherman who once lived within the house.

His name was Alex Batchelor, an eccentric of the 19th century who also covered his coffin in shells. Robert Louis Stevenson on visiting Anstruther as a child around the 1860s remarked on this house in his Fife Journals, commenting on the 'agreeable eccentric who covered his house with pebbles.'

The shell covered room within the house has also been prone to those sudden bouts of coldness customarily associated with a great many hauntings.'

This is similar to Lady Buchan covering the interior of the cave in shells. Anne told me other rooms in the house are also covered in shells. Unfortunately, the box bed isn't there anymore, just the recess where the bed sat. She wasn't aware of what haunts the building but some of her guests have been reluctant to go into that room.

Anne also spoke of a house opposite which has a ghost. An occupant awoke in the bedroom to find a man standing at the bottom of his bed. He was wearing a ship captain's hat and a blue duffle coat. Not long after, workmen were conducting alterations in the house. In particular, one was working on a walk in wardrobe for this same bedroom. He heard someone behind him and called to his workmate to pass him a tool. When there was no reply he looked round and standing behind him was this same ship's captain. He then couldn't get out of the cupboard fast enough and bumped his head on doing so.

**The North Castle Street Monk**

The figure of a monk was seen walking along North Castle Street towards the Bishop's Palace by a man in the 1950s. I was told he was of sober mind and in possession of a very matter of fact disposition. He wasn't readily prone to accepting such things but he saw the figure nonetheless. When nearing the Palace, the figure just vanished in front of him.

**The All Saints Church Photo**

North Castle Street 2012

In 2012, Marysia Denyer of St Andrews took a photo of four of her friends in the courtyard of All Saints Church along North Castle Street. In the photo are at least 10 faces which I believe are the spirits of those who died in a battle that took place on this site in 1746 between Jacobite's and Hanoverian troops. The photo and full details commence from p.546.

I speak later of the coach and horse phenomenon in St Andrews. As an observation, there has been reports of a coach and horses/horse along South Castle Street but none North.

**From tan, to soaked, to seeing a ghost all in a minute or two!**
August tour 2019
The following from one of my tours all happened in the space of only a minute or two.

I had a coach party of 35 Americans on a private tour. It was a very hot afternoon, 40 degrees with blue sky and a light breeze. We were standing by the monogram of the Protestant martyr George Wishart on the road in front of the Palace. As I was talking and everyone was enjoying the hot summer sun, a monsoon came down. Within a few seconds the road became a flash flood. One in the party said, "Where the hell is the cloud!" which I found hilarious. There was no warning, no cloud and no shelter, so I suggested we walk as quickly as possible toward town. I was on the road and the party on the pavement.

As we were passing the front of the Palace some of the group started talking amongst themselves and slowing down rather than speeding up. This then spread amongst the others and they all pretty much stopped. The rain was coming down hard and we were all completely drenched. A few then said, "Richard, did you see that?" I didn't know what they meant. They said a young man wearing a tweed suit just passed them on the other side of the road. There was no sense of urgency about him and he was bone dry! Then when he reached the corner of North Castle Street. He didn't go around the corner, he just vanished at the corner. He appeared just after the monsoon started and walked passed the ivy-clad building of Castlemount Bed and Breakfast.

This was a random coach party. 35 American tourists of varying adult age getting soaking wet. Most of them saw the young man, and also saw him disappear. I was the only one who didn't see him as I was on the road facing the group as we walked. All I saw was their unfolding expressions. We sped up again just as the offending cloud appeared from behind Gannochy House (a University Hall of Residence), and made our way through the north garden grounds of St Salvator's College. We sheltered under the open cover of the chapel, although by then we were as wet as if we had all fallen into the sea. A few were talking of going back to their hotel to change once the rain stopped. It marked the end of the tour, but it wasn't the rain that fazed most of them. That became secondary to the conversation about the young man. It was an experience none of them will forget. From tan, to soaked, to seeing a ghost, all in the space of a minute or two, only in St Andrews!!

I have no suggestions as to who this young man was or what time-period he was from, other than to say tweed suits were an especially popular golfing accessory in St Andrews through the late 19$^{th}$, early 20$^{th}$ century for their hardwearing properties.

**The Castlecliffe House Soldier**

In GOS I give brief details of the ghost of a First World War soldier at Castlecliffe who fell to his death whilst cleaning the windows. The actual article spans a few pages of a University magazine and most of it comprises the family tree of the said unfortunate individual (refer to GOS p.66).

This was an auxiliary hospital for those unfortunates injured during the First World War, so it is just as plausible, if not more so, for the ghost to be one of those who lost their lives here than someone falling off a ladder to their death.

Something that does run in favour of the window cleaner is when the cleaners enter the building in the morning they always say "Morning Tommy!" (may now be past tense). This is in acknowledgement of their resident ghost. If they don't say this, the ghost habitually causes all manner of mischief; cleaning aids disappearing and reappearing, vacuum cleaners switch themselves on and off, lights doing the same, and footsteps where no one is present. They call him Tommy because during the two great wars, the British were the 'Tommy's,' the Germans the 'Jerry's.'

I have people on my tours from every walk of life, and when I mention Castlecliffe, a surprising number then share their own experiences from all parts of the world of a similar nature.

For the most part these are experiences that will never hit the press, after all, why would anyone be interested in anything that doesn't involve murder or possession, yet they hold no less importance.

**Principal's House (University House)**

The house was built from 1863 to 1865 as a Scots Baronial residence for the Principals of the University.

I write in GOS p.63, about the sound of bagpipes that were heard by Heba Watson, wife of the Principal at the University in 1980. The headline of the Sunday Mail was the '£200,000 Ghost.' A St Andrews Coastguard on a tour in March 2016 said, "Following a report of someone disappearing over the cliffs late one night, I was called out along with police and paramedics to the garden of the house.[ix] Whilst searching the grounds and cliffside area we found no sign of anyone. Then, as we were finishing up our search, we all heard bagpipes coming from within the house. This spooked all of us and we couldn't get out of the grounds quick enough." The house was in darkness at the time as we were between principals.

There is also the sound of footsteps in the house.

**The Swallowgate Ghost**

Saturday 14th November 2015

At about 10:20pm on a tour with a group from Yorkshire, a gentleman said he felt someone brush past him on the tour. He didn't mention it until after the tour as I was speaking at the time about the Principal's House and he didn't want to interrupt. He said it was just before we turned the corner into the lane (Butts Wynd).

I smiled and said I also experienced something and didn't have chance to mention it because I was talking. I heard someone running up behind us. We have a lot of joggers on the Scores, so while I was talking, I stepped aside to let whoever it

[ix] The house itself was closed at the time as we were between Principals so all was in darkness. Louise Richardson had moved to Oxford December 2015 to become the Principal there and her successor had yet to be appointed.

was past, no one did and the sound stopped at the moment I thought they would pass.

So, I heard someone running up behind us and the man from Yorkshire felt someone brush past.

This is an unusual one because it is the only tour I can recall where a group of us have been relatively closely bunched and only two of us experienced something of this nature.

The experience was picked up by our senses in different ways, the gentleman from Yorkshire felt it, and I heard it, even though I was talking at the time. Seems subtle or inconsequential perhaps, but until this happened there was only one aspect of the paranormal per se I was unable to explain, and that was a big one: Why do some of us remain when there appears to be no motive other than enjoying familiar surroundings? Sounds such a simple question but the answer is complex, and it took a while to get to grips with it, which I did, and I am sure you read the answer earlier in the first section.

The answer to the present anomaly also took a while to work out. For it to only be myself who heard the footsteps, means that my awareness was more acute than the others present. For the sensation of something brushing past, it was myself and the gentleman who were on the north side of the pavement, this is a cycle lane and often used by joggers. Because I heard it I stepped aside thinking someone was coming up behind us, the gentleman from Yorkshire didn't, so he was now the only one in its path. Had the others been in the same line, chances are they would also have felt it, and myself had I not moved. There is always a logic to the paranormal.

**Another Swallowgate Experience**

As I started an evening tour on Wednesday 17th February 2016 with a group of people I had no idea I was soon to be given another piece of an ongoing puzzle. Allan Taylor who has West Burn Court Bed and Breakfast I spoke of earlier about his experience in the Square Tower, came up to me very excitedly in South Street. I think his enthusiasm caught my group off balance, and me to an extent. He had an experience earlier that day and wanted to tell me about it. I always remember it was a very bright and fairly warm day, which in the past would have been an unusual anomaly in itself for this time of year.

He was cycling west along the Scores Path and was about to turn up Butts Wynd when something white flew around the corner nearly knocking him off his bike. It was around five feet high and around five feet off the ground. He said it was like a person covered in a white sheet. A "spectre" he called it. It flew  quite fast past him and left him a bit shaken. He said he went back for a look around but there was nothing to account for what he had experienced. He then bumped into me and asked if I had any reports from that locality. I told him of my earlier experience there, but this was different. This was very reminiscent of a white figure that flew out of the Eastern Cemetery knocking Betty Wilshire off her bicycle in the 1970s, refer to GOS p.99. Something more recently happened at the cemetery that ties in with Allan's experience...

**Swallowgate and the Eastern Cemetery Angel**

There is the legend through the town of an angel at the Eastern Cemetery flying by night and strangling its victims. The angel is a statue sitting at the top of the cemetery above a family grave.

A woman I had on a tour who has experienced quite a few paranormal anomalies in her life, said she was walking up the Pends Lane a few days before the tour and heard a male voice while passing the entrance to the Eastern Cemetery, "I was strangled you know!" There was no one around and she knew nothing of the legend, of the angel, or Betty Wilshire's experience. Understandably she felt a bit upset and couldn't work it out, so she came on a tour to speak to me about it.

Some interesting parallels are taking place here. The legend of the angel, the voice, Betty and Allan describing the same large white humanlike shape, and they were both on bicycles which adds its own a quark. Betty was knocked off her bike and Allan was nearly knocked off his. Both experiences were too similar for there not to be a connection. There must surely be something that ties both locations together?

With keeping the tour's current, I spoke of Allan's experience on a few of the subsequent tours, and each time I mentioned it I was trying to figure it all out. I explained to the tour groups that this was a work in progress. "Why just here on the Scores path?" I would say rhetorically, "what is the connection between here and the Eastern Cemetery?"

When mentioning this on a tour a few nights later I realised we were standing in front of Swallowgate, the School of Classics for the University. The direction the white shape came from was this building. It then clicked, the Archaeology Museum is within this building. Open to the public in the 1980s, I had access to the exhibits back then as I was an artist based in the Crawford Arts Centre in North Street. I used to draw the exhibits housed in the Archaeology Museum here, the University's Bell Pettigrew Zoology Museum, and the Crawford Arts Centre for school exhibitions etc.

I believe there is an archaeological artefact in the museum originating from the cemetery, that by association, has a direct bearing on what both Allan and Betty experienced. I have not yet been able to find what it is, but when I do, I believe it will shed more light on the matter.

For the dark words to be spoken by the unseen man implies the spirit of the person is still at the site of his murder. So too is the figure in white who could be the murderer? If this were the case, it is the murderer we are looking for here. Could the figure in white have been part of the early Céilí Dé community? Could the bones of the murderer now be in the archaeology museum? And the link is the bones of the spirit and the site of the deed?

There is also an elderly woman wearing black who stands along the wall near the Eastern Cemetery gate (refer to p.390), but I think to link her in would be a red herring, unless she was the wife of the person who was murdered and is wearing black in mourning for her loss! Ah, the potential, but that is tenuous.

Being a paranormal historian, putting all the pieces together is reliant on recognising what pieces form part of the same puzzle. The development of theories is an important aspect of this. As more information is gathered the theories change or modify accordingly, and until all the information is in place, historical conclusions will always be subject to conjecture and change. The difficulty is in knowing at what point we can say we have all the pieces to give unfaltering historical conclusions. I can say, that it is not an uncommon process to receive reports then to find obscure historical events that tie it all together and confirms the historical validity of experiences. It is a process that often takes years.

**Eastern Cemetery & the Holy Well Monk**

The area now occupied by the Eastern Cemetery was once a fish farm run by Augustinian monks. With the most spectacular views across the East Sands and the coastline of Fife, it was originally a holy sacred garden with a focus on a sacred spring from the time of the Picts. Believed to have healing properties this is the Holy Well or St Leonards Well.

Sited halfway up the left side of the present cemetery, from a distance it just looks like a grass covered mound.

The spring is underground, protected by a manmade vaulted chamber with stone steps leading to its open entrance, which has a niche on the lintel above for a statue, St Leonard? Once inside there is a stone seat and a trough for the spring water.

A monk has been seen walking up the narrow winding stones steps. He then walks downhill slightly and disappears through the western partition wall.

Part of the wall is all that remains of the granary from the days of the priory precincts. A large imposing building some three stories in height. It is also the direction of the Earl of Moray's former residence which was sited opposite the former New Inn (Hospitium Novum) on the Pends. Moray was a Prior of the Cathedral in the sixteenth century but I make on suggestion that the ghost is of this prior.

# *The Coach/Horse Phenomenon*

## 22 Reports – Audible / Visual

**David Octavius Hill, 1843**
Courtesy of the Scottish National Portrait Gallery
Accession number: PGP HA 4042

I wrote the following for GOS, pp.147-148. Completed in 2013 it serves as an adequate introduction and background to a wealth of new material having emerged over the last 7 years.

# *The Coach/Horse Phenomenon*

**Reports of Phantom Coaches – Introduction**

'Phantom coaches are a perpetual talk of the town when it comes to the ghosts of St Andrews. There has been various sighting over the years alongside even more reports of the unmistakable sounds of a coach and horses being heard in the still of the night [now also during the day]. The locations have been the quiet outlying areas towards Strathkinness and around the precincts of the old town itself, especially along the cobbled east end of Market Street, near to where the old tolbooth once stood that saw various body parts being displayed from executions here and elsewhere. The occupants of these large black coaches range from Archbishop Sharpe and Cardinal David Beaton, to Hackston of Rathillet. All are being driven to hell with the Devil beside them as their final companion! [The latter of course is Linskill at his best. Always remember his stories are nothing more than fiction, written around events that have, and still are being experienced around St Andrews.]

There are several locations where a Phantom Coach has been seen or heard in and around the St Andrews area. It is not until the list is put together that the extent becomes apparent.

[The following page references are for GOS]:

**Locations of phenomenon**

|  |  |
|---|---|
| Strathkinness – St Andrews Road | p.203 |
| Argyle Street | p.173 |
| South Street | p.174 |
| Market Street | p.160 |
| Abbey Walk | p.148 |
| The Pends Lane | p.110 |
| Castle Sands | p. 85 |
| East Sands | p.203 |
| St Andrews Bay (non-specific location) | p.258 |

**Additional locations recorded here since GOS was published in 2013:**

Magus Moor (not Linskill)
Hepburn Garden's
Queen's Gardens
Church Street
North Street
South Castle Street

**Echoes of the past**

We receive the idea of (Sharpe's) phantom coach and horses making its way from the direction of Magus Muir towards St Andrews Bay through Linskill. From GOS p.203: 'He relates to us three fictional stories concerning the Phantom Coach; two stories featuring the Strathkinness to St Andrews Road where one ends its journey in St Andrews Bay, and a third giving mention to a Phantom Coach being seen in St Andrews Abbey Walk.'[x]

Most of the reports for the coach and horses are in the centre of St Andrews focusing especially on the East End of Market Street, which was a hub for coaching Inns and stations with no correlation to Sharpe. There does however appear to be a link with Sharpe's coach through other locations where it has been heard or seen, as it marks the route he would have taken had he completed his journey that fateful day.

It has been seen and heard at Magus Moor (where he was murdered), then heard on the Strathkinness Low Road, Hepburn Gardens, Argyle Street, South Street and the Pends

---

[x] Refer to GOS and Linskill's stories:
*The True Tale of the Phantom Coach*, GOS p.340
*Related by Captain Chester*, GOS p.287
*Concerning More Appearances of the White Lady*, GOS p.283

Lane by one of his former residences. Interestingly, all these particular reports have it going in the same direction – west to east. Additionally, there are no reports at all of a coach and horses being heard on any of the other arteries into town: St Andrews/Guardbridge Road, Largo Road, Crail Road, Anstruther Road or indeed the Grange Road.

Sharpe's murder deeply affected everyone. While the town and Scotland were split between the Episcopalians and growing unrest by the Presbyterian movement, despite a previous assassination attempt, none could have pre-empted the death of this prelate, not even those who would go on to commit what was a frenzied attack driven primarily by anger. [xi]

Of all the experiences for the coach/horse, it is very rare to see. Indeed, apart from Linskill's stories when I published GOS I only had one report of the coach being seen which I mention later. I now have another report, as follows:

## Magus Moor

**Report 1.**

**Large black coach – seen but not heard**

I get the wheels rolling this is a very rare sighting Linskill would be proud of. It was recounted to me by a couple whose testimony is not out of sync with something Linskill would have incorporated into one of his fictional stories. It is surely one of the more remarkable of accounts for this phenomenon.

It was by the village of Strathkinness at Magus Moor a few years ago when a couple walking through the woods one winter's morning saw the phantom coach. It was cold, dry and crisp. The snow on the ground was about six inches deep. As they started walking through the snow across a clearing in a field by the woods of Magus Moor, they saw it. They were overtaken by a large black coach and four huge black horses

[xi] Refer to GOS p.196, for a background to Sharpe's murder and the violent repercussions and HOS for additional material.

travelling at high speed. It came from behind and really shook them up. They had no notification of its approach and the only sound was from their gasps as it passed. As it disappeared in the far trees it left no imprint in the snow. Their extraordinary experience has left a profound mark on them to this day.

**Report 2.**
**Coach and horses – heard but not seen**
Another account for Magus Moor is from a woman I met who was taking a stroll through the woods here one afternoon in 2016. She was nearing the pyramid cairn marking where Archbishop James Sharpe was murdered on the 3rd May, 1679. It was in the afternoon and she distinctly heard, "Many horse's hooves, and the trundling of wheels." She said, "It was unmistakable, and only stopped when I looked to find where the noise was coming from."

You will find as I progress with the reports for the coach/horse phenomenon, this is the same with all who hear it.

## Hepburn Gardens

**Report 3.**
**Hepburn Gardens 2018**
It has been heard halfway along Hepburn Garden's near Saint Leonard's Parish Church by a couple of students. They were walking into town around 9 pm, November 2018. Apart from the odd taxi the road was quiet. Following the same pattern, they heard a coach and horses coming along the road quite fast from behind, when they turned to see it the sound stopped and nothing was to be seen. There was nothing that could have made the noise. They came on a tour the following day to tell me their experience. They didn't know what to make of it and hadn't heard of the 'ghost coach' as they called it.

## South Street

These accounts are reminiscent of a newspaper report from the 1890s and reproduced here for the first time...

**Report 4.**

**St Andrews Citizen – Saturday 26 May 1917**

Published a week after a brief article called the *Reappearance of the White Lady* I reproduced in part earlier on p.151, as follows:

*The Re-Appearance of "The Phantom Coach"*

'It is high time that a psychical research society was formed in St Andrews. The other week several citizens reported that they had seen "The White Lady of the Haunted Tower," and now "The Phantom Coach" has made its re-appearance. The following letter we have received from a reader gives the particulars:-

Church Street, 19th May

To the Editor – Sir, - The mention in your columns of the White Lady's re-appearance suggested to me that some of your readers and certainly the Dean of Guild Linskill would be interested to hear of a recent ghostly experience of mine. I knew that Archbishop Sharp's carriage was occasionally heard in South Street. On Sunday night I was working late, and retired to bed about half-past one on Monday morning (14th May). I had just got into bed and had not fallen asleep when I heard a carriage rumbling along South Street. The noise of the wheels was very distinctively heard. On examining the experience afterwards, I was rather surprised at having no recollection of hearing horses' hoofs. In a hazy way, I connected the experience with the stories I had heard of Sharp's carriage. Next morning, I told the story to two friends, 'But, they said, "It is only heard on the anniversary of his murder." We looked up and found that he was murdered on 3rd May. This knocked that on the head; till someone recollected that the calendar had been changed in (I think) George III's reign. We looked this up also. The change was of eleven days. The third would now be the fourteenth. – I am, &c., CIVIS UNIVERSITATIS.'

As a footnote to this report, there are various myths about the ghosts of St Andrews that happily do the rounds. From the reports, the sound of the coach and horses is not an anniversary phenomenon although this account is suggestive. 11 days is correct and it was George II in 1752 when it changed.

**Report 5.**
**South Street – Madras College 1960s**

It was related to me by Anne of the Preservation Trust I introduced earlier (p.221), that Dr Thomson, a former Rector of Madras College in the 1960s, heard the Phantom Coach careering along South Street on cobbles that no longer exist. He was in his study at the front of Madras College East House when he heard the disturbance.

**Report 6.**
**South Street – by West Burn lane**

A man walking along South Street had a few back to back experiences when the haar was entrenching itself through the town. I spoke briefly of part of his experience at the start of this volume, and mention it in full on p.303, He turned right into West Burn Lane from South Street, and as he walked towards Queen's Terrace he heard the sound behind him of horses and a carriage coming toward him. He turned, and as he did so the sound stopped as soon as it had started. There were no horses or carriage.

## Queen's Gardens

**Report 7.**
**Queen's Gardens 2017**
Monday 17th April
At the start of an evening tour, a family from Saudi Arabia (who have the awareness), spoke of what they have been experiencing over the previous few days whilst visiting St Andrews. They were staying in a flat at the top end of Queen's Gardens and heard galloping horses travelling along the road at night. They also feature in two another reports, p.243, p.268.

## Church Street

**Formerly Kirk Wynd**

**Report 8.**
**Church Street 2014**
December
The unmistakable sound of a galloping horse was heard by a woman at the beginning of December. She turned to see this unusual spectacle, but there was no horse. She said the sound was drowned out by a car, but given the pattern of experiences, if a car hadn't come along at that moment, the sound would have ceased anyway as she turned to look.

**Report 9.**
**Church Street 2018**
Saturday 13th January, 9 pm tour
I had a young couple on a tour visiting the town for a few days. At the end of the tour I spoke about my own experience of the coach in 1982 (p.249), and relayed a few of those above. As I spoke of the 2014 experience in Church Street, they looked at each other, then to me. I have seen their expression before – a lot, including the woman who heard the coach in Market Street p.251 you will read about shortly.

Paul said just before the start of the tour they heard the same as what I was relaying. They were at the TSB on the corner of Church Square and Church Street. While getting money out of the cash machine they heard what they thought was the clip-clop of high heels coming along the street. They thought the street was deserted, as was most of the town being January, so it alerted them even more. The exact moment they looked, the sound stopped – nothing in the street.

**Report 10.**
**Church Street 2019**

The same thing happened again a year later. This time it was on a 4pm tour during the summer, with a bright sky and a vibrant town. There were a lot of people on this tour and when we got to the end in College Street, a teenage girl piped up and as she pointed towards Church Street said, "I heard that when we crossed the road at the start of the tour." She heard a horse coming along the road. A few others then also piped up and said they heard it as well. They had turned to see but there was no horse, and again the sound stopped at that moment.

As we were walking across the road I was talking to those at the front about how dangerous crossing a road in St Andrews can be. Those of us at the front didn't hear it as we were a good twenty feet ahead of them, so when they were crossing Church Street we were walking past the Citizen Office.

**Report 11.**
**Church Street 2020**

At the beginning of October, a taxi driver one afternoon told me he had just had a fare from three people, who, shortly before were walking along Church Street and all heard the trotting of horses and the rattle of a carriage coming along the road. When they turned to look the sound ceased. They knew nothing of this phenomenon in St Andrews and were not in town for long.

## South Castle Street

(Formerly Ratton Raw – meaning raw rat! c.1450)

**Report 12.**
**South Castle Street 2017**
Saturday 15th April
A couple of days before their tour, one of the Saudi girls and her mother I mentioned regarding Queen's Gardens, were cycling along South Castle Street when she heard this same sound of a galloping horse behind her. When she turned the sound stopped. She thought it odd but didn't mention it to her mother thinking she may also have heard it and shrugged it off. She didn't think it was supernatural, but as she dwelt on it she began thinking there could be no other explanation. Like most

others, they knew nothing of the history of the town which is one of the reasons they came on a tour. They also wanted to tell me their experiences, which they told me before the start of the tour, and were amazed when I told them others had also shared the same. Refer also to p.241 and p.268.

**Report 13.**
**South Castle Street 2018**

Saturday 20th January

Exactly one week after Paul and his partner's experience in Church Street, Holger Fangel, a scriptwriter for television commercials in Norway, came over for a couple of days to make a short film of myself and the town. He came on one of my tours a year before with his family and was taken aback by the history of St Andrews and the paranormal that accompanies it.

He had managed to find a rare window to spend time doing something for himself away from his work commitments and wanted to come here again. For his film, he was looking to understand from me why there is so much paranormal activity in St Andrews. We met for a coffee in Jannettas to work out a plan for filming.

He filmed the start of one of my tours that night, then we spent Sunday afternoon filming in various locations around St Andrews and doing voice overs. When we met on Sunday he told me he had an experience after we met on Saturday. After a few hours filming around a very cold St Andrews, he was at the far eastern end of Market Street when he heard what he thought was someone walking along South Castle Street wearing stiletto heels. He looked around, no one was there. I asked if the sound continued, he said it had stopped the second he turned.

**Report 14.**
**South Castle Street 2015**

11:30 am on Tuesday 14th July

I had a golfing party from the States on the 9 pm tour. This was the week of the Open Golf Championship in St Andrews. Tiger Woods had arrived and the town was buzzing. They had rented what I imagine was a reassuringly expensive apartment on South Castle Street for the week.

One of the American women in the group wanted to explore some of the historic areas of St Andrews before heading to the golf course. She left her apartment at 11:30 am and was walking along South Castle Street making her way to the Palace, when she heard a carriage and horses hooves coming up behind her. Her first impression was one of delight. She thought it could be a horse and carriage taking visitors around the town as this was a common occurrence where she was from in the States and would have taken a ride in one. She stood to one side to let it pass. As soon as she turned to see, the sound stopped dead and there was nothing to explain the noise. She mentioned it to the others when they met up later and they all came on a tour that night after their dinner so she could to tell me what she had experienced. They were all interested to find out if I knew anything about what she had heard. My reply was, "Where do I start!"

# North Street

**Report 15.**
**North Street, Deveron House Hotel 2015**
Sunday 31st May
Two weeks before the experience of the American woman in South Castle Street I had Dan and his golfing party from Canada on a tour. At the end of the tour I was talking about the experiences of myself and others hearing the phantom coach and horses. At the end of which, one of the women on the tour asked her husband why he was smiling. He turned to his wife and said, “Remember last Sunday at breakfast.” He explained to me that one of their party hadn’t come on the tour as he was from Quebec and spoke French, but very little English. That morning he joined them all for breakfast at Deveron House Hotel along North Street. He told them he had been woken early that morning by what he called “horses and buggies” trotting along the road. He couldn’t get back to sleep as the sound, which was loud, just carried on annoying him. He said it made a clip-clop noise and demonstrated the same with his downward turned cupped hands. The gentleman on the tour gave the same gesture.

There were no horses and carriages along North Street that morning, but they were unaware of this. None of the others heard the noise, and until they came on a tour, they were unaware of these ghostly carriages being heard in St Andrews.

Without realising, the golfer from Quebec had heard the phantom coach and if the others hadn’t come on a tour, he would never have known that what he heard that morning was not of the physical.

## The Pends Lane

**Report 16.** 1973
GOS p.110: 'Andrew Green mentions a phantom coach being seen in St Andrews. Although the exact location isn't mentioned in his article, the coach in question was seen along the Pends Lane: 'When on an assignment here in 1973 I was assured by a local historian, a Mr. McKenzie that on "the road down to the bay one or two people, including some golfers, have seen what appears to them to be a coach drawn by two horses." The time the vehicle was seen was somewhere between four and five in the afternoon.'[27]

**Report 17.** (19th C.)
Helen Cook in her article *Haunted St. Andrews* in the Scots Magazine of November 1978, says 'a figure wearing a green riding habit on horseback was seen by a police sergeant in the 19th century. The horse and rider rode down the Pends before disappearing through the Priory wall.'[28] GOS p.101.

It disappeared to the right, near the bottom of the Pends Lane through a blocked off entrance that once led to the Teind Barns and stables for the New Inn (Novum Hospitium). In GOS p.100, I have a report of a monk disappearing through the wall of the same entrance in 1981.

**Report 18.** (19th C.)
I have another report from a Victorian policeman at the tail end of the 19th century. One evening while on his beat he heard a coach and horses coming up behind him. He moved near the wall, turned, and the moment he did the commotion stopped. The Pends Lane was empty.

## Market Street

Sound of a Phantom Coach, Horse or Horses

East End

The configurations of a coach and horses, horses, or a horse, have all been heard in Market Street and it is always centred on the East End.

**Report 19.**

**MacGregors** Market Street

Ronnie Howe's experiences feature in a few places throughout this book. The following is from the early 1970s when he was around five years old. Ronnie is the son of an undertaker and they stayed at the time in Market Street next to MacGregors.

In the early hours of an August morning he heard a coach and horses moving high speed westwards across the cobbles along Market Street. As soon as he looked out of his bedroom window the sound stopped. He said it was like pea soup out there. The haar was well into the town, but he could see there was nothing in the street to make the noise. Refer to p.75 and p.261 for Ronnie's other experiences.

**Report 20.**
**Market Street 1982**
When I heard the coach and horses…
In GOS p.160, I wrote about one of my own experiences from around midsummer 1982. At that time, I was staying in a flat above what is now Luvians Bottle Shop in Market Street. Neither myself or Ronnie knew until he was speaking about his experience that we had both experienced the same thing, in the same location, 12 years apart. We were living on opposite sides of the street, both late at night, and it was travelling in the same westward direction.

'In the early 1980s, myself and John Briton shared a first floor flat towards the east end of Market Street where we heard the phantom coach. We were in the living room of the flat facing onto Market Street. The time was around 1 am. The windows were open to allow a cool breeze to enter from a hot summer's night. We were chatting away when we heard a coach in the dead of night. The sound was unmistakable as it trundled across the old cobbled stones, with the echoing sounds of several horse's hooves accompanied by heavy rattling chains making its way along Market Street, travelling east to west.

As the unusual sound began to register we looked at each other and flew to the window to see what it was. There was nothing to see, the street was as deserted as it ever is at this time of night and the silence had returned, barring the faintest sound of a distant car in North Street or South Street. Immediately we went out the door of the flat and down the steps excitedly describing to each other what we had heard. We concluded it was the sound of an old horse-drawn coach, it was unmistakable. Once in the clean fresh air, we looked up and down the street. My flatmate looked down Union Street and I looked down Church Street but there was no sign of any horses, let alone a coach or any sign of movement to be found. There was no other explanation than it being the Phantom Coach we had heard that night.'

**Report 21.**
**Market Street**

The coach is heard again

The woman in the following account was staying in a flat above what was Hogg's Shoe Shop at the time, and is now the Subway in Market Street. I met her not long after the experience of John and myself which is how it came up in conversation.

In GOS p.160, I have: 'Independent of our encounter [myself and John Britton] with the coach, and with a description correlating with the same, a resident of St Andrews when living also in the east end of Market Street heard the Phantom Coach on two occasions. The first time she heard it was before hearing any of Linskill's stories, or indeed hearing any tales of the coach at all.

At night when all was still, she heard the loud clattering sounds of horse's hooves accompanied by the echoing trundle of a heavy carriage travelling at some speed along the cobbled road. Only lasting a few seconds, the sounds died out as rapidly as they started. She could give no physical explanation for the eerie sounds and saw nothing that could have made them when she looked out of her window.

One of the things Linskill mentions in connection with the phantom coach is when heard it foretells death or illness. After each experience with the coach she always felt ill and slept uneasily. To date, this is the only mention of anyone suffering any ill effects after their experience.

**Report 22.**
**Market Street 2017**
Wednesday 5th April, 7:30 pm tour
When I mentioned the sound of coach and horses to a family at the end of a tour, the mother of the family gasped. Her face went white and her eyes were wide. She explained that during the day they had been walking along Market Street. Amid the general noise of the traffic, people and seagulls, she heard a coach and horses galloping behind her. She turned to see this unusual sight. She didn't think the sound suddenly stopping as she turned was unusual as she was looking to see where it had stopped, but there was nothing of the coach and horses to be seen.

She didn't dwell, or rather have time to dwell on the incident as she was busy browsing and shopping along Market Street with her family. It wasn't until she was on my tour that evening and I mentioned the coach and horses that she realised she heard the same that afternoon. This is such a common feature of people's experiences, as I mentioned earlier for the disappearing person we saw by the North Gate, p.130, fleeting anomalies rarely stick when they occur during our daily preoccupations. To remember it happening then takes a trigger, which is what I gave her through my reports of the same.

# Coach/Horse - Patterns of Experience

❖

Some of the reports describe the sound of high heels rather than a horse. I was chatting outside the Greyfriars Hotel (now Greyfriars Inn) one evening with a friend of mine, Mr James (Champagne) Cantley of St Andrews. "There's your phantom horse", he said with a wry smile as a woman walked towards us down Greyfriars Gardens. Her high healed footsteps clopping on the ground made a similar sound to horse's hooves. It was an interesting observation. They had a hollow echo as she walked down the empty street. This got me thinking. Maybe it isn't a horse everyone hears, maybe some of the phenomena is explainable as simply being someone walking along a road?

Certainly, Paul and his partner heard the clip-clop of what they thought was high heels and Holger from Norway thought someone was walking along South Castle Street with stiletto heels.

This theory though soon becomes problematic when correlating the reports. Firstly, the phenomenon isn't random from around the town, which it would be if it were the sound of high heels. A lot of people in St Andrews wear high heels and logically a lot of people hear high heels, but it *only* occurs in certain locations, which are the same locations as the sound of a galloping horse or the sound of a coach and horses. Secondly, and crucially, the sound then stops at that exact moment, that split second the recipient/s turn to the direction of sound, and there is never anything present to be suggestive of a source.

# *The Coach/Horse Phenomenon*

When we hear a sound, our mind analyses the sound pattern and by association, we call up a match most familiar to us. A horse isn't something we would expect, so we are more likely to associate the sound with someone in high heels and it only applies to a trotting sound. The suggestion of high heels has never been entertained when a galloping horse has been heard.

Every experience on hearing the coach/horse phenomenon from Victorian times to present day St Andrews share these same commonalities. Like all the correlative patterns I mention throughout this volume, the patterns here are not something *anyone* was previously aware of. For the sound of a coach and horses, the sound of horses or the sound of a horse the patterns are always the same:

Typically, loud and fast.

The *instant* those hearing it turn to the source it stops at the instant, and there is never anything that could have made the noise.

The occurrence is always spontaneous.

It always happens as an additional circumstance to our everyday lives. Many are here on holiday or a day trip, and are often thinking about golf, not ghosts! and know nothing of this phenomenon.

It can happen during the day as well as at night.

The majority of those who experience this have never heard about the phenomenon here before.

This is Group A. an echo in time. Like the observance of a Group A. ghost or scene, it is about being in the right place at the right time, coupled with the subtle mix of localised energy and receptivity. The difference here is its fragile nature. Why the sound stops the moment we look to find the source is complex. Unlike other aspects of Group A. phenomenon, no one has continued to hear the sound after looking for the source, which serves as a distraction that breaks an already tenuous link. When outdoors it has never been heard in front of you, always behind or to the side.

It was asked of me at the end of a tour on the 28$^{th}$ August 2020, if others, say in North Street had also heard the sound that morning along with the golfer from Quebec in his hotel room, would the sound have stopped for him if they had turned to the source of the sound?

The sound would have stopped for those in the street but would the golfer still be able to hear it from his room? It got me thinking as it could potentially bring in an additional dynamic to the nature of paranormal phenomena in general.

I can say, for all my researches everywhere, I have not had two or more people coming forward with the same experience happening at the same time from completely different vantage points. It is not to say this hasn't happened, but given the volume of testimony I have amassed over the decades from across the world it is highly unlikely. So, it is the subtle vibratory framework of the immediate locality or vantage point of the recipient/s at that moment that is affected. There is also an additional anomaly, there are instances where not everyone occupying the same vantage point hears anything at all out of the ordinary. This is different to a group scenario when encountering a ghost for example where everyone will experience, unless you happened to be looking in the wrong direction (refer to p.352). The woman who heard it in Market Street with no one else in her family or anyone else around her hearing it. The same with the girl from Saudi Arabia who heard it in South Castle Street while her mother didn't. So, how can this be?

The first thing to understand is how phenomena in general terms, excluding poltergeist activity, is happening all the time, it is ever present but operating on a different vibratory frequency to anything of the physical realm. The manifestation of phenomena is a mix of vibratory energy coupled with the awareness of the recipient/s, who, for a moment have unconsciously tapped into this same frequency. Recognition is dependent on awareness and in these brief moments the awareness is in sync with the phenomena. This then opens other associated aspects as to the cause of this syncing in of frequencies. For more than one to experience presupposes they too have tapped into this same frequency. The audible nature is very subtle and can be thought of as a brief gust of astral wind sweeping through the locality from a different time, and lasting just long enough to be consciously registered.

The subconscious absorbs all the reality in the vicinity of its sphere of involvement like a sponge, including localised paranormal phenomena, and everything is eternally retained. So, all reality is available to us, but only a fraction is filtered through to our consciousness as a partial isolation of this potential entirety. There is a selectivity in what is filtered through to our conscious awareness which is then stored in our short and long term memory. This selectivity is focused and directed on expectation, and what we believe to be important at any given moment. As our focus shifts, so too does this ever shifting pool of sensory reality.

For example, in a busy environment we can hone in on a particular conversation that then blocks out all extraneous background clutter. The influx of information and the rate it is received to our consciousness is the reason our minds can occasionally feel overwhelmed as the influx of information is too great to comfortably take in and process at the same time. This filtering is a safety mechanism. If it were not in place, we would render ourselves instantly insane. As I mentioned earlier, we would be instantly overloaded, in the same way a computer blows a chip, which brings about an important reoccurring theme: This relationship between the dynamics of spirit, the subconscious and consciousness.

Recognition begins silently behind the scenes with awareness in our spirit. The influx of reality then flows to the subconscious which you could think of as a reservoir, filtrating reality through to consciousness. Infinite variables determined by disposition and circumstance among other dynamics are at play here. There is a direct link between phenomena and the spirit of the recipient/s. While the subtle realms are ever present, they are generally beyond conscious remit. Occasionally, elements of phenomena bypass the subconscious filtration, and when they do, the receptivity is immediate and impacting. There is a familiarity, but our conscious mind immediately processes for recognition, which conflicts with our conscious presuppositions and results in confusion. While experience is undeniable, paranormal circumstance remains unexplainable by the majority who experience it.

It is all about this awareness, ultimately stemming from spirit, and the awareness is always operating with a greater proficiency when it is not being constantly bombarded by an influx of mundane baggage. The less baggage, the more space or openness of mind there will be to appreciate these subtleties, which is why children and mediums are able to utilise more of this awareness. There are different techniques as to how to this can be consciously achieved as we are all have mediumistic abilities. A medium of note opens a channel allowing these subtleties of spirit (our spiritual nature) to flow directly as a conduit through to consciousness. This again bypasses the subconscious filtration, which I mentioned is complex as it is feeding the sum-total of everything we *think* we are, everything that makes us – us, including all our life's involvements, thoughts and persuasions of being, but many of these are physical traits, it is the spirit that carries the true blueprint of who we are. It is the spirit who knows who we really are.

# *Market Street Phenomena*

## (Mercat Gait)

**Student flat in Market Street**
Before embarking on the east end, students sharing a flat above the shops near Greg's the Bakers came on a tour to tell me about a ghost they have in their flat. Some give them names as familiarity cushions uncertainty. They call theirs Ali. Things will go missing and no matter where they search they can never find the missing items, but a few hours or days later they will reappear. Never in the same place, and always characteristically in places impossible to overlook.

## East End Ghosts

Most of the activity in Market Street is centred on the east end. Forming part of the older quarter, this was the fringe of a young city that would soon have designs on expanding further west.

**66 Market Street**

I had a student on a tour staying in a student flat at 66 Market Street above Luvians. There is a fairly persistent sense of a presence throughout the premises. At night she has seen the ghost of a monk appearing in the corner of the living room. Standing motionless, it vanishes when the light is turned on, when the light is turned off it reappears.

Her account was uncannily reminiscent of the *moonlight monk* I recorded in GOS p.123, from the pages of James Wilkie in 1931, as follows:

**The Moonlight Monk**

A story mentioning a ghostly monk tells of a lady who took lodgings in a house and was woken during the night to find a monk standing in her room surrounded by moonlight...

'Among the many tales of monkish figures still manifesting themselves in the environment they knew so well of old is one concerning a lady of position in the county who took rooms in a house which, though not of itself of any great antiquity, succeeded an earlier building. She entered on possession at a time when night was left to the stars. Some hours after retiring she awoke to find the room flooded with the pale light of a full moon which shone in at the window – despite the calendar. In its silver radiance stood a monk.

She switched on the electric lamp beside her. Moonlight and monk alike were gone. She shut it off again, and their appearance was repeated. She had no feeling of fear, simply of wonder, and that chiefly because she remembered there could not even be a crescent in the sky for an evening or two to come.

In a casual way she made an inquiry to her landlady as to the monastic associations of the site. The other showed embarrassment and a desire to evade a direct reply. The vision was then mentioned. It was elicited that the phantom and its accompaniment were occasionally seen, and an undertaking was given that the house should not be identified lest the story interferes with the letting of the room.'[29]

The story relates to St Andrews and was recounted in 1931, but the experience may have a far older origin. The location of the disturbance was kept quiet at that time for fear of not being able to rent out the lodgings. This is not so much of a problem as it once was, but there are still those who have their concerns. Refer to p.412.

The two accounts are compellingly similar. Both involve the ghost of a monk, both appear to be standing motionless. Both disappear when the light is turned on and reappear again when it is switched off, and the student had no idea of Wilkie's 1931 account. This must be where the woman lodged.

**82 Market Street, Le Rendez Vous (Group B)**

No.82 along with neighbouring 84a Market Street was the site of the Albert Hotel until 1844.

The staff of the cafe have spoken to me a few times over the years about it being haunted. They have poltergeist activity here in abundance but have never seen anyone. Whoever is causing it is very active. They have the sound of footsteps, doors slamming shut when no one is around, and the constant feeling of a presence that also extends to the close next to the shop.

The most recent event was on 10th December, 2020. One of the staff was in the kitchen off the back of the café and heard the toilet in the café flush twice. He asked another staff member if he had been in the toilet as there was no one else on the premises at the time, but he hadn't. In trying to work it out he thought it might have been from the flat above, but it is not something they ever hear in the café.

All the staff have experienced these things and more. Like most anomalies I mention in this volume, everything is still taking place. Phenomena is far from 'appear on demand' but if you fancy a coffee and a bite to eat, spend some relaxation time here and just observe.

**77 Market Street, Central Bar**

The Central Bar at 77 Market Street has seen its fair share of St Andrews history over the centuries, and is one of St Andrews more prominent social landmarks. Until Paul Gray arrived as the new Assistant Manager in 2016 I hadn't heard of anything happening in the bar itself.

Paul, stayed in the brewery flat above the pub with his partner, baby and dog. He told me things began happening not long after starting here. He wanted to come on one of my tours but said he attracted these things and didn't want to tempt fate. I cannot disagree, receptivity does bring its own attractions and Paul is in-keeping with this.

One of the most common incidences he experienced is the gas taps for the fonts switching off. Each morning while preparing the bar for opening he went into the cellar to check all the gas taps were on and that everything was in order. As an example of a fairly frequent occurrence; on the morning of 14th July, 2017, he did the same, but when they opened, the beers were not pouring properly. He went down to the cellar and the gas taps for all the fonts barring two, had been switched off.

The two left on had longer leavers and were at either end of the others. No one had been down there since himself.

He has heard footsteps when no one else is in the bar, the feeling of a presence, and every so often someone flitting across the east side of the bar as if they have just come in through the main Market Street entrance, but the door is locked.

In his flat upstairs, there is also the occasional sense of not being alone. It has become extremely cold for no apparent reason, and a heavy closed door is often found open.

**Ronnie Howe**

This is just by Ronnie Howe's former family home. Ronnie remembers in the 1970s while his father was in the old Central bar seeing a Victorian lady in his home sitting in his father's chair. It was just Ronnie and his mother in the room at the time. Ronnie experienced a few things in this area when he was young. Another of his experiences is as follows:

**Ronnie Howe - The College Street Town Crier!**

As a boy in the 1960s, Ronnie and his sister were playing with a football in College Street just by the Central. He said, "It was the safest place to play as there was rarely any traffic."

He saw a large man coming toward him wearing a large dark overcoat and ringing a bell that made a loud noise. In an equally loud, deep voice, he was repeating the words, "All is well, all is well." Ronnie carried on playing with his ball but when he looked up again he was gone and the street was silent. He mentioned him to his sister who saw and heard nothing.

Public announcements were made from the Mercat Cross only yards from where he saw the town crier. Refer also to p.75 and p.248, for Ronnie's other experiences.

**Nando's, 73 Market Street**

In December 2014, I was told of something strange that had just happened in Nando's Restaurant in Market Street. I went around and spoke with Graham, the manager. He said when he arrived to open that morning, the fire door through the back of the restaurant was open. He closed the door and checked the premises for burglary or vandalism but everything was in order. He was somewhat puzzled as the fire door can only be opened from the inside by a long push bar. The building, including the fire door is alarmed, but the alarm had not gone off. On the outside, the fire door leads to an enclosed path separating part of Nando's from the Central and runs down the side of the building. A security camera is trained on the fire door from the inside, so he checked the CCTV footage from the time he closed the restaurant the night before to his arrival that morning.

At around 3 am, the door slowly opened by itself to about 2 feet wide, which is how he found it in the morning. The push bar hadn't gone down. There was no physical way the door could open. He then checked the security alarm and all was in order. He called the alarm company and told them what had happened. They asked if the alarm worked, he said it did. Of course, they then said there was nothing they could do as there was no apparent problem. He had transferred the footage to his mobile and showed it to me when I arrived. Sure enough, the door slowly opened from closed and the bar did not go down. There was no one around at all that could have done it and what we saw wasn't physically possible. On the night it happened there was no wind or rain, so it wasn't as if it had been left ajar and had blown open. In any case, the alarm won't set unless it is locked and completes the circuit.

71 and 73 Market Street was originally one premises. This was Macgregor's auction and furniture house. Next door at the time, at 71 Market Street was Macgregor's coffee shop/café. That became Sainsbury's in 2012. The Nando's side became Little John's Restaurant, owned by Simon Littlejohn. There was a school to the east of where the door opened, behind the Martyrs Kirk (Free Church, now the Special Units Research Facility for the University), but there is no phenomena associated with it. There has not been any other activity on the present Nando's site, but with the immediate localised vicinity having the ghost of a Victorian woman, the shadow of a figure, and poltergeist activity, there is more than likely to be a connection here, especially with the Victorian woman.

**Buchanan Building**

St Andrews had its slums, and they tended to be occupied by fisher folk. The area now occupied by the Buchanan Building running alongside Union Street was one of them until 1835, when, as Fleming put it, 'a clearance scheme was carried out.'[30]

The fisher building on the corner of Market Street and Union Street was known as the 'Double Decker,' so named for the two rows of dormer windows in its roof.

It is here the ghost of a fisherwoman was seen standing at the corner. Cathy Buchanan (p.74), was telling me her grandparents lived in the Double Decker with their six children. When her mother's cousin, May Cunningham, stayed there in the 1920s or 30s, she saw a ghost at the entrance that terrified her. She always believed it to be John Knox. There are certainly five other locations where Knox has been seen and they are all in the area from St Salvator's to the Cathedral (refer to p.383). The closest location to the Double Decker is outside the former Cinema House in North Street, so the area does fit.

Conditions for the fisher folk back in the day were harsh. To give an idea, a close running along the back of the buildings from Market Street to North Street was called 'Dirty Lane,' and

'Foul Waste' was the official name for the street Playfair changed to Union Street. It is hard to conceive (or maybe it isn't) that these were literally only yards from more affluent quarters, in most cases just across the street, as everything in St Andrews was at close quarters, and the smell, especially on hot days was ever apparent. A passed down remark through many generations says that you knew when you were in St Andrews because of the smell, and is why I have a chapter in GOS titled 'Dung Hills and Herring Guts!' about a missing period of St Andrews history spanning three centuries to 1855.

# Market Street / Logies Lane

**Star Hotel, 92 – 94 Market Street**

Since writing about the Star Bar in my previous books, a few new reports have come to light, including the ghost of a woman in one of the former hotel bedrooms that was relayed to me by Johnny Hughes. His parents owned the hotel for several years along with the St Andrews Golf Hotel on the Scores (p.423).

The Star Bar stood at 2 Logies Lane, as the public bar of the hotel. On closing its doors in the early 80s it was a sorely missed watering hole in the town, not least my myself! What I wasn't aware of when I published my previous books, is the bar was originally called the New Bar. I referenced earlier that it became the Star Bar in 1921, which is the same year a photo I had on the cover of *A St Andrews Mystery* (now HT) was taken of William Linskill, Captain Wilson and Mr Ferguson, the then owner of the hotel, all standing proudly at the bar. This couldn't have been a coincidence. It would make sense why the photo was taken at that time. Linskill's local had just changed its name! Whether this was accompanied by a refurbishment of the bar I do not know. Maybe they just washed the windows!

Excavations here in 1982 recorded three human burials and a sealed well. Workmen building the row of shops on this site found more burials. This was the northern part of the burial ground for Holy Trinity Church.

Ian Wilson of St Andrews (Dexy), told me when he was there, a large charity money bottle sat on the far end of the bar. A few of the staff left the pub one night and on entering again the next day the bottle was on the floor by the bar's public entrance. It was still full of coins, and the door was locked. There was no explanation as to how this could have happened.

Iain Thompson, an old friend of mine of St Andrews, had the feeling that something went through him one night in the bar after it had closed for the night. This gave him a shiver and, "goose pimples on goose pimples," as he described it. His parents worked in the hotel and after this their dog never entered the public bar again, and Iain never went into the bar after it had closed for the night to the public.

The following is an excerpt from a piece I wrote in GOS p.162: 'A former barman briefly went through to the hotel and on his return, all the tables and chairs throughout the pub had been disrupted. Some were lying on their sides; others had either been upturned or were now piled on top of each other in the middle of the room. The door to the pub was locked and there was no one else present. No sound had been heard and no one could have entered the bar through the hotel without passing by him first.'

**Little Italy, Logies Lane**

Situated on the site of the iconic 'Star Bar' in Logies Lane, the manageress of the popular Italian restaurant Little Italy, told me not long after they opened, wine glasses would randomly start shattering in the restaurant. The glasses would either be behind the bar or on the tables. No explanation was ever found as to how this could have happened. Eventually, she had enough of this and told it to stop. They have never had any trouble since.

They were aware of bodies being found under the location of the restaurant when the Star Bar was demolished, but they were unaware they were from the cemetery that surrounded the church. To this day, the remains of well over 200 people are still present only two feet under the area surrounding the church.

This was the parish burial ground for the town c.1412 to possibly the late 16th century, a few decades following the Reformation. Built here as the focal point of the town on the site of a 13th century church, around the 1850s the grounds around the church precincts and South Street were levelled down by four feet in places and the burial ground cobbled over. This was part of Playfair's bid to landscape the town and rid it of around three centuries of rubbish having accumulated following the Reformation. Being former arable and estate land, the centre of St Andrews was originally more undulating than we know it today. Some of the area was higher, other parts lower, but it has all changed so much and is now more or less all levelled out. Many medieval gardens at the back of the buildings in the centre of St Andrews - the old rigs, are still around three or four feet higher than present street level.

In 1991, excavations by the Scottish Urban Archaeological Trust (SUAT) found 'five earlier street surfaces'[31] at the South Street end of Logie Lane alone. They also found '101 articulated human skeletons belonging to the graveyard of Holy Trinity Church.'[32]

During one of the council's many acts of vandalism over the centuries in St Andrews, in the year 2000 they gutted what had been the Hay Fleming Library since the 1930s, 'archaeologists found 76 burials alone in the south section of the building designated for a lift shaft.' [33] They dated from the fifteenth century, so not long after the church was built.

# *Queen's Gardens*

## Originally Queen Street

**2 Queen's Gardens**

February 2017

The following is from a flat just off South Street at the top end of Queen's Gardens, next to the Town Hall. Students came on the tour and excitedly said, "We have someone else in our flat!" They have not seen the person but they know they are there and it makes them feel very uneasy.

They said, "The feeling of being watched or sensing we are not alone is very common. It's the same feeling as you know when someone is standing behind you."

**Queen's Gardens flat**

Monday 17th April 2017

The family from Saudi Arabia I recorded earlier (p.241 and p.243), spoke of what they have been experiencing over the previous few days around St Andrews. They were staying in a flat at the top end of Queen's Gardens and heard the chime of bells ringing, but these were not the town bells. They said it was at odd times of the night between the regular quarter and full hour church bells. This is reminiscent of the legend of the Cathedral bells being heard through the town, p.204.

**Phantom Car!**

There is also a phantom car in Queen's Gardens witnessed by Greta Boyd (p.91, 268, p.484 and GOS including p.163).

Refer also to St Regulus Hall of Residence p.474.

# *South Street*

## (Southgait or South Gait)

## *West of Holy Trinity Church*

**118 South Street, Southgait Hall**

The Royal Hotel originally stood within a large three-storey complex called the Albert Buildings at 109-121 South Street. In 1857 it moved location to 118 South Street across the road. Built in 1854, two large pillars surmount a now blocked off door. This was the main entrance to the hotel. The section of the building with the entrance for horse-drawn carriages was an extension for the hotel built in 1894. In 1963 the building was sold to the University and became Southgait Hall of Residence for students. In 2002 it became private flats and remains the residence of students and residents alike.

There is the ghost of a young man in the building who flits between two particular rooms on different floors, one above the other. Those experiencing the phenomenon are always unaware of other reports, and these span several years through different student occupants.

One of the residents observes a pink mist in his room that sometimes takes on the form of a person. Another student had a shadow flitting around her room. While another student has also seen a dark shadow.

The most reported and disturbing experience in this room is the sense of being watched which makes those who experience this feel very self-conscious. A female student often covered herself up whilst undressing for bed. She said, "It sounds crazy but I just feel so uncomfortable, I get an overwhelming feeling of being watched sometimes." Again, she had no idea of the other reports.

The phenomenon is still taking place.

**129, 127, 127b South Street**

This immediate location is a bit of a hotspot when it comes to fine dining. It is also a hotspot of history and activity.

There are two buildings at 129 South Street, one behind the other. The one closest the street was originally built for a shop. It then became a watchmaker's run by a Mr Foster, and in 1907 the Post Office temporarily moved in. For the last few decades it has been a food outlet that has seen its fair share of incarnations. It occupies the site of a former walled garden lined with pear trees for the white 18th century building standing inconspicuously behind it.

Fleming believed this was the residence of Kate Dalrymple, which is also the name of a famous traditional Scottish reel written about her. The words for the tune were added in 1750 by William Watt of East Kilbride, and was initially titled 'The

New Highland Laddie.' Robert Burns called it the 'Old Highland Laddie.' The Scottish folk tune was given a wider audience through the Corries. As a popular Ceilidh tune many have danced to it at a wedding without realising. It was also used as the theme tune for BBC Radio Scotland's show 'Take the Floor' for many years.

There is speculation that Kate was a fictitious figure, however, it would be out of character for Fleming to state something without qualification. If she did stay here, there is no indication as to how long she stayed for, but the 18th century is the period when she was said to be alive and it fits with the age of the building.

The building of 129, and the extensive gardens to the rear have been haunted for centuries by the ghost of a woman who is also the source of the poltergeist activity in the building.

**Drawing of the 18th century building**
From David Hay Fleming's St Andrews Standard Guide, 1881

In 1840, everything to the right of the front door in this drawing was demolished. The photo on the following page shows the remaining left section. The demolished section was to make way for a townhouse that became 127 South Street.

**This is the existing left half of the building, photo 2020**

**Photo by Dr Adamson, 127 South Street, 1862.** Courtesy of the University of St Andrews Libraries and Museums, ID: ALB-8-67

This was home to Dr John Adamson, a physician from St Andrews who stayed here with his family from 1848. St Andrews was one of the early pioneers of photography. Some of the earliest photographs in existence are from here. Along with being a physician, Dr Adamson was one of these early pioneers. In 1841 he took the first calotype portrait. He took the photo opposite of his family and staff in 1862.

In the early 1900s, the ground floor of 127 became the Victoria Café, the landscaped garden was partially transformed to become the Victoria Café Summer Garden. Run by Miss Jane Blair, it served afternoon tea in-keeping with the former regal tradition of the property. (This was the sister venue of the Victoria Café at 1 St Marys Place.)

In 1907, it changed occupancy again and became the Post Office that most in the town are familiar with. Then 101 years later in 2008 it moved to its new location across the road into W. H. Smiths, however, few will realise Smiths is the fifth location for the Post Office on South Street.

In 2012, the 127 South Street site opened its doors to its new host, The Adamson, so-named after its ground-breaking occupant. The restaurant was soon embraced into the town and quickly became one of the top restaurants.

The ghost of the woman is still here, and the poltergeist activity remains. It appears she is not alone and it is not just relegated to 129. Buildings and people come and go, while phenomenon tends to remain. Build on the same location and the new property will invariably be affected with the same, often with more activity than before if stasis spirits are involved. They do not like change. This is born out with the Adamson building where the chefs have experienced poltergeist activity in the kitchen of the restaurant. Their experiences are not isolated. I would wager the Adamson children certainly saw her, and no doubt there were rumours between staff members.

Restaurants are like hotels, they both have a high turnover of staff, and being always busy it is not so easy to nail down those who have experienced phenomena in these establishments. In the same vein, there are those who do not believe it exists because after being in the same location for many years they have not experienced for themselves (p.412).

In the drawing of 129, the front door is now the close entrance through to the Adamson Cocktail Bar. This is the former telephone exchange and sorting office for the Post Office at the back of the Adamson building.

Properties in the centre of St Andrews hide a great many secrets and treasures. For the most part these formed extensive gardens (rigs), but with real estate being at a premium and space being what it is in St Andrews, many have been developed with additional housing and the occasional business tucked away down a myriad of closes and lanes.

Running lengthways behind the Adamson, north to the boundary wall for the gardens of the Market Street properties, are a modern terrace of two houses. 127a and 127b South Street. Each has two bedrooms and part of a walled terrace. The Long Bar and the two properties occupy half of what was the garden of the 18th century building. With the advent of the Victorian townhouse, this section became an extensively landscaped patio garden.

With both 129 and 127 being haunted, it shouldn't surprise that 127b has the same phenomenon. On Saturday, 22 December 2018, I received the following email:

Dear St Andrews Ghost Tours,

I am a former student at the University, and I am inquiring about whether you guys have heard anything about paranormal activity happening in the houses just behind the Adamson.

I lived in one of them last year and am still convinced that my house was haunted, but haven't gotten any closure about this since moving out.

I would really appreciate any info you might have!

Best Wishes and Happy Holidays,
Anna

On Friday, December 28, 2018, I sent an email that there is a woman who haunts this area, and there is currently poltergeist activity in the Adamson. She replied with the following email just before the turn of 2019:

Monday, 31st December 2018

Hi Richard,

Thanks so much for your response. Your mentioning a female spirit is quite chilling, as a lot of what I experienced led me to believe I was haunted by a woman. My address was 127b South Street, and it's just down the alleyway behind the Adamson.

My own encounters started nearly as soon as I moved in. I would randomly catch strong whiffs of the same woman's perfume in particular areas of my flat (and my flatmate nor I wore perfume). I also suffered from bouts of intense and unexplained nausea, only ever in the living room, that would go as quickly as they came. Additionally, I experienced intense nightmares usually involving the flat itself or the alleyway behind the Adamson, from which I would always wake up at 3 or 4 am. This was especially strange because I'm not prone to nightmares and only ever experienced them living in that flat, in that particular bedroom.

My flatmate and I also experienced very strange electrical issues in our flat, as well as doors opening on their own, alarm clocks going off when no one had set them, and shuffling noises coming from upstairs bedrooms when we were both downstairs.

Lastly, (and the most shocking instance of all) my mother came to visit me and had to spend a night alone in the flat, where she decided to sleep in my bedroom. She woke up at around 3 am to a strange noise, and found herself completely paralyzed, and hearing a deep man's voice in the room, and other voices whispering around her, but, of course, no one else was home. When she could finally move her muscles again a few minutes later, she jumped out of bed, turned on all the lights and started making a bunch of noise (clapping, banging on pots, etc.) to disrupt the voices. She told me she had never experienced anything so chilling (she's a total sceptic and hadn't really believed in anything that I had experienced before that).

Needless to say, we were both happy when I finally moved out of the flat at the end of the year!

I've never been able to get much information about the land the property was built on, or the property itself from the internet, so any info you could provide would be helpful!

Happy New Year to you.

Kind Regards,
Anna

**143 South Street flat and Cancer Research UK Charity Shop**
A few doors west of 129 is 143 South Street. The building dates from 1800 and it shows from the architecture when inside. I lived at 143 for a few years in the 1980s. It still retained some of its old charm from that period with large rooms and high ceilings. The charity shop below extends through the back with an attic above the back section on the same level as the first floor

of the maisonette. Within the attic is the ghost of a man who has been there for years.

In 2014, when opening the shop in the morning, staff heard the gushing of water. On walking through to the stockroom, the tap in the toilet at the back was found full-on and the floor flooding. This happened a few times. When they lock up at night the tap is always off and there is never any evidence of intruders.

During the summer of 2014, a few of the staff members and Mo from the former Happy Hacker (141, Jurek Pütter's former studio), were in the courtyard of Burghers Close behind 143 having a barbeque. They were sitting chatting. It was early evening on a bright summer's day. The shop was locked up for the day but the side fire exit door to the stockroom of the shop facing the courtyard was open. While enjoying their barbeque they saw someone in the stockroom walk passed the door to the toilet. Immediately they called out. There was no answer, so the manageress went in to see who it was, and what was going on. There was no one in the toilet and nowhere for the figure to go.

A gentleman from the Baptist Church in South Street came to see if he could ascertain the cause. As a spiritualist, he realised the premises has the spirit of a man living there. He spoke with him and he seems quite happy being there in the attic. The disturbances have calmed down since then but occasionally it still occurs. The manageress of the charity shop also speaks to the ghost and that also seems to calm him down. Before she leaves for the evening she tells him not to switch the tap on!

Spirits are looking to attract your attention to notify they are present. If you acknowledge them they generally stop.

In the shop itself it is common for things to move around, especially scatter cushions (appropriately enough), that will fling themselves onto the floor – that happens a lot.

I featured the 143 flat above the shop in GOS p.165, about the floating head of a man from the early 1980s. I didn't start hearing about the charity shop phenomenon until 2014. The 143 flat shares the same address and is quite possibly a partial manifestation of the man whose dwelling is only yards away.

The account is as follows:

**The Floating Head in a South Street Flat**

'Along South Street from the West Port is an old flat above shops opposite Blackfriars Chapel. The flat is the haunt of a dark shadow-like form drifting around the walls. The spectre is usually accompanied by areas of extreme cold and the large head of a bearded man has been seen floating around one of the rooms – much to the surprise and shock of those who have witnessed this gruesome spectacle. One night an occupant in one of the bedrooms on the second floor awoke to see the head hovering just above her face. On waking the other occupants with a scream, they rushed in to see what had happened, but by the time they arrived the apparition had disappeared. Various people staying in this bedroom have experienced the same.'

I never saw it while I was there, but I was present on those occasions. Something woke them up and on opening their eyes, there he was. Staring at them, his face just above there's. He vanishes as soon as they scream.

There is an acknowledgement to a floating head in Linskill's book where he attributes a floating head to Lausdree Castle – a fictitious castle somewhere close by St Andrews. I have always believed Lausdree to be Earlshall Castle near Leuchars. It does have its ghosts which you will find in GOF p.110, with a few matching the activity portrayed by his fictional story.

Linskill collected paranormal experiences of St Andrews, Fife and beyond, and his fictional story: *The Hauntings and Mysteries of Lausdree Castle,* incorporates a real hotchpotch of activity where he took odd snippets of information and put them all in one place. They are a mix of information from locations where he wanted to protect their privacy and reports that include very little information. Sometimes there is only a suggestion, the 'floating head' being one of those snippets he heard about but he had no location for, which is why there are no accompanying details for the head in his story. I have a number of these which can and do sit for years in a word document awaiting an eventual match with other incidents. When a match appears, it can give additional information for the same locality or reveal the locality itself, which we have here. For all the activity we have at Earlshall Castle, there is no floating head, it was 143 South Street he was referring to.

The same with the Moonlight Monk from Wilkie in 1932, and subsequently with the student's experience of the same at 66 Market Street (p.258). It is through this correlation that the patterns I often mention then start to emerge.

Another potential tie-in is as follows:

### The South Street Pedlar & Aikman's Bar and Bistro, Bell Street

Before continuing along South Street, just along Bell Street is Aikman's Bar and Cellar Bar. It first opened as the Wine Bar and just occupied the lower floor. Originally this was part of the storage cellar for the grocer's shop, Aikman and Terrace[xii]

---

[xii] Sited at 165 South Street, on the corner of South Street and Bell Street.

(1837 to 1981), which ran partway under the buildings along the west side of Bell Street. The Wine Bar was opened by a salvage expert who designed it to be like the interior of a ship. Full of nautical memorabilia, it featured parts from one of the Titanic's sister ships.

When long term owners Barbara and Malcolm bought the property, they created the upper level which became Aikman's Bar and Bistro. The lower level was changed to the Cellar Bar and still has a copper facing along the top of the bar from the Wine Bar days which is from the Titanic's sister ship.

The ghost of an elderly man sits motionless in the corner of the seating area next to the door to the left when entering the Cellar Bar. He has been attributed as being William Aikman, also known as 'Bill,' who, for many years ran Aikman and Terrace, but there is another attribution for the same location. A historic ghost in St Andrews called the 'beckoning ghost.' A 19th century South Street pedlar, who was first seen in the street in front of the premises where he was murdered in its cellar. I believe this was on the former Aikman and Terrace property and would make sense of the figure and disturbances.

There are a few paranormal attributions here with characteristics shared with what is now the The Räv in North Street (p.406). Before they have opened, or after they have closed to the public for the night, staff in the Cellar Bar have heard footsteps of people walking around the bar above. A large mirror sits at the back of the bar on the upper floor and it is common for them to see someone out the corner of their eye in the mirror, flitting across the public side of the bar behind them. They have also heard footsteps walking past the bar, but when they turn no one is there and the sound ceases.

**170 South Street**

The Saint Bar and Kitchen, formerly West Port Bar and Kitchen, the Britannia Hotel, the Blue Bell Hotel, Blue Bell Public House and Spirit Dealer run by George Sams, c. 1903.

# South Street - West

In GOS p.175, I wrote:

'The ground floor and especially the garden area was the haunt of a well-dressed middle aged gentleman wearing a dark suit. He would appear to residents around dusk, either standing or seated and would always appear quite motionless.

Occasionally things in the bar would move around without any intervention and both the bar and the guest rooms were prone to an unnaturally cold chill. Sometimes a particular area, [now halfway down the bar on the right, at the foot of a few steps leading up to a restaurant area] would become very cold, and no amount of heating would solve the problem. The two elderly sisters [who owned the hotel when it was the Britannia] were aware of this. It is why they kept the heater there until someone came in. This was once the area at the end of the bar which ran along what is now a partition wall between the bar and restaurant. The lights in the bar, the toilet and other parts of the hotel would flicker or go off at times, as if something was trying to notify of its presence. It would happen just for a moment when someone was doing something they needed to see by, such as going to the toilet, or walking up or down the stairs. No electrical faults were ever found. The ghostly gentleman was believed to have been a guest who died in the hotel many years previously.'

The following is an update from Nicky Irvine, the former manager here when this was the West Port Bar and Kitchen. He has felt a presence at the foot of the stairs leading to the upstairs bedrooms. The presence has also been felt in the office on the ground floor adjoining the stair. When he showed me a small corridor now leading to two of the guest rooms, we both agreed the area had a very heavy oppressive feel to it. A kind of dry charged atmosphere with little air which is an indicter of increased energy bordering on imminent activity. This is where the figure of a young man has been seen. The rooms have been structurally remodelled over the years. The corridor was originally part of one of the rooms where I believe he died.

Paraphrasing from GOS: When this was the Britannia Hotel there was something quite unusual about it, and it wasn't because of its continental feel. It was something only noticeable once inside. Two elderly sisters greeted the customers. On ordering drinks, you gave your order to one, who then took your money while the other poured your drink. Sounds simple, but this would turn into an operation that would somehow take around 10 minutes to accomplish, despite our being the only two in the bar. They had a strange knack of somehow bamboozling you with their many quirks.

A small black tube with coloured circles sat as a 70s disco icon at one end of the bar. This would come to life at the weekends and it was always a big deal when they turned it on, almost ceremonial, and like the big turn on of the Christmas lights (or turn off where St Andrews is concerned), they always looked forward to the weekends so they could switch it on. They would get more excited than the punters as it created whirling flashes of colour across the very dimly lit room. It certainly gave the bar with a 70s disco ambiance, but what I forgot to mention in GOS is there was never any accompanying music! We always used to sit to the left when you entered the building. Can't do that anymore, there is a bit of a bar situation going on there.

There was always something odd about the place I could never quite fathom, or perhaps it was just the eccentricity of the elderly sisters that carried an air of Victoriana.

Following the release of GOS, I was told something about the hotel when it was the Britannia which then made complete sense to me, and was one of the missing pieces of the puzzle for its quirky feel. There were four rooms in the hotel. Every time I was in there I remember the rooms were always full. At least when anyone turned up looking for a room that is what they were told. But it seems the rooms were always empty. They never let out the rooms! I have reports of residents seeing the ghost of the well-dressed man so I don't know how long they had the hotel, but before the Britannia it was called the Blue Bell Hotel. If they had it since the name change, the residents I refer to in GOS were either staying there before their arrival, or perhaps it was in the latter days of the Britannia when they stopped letting out rooms perhaps due to their age.

It all reminded me of an award-winning story written by Roald Dahl called 'The Landlady' which was originally going to be Dahl's only ghost story, but he changed the ending! I am sure you have read it. If you haven't, I would advise skipping to the next paragraph. In brief, a bed and breakfast run by an eccentric and seemingly absent-minded elderly lady, attracts the attention of a 17 year old youth for its extremely cheap price. He notices in the guest-book two other guests are also staying there. The landlady invited him into the living room for a cup of tea. While he is drinking his tea, he notices there is also a dog and a parrot in the living room. "I always stuff my pets when they die," she said, as he was finishing his tea, which unknown to him was laced with cyanide. The other two guests who were also of his age had gone missing a few years before. The Landlady now had a third guest staying in her bed and breakfast.

The hotel has had its fair share of ownership and name changes since the two elderly ladies ran the Britannia. It has also seen its fair share of structural changes, and as you will by now be aware, this tends to accentuate phenomena. The well-dressed guest wearing a dark suit is still present and the disturbances don't stop here…

**172 South Street**

One of the flats next door at 172 South Street had a shadow flitting across the walls, the strong feeling of a presence and persistent poltergeist activity. Things disappeared and reappeared, things flew around the rooms, and there were increasing areas of extreme cold – freezer cold. The student couple who stayed there in 1989 were unaware of the disturbances taking place at the same time next door in the hotel. On one occasion after going to bed, Jane became extremely cold down one side of her body as if someone or something very cold had just laid down beside her.

When I went around there to interview them I will never forget how scared they both were. The anxiety they were suffering was very palpable. Their time in this flat affected their studies, their sleep and their lives. They were living a literal nightmare. They had stopped using the other rooms because the disturbances had become so extreme and persistent. Room by room they took out what they needed and never went back in. So, when I went around they now found themselves relegated to spending their waking and sleeping time in the living room. It was the only room where there didn't appear to be anything happening. The kitchen and the toilet for example, were rooms where did still enter, but would spend as little time as possible in them.

They couldn't wait to move out, which they did with a great deal of emotional relief a few months later. The phenomenon is related to the hotel/bar next door, and the activity didn't stop with them moving out. It just continued.

Dark shadows flitting across the interior walls of dwellings are a common feature of many disturbances. They are especially common as an accompaniment to poltergeist activity. This is to do with the energies present at the time. The fleeting shadow/s are partially manifest spirits when the energies are not of a degree to enable full manifestation. The spirit here used all it could from the atmosphere to cause the activity, hence the extreme cold. While they will not physically harm you, they can carry an overbearing heavy air (Group C.) that will be easily picked up and disturb the psyche. As if death itself is paying an unexpected and most unwelcome visit. Their appearance is always sudden, and where the great unknown is concerned, the invasion of privacy can be very frightening for those involved.

**Gibson House, Argyle Street**

4th August 2019

Before heading along South Street east of Holy Trinity Church, there is a location nearby I want to give a brief mention to. Through the West Port, across the road on the corner of Argyle Street and City Road is Gibson House, a residential care home.

The home was a gift of the late William Gibson, for aged, infirm and sick persons and opened its doors in January 1884 as William Gibson Hospital.

I received an email from James Drury who experienced something along the Pends Lane following one of my tours (p.387). He also included another experience tagged onto it he had in St Andrews on another occasion:

'I personally feel very uneasy and get a sick / nervous feeling whenever I walk or drive past the Gibson Care home/hospital, do you have any Haunting / ghost info on this place? I have had this feeling only a few times in my life in relation to the buildings / areas and I simply refuse to go near them or stay in them out of a pure primal fear!! I have a similar experience when I pass an old care home in Lanark.'

Thanks again for the great tour, James Drury

These Group C. feelings tend to be associated with a subconscious recognition of something having taken place at the locality. Something the spirit through the subconscious recognises and can directly associate with - sometimes through its own experience. It may never be found what this is, as it doesn't have to relate to something in this life, so the scope is more often too broad for anything specific to present itself. However, when fear is expressed in this manner, it tends to be something extreme that happened. Whatever it is, it is not something others could readily also pick up. It is personal and impacting, such as the manner of death in a previous life, hence the care homes. It is partly why we have the expression 'Someone just walked over my grave,' this is because, metaphorically through empathic recognition, you have just walked over your own grave.

**The City Road Ghost by Gibson House**

I don't have anything for Gibson as such, but a few years ago I received two independent reports about a figure sitting on one of the benches by the corner of the grounds on the roadside looking onto the mini roundabout. On both occasions, an elderly man was seen sitting on the bench then promptly disappeared. One was from a student who was about to cross City Road from South Street. She said "It was just someone sitting there on the bench, I glanced along the road to see if there was any traffic and when I looked back to cross the road he had gone. I only looked away for a second. There was no time for him to have walked anywhere."

The other report was from a woman working in the town and was driving south along City Road, when nearing the roundabout, she noticed a man sitting on the bench. She waited for traffic to go through the Port before heading off and when she looked to make sure the traffic was clear he had gone. She questioned her mind and wondered if she had seen anything at all, but there was definitely an elderly gentleman sitting on the bench. When she set off she was looking along the road and Argyll Street but there wasn't anyone around. There was a red phone box on the corner at the time but it was empty. Neither were aware at all of the others experience, and like the majority of experiences through this volume, this is the first time they have seen print.

**64B Argyle Street – Makeover Rover**

Ailda Brill has a pet grooming parlor here and herself and the staff have seen a dark figure in the corridor and reflected in a mirror. There have been numerous bouts of poltergeist activity, often preceded by the strong smell of incense. The washroom is always freezing cold which seems to be where the spirit is localised, but in the grooming room things will disappear then reappear in the most unlikely places. One of her ear pieces fell out and despite searching it was nowhere to be seen. It then turned up hanging under the air conditioning unit across the room. She dropped a pair of scissors which turned up behind things on a shelf. There was also another spirit with an oppressive feeling which she did manage to get rid of. The spirit that still remains is neutral and when they tell it to stop it does.

# South Street

## (Shoe Gait)

## East of Holy Trinity Church

**99 South Street – The Criterion**

Run by Steve and Hazel Latto, a vibrant, friendly, and ever welcoming couple. Candlelight and a keen ear for good music add to the congenial atmosphere and ambience of this warm award-winning bar. When anyone asked if the place had any unusual activity, I always responded in a kind of surprised tone that I'd never heard of anything, so this next account was a surprising one, not least because myself and Hazel feature in it.

One evening in 2015, I was sitting along the middle of the bar chatting to Hazel after a tour. There was no one else in the bar apart from us. While we were chatting a long vertical black streak or fleeting shadow, the height of a person, came diagonally from across the public side of the bar and brushed past the right side of Hazel. It came from the left of where I was sitting, and it was quick.

Automatically, Hazel jolted, gave out a yelp, and said, "Oh Richard!" whilst brushing her head with her right hand as if a bee had just flown into her hair. She said, "Something just brushed past my head!" We both saw the shadow and it vanished as it brushed passed her.

It came from the direction of the main entrance door from South Street. The door never opened and there was no wind, draft or accompanying sound. The whole thing lasted no more than a second or two. Quite shaken, she didn't want to close the bar on her own that night.

If it were a person it would have been around 6 feet tall, and that is exactly what it was, a person. I briefly spoke about shadows earlier for 172 South Street. Stasis spirits generally appear as real as you and I. They are as solid as you and I, and unless they defy the laws of physics, you may never know they are not of this realm. If the energy in the locality is weak, they can also appear with a transparency or as a shadow with no distinguishing features. The latter two are not so common, despite their transparency lending to the stereotypical perception of what the majority in the West think a ghost will look like. With a rapid movement we don't see the full girth of the body, hence the shadow appeared very thin. The energies here and at 172 and elsewhere are not apparent enough to formulate a full manifestation, as I mentioned earlier, hence the shadow, and why it can become icy cold, as they are utilising all the energy they can. However, the latter is not a requirement of phenomena, and it is fairly rare to experience by comparison.

To date, that is the only time this has happened in the Criterion and the cold was not an accompaniment. There was nothing immediate to account for who it was. The location in the 1800s was a residence, a library, a shoemakers, a restaurant and a public house.

The following year, something happened of a different nature that may give a clue. A large old clock sits on the wall above the coffee machine at the end of the bar. It isn't original to the premises and appears not to have worked properly for years. It sits there more as an aesthetic feature. The hands were always pointing at 10:30, no doubt marking last orders in days gone by.

Steve, the owner, and Andy, a taxi driver in the town, were both sitting at the far end of the bar near the clock one evening in October 2016. Andy asked how many years it hadn't worked. While Steve contemplated this, there was a loud clang and to their amazement the clock started working again. It was a moment that struck them both as "freaky."

By the sounds of it, the clock was overwound at some point and the clang was the mechanism releasing itself, which, albeit briefly kick-started it back into temporary life. A fair assumption of the noise, and how it started working I would have thought, so nothing unusual on that front. However, it does not explain why it started working the moment they were sitting having a conversation about it.

This was not a dramatic incident, while it could leave a niggling unexplainable residue in the mind, in a grander scheme it could be thought of as an arbitrary occurrence that won't change any lives, but it was certainly coincidental and they did think it as "freaky", and that is the point. That is the bit we miss.

By default, energy and synchronicity are the underlying themes of this volume. the complexities are very subtle and always operate on their own terms.

The connectivity and meaning between paranormal causality and synchronicity are involved and its occurrence operates on the mundane physical through the occult levels of energetic interaction. Lyall Watson published his 1973 international bestselling work *Supernature – The natural history of the supernatural.* As a scientist and rationalist, Watson correctly dispenses with the distinction between the natural and the supernatural and focuses on supernature, 'phenomena that are not wholly paranormal, but which are not classified as natural occurrences according to 'traditional' science.'

It brings into play the inadequacy of terminology through the labels we use to pigeonhole various aspects of phenomena. The tendency is to give paranormal associations an abstract stance, one divorced from the self and one's natural surroundings. When in fact what they represent is seamlessly integrated within the self and throughout reality. The interaction of their energetic dynamics is a constant in our lives with influences coming to us via avenues we will rarely, if ever be aware of.

**Parliament Hall**

GOS p.153, 'The room above Parliament Hall in the northern building is the Long Gallery, which housed part of the library and was mentioned by Theo Lang in 1951:

> 'In an upper hall is an inlaid line crossing the floor diagonally, following the line traditionally stated to have been scratched by James Gregory as Scotland's first meridian line. Gregory, inventor of the reflecting telescope, carried out many of his experiments in this hall. In the recesses behind the bookcases on the north side – where once were windows – a ghost is reputed to have constantly appeared.'[34]

James Gregory was the first Regius Professor of Mathematics at St Andrews. A post he found difficult to fulfil as his mathematical understanding was more advanced than the University were prepared to digest at that time, so he eventually settled in Edinburgh where his work was recognised for what it was, and unlike St Andrews, he was embraced with academic accolades. His workshop, or laboratory, was in the Upper

Parliament Hall. He was also a noted astronomer and in 1673 he created Britain's first meridian line, way before Greenwich.

A brass line runs diagonally across the pavement in South Street outside the front of the building. The line was laid in 2014 as a direct continuation of the meridian line running across the hall above. I have so many from the town on tours who had no idea of its existence until they came on a tour. Some have even walked over it twice a day to and from work, five days a week, and the first of them seeing it was when they came on a tour. That is how aware we are. It could do with a polish!

A short fictional Victorian ghost story was written in 1896 by Mrs Margaret Oliphant, a popular Scottish writer of the 19th century. It concerns the appearance of a ghost in the King James VI Library referred to by Theo Lang in 1951. Her story is a long, somewhat melancholic tale of obsession and unrequited love called *The Library Window – A story of the seen and the unseen.* I reproduced the story in GOS p.208.

The following is an unravelling for the potential identity of the Parliament Hall ghost.

**The University Postman**

Russell Kirk in 1954, relates to us a gruesome piece of local history associated with this quarter:

'One of the most macabre touches in old St. Andrews formerly clung to this gallery. In 1707 the University porter hanged himself from the balustrade of the stairway to the gallery; and the Senatus,[xiii] then still possessed of remarkable powers and being wrathful at this sacrilege, resolved that the suicide should hang in perpetuity "and be forever without a name." The wretched man's bones, suspended in a case above the stairway, languished after the fashion of Mahomet's coffin[xiv]

---

xiii A senatus is Latin for a chamber or parliament.

xiv Mahomet's coffin refers to a legend where Muhammad's coffin was suspended in mid-air by load stones from the ceiling of his tomb.

until 1940, when they were given decent burial. He may or may not haunt this area."[35]

Kirk in 1954 was the first in recent times to give mention to a member of University staff hanging himself in 1707. If Kirk is correct it was from the balustrade of the stairway to the gallery which is through the far right windows in the photo of Parliament Hall.

There was certainly a suicide, and the balustrade of the stairway appears to have been the location, however, there are a couple of inconsistencies with Kirk's account, he was removed in 1941 not 1940, and being given a 'decent burial' maybe a little premature which will become apparent later.

True to their word, the identity of the suicide was never [directly] disclosed, and any initial suggestion would have been erased.

The Senatus had paid for his body to be taken to Dundee where it was dissected, turned into a skeleton and a case commissioned to house it. The display then hung in view down the central column of the stairway to the library. There is a small circular recess in the ceiling directly above the central area of the gallery where it is possible a housing with a hook was attached for the case to be suspended.

**David Murray**

In GOS 2013, I give mention to Dr Norman Reid, Keeper of Manuscripts and Muniments and Head of Special Collections at the University (Honorary Research Fellow, School of History, St Andrews) who wrote an article about this for the 13th edition of the University Staff Magazine *The StAndard* in March 2008. Titled 'The Skeleton of St Mary's' the article is now online[36] and is well worth a read as it gives a detailed insight into the same incident related briefly by Kirk. He gives the name of one David Murray who became the University Messenger (postman) in 1704.

Hanging him in perpetuity where he hung himself with the caveat that he would, as Kirk put it, 'be forever without a name' could not have been more damning. They were in a frenzy over his actions. The church never understood suicide, they couldn't work out why anyone would go against God. It was a mortal sin. Aquinas believed suicide took away God's control. For these, and a whole host of other theological reasons, there are periods in time where suicides were not given Christian burials.

Suicides were classed as criminals, and in being treated as such they would often be buried at crossroads. There was a fear that both could haunt the living, so being buried at a crossroads confused them. In not knowing which direction to take, their spirits could not then roam freely and haunt the living. Being a Christian ideal, it inevitably brings into play the traditions and superstitions relating to the Devil. As a mortal sin, suicide was turning your back on God, thus favouring the Devil in becoming one of his consorts.

Reid says 'workmen were commissioned to make a case for the skeleton'[37], so there was a degree of elaboration. It could have been made of wood, glass or both to allow the unfortunate dissected soul to be viewed. I would wager a wooden framed glass display case, otherwise there would be no reason to even have a skeleton inside, no one would be any the wiser.

For all their ingenuity, time and expense, their elaboration wasn't just to satiate their own anger at what he had done, this was an example of a suicide, this was a deterrent, lest others dare attempt the same, which adds an interesting twist. Why would they go to so much trouble and elaboration for a suicide at that time? It was surely not the first unfortunate to have committed this act on their watch in nearly 300 years?

While all this was taking place, something else was happening in this building. A piece written for a University webpage titled '400 years of the King James Library'[38] records: 'From about 1700, a collection of what were then termed 'curiosities' – items of interest to the curious mind – was gradually accumulated in the University Library. These included geological and zoological specimens. There were also artefacts illustrating different human cultures, collected from the various continents. Materials ranged from baskets and gourds, shoes and jewellery, to musical instruments, weapons and religious pieces.' There was also a growing anatomy and pathology collection.

In essence, the timing of the suicide fitted with the influx of exhibits and curios being drawn to this building from different quarters of the world. As a backdrop, this is what perhaps gave them the idea to fashion the case for its unfortunate occupant, as there would have been quite an industry here at this time with workmen fashioning cases for the newly arrived exhibits.

Ironically, it would easily become swamped as just another curio amid the mountain of exhibits and historical artefacts to be found at every turn. For all the great lengths the University went in carefully preparing the body ready for display, memories fade pretty quickly, and with a high turnover of students the impact could soon lose the potency of its cause.

I always thought there might be a photo of him hanging in the case down the stair. After all, St Andrews was one of the early pioneers of photography, but it is a fact that we don't tend to take photos of things we take for granted, and he had hung there for so long he was almost becoming part of the fabric of the building.

I have never found a photo of him hanging in the case, nor a reference to one existing, but a photo had been taken of an inscription that was written in 1714 by the surgeon who originally fashioned his bones. Reid mentions the inscription was then attached to the case housing the corpse. The following is the inscription on the case from Reid's article:

*'You behold the remains of an unfortunate and infamous man, once the Messenger of this University of St Andrews and thereafter never to be named for all time to come: incensed at his monstrous action, in that he*

*laid wicked hands upon himself and sought death by hanging, the sacred University, desiring to obtain the greatest advantage from one who had so criminally destroyed himself, resolved, first that his corpse should be publicly submitted to the dissecting knife, then that his bones should be articulated into a skeleton, on the 25 January in the year 1707 of the Christian Era; employing for that purpose the zealous services of one who at that time was Pharmacological-Surgeon and Botanist of the Dundee Society but now is a Doctor of Medicine of the Royal Society, Patrick Blair.*'[39]

Losing its meaning over time and becoming just another curio amid the accumulation of artefacts would give a plausible reason for a note to be written and placed on the case seven years after he was first hung on the stair. It would remind people of why he was there. However, unless scrutiny were paid to this small inscription, few would still have any idea. Without reading it, they could easily suppose it to be a descriptive note about articulation and think nothing more of it.

Reid mentions 'He was still there in 1889 when an article about the incident was published in The University News Sheet, (although by then he had been placed in a cupboard, rather than in full view)... By 1941, the box [as Reid describes it, quoting I think from an earlier source] and skeleton were in the loft above the top of the staircase on which the poor man reportedly had ended his days. It was removed on the instruction of the University librarian [George H. Bushnell] and Mr J. B. Salmond, a member of the University Court. The skeleton was passed to the Professor of Anatomy, who (having first studied the method of articulation used in the early eighteenth century) arranged for the proper disposal of the bones.' [40]

The professor was based in the Bute Medical Building, and by using the word 'disposal' rather than 'burial' as suggested by Kirk, points more to the method of his 'proper disposal' being by the furnace than in the ground as could be assumed, and which Kirk had presumed, and which they had in the Bute for such purposes.

The connection between the suicide and David Murray is that he was the messenger from 1704, and the suicide was the messenger taken to Dundee in 1707 to appease the wrath of the incensed Senatus. Presuming it was Murray who committed suicide in 1707 from the balustrade of the stairway, and there is no reason to believe it wasn't given the time period, why was suicide his chosen option? And equally, why do it on University property? There were and are far easier methods, throwing yourself over the cliffs for example being one of the easiest ways in St Andrews, or swimming out to sea. Doing it where he did was certainly a statement, one pointing more to a disgruntlement with the University.

Nothing is known about Murray, including the social implications surrounding his death. Norman Reid gives details of no less than five finding their role as messenger short lived in the space of only a few decades. Murray a suicide, the rest dismissed through various misdemeanours including drunkenness and embezzlement. It certainly seemed to be a role given generously to the unreliable and untrustworthy, and there is no reason to suppose this was a pattern that would skip Murray. The note on the case states 'infamous man'.

This is conjectural, but given the pattern of those the University employed for the role of messenger around this period, if he too were dismissed on similar grounds, it could give a contributing reason for his committing suicide. Losing a job can cause shockwaves in directions only they will be aware of. The location of his final act may have been his personal retribution for his being dismissed, as he will have been more than aware of the implications of shame a suicide would bring to the University.

Whether my theory is correct or not, the Senatus of 1707 were so affronted, the shame of his act succeeded in completely overwhelming them.

### *The Ghost*

In the last seven years, I would say around thirty students studying within the building have come forward independently on my tours to tell me what they have experienced on the stair leading to the first floor of the King James Library. They also wanted to find out if I know anything about the stair. The reports are always a variation on the same theme, a mix of being watched, an extreme cold, or of something brushing past them when going up or down the stair.

For these occurrences to be present, the ghost on the stair is the spirit of a deceased person. It does appear David Murray was the suicide the Senatus deemed would languish "forever without a name." I would also attribute him as being the ghost referred to by Lang and Kirk. The same stylised by Oliphant in her 1896 fictional story, and the very same ghost experienced by over thirty students independently in recent years alone.

Of the many reasons for the deceased remaining in the physical following death, suicide always ranks as one of the more obvious, being the motivations of a troubled spirit etc.

The stair to the King James Library is the only part of the building where people have experienced something unusual enough to then warrant a mention to myself. None of the students were aware of other people's experiences, so none were aware they all shared the same experience in the same location, and none knew what was hanging down the stair for around 200 years then subsequently hidden in the loft above the stair until 1941. Respectively, David Murray had no idea that following his death he would be taken to Dundee, dissected by one of the finest surgeons of his day, put in a case, and exhibited for the next few centuries down the stairwell where he hung himself. Well, no one would think of that one! It is why he is still here and fits uncomfortably well with the many gruesome, bizarre, and sad episodes St Andrews has experienced in its long and not always so illustrious history.

It is also why I sometimes mention David Murray near the start of my tours. It is the only way I can think of easing people gently into the town!

As an aside to the provenance of the ghost, and as fate should have it, through Norman Reid's research and my tours, many thousands of people from all quarters of the world are now familiar with a name the University in the 18th century went to so much trouble to erase from history – one David Murray.

**Bute Medical Building**

Located at the southern end of St Mary's Quad with a West Burn Lane address, the University through John Patrick Crichton-Stuart, 3rd Marquess of Bute, started construction of the Bute Medical Building in 1897. It was completed in 1899 as the medical school for the University. The Marquess was Rector of the University at the time and his daughter Margaret, attended St Leonards School for Girls in 1890.

Monday, 22 June 2015

Hi Richard

I was on your tour at 7:30 pm yesterday and I would like to give you more information about my sighting in the Bute Building. First, I would like to say we all enjoyed the tour, I've only ever been on one other ghost tour in the Edinburgh vaults and it was full of cheap scares and little history, however yours I really enjoyed and I shall write a review on tripadvisor shortly.

I'd never experienced personally any ghostly activities in St. Andrews or in my life until I started to work and study regularly in the Bute Building. Last January I left my books in the C21 lab [geoscience] and went to get them at around 4:30 pm before it closed. I know the lab is quite old because there is an old picture of it in the Bell Pettigrew Museum in the Bute building on the first floor where the telescope exhibition is. I can't quite remember what it said about the room but I can go and check when I have time. It was dark so I turned on the lights and no one was there, I went to collect my books off the bench at the far side of the room and when I turned around towards the glass cabinets I saw my full reflection and half of a reflection of a bald man in his late 30s early 40s in an off pink shirt standing behind me, it felt like a while but it only must have been a second before I turned around and no one was there. I didn't feel threatened, partly because I didn't quite believe it. But I walked out and didn't experience anything and have never been alone in the lab since until I started to work in the Bute building regularly as an intern where I work today. The lab I work in, a different lab to C21, is newly refurbished so I'm not sure what it was before. I've never seen anything but a lot of things go missing or are transferred across the room when you're out. This is only when a couple of people are in the lab and you also need a key card to access the lab.

I asked my supervisor if she experienced anything and she said the same. It mostly happens when she is alone and passes it off as moving things by accident etc. She also says sometimes the motion sensor lights come on when she is at the other side of the lab or in the room next door (refer also to p.350). I also work on my own in the lab in the morning and I feel uncomfortable like something is watching me or something is there with me and I see quick movements in the corner of my eye reflected in the many fume cupboards. But I must admit I mostly pass these things off as me being tired.

Sorry for the long email and thanks for the tour,
Elizabeth Pinder

My reply, 23rd July 2015

Hi Elizabeth,
I always knew there had to be something in that building. With the mainstay of phenomena being so subtle, most don't immediately associate it as being paranormal in origin so the reaction is usually to try and dismiss it as the imagination, even though to tentatively question an experience is to know it is not. We only question ourselves in those environments where these things are occurring. It is normal to question, and it is often only when it emerges that others have experienced the same that the validation process begins. Not everywhere is haunted which holds its own testimony, and seeing things out the corner of the eye is also a fairly common feature. I used to work in the small cottage to the left of the University building in North Street that used to be the Crawford Arts Centre, to the left of the walkway to the library. I used to see a small girl in the corner of my eye flitting across the walls. The complex used to be St Katharines junior school for girls [1894]. Part of St Leonards School.

Many thanks and kind regards
Richard

Seeing half a person anywhere else would be a suitably disturbing sight, not to mention odd, but knowing the purpose the Bute has served it makes sense, and gives away the nature of the phenomenon. What Elizabeth saw was an impression rather than the spirit of a deceased person.

There are a few qualifications for this. Unlike horror fiction, and by way of example, if the spirit of a person having been in a fatal accident is viewed they will look as they were before the accident took place, whereas with impressions, the person will be seen as they were during or following the accident itself. What you are observing is a snapshot in time of the moment it happened. For this instance, we know dissection is commonplace at the Bute, so for it to appear in this manner, it is the impression of a cadaver in one of its phases in death having been cut in half in the Bute. But why would it appear here?

On speaking with someone else connected to the Bute, they said there is half a man's head in a case fitting the same description. Elizabeth could not have been aware of this otherwise she would have mentioned about there being one in the building, and would certainly have known if it were in a case in the room where she was working.

The man was only seen long enough for it to register before it disappeared and crucially she thought it was standing behind her. Her observation would figure if the exhibit had been originally housed in this case and was moved when the room changed purpose to its new location. It would appear the impression she saw was an energetic imprint from when it was in that case. A bit like the afterimage on a computer screen, which her mind in its cognitive way took as being the reflection in the glass of half a man standing behind her. Her mind was filling in the gaps, rather than being behind her, she couldn't see his body because it wasn't present. She said she 'didn't feel threatened' which also points to an impression rather than a spirit. Poltergeist activity in the second, newly refurbished lab she works in is caused by the spirit of a deceased person. Perhaps the refurbishment revitalised the spirit for the disturbances to happen. As I say often, they don't like change.

Elizabeth's experiences lift the lid slightly on the activity of a building that has been the keeper of secrets since it opened its doors in 1899. There will be a lot more here, both historical and current. To the extent that it would surprise me if any having worked in that building have not had at least one experience they are unable to account for, and in over 100 years of operation, a great many people both living and deceased have passed through its doors.

In the 1980s I used to spend a lot of time drawing exhibits in the Bell Pettigrew Museum in the Bute for exhibitions. There were moments where I had a feeling of not being alone, or of being watched despite knowing I was the only one in there. In my peripheral vison there was also the occasional fleeting movement of something, but who or more the point what it was is not something I could ascertain as I was in the company of literally thousands of taxidermied animals!

**Psychology Building – St Mary's Quad**
Elizabeth Pinder also experienced something brushing past her a couple of times in the Psychology building, situated on the left side of St Mary's Quad when entering from South Street.

### West Burn Lane

Formerly West Burn Wynd, Butler's Wynd.

**Report 1a.** (Part of this I relayed near the start of this volume) A gentleman was walking eastwards along South Street past the Town Hall just as the skyline began disappearing amid a thick haar coming in from the sea. Rapidly enveloping everything in his line of sight, his attention was diverted by the sound of someone coming up behind him wearing what he thought were segs on their shoes. They were making a loud noise on the pavement as they walked. Walking faster than he, the footsteps grew louder as the person approached. Then just as he was turning into West Burn Lane, the footsteps continued passed him, but there was nobody accompanying the sound… His report continues:

**Report 1b.**

The haar was thick by now and the street lights had a hazy glow. Whilst walking down West Burn Lane towards Queen's Terrace he heard another sound behind him, this time it was the sound of horses and a carriage. He turned, and as he did so, all sounds stopped as soon as they had started and there were no carriage or horses.[xv]

**Report 2.**

Over the last 12 plus years, Allan Taylor and his wife Sharon I mentioned earlier (p.95, p.228), of West Burn Court Bed and Breakfast, have become quite accustomed to ghosts in their lane. They have not heard the coach and horses but during the winter months at around 11 pm, they have regularly witnessed the shadowy figures of adults and children walking southwards from South Street. They have never seen them walking in the opposite direction. They see them for a few moments then they just disappear.

[xv] Segs protect the soles of shoes and have been around since 1880.

**Report 3.**

Mark Rogerson, the father of a family on a tour August 2020, was a student in St Andrews from 1968 to 1972. He asked me if I had anything for West Burn Lane. He stayed in a house along the lane with a few friends whilst studying here and said his friends had seen a woman a few times walking along the lane who then just disappeared. I asked for a description, unfortunately, he couldn't remember any other details.

**The importance of West Burn Lane**

I spent a long time trying to figure out why there would be phenomena in West Burn Lane, as it is an unassuming lane with no apparent reason for their being a fairly diverse range of ghosts.

In brief, what I found was that there are two lanes sharing the accolade as being the oldest lanes in St Andrews. These are West Burn Lane and Baker Lane diagonally across South Street. This was originally a well-trodden cart track.

There were nine ports or gates (gaits) into the town. One of them stood at the bottom of West Burn Lane controlling general access from the south to the town. Called the West Burn Gait or Port, this was the only route that led directly into the centre of St Andrews until the 19th century, so this lane was well used and had great importance. It was called Butler Wynd and led to the following building across the road in South Street.

**69-71 South Street**

**St John's House – House of the Knights Templar**

Directly opposite the South Street end of West Burn Lane is St John's House. The building was originally a wooden structure built in 1100. Standing in its own grounds, none of the current surrounding buildings existed. In 1160 it was bequeathed to the Knights Hospitallers, the Knights Templar, Knights of St. John as temple land by King Malcolm IV (Mael Coluim IV). This was the same year he authorised the construction of the Cathedral. In 1450 it was replaced with stone and has seen subsequent alterations. The accommodation was on the upper floors with an ornate stair leading to the first floor from South Street. The ground floor was for business.

David Hay Fleming records in a pencil footnote to one of the books in his library that this was the first residence where Mary Queen of Scots stayed when she visited to St Andrews in 1561. She loved St Andrews so much she stayed here for a week as a guest of Sir James Sandilands, a relation and Commander of the Knights in Scotland. Enjoying court favour, Sandilands by her hand in 1563, became the first Lord of Torphichen – the headquarters of the Templar's in Scotland which oversaw the Templar's and the Templar lands.

**c.1846, photo taken by Sir Hugh Lyon Playfair, featuring some of his family**
Image Courtesy of the University of St Andrews Library
ID ALB-8-2-2

In the 19th century, it became residence to the influential Playfair family of St Andrews. It is now the Medieval History Department for the University. With the remarkable history this building has to offer I knew there had to be something lurking within its walls. The first two reports here were given to me completely independently of each other on the same day by students witnessing the same activity:

**The St John's House Poltergeist**

During the summer of 2015, I had a medieval history graduate on a tour. She studied in the building over four years from 2011. During her time here, she had unaccountable experiences in two of its rooms. One of the rooms would become extremely cold. It would happen extremely quickly with no source as to the cause and was accompanied by an overwhelming sense of depression (Group C.). It happened a few times over the years. After the second time she realised the cold and the feelings of depression were connected, whenever the temperature dropped, it gave her time to get out of the room or even the building. She told me the feeling was always one of being overcome with an extreme sense grief and sadness. She spoke of one of the other rooms where they were studying. There was the sound of a heavy thud on the ground. When they looked a book was lying on the ground. This was followed by other books flying off the bookshelves across the room toward them, but they never hit them and they soon got out of the room.

Generally, the only physical harm is from scratches, wheel marks or tooth marks etc., on the body. The rest is psychological, and as I mention elsewhere, they aim to miss!

Following the tour, I was speaking with a few history students in the Whey Pat, who were aware of the tours I do. Independently, one of them described what she has experienced in the building – it was the same. The feelings and the poltergeist activity are related to the same spirit. Nobody has thus far been seen in the building, but they have been seen in the garden.

**St John's Garden Monk**

Just before Christmas 2014, a few students came on a tour. They wanted to know if I knew anything about St John's Garden being haunted. They stayed in a flat on the ground floor next to the gardens at the back of the building. They didn't have access to the gardens but their living room window overlooked the grounds. At around 2 am the night before they came on a tour, they saw a cowled figure in black carrying an old lantern light wandering around the garden that scared them. One of them said the gates were locked and the building was in darkness so nobody would have been in there at that time, and they all described the same form. I was able to tell them it was the ghost of an Augustinian monk.

The gates were always locked at night, so in the garden he was mostly seen during the day before the University had to close the gates for good c. 2015, following what I believe was too much rubbish being left by a customary ignorant few, who, since the advent of the current plague are multiplying.

He has also been seen standing at the gated Market Street entrance on the outside by residents of the flats opposite, and by passers-by walking along the narrow Market Street lane toward the centre of town.

Other than being an Augustinian monk and a history spanning many centuries, it is not possible to be more defined. Whoever the spirit is in the building, it does appear to have been a former resident. Whether the activity within the building has any connection with the monk I do not know.

**42c South Street**
Student flat, top floor

The building itself dates from the early 1500s and has Hepburn's coat of arms on the South Street frontage. It was remodelled in the early 1800s, and by the mid-1800s had been converted to flats which remain its primary function to this day.

A student I had on a tour in February 2017, lived in a student flat down the close near the Byre Theatre. He told me about them all hearing a crashing sound in the night. All the doors in the flat were flung open and all the drawers in the kitchen were the same. There were spontaneous bouts of extreme cold in one of the bedrooms and the electricity board said there was nothing that could make the room so cold. Objects occasionally disappear and reappear in obvious places, and when one of the students came back from the Christmas holidays all the windows were fully open and the heating was on full blast. He doesn't know how long it had been like this but there were no birds in the flat. He contacted the letting agents but none had been around and only the agents and students had keys. The other students were still on holiday and when they heard this they were as dumbfounded as the student discovering the scene.

The ground floor flat at 42a South Street also has its activity. The ghost of a woman stands looking out of the ground floor window by the entrance steps. She was last seen by students occupying the flat in 2015.

**Patterns:**

**An observation – Poltergeist Activity – No half measures**

There are never any half measures with poltergeist activity, it is everything or nothing.

The deceased can affect the physical by utilising the energy in the locality, but they tend to have little control over the energy once set in motion. If something flies across a room it is rare that it will intentionally hit anyone. In the same way, if someone under hypnosis were instructed to kill themselves, they would never do it through hypnosis alone.

In the above report, the central heating in the flat was on full blast, all the windows were fully open and all the drawers were out as far as they could go. This was the same as a flat in Edinburgh I visited back in 2003. The drawers in the kitchen area were open all the way, and all the pots and pans were stacked on top of each other in the middle of the floor (p.575).

Each time they opened the Cancer Research Shop in South Street in the morning, the tap in the toilet through the back was not just on, it was turned on to its maximum causing the floor to flood (p.276).

Mobile phones at the Haunted Tower are always completely switched off, never just put on standby.

The television in a guest room at the New Inn was again not just turned on, the volume was always up as full as it can go. So much so, when the room wasn't being occupied they had to unplug the TV from the wall to stop it happening (refer to GOS). The gas taps for the beer lines in the cellar at the New Inn, the Central, Whistle Binkies in Edinburgh as examples, and many bars and restaurants across the world share the same pattern, they are not just turned halfway off, they are always turned all the way off as a universal characteristic.

Pete Rankin who has a few entries in this book stays in a former morgue in Arbroath. He has had his fair share of experiences over the years in properties he has stayed in. His current residence has the spirit of a man who is always active. When he arrives home the digital radio in the kitchen will switch itself on the moment he enters the house and it will always be on full blast.

**33 South Street**

24th September 2014

Across the road in South Street from the student flats is the famed Jannettas Gelateria. A much-loved family-run business spanning four generations. A lot of students are staying in different residences in different terms. They often come on my tours to tell me about what they are currently experiencing. As I mentioned earlier, it has reached the point where they will tell me what they are experiencing and I will tell them their address. That is how specific they can be. While phenomena tend to share in similar characteristics, there are often qualities unique to that environment, and they rarely have any idea of its history or previous occupants.

When you move into a property you are just inheriting phenomena. They have been here a lot longer than we have.

I had Lauren and three of her flatmates on a tour not long after the start of the new term 24th September, 2014. They were telling me about their current experiences in the flat they were staying in above Jannettas. She was saying they have a presence in the flat, and the fire door, which is large and heavy, would open and slam shut when no one was by it.

They have a patio through the back of the flat enclosed by walls above the kitchen of Jannettas. "Tables, chairs and a plastic street cone were flying around the courtyard. It was windy but not anything dramatic enough to have caused the objects to fly and bang against the walls of the patio area. They are heavy items and it would have needed a hurricane to do that." This is the same phenomenon we have experienced at North Gate (p.128).

They adopted the name Rebecca for the ghost. They never saw it physically, so if it were four males living there, maybe the ghost would be called John or Patrick!

When I spoke of this to a family I had on one of my tours in May 2015, they all pretty much at the same time looked at each other, and turning to me said, "I knew something was wrong with that flat!" They had stayed there for 10 days during the summer two years previously. The property was a holiday flat during the summer and students the rest of the time. They said it was just small things that would happen. Things would go missing or disappear and were never found.

When something disappears, it can be a momentary disappearance and reappearance in another location. The majority tend to reappear between 1 and 3 hours later, but there are occasions where it can be years before an item reappears. Perhaps they should stay here again one summer and see if their belongings reappear, which isn't as farfetched as it sounds. It has never happened where something disappears then say a few years later objects start appearing to those who wouldn't recognise them. It is a quark of poltergeist activity that when objects reappear they always belong to those who discover them. There is always a personal involved, and that is the connection.

I had a large party outside Jannettas late one summer and was talking about the upper flat. There were two girls hanging out the window. They could not hear what I was talking about but eventually realised it was a ghost tour, so they started going, "Woooooooo." I turned to the group and said, what they don't realise, is what I am talking about is behind them! So, the group laughed, I laughed and the girls laughed, but they thought we were laughing for a different reason.

**29c South Street**

On Thursday 6th February, 2020, I had four adults on the 7:30 pm tour. Graham Winter spoke to me about a few experiences at 29c South Street – top floor. He lived there for 8 years from age 5 around 1980. He remembers there were always shadows on the stair and his mother would never go into the room at the top of the stair. They were standing on the landing when sick just appeared in front of them all over the landing floor. It had appeared from nowhere. No one had been sick. There were also other things happening during his family's time there. He remembers his parents talking about things between themselves

every once in a while, but it was too long ago to remember the specifics and they never speak about it.

**Byre Theatre**

The Byre Theatre sits just off South Street along Abbey Street as the main theatre in the town.

An Asian woman came on a tour in 2016 to find out what I knew of the Byre Theatre. She was a cleaner at the Byre and was telling me late at night she sometimes hears music playing. It is quite faint and she can't make out the tune but it always spooks her. She said hearing it is her queue to lock up and get out of the building. She was completely unaware of the following which I reproduce in GOS p.150, from the pages of a book called *Theatre Ghosts* by Roy Harley Lewis, 1988:

.'...Perhaps the most intriguing incident was in the new theatre when the company was working on a change-over late on a Saturday night. Suddenly the familiar mix of scenery and lighting changes was punctuated by the record/tape player which started to play one of Charles Marford's favourite pieces of music. Nan Eagle, the caretaker who is still with the company,[xvi] remembers those startling few seconds vividly- although she cannot recall the title of the music.

The backstage team stopped, transfixed, and when it ended Andrew Cowie,[xvii] the stage manager went over to the player to investigate. On it, he found, not the tape they had heard – but the one that had originally been set-up for the interval earlier – a different piece. Yet years later Nan remains convinced that what they all heard was Marford's favourite – however it was relayed!'[41]

I have never been able to find out what Charles Marford's favourite piece of music was. He was an early actor and co-founder of the Byre along with Alex Paterson. Known as 'Chas' he is also believed to haunt the locality even though the present building is not on the same site as the original. Refer also to The Byre Theatre, GOS p.149, where I have more details of various experiences and a brief history of the Byre.

**South Street/Abbey Street**

A woman on a tour mentioned to me something her father told her. He was a policeman in St Andrews. One evening in 1952 whilst on his beat he saw a man standing at the top of Abbey Street. He was smoking a cigarette and his hand was shaking. He'd left the Byre Theatre and the ghost of a Bishop complete with Mitre had walked past him in all his regalia. I am informed it was in the newspaper of the time, but following extensive searching I have been unable to find it. (Refer also to p.75).

In early 2017, Willie Mcintosh, a mine of information about the residents of St Andrews played host every Thursday night to Eric Flintney, a Jazz drummer who stayed with him after playing open Jazz sessions in the Byre Theatre. Willie was in his

---

[xvi] Nan Eagle performed in some of the plays within the theatre and together with her husband was a caretaker in the Byre Theatre for many years. She passed away in the latter half of the 1980s.

[xvii] Andrew Cowie passed away in 1980

kitchen one-morning making breakfast for himself and Eric. He heard a noise behind him of someone coming into the kitchen and clearing his throat said, "Good morning Eric!" When he turned no one was there, Eric was still upstairs.

Willie also saw a figure in white in the Pends in the 1970s. Refer to HT p.230, and experienced poltergeist activity in Queen Mary's House p.340.

Sadly, Willie passed away in 2019. He loved talking about aspects of St Andrews history and was always so enthusiastic about my research into the underground passageways. I certainly miss him, and miss sharing our enthusiasm for the town over a coffee or a beer.

**24 South Street – The White House**

The white harled burgh house situated on the corner of South Street and Abbey Street dates to the early 17th century. It was restored in 1973 by the Preservation Trust.

In 1904, David Henry was commissioned by a Mrs Stirling to convert 24 South Street into a public house. The building that stood in front of this before Abbey Street was widened had a club. So, it is possible this property then adopted the address.

In the 1980s, students staying here had poltergeist activity. It was localised to the area of the kitchen which would go very cold, and things started disappearing then reappearing at different times. There would also be the sense of a presence. This was felt throughout the building, but it was especially strong in the kitchen where they felt like someone was standing behind them while they were making food.

Their experiences were occurring at the same time as the poltergeist activity I recorded earlier about two fourth-year students in their flat at the other end of South Street p.284 and GOS in full, p.177.

There is a report from a family that stayed there in the late 1960s. The parents would go to bed and sometimes the ghost of a man would appear, standing motionless at the foot of their bed wearing a white nightdress and a white nightcap. He would just be standing there, eyes glaring at them where they lay as if to say, "What are you doing in my bed!"

Until late 2019, the property was owned by Sandy Bremner and his wife who lived there with their wee dog. They did an amazing job on the property over the years, converting the interior between 2008 and 2009 near to what it would have looked like originally. The only area they couldn't convert back to its original was the kitchen as it would have been too small for the amenities!

The experiences continued while they were here and again appeared to be localised to the area of the kitchen with objects disappearing and reappearing. From the early part of 2017, there was also the smell of tobacco and neither of them smoke.

It is such a great property and occupies one of the best locations in St Andrews, not that I am jealous of who stays there you understand, but when Sandy sold it, the three-quarters of a million pound price tag was just out of my price range. It will be interesting to see how the new occupants fare.

**1 South Street, The Roundel**

The Roundel sits as a feature on the corner of the east end of South Street and neighbouring Deans Court at 1 South Street. The building dates to the late 16th, early 17th century. Originally a three-storied angle stair tower it has since been developed. The property is now owned by the University, and is the 'dedicated study centre for research postgraduate students in Divinity.'[42] The upper stair has been removed and now forms an extension of the rooms on each floor.

Gillian Falconer, sadly no longer with us, was an honorary vice-president of the St Andrews Preservation Trust, and a font of knowledge about some fascinating aspects of St Andrews. She had a few paranormal experiences herself (refer also to p.329, p.340) and was a friend of William Linskill's granddaughter, so in my eyes that makes her a bit of a celebrity!

Gillian was first told about some of the legends and traditions in St Andrews from her grandmother, who in turn received the information through her mother, Gillian's great grandmother. So, an unbroken chain to myself from the late $18^{th}$, early $19^{th}$ century. Their origins will be older still.

The legend concerning the Roundel is a skull that used to bounce down the stone stairs.

When I heard this, I began researching the tower and discovered something fascinating about it. At the top of the tower is a balustrade surrounding the level roof. Following the Reformation, the Cathedral precincts became a quarry for the emerging town. Using the stone to replace old wooden structures and build new ones, it was used in this way for over two centuries. This is one of the buildings constructed from the Cathedral stone.

I found the balustrade was constructed from tombs originating in the Cathedral precincts. Around 200 graves were desecrated during the Reformation. The Protestants recycled everything. These were 'tomb balusters' originally supporting large stone horizontal tomb slabs taken from the graves of Canons following the Reformation. Some of the existing tombs in the Cathedral dating from the $18^{th}$ and $19^{th}$ centuries have very similar balusters supporting stone tomb slabs, no doubt either modelled on those at the top of the Roundel, or they are original to the Canons before them. With finding out about the balusters coming from graves, it was like finding the birth of a legend, as it is easy to imagine where the connection with the skull bouncing down the stairs came from.

On Saturday $28^{th}$ December, 2019, I had Karen Kiefer on a tour. She is a Divinity Postgrad at the University and came on the 9 pm tour. At the end of the tour, she told me her office is the first floor of the Roundel. When she leaves each evening, she switches off the light and locks up the office for the night. When entering in the morning the light is on. She knows no one could have been in as she has the keys and everything else is the same.

On several occasions when passing the Roundel later in the evening she has noticed the same, the office light is back on. She unlocks the door and checks but again everything is fine.

The light of her office was on when we were on the tour which I think made her a little uncomfortable. She hasn't noticed anything else happening thus far, and thinks of it as being odd more than anything else, but there is no physical explanation. She mentioned all this to me at the end of the tour then headed back to the Roundel to switch off the light.

I knew a gentleman who lived here many years ago. On a lazy sunny day he would take himself to the top of the Roundel, set up his deckchair and just watch the world go by along South Street and across the Cathedral precincts. A great vantage in a time when the traffic was not as chaotic or as noisy as we are now accustomed to along here.

# *St Leonards School*

## Queen Mary's Haunted House
**The most haunted building in Fife**

Energy Centre 6.

**4 South Street**
Following my researches up to 2013, and my publication of *Ghosts of Fife* (GOF), which remains the only book written exclusively about the paranormal in Fife, I gave the accolade of 'Fife's most haunted building' to Balgonie Castle near Markinch. With at least 14 different ghosts in the vicinity, I wasn't aware of anywhere else in Fife with the same degree of activity, although Earlshall Castle has its fair share. Balgonie is still the most haunted castle and the most haunted inhabited dwelling in Fife, but the most haunted building has switched to

Queen Mary's House/Priorsgate, with at least 18 ghosts plus poltergeist activity. There are also at least 13 further ghosts in the immediate vicinity of Queen Mary's House and St Leonards grounds only yards away, totalling 31 different ghosts plus poltergeist activity in this locality alone.

As an aside, I conducted a survey on my tours through 500 people from across the world as to what they thought was the most haunted building in the world. The most common answer through about 97% was the Tower of London, but that has around 13 ghosts. It gains a lot of coverage and it has some of the most famous and publicised ghosts, but that doesn't translate to the most haunted building. The answer is Glamis Castle in Angus, Scotland. It has been dubbed by a few as, "the most haunted building in Scotland," but it is actually the most haunted building in the world. With over 90 independent ghosts nowhere else comes close. Like many, the occupants are aware there is a lot taking place, but none will be aware of the extent before reading this. I spent a few years concurrently researching the paranormal in Scotland along with that of St Andrews and Fife. It took around six months to correlate everything for Glamis alone. However, in 1999 I moved flats in Edinburgh and had quite a clear out of 'stuff' I had amassed over the years. Over four hundred pages of handwritten manuscript for *Ghosts of Scotland,* complete with all the notes and reports went into the skip by accident. I haven't attempted to rewrite it since.

I cover Queen Mary's House in some detail in GOS and HT, so I don't want to go over too much repetitive ground here, as I have a lot of new information since the release of those publications. I will however give details where necessary as a background to this property, and some of the relevant activity I published in those volumes.

Between 1562 and 1566, Mary Queen of Scots stayed here for a few weeks at a time when she visited the town (first visit

1561 in St John's House for one week). She lived more the life of a bourgeois housewife than a Queen and loved St Andrews.

In 1926, St Leonards Girls School bought the property and after subsequent restoration, the building became known as Queen Mary's Library (so named after Mary Queen of Scots) for the Girls of St Leonards School. The library was opened in 1927 by the Duchess of York, future Queen of George VI and mother of Queen Elizabeth II. She attended St Katharines primary school, part of St Leonards in North Street for a time. Those grounds are now occupied by the University Library and further University buildings and grounds.

For Queen Mary's House, I wrote in GOS: 'The building was or perhaps still is subjected to what may be termed the 'classic haunting.' There have been many ghostly inhabitants and associations with this old house.'

As an update I can confirm the rooms are still subject to what may be termed the 'classic haunting,' and like most locations it is far from frequent but it is all still present. What you will read in the following pages spans many years.

The following short account is from Russsell Kirk's *St Andrews*, 1954, from GOS p.144. I reproduce it here to give a little relevant background to current phenomena together with an update for Kirk's details. 'The library was haunted most disturbingly and girls who sat here to read, in the gloaming, were terribly oppressed by some presence. Sometimes the figure of a little woman in dark clothing was seen scurrying out of the building into the garden, of an evening – seen by various people on various days. All this was vexatious; the Bishop was brought, with bell, book, and candle; now, it appears, Queen Mary's and the adjacent house are undisturbed.'[43] The exorcism succeeded it seems in allaying more the fears of the occupants for a time than the disturbances. An exorcism wouldn't work on anything in this building. It is debatable if it would at all for buildings. They can potentially neutralise the atmosphere of a location, thus ridding the air of any negative energy if the exorcist is worth their salt, but not spirits of the deceased. Exorcisms are more suited to personal possession, and genuine occurrences of these are a lot rarer than horror films, and to a degree, the Catholic church, or your casual exorcist would have us, or them believe. Misattribution is a commonality here.

I found out the exorcism at Queen Mary's House took place in the 1930s. It was conducted to rid the house of its spirits and allay the fears of the occupants, but it took place at the start of the summer holidays when there was nobody in the building. It did allay the disturbances for a month or two, but logically this was only because, being the summer holidays there wasn't anyone in there to experience the phenomena! When they all came back for the start of the new term, the disturbances just carried on as before, and as they have done to this day.

The following is a brief history to give a background to its many ghosts from GOS p.140 – updated: 'A wealth of history is to be found at a three-story mansion located by the Cathedral precincts at 4 South Street. The house was originally built in 1523 for Alan Meldrum, Canon of the Priory and Professor of Theology at the time. The house was built on the site of a fifteenth century house called Smalmonth and excavations have shown that a building has continuously occupied this site since the twelfth century. The eastern section of Prior's Gate was rebuilt in 1783, with the western section at 10 South Street also being built at around the same time.

When Mary Queen of Scots stayed here there was a coach works on the grounds. For her second visit to St Andrews in 1562 (and her first stay in this house), she had her coach repaired here from damage caused by the inadequacy of the roads, or more the point the lack of them at the time. Most of her travels across Scotland with her 30 to 40 strong retinue were on horseback for this reason.

The house has seen many alterations over the years, especially in the seventeenth century when it was called Scrymgeour House, so named after Hugh Scrymgeour, an influential merchant in the town. In GOS I had Scrymgeour as building it in 1523, which I took from the Royal Commission on the Ancient and Historical Monuments of Scotland (RCAHMS), and has been misattributed by others quoting the same source, including Canmore, but as you have just read it was built for Alan Meldrum, Scrymgeour came a century later. Mary Queen of Scots great-grandson Charles II stayed here as a guest of Scrymgeour when he visited St Andrews in 1650 as King of Scotland, just one year after he was proclaimed King of Britain and Ireland in Edinburgh – which was denounced by Cromwell favouring a republic in England. He stayed here for 3 days from the 4th to the 6th July of that year. The name of the house was changed to Queen Mary's House at a later period, not following her first visit as some have suggested.

Around the turn of the twentieth century, it appears the building was rented out to an American woman.

The mid to late sixteenth century stands out in particular as one of the most fascinating, complex and intriguing periods of Scottish, if not international history. This was a period of great turmoil. Following the Reformation in Scotland, Mary Queen of Scots and John Knox took centre stage.

The building houses historic furniture but it is not a museum. This is a functioning building of the school. Mary Queen of Scots' bed chamber is still intact and her bed (quite probably a reproduction) is around 4 feet long. She was 5' 11," the same height as her cousin Elizabeth I. I always thought she must have slept diagonally or on the floor. Surely, they would have a bed large enough to accommodate her?

We see these short beds in stately homes and the small doors and low beams in houses, and we all assume most were not very tall back in the day. Well, they were small, tall and everything in between. The same as today. It is genetically impossible for us to stretch on mass in only a few centuries. This is a logic we never think about. The reason the beds are so small is they slept sitting upright. It was a bad omen to sleep lying down. The only time they saw someone lying down was when they were a corpse. It also helped their bronchiole problems, indigestion and heartburn from the rich food of the time.

The low doors and ceilings were a practical reason to keep the heat in. Only larger properties had large entranceways such as churches and mansions and the likes, as they could generally afford to heat them, so it was also a symbol of wealth, which tended to go hand in hand with power.

# *The QMH Ghosts*

**List of Phenomena at Queen Mary's House**
(G) Ghost, (P) Poltergeist activity

The title of the ghosts comes from the colour of their attire.

| | |
|---|---|
| Main Stair | (**G1**) Presence |
| Main Stair | (**P1**) Feelings of being pushed |
| Chancellor Room | (**G2**) Room transformation, Victorian scene of gentlemen chatting |
| Upper floor room | (**G3**) Figures having a meeting from the 16$^{th}$ century |
| Room in building | (**G4**) Figures of four monks |
| Room in building | (**G5**) A dog by the fireplace & former fireplace |
| Garden | (**G6**) Ghost of a man fitting the description of John Knox |
| Garden | (**G7**) Ghost of a nun |
| Garden | (**G8**) Ghost of a woman wearing a dress (no colour) |
| Garden | (**G9**) Ghost of a small woman in dark clothing |
| Within the building | (**G9**) Woman in dark clothing |

## *Ghosts*

| | |
|---|---|
| Mirror | **(G10)** Woman walking through a mirror |
| Mirror | **(G11)** Man walking through the mirror, identified as James Hepburn |
| Mirror | **(G11)** Man seen in mirror standing behind a pupil, identified as James Hepburn |
| Same room | **(G12)** Ghost of a woman in green dress |
| Within the building | **(G13)** Ghost of woman in a purple dress |
| Within the building | **(G14)** Ghost of woman in a blue dress |
| Within the building | **(G15)** Ghost of a woman in white flitting through the rooms |
| Bedchamber | **(G16)** Mary Queen of Scots in white seated at tapestry |
| Within the building | **(P2)** Poltergeist Activity:<br>Doors slamming, footsteps, something pressing on shoulder and odd feelings |
| Adjoining room | **(P3)** Grandfather clock behaving Strangely |
| Priorsgate | **(G17)** Victorian woman wearing a large purple dress and a purple bonnet |
| Priorsgate | **(P4)** Doors slamming, footsteps, woman's voice, feeling of being touched |
| Priorsgate | **(G18)** Ghost of Lord Darnley? |

### Main Internal Stair

A narrow stone spiral staircase leads up to Queen Mary's chamber and various study rooms on the first floor. The stair has more the feel of a servants back stair than the main access stair to these important rooms. A few have felt a presence on this stair when walking up or down between floors. I was told how a former gym teacher of St Leonards, when walking down the stairs felt something trying to physically push her back up, as if whatever it was, did not want her to leave that floor.

Another woman I had on a tour was a pupil at the school in the 1960s and she experienced the same on more than one occasion.

### The Haunted Chamber – Chancellor Room

Opposite Queen Mary's chamber and up a few more steps to the left is a smallish room that also has that customary 'creepy feeling.' Over the years the room has gained the reputation of being haunted by those studying within this chamber.

Gillian Falconer I introduced earlier, was a pupil at St Leonards during the Second World War and knew of the room being haunted. She enjoyed studying here all the same because of the relative peace and quiet she felt within its walls. She said she didn't think the ghosts would bother her as much as the other pupils and knew she would have the room to herself.

She was walking up the spiral stone stairs one-day when she heard a commotion of male voices coming from the haunted room. This struck her as unusual, not least because this was a girl school. The door to the room was closed. When she opened it, she described the room as being thick with smoke. The room, she said, was full of men from an earlier time (Victorian), standing around chattering between themselves and smoking long white clay pipes. The room also looked different. The books, desks and chairs had all disappeared. She immediately closed the door, when she did, the commotion of their voices stopped. Picking up courage, she tentatively opened the door again; the whole scene, including the smoke had disappeared, leaving the room back to its normal state. It would appear during the Victorian period when the building was a private residence, occupants would have their dinner downstairs then the gentlemen would retire upstairs to this room. This was there after dinner smoking room. What she had experienced was an imprint in time of an earlier age. Hence the disappearance of the furniture.

**The 16th Century Meeting**

One of the janitors of the house quite a few years ago told me a woman visited the library. She was a former pupil and wanted to view one of the books. The member of staff consented and she went upstairs. When the woman entered one of the rooms, there were several people seated around a table. She apologised for interrupting their meeting, left the room and closed the door. On arriving back downstairs the member of staff said, "could you not find the book you were looking for?" She explained that a meeting was taking place in the room and would come back later. This puzzled the member of staff who informed her no such meeting was scheduled, and no one was up there. Somewhat worried, they both went upstairs to check the room. When they entered, the room was empty. It then struck the woman the occupants were wearing what could be considered sixteenth century costumes, and she had apologised to ghosts for interrupting their meeting.

GOS p.146. Two reports recorded by James Wilkie in 1931:

**Monks**

Wilkie Report 1.

'A lady saw in one of the rooms a small table, seated at which were two or three monks, while another stood with his back to the fireplace. She was accustomed to abnormal experiences and after contemplating the scene quietly withdrew.'[44]

**Ghost of a dog**

Wilkie Report 2.

'For many years there was the form of a dog stretched out in front of a fireplace, it seemed to enjoy the heat whether a fire burned or not. An eminent churchman, who saw it, said some words of blessing and the apparition was seen no more.'[45]

With these being published in 1931. If this were the same churchman who performed the exorcism, it would place the exorcism as 1930/1 depending on his publication date.

**Another report of the dog**

As I mentioned, the exorcism didn't work. The dog was last seen in the building in 2015 by a pupil who came on a tour. She had been reading and said it was just for a moment, lying on the floor. This time there was no fire for it to lay in front of. An exorcism can catch the curiosity of a spirit but will do nothing at all for impressions.

**A few Garden Ghosts**

The private walled medieval garden is sited between the house and St Leonards Chapel:

**Garden – Minister**

GOS p.143, 'The garden has the ghostly figure of an old minister dressed in black. The figure has been seen pacing around the grounds between the house and the chapel of St Leonards and is thought to be one of the apparitional sightings of John Knox. He enjoyed walking through the garden and grounds of St Leonard's College when he stayed in The New Inn just nearby on the Pends Lane.'

**Garden – Ghost of a Nun**

HT p.245, The ghost of a nun has been seen walking out of Queen Mary's House into the garden, just behind St Leonards Chapel and the Nuns Walk.

(A lot more about the nun to come in the next section on St Leonards Chapel and Nuns Walk.)

**Garden – Ghost of a Woman**

The ghost of a woman has also been seen wandering around the garden wearing a dress, but no description of colour.

**Garden and house – Black Lady**

GOS p.143: 'The ghostly figure of a little woman in dark clothing has also been seen throughout the building and garden.'

**Mirror**

This following short piece, was also written by James Wilkie in 1931, and is reproduced in GOS p.145:

'A certain old house in the City was on one occasion let for a few months to an American lady who moved out sooner than she would have liked. She was sitting in the drawing room on the first floor looking out upon the garden, when a tall man in a garb seen only in pictures of later Stewart Scotland walked in through a great mirror on the wall. In earlier years the banqueting hall of the mansion comprised the room itself and the apartment adjoining, now separated from it by a partition to which the mirror was affixed.

[I mentioned the American woman earlier. She occupied the property in the early twentieth century. So, according to Wilkie's report, the ghost is the reason she left.]

In the same house the proprietrix had on one occasion a child of about five years old staying with her. They were sitting in the drawing room when the child pointed to the door, trembled and burst into tears. The lady herself could see nothing, but was told in faltering tones "a man was standing there." The girl was too young to give any coherent description of him.'[46]

When I reproduced this in GOS I put it in the section I had written about Queen Mary's House as it seemed to fit here more readily than any other location. My hunch proved correct. Since publishing GOS I have had three independent reports which not only verify the location, they verify the testimony written by Wilkie back in 1931.

A large mirror once stood in the English room on the first floor against the wall adjoining Priorsgate. It has since been moved to a classroom in the main St Leonards building. Without knowing any of the above, it was apparently moved as it was disturbing the pupils too much.

A teacher saw a woman walk across the room and disappear through the mirror, but I have no description of what the figure was wearing.

A pupil walked into the room and a gentleman did the same thing. From her description it fitted that of James Hepburn, 4th Earl of Bothwell, Mary Queen of Scots 3rd husband. This is the figure from later Stewart Scotland recorded by Wilkie that the American woman and girl also saw. A few years later, another pupil walked into the room and when she looked in the mirror, he was standing behind her. The mirror was then moved not long after.

I always thought it was a large mirror above a fireplace. It is actually almost floor to ceiling, about 7 feet wide and 9 or 10 feet tall, with a plain light wooden surround and had been used as a ballerina mirror for a time. Still afraid of the mirror, the school pupils covered it in paper and used it as their quote wall.

When they took the mirror away they realised it was hiding a blocked off door which made sense of the figures passing through. They were walking through the former door. It now has a bookcase against it and the figures are still seen walking through the bookcase. This was originally part of the banqueting hall. The partition with the blocked off door is the wall now separating Queen Mary's House from Priorsgate.

Fil Dearie, a cleaner at the school said there was a "vibe" about the room and especially in the doorway to the room. There is also the feeling that there are people in the room, like they are hiding, poised to spring out for a birthday surprise.

**Purple Lady**
There is also the ghost of a woman wearing a purple dress, flitting through the rooms.

**Blue Lady**
The ghost of a woman has been seen throughout the building wearing a blue dress. No other reports or details. Refer to p.405.

**Green Lady**
In the English room that had the mirror, there is the ghost of a lady wearing a green dress looking out of the eastern window. She is seen by those entering the room then disappears. To date she has never been seen by any passing along South Street, or perhaps she has, but if you were walking along and saw someone looking out of a window you wouldn't think anything of it.

The adjoining building of Priorsgate is living quarters for staff of the school. On a tour a few years ago when the whole building was in darkness, I didn't have time to mention that. I was talking about the woman in the green dress, then I mentioned about the mirror. 30 people were on this tour, they were facing the building and I had my back to the building facing them. As I pointed to speak about Priorsgate, everyone screamed. This was followed by another scream and I didn't know what was happening. A woman in Priorsgate heard my voice and came to the window to close her curtains before she put the light on. Everyone thought it was a ghost! So, I mentioned about the woman appearing at the window in Queen Mary's House, the woman appears at the adjoining window in Priorsgate, everyone screams, she screams because they scream, and I thought I was going to have to call a paramedic for 32 people!

**White Lady**

In GOS p.143 from Wilkie: 'Dressed in white the apparition of Mary Queen of Scots has been seen either seated at her tapestry or flitting around the building 'with noiseless steps.'[47]

These are impressions of her from an earlier time (Group A), they are not her spirit.

The bedchamber of Mary Queen of Scots is where she has been seen seated at her tapestry, which is no longer present in the room. She has also been seen roaming the chamber.

There is also the ghost of a woman who stands just by the Eye of the Needle security entrance inside the Pends entrance wearing a white dress and another with a white or grey dress (p.382).

**The White Queen**

When Mary and her four Maries visited St Andrews, they wore white in mourning for the death of three of her close relations who all died within the space of eighteen months, resulting in her coming back to Scotland from France. These were her father-in-law Henry II (July 1559), her mother Mary of Guise (June 1560), and her husband Francis II (December 1560).

Wearing white, she became known as the 'White Queen.' White was the colour of mourning for the French Queens of the time and was known as deuil blanc (white mourning).

Despite this, it was also her favourite colour, so she wore white to the wedding of her first husband Francis II at the Cathedral of Notre Dame in Paris in 1558 which caused quite a stir.

This was later picked up by Queen Victoria, who wore white to her wedding. It was Victoria's wedding that then started the tradition of the white wedding dress we now have today, but it was Mary Queen of Scots who started the precedent.

Linskill fancied Mary as a prime contender for the White Lady. He never made any mention of any ghosts at St Leonards other than the nun, even though there are at least 31 of them. His association has Mary at the Haunted Tower. He also gave a mention that he thought the White Lady was one of her Maries, so his suspicions switched depending on his train of thought when he wrote his articles. The White Lady of the Haunted Tower is not Mary Queen of Scots, or one of her Maries, and to throw something else into the cart marked 'discarded speculations', the ghost of the nun at St Leonards is also not one of the Maries, which was also a suggestion Linskill proposed at one point.

**Ghost of Mary Queen of Scots**

Andrew Lang said of her: 'Mary Stuart is the fairest and most fascinating of all the historical shadows which haunt St Andrews.' I wholeheartedly agree. She remains one of the most enigmatic figures of any age.

I recorded earlier when Mary Queen of Scots visited in 1561, 'she loved St Andrews so much she stayed here for a week' (St John's House). This building then became her holiday residence generally around September when she was able to come here for her visits. Some of her love for the place came through the association of her parents James V and Mary of Guise who were blessed in the Cathedral. Mary of Guise spent her later years here in her Palace of the New Inn (Novum Hospitium) before fleeing to Edinburgh during the ensuing chaos of Knox's Reformation.

**The Identity of Ghosts**

There is a potential trap I am always mindful of when people ask if I know the identity of the many ghosts here and elsewhere. Patterns of genuine phenomena are shared across the globe, likewise patterns where the mind dupes itself into giving paranormal attributions to physical phenomena. As the mind is prone to distorting reality, the mind is also prone to attributing a ghost to the most famous person who ever set eyes on a locality. This is especially common with old hotels. Of course, this is nonsense. It is a universal trait because we like answers, and it lends an additional air of historical standing to a property. From this it would be easy to think most ghosts are of royalty, nobility or the famous amongst us, when in fact, the majority are of those with no grand associations or titles. Without defined descriptions to uphold these suggestions it can be nothing more than speculation or wishful thinking, and the potential commercial benefits cannot be ruled out which only serve to hamper any reasonable conclusion.

Despite the answers we seek, for the most part we will probably never know the true-identity for most reported ghosts in any location. It is always dependent on the level of detail given, coupled with the circumstances of their behaviour, personal association, and any directly connected historical associations of the locality. I do believe the ghost of the white lady in her chamber is of her. Being seated at her tapestry gives a direct personalisation and historical context, and ties in the ghost wandering the chamber as being the same person. The description of the other female ghosts in and around Queen Mary's House lack the necessary detail to make any positive judgement or conclusion. The house has a long history. To tie in all the female ghosts as being the most famous person having stayed here, would at best be a glamorous notion in the absence of more defined details to make a positive identification.

If I were to attribute any of the other ghosts to her, it would be the ghost of the women wearing a green dress and the ghost wearing a blue dress. While white served the early period of her visits, she would have worn other colours of dresses as her visits progressed. She loved her masque balls, and her retinue would carry at least thirty dresses of varying colours for her as she explored the many quarters of Scotland. Again, all was conveyed on horseback. As a process of elimination, the woman wearing dark clothing is too small to be Mary. The woman with the purple dress could be her, unless she is the same ghost I shall mention for Priorsgate, in which case, again it is not her.

There are so many reports of Mary's ghost being seen around Scotland through at least 20 different locations. Some of these are defined sightings fitting her description. Others are pretty thread bare, with no other association than she stopped to powder her nose en route to another destination. Where it has been established as being Mary, it is a Group A. impression, which is why it is possible for her to be seen in multiple localities.

There is quite a mix of activity at Queen Mary's House. The majority have never acknowledged or looked at any observing them, and they display the same Group A. characteristics. For example, walking through the mirror/bookcase where the door behind has been blocked off, flitting through the rooms, looking out the window or walking into the garden.

There are also the four displays of an overlapping of time in the house: one where a room was transformed with the monks, the Victorian gentlemen in the Chancellor room, the room with the 16th century meeting, and Mary seated at her tapestry. These are all Group A. Then there is the poltergeist activity:

**Poltergeist Activity (Group B.)**

There is at least one spirit lurking around here that puts their hand on people's shoulders, tries to push people up the stairs, and is the source of the presence being felt. There is also the following, firstly from GOS p.143:

'In the late 1980s a workman carrying out minor repairs within the building vowed never to enter again after an incident there. He was working late one night after everyone had left the building and had nothing more to disturb him than the faint sounds of traffic outside. Around 11pm though he was startled by the loud constant banging of doors slamming shut throughout the building and the sounds of footsteps echoing all around. Knowing he was alone in the old building the commotion immediately brought him to his senses and a shiver ran down his spine. He stopped what he was doing and cautiously surveyed the rooms for its source, but found nothing to account for the noises. Somewhat bewildered, he felt the commotion must have been his imagination and decided to resume working. But soon after, the noises started up again in the same manner as before, loud banging and almost equally loud footsteps echoed throughout the building. Becoming very unnerved, he looked around again but still found nothing to account for what he was hearing. On his return a second time to the room where he was working, the furniture within had been left untouched but his tools had now been scattered all over the room. His pots of paint, although in the same places as before, were now standing upside down. This was all too much for the workman who panicked and fled the building – never to return.'

Fil has heard unexplained bangs and a lot of footsteps in QMH and all over the school including the classroom buildings. On one occasion he heard footsteps walking up behind him on the first floor of QMH, there was no one there and they carried on right past him. He and other cleaners have heard curtains being drawn apart then back together again right next to the mainstage.

On the first floor he sometimes has the feeling that something doesn't want him to be there. He heard a growl and half dismissed it as pipes, but he has only heard the sound once – it wasn't pipes.

He thought there may be something along the first floor that is attracted to those unhappy or depressed that feeds off their negativity, but this is unlikely. It is more a case of our trying to make some kind of sense for what we are feeling or experiencing based on what we are familiar with, and that is generally through the genre of the stereotypical horror format.

People don't like to be on the first floor by themselves and it seems to be pretty uniform across the whole floor including that of the neighbouring Priorsgate.

The vaults in QMH houses quite a number of library books but this was once a utility and storage floor. Fil has had no negative feelings there but he has had the smell of tobacco from a pipe, cooking smells, and the smell of old wine like a rich claret. Willie Mcintosh who I mentioned earlier, experienced the phenomena in the building. The gas meter is in the ground floor vaults. He worked for the gas board in St Andrews and said, "It got to the point where the engineers would draw straws to see who was going to go in and read the meter." He heard the deep hollow of footsteps and felt someone else was with him when he was in there on his own.

**The Grandfather Clock**

The room adjoining the English room that had the mirror has a grandfather clock against the wall. There have been occasions where the hands have been seen flying around at great speed. Gillian Falconer saw it happen when she was a pupil here. She couldn't believe what she was seeing. There was nothing to account for it, but it is in direct alignment with the blocked off door at the far side in the English room which was all open plan originally.

**The Sleepover**

I sometimes jokingly mention on my tours: "It is well known Queen Mary's is haunted, so, in the mornings during term time, everyone is dragged kicking and screaming into the library... and that is just the teachers!"

A few years ago, some teachers had a sleepover in Queen Mary's House. The details of that night are sketchy, moderately conflicting and border on the mythical, if not the legendary. It appears they were looking to do it for charity. A worthy cause any could suppose for spending time in Fife's most haunted house through the wee small hours, although they were not aware as to the true extent of the disturbances. As it turns out, none of them lasted the night. Leaving at different times, they all kept their experiences quiet. Outside the obvious placebo effect, which would have been accentuated by the slightest natural creak and groan of a building settling down to rest for the night, there are no shortage of possibilities for what may have happened. In fact, take your pick from any of the above.

Their sleepover that night simply adds another dimension of mystique to a unique and very special Scottish school, set in what amounts to be an idyllic, historic, and very haunted setting.

Steeped in history, the library is part of the functioning school and is not open to the public.

Poltergeist activity here is more sporadic and infrequent by comparison to its visual counterparts. The cause of the activity is possibly the ghost of the woman in the purple dress I intimated earlier, the reasoning for this will become apparent as we now turn our full attention to neighbouring Priorsgate.

# *Priorsgate*

## Once part of Queen Mary's House

Priorsgate at 2 South Street, adjoins Queen Mary's House on the right in the photo. Located just beside the Pends, this is the last eastern dwelling on the south side of South Street. It was shortly after 1783 when the east wing of Queen Mary's House was partly taken down and rebuilt in an L shape as Priorsgate. The rebuilding of this section, complete with vaulted cellars doesn't make it any less haunted. If anything, it served to increase the activity, and it is always the location that carries the general importance, not necessarily the reconfiguration of its structure. As with Queen Mary's House, the ghosts here appear to span a period from the Stewarts to late Victorian.

Between 1888 and 1890 it became one of seven 'houses' for girls at St Leonards. It is now living quarters for some of the teachers and staff of the School, but will soon become apartments for holiday makers. I look forward to hearing of their experiences!

**Report 1.**

A number of years ago, a professor and his family stayed here. One day, the professor heard his son talking to someone. He knew there was no one else in the apartment and went through to his room. He asked who he had been speaking to. His son said, "With my grown-up friend." So, the professor believed he had an imaginary friend.

A while later, the family were invited to a reception at Holyrood Palace in Edinburgh. They were walking along one of the corridors when their son pointed to a painting and said, "That's my friend from home!" It was a portrait of Lord Darnley, Mary Queen of Scots second husband, and he was too young to make any historical connection.

Lord Darnley, was murdered on 10 February, 1567, being one of the greatest unsolved historical crimes it remains one of the great medieval mysteries of our time.

One year following what would be Mary's last visit to St Andrews, a band in the dead of night, seized Darnley's house at the Kirk o' Field[xviii] in Edinburgh. They packed the cellar full of gunpowder and blew it up. The explosion killed some of Darnley's servants, but Darnley was still alive. Narrowly missing death, he fled into the grounds in his night attire just as his house by all accounts completely collapsed. In the ensuing chaos he was captured and duly strangled by unknown assassins in his garden along with his valet. When they were found they were lying on the grass amid an orchard with a chair beside his body. Many believe his murder was in retribution for Darnley murdering David Rizzio in 1566 at Holyrood Palace. Rizzio was Mary Queen of Scots secretary. A heavily pregnant Mary was present at the time of the murder and Rizzio's blood still stains the wooden floor where he was stabbed to death.

James Hepburn and Mary Queen of Scots were implicated in the plot to murder Darnley which was never proven, but

[xviii] The site is now Chambers Street in Edinburgh, in front of the Museum.

Mary's reputation was tainted by the event for the rest of her life, especially as it was believed she was seen playing golf shortly after his murder. Whether true or not, she did marry James Hepburn only three months later, and her reaction to his death was certainly different to that of her first husband Francis I.

I have thus far been unable to find an official record of Darnley visiting St Andrews, and this poses a problem. There are two possibilities here. Either the familiarity in the portrait he saw was through what he was wearing, which means it was someone of that period and not necessarily Darnley. Or this is another instance of a paranormal report emerging before a historical verification, which would not be the first time. Not all the details of their travels were recorded, and not all those that were have survived. However, the boy was in conversation with a spirit which is also somewhat problematic. If Darnley had visited, it must have been a low key event, but why would he still be here? He didn't die here. Of course, an intense emotional incident can hold a spirit as readily as a major physical event like death, but, given the number of dramatic incidents we are aware of in Darnley's complex and short lived life, it just doesn't figure. Hepburn stayed here and has been seen walking through the mirror, but again he didn't die here. Hepburn's ghost is a Group A. impression. The boy was speaking with a Group B. spirit, dressed in similar attire from the Stuart period and whose identity is currently unknown.

**Report 2.**

The Cantley family who resided on the second floor at Priorsgate had children visiting during the summer holidays of 2015, and again in 2016. Ian Cantley, a former porter at the school, was telling me the children were visited by a Victorian woman wearing a large purple dress and a purple bonnet. She sits on the beds and they have a conversation, but they can't hear what they are talking about. There is the ghost in Queen Mary's House also wearing a purple dress I mentioned earlier which is suggestive of they being the same person. Like Queen Mary's House, the sound of footsteps has also been heard, and there is a presence in one of the rooms, which will be one of these spirits.

So, we have two Group B. spirits in Priorsgate. A man from the later Stewart period and a Victorian woman. Could one of these, or both, be the cause of the poltergeist activity in both sections? Of the two walking through the mirror from QMH to Priorsgate, one is Hepburn, the other an unknown woman. Eliminate Hepburn who appears to be a Group A. and we have the woman in the purple dress as the possible cause. It is still happening, so it is a case of waiting for more definitive reports to tie down the source. If it turns out the woman walking through to Priorsgate from QMH is wearing a purple dress, then we have found the source of activity in QMH.

**Report 3.**

James Cantley was telling me there is a particularly heavy door with a good lock that keeps opening by itself, which is perplexing and more annoying than disturbing. The same as there is in the flat above the Central.

**Report 4.**

A janitor staying on first floor heard his front door bang, it then did it again, he jumped up and looked but there was nothing to see. It was occupied for a few years by a family. When they moved in, I knew with a lot of children it would be bedlam. There are ghosts here, but with so much activity from the patter of small feet there would be little scope for phenomena to get a look in. I was speaking with Fil a few years ago and he asked if I knew of anything about the garden of Queen Mary's House. I told him there are at least three ghosts. The ghost of John Knox, a nun and another woman. He said, some evenings when the children go to their beds, they look out the bedroom window and a woman is wandering around the private garden.

I hadn't thought about something so simple but people never liked staying there.

**Report 5.**

Fil Dearie, lived in the ground floor flat of Priorsgate. Originally this was one large space before creating false partition walls for a flat.

Like QMH, he mentioned the banging of doors that are already closed. He heard the same coming from the first floor after the family moved out and things would go missing, which they also do on the first floor. He would wake up at 4am or 5am after hearing someone speaking or moving about in his flat and thought he was dreaming. Until one occasion when someone was holding his wrist and stroking his arm with long finger nails - he then realised he hadn't been dreaming. One night when he went to bed a woman started talking to him. The voice was right next to him but it was too dark to see anything and he couldn't feel any breath, that is how close she was. He didn't take in anything she was saying as he jumped out of bed and in the pitch dark, scrabbled around the room for the light switch and the door. All the while she was still talking to him. Disoriented and panicked she then gave a long sigh when he found the door and ran out of the room. He actually ran clean out of the building in terror and said to himself, "What was that?" He kept repeating, "What do I do? What do I do? Ten minutes later when he collected his thoughts he cautiously went back in and slept on the couch. He didn't sleep in the bedroom again for two weeks, and when he did it was always with a wary reluctance. He had no sense of any threat or harm which again is in-keeping. It seemed more as though she just wanted to communicate. Fil thought it was a woman who died in that bedroom in more recent times, but associated experiences were taking place long before then. I believe it is the Victorian woman with the purple dress who was speaking with the kids on the second floor. The patterns are too similar.

# *Further St Leonards Ghosts*

Along with the phenomena of Queen Mary's House, Priorsgate and garden, there are two ghosts and poltergeist activity at the side security gate to the Pends Hall next to Priorsgate (p.379). Then in the immediate vicinity within St Leonards School and grounds there are the following ghosts with accompanying reports through the next few pages.

1. Motion sensors activating the classroom lights in the main classroom building

2. Art department (was science department), voice of young girl saying "excuse me sir can you help me please?"

3. Outside the IT dept, east wing of school – horrible 'historical' odour described as rotting corpses

4. Ghost of a girl in front of the garden gates

5. Ghost of a girl by the chapel entrance

6. Ghost of a woman and a girl at the corner of the Chapel (2 reports)

7. Ghost of a nun by the tree opposite the chapel

8. Ghost of a nun at the chapel (3 reports)

9. Knocking noise from within the chapel

10. Ghost of a nun in the Nun's Walk (4 reports)

11. Ghost of a girl in the Nun's Walk (12 reports)

12. Monk seen standing at the Pends Lane entrance to St Rule dormitory (2 reports)

**The Foundation of St Leonards Grounds**

The grounds of St Leonards have a deep-rooted history. This is the site of the former Augustinian Priory Precincts of the Cathedral, with vast numbers of pilgrims over the centuries staying in the Guest Hall on the site of the current school dormitories. The hall was said to have held up to 5000 at its peak (refer to p.376).

Ronald Cant wrote: 'St Leonards College was founded in 1512 on the site of a former hospital[xix], originally intended for pilgrims, and later housing elderly women.'[48]

By the early sixteenth century, pilgrims were not now arriving in the same numbers the previous centuries had enjoyed. With diminishing funds, the college was formed on the priory grounds and run with very strict disciplines and suitably harsh conditions.

Following the Reformation, there was little reason for any to venture here. Unlike its former pilgrimage days as a major destination for the Cult of St Andrew, it was now completely off the beaten track. With religious and political turmoil, many uprooted and left. The University were struggling to recruit new students, funds were drying up and the town was broke (GOS pp.91-98). By 1697/8, everything had deteriorated to such a degree, a consideration was made to relocate the University to Perth.

One of the inevitable concessions with the University came in 1747 when St Leonards College amalgamated with St Salvator's College, becoming the United College of St Salvator and St Leonard in North Street, leaving the St Leonards site and Chapel abandoned.

St Andrews remains off the beaten track, so uniquely, unless you are lost, most arriving here, are here for what St Andrews has to offer, even if it is not their final-destination.

---

[xix] Hospital – a medieval hostel providing hospitality as its main function, and it was free.

# *St Leonards Ghosts*

**The Foundation of St Leonards School**

In GOS p.118, I record the school as opening here in 1888, so my apologies for rippling the waves of time! Founded in 1877 as St Andrews School for Girls Company or St Andrews School for Girls Co. Limited, they leased a building at the foot of Queen's Garden's (now St Regulus Hall of Residence, p.474).

Expanding rapidly, they adopted the former college in 1882, and opened in 1883, changing its name to St Leonards School for Girls. They started admitting boys in 1999.

With ties to St Andrews University from its initial founding, this is one of the finest private schools in the world.

We have HRH Queen Elizabeth, the Queen Mother attending primary school here for a time, and Queen Mary's House with its additional royal connections through Mary Queen of Scots, a very young future James VI, and her great-grandson Charles II having stayed within its walls.

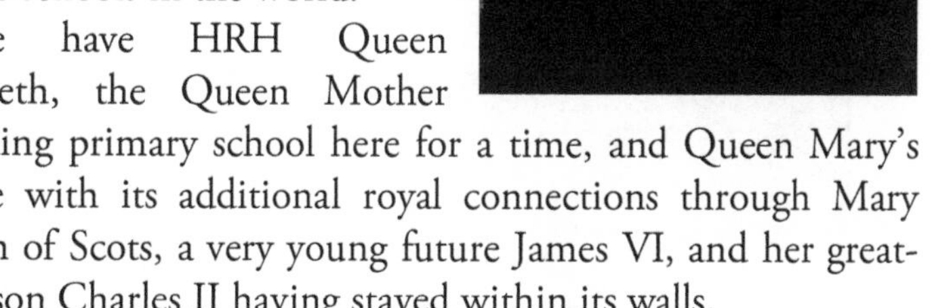

With such an extraordinary history, it is not surprising there are ghosts at St Leonards. As I mentioned in the introduction for Queen Mary's House, at the last count there are 31 ghosts plus poltergeist activity, but that is not all of them. There are more in the dormitories and a lot more in the surrounding area.

**Motion sensors in the classroom building**

Ian Cantley was telling me every night he checks the school building before locking up for the night. He does a sweep of the classrooms for any stray teachers falling asleep doing the marking, then locks up. There are motion sensors through the building so the lights come on when anyone enters. Once Ian has checked the building and locked up, he can be walking along the grounds by the classrooms and one by one the lights on the ground floor rooms come on. Someone has activated the sensors and is following him from the inside. (The same as at the Bute.) He hasn't seen anything on his rounds but as with my tours, I know he is often being watched.

**St Leonards Chapel**

David Henry believed the chapel was built in 1413[49]' (HT p.243), just after Holy Trinity Church was built in South Street, and the same year a school for higher studies (1410) based here, became the University of St Andrews. It stands on the site of chapel and Céilí Dé Hospitium built c.1112. This is the last part of the St Leonard's complex still owned by the University. The roof of the chapel was removed in the 1750s following St Leonards College merger with St Salvator's College in 1747. It wasn't long before the walls then started crumbling.

**Drawing by John Oliphant, 1761.** Image courtesy of the University of St Andrews Libraries and Museums, ID: OLI-15

The drawing is looking north. The current space between the chapel and school is where the bell tower and part of the building once stood. Samuel Johnson in 1773 wrote that it had been converted into a kind of greenhouse. By then the bell tower on its western side had also gone. This is only some 12 years after Oliphant's drawing.

**Victorian drawing of St Leonards Chapel in ruins.**
David Hay Fleming, St Andrews Standard Guide, 1881

The University started tentative reconstruction of the chapel in 1853. David Henry 'was commissioned to make architectural alterations to St Leonards Chapel in 1899. In 1910, although Henry wasn't involved in this aspect of the project, a new roof was put on the Chapel. Work then continued in 1948.

Now the western gable of the chapel, this large space is where the bell tower once stood. The chapel is shared between the University and school and is used all the time for services, events, orchestral, choral and organ practice.

**Ghost of a girl – garden gates next to the chapel entrance**
Two visitors on a tour glimpsed a girl standing by the gate.

**Ghost of a girl by the chapel entrance**
In HT p.244 I wrote: There is 'a small girl standing motionless outside the southwest corner of the chapel.' In 2016 the following occurred:

**Ghost of a woman and a girl at the corner of the chapel**
At 9:30 pm one evening in March 2016, myself and a tour party were standing at the head of the South Street entrance to St Leonards School. It was dark but there was a very bright halogen light on the building wall at the bottom illuminating the lower part of the avenue. While I was talking about the school complex, the silhouette of something appeared by the corner of the chapel down the avenue. It walked, or more the point drifted across the courtyard

to the middle, then to the left back to the chapel. It was about five feet tall and went down to around three and a half feet tall on the right side. We all saw it on the tour barring two people. A conversation soon broke out between everyone and it became apparent the only reason two didn't see what the rest of us did, is they were looking at me rather than down the avenue.

One afternoon three weeks before, a porter and one of the workmen for the school saw a woman and a girl standing by the corner of the chapel, they then completely disappeared in front of them. That made sense of the two different heights of the silhouette shape we saw on the tour. This was the same southwest corner of the chapel where the small girl was seen nearly a year before in 2015.

There was a degree of debate between nineteenth century antiquarians as to whether there was a nunnery here. David Henry was part of the reconstruction project for the chapel, and had an interest in its history. He wrote the following reproduced from HT p.244: 'The conclusion is not unwarranted that the church of 1413, then recently built, was for the old ladies who succeeded the pilgrims – a church or convent chapel being for them a necessity. Other meetings are mentioned as being held in the church, but the Canons who built it, and who administered the affairs of the sisterhood, may very well have had the use of it when they required.'[50] He continues, 'There is a "priest's door" for him into the Church when ministering at the altar, but probably he read the daily services from the so-called passage in the wall behind the altar where there is a sufficiently large opening – in which some grate or screen concealed him, but did not obstruct his voice.'[51]

There was enough of the structure remaining for the University to build it to the standard we see today but they removed the east partition wall mentioned by Henry that created the concealed passage for the priests.

# *Sightings of the Nun of St Leonards*

## Dispelling the Linskill myths

### St Leonards Chapel Ghost

In GOS p.117, my only mention of the ghost of a nun at St Leonards is, 'A small figure in black clothes has been seen either wandering into the chapel or within the chapel itself. It is believed to be the ghost of a nun and is almost certainly part of the inspiration behind William Linskill's story *The Veiled Nun of St Leonards* [reproduced in full GOS from p.344], roaming the nearby approach to the chapel.'

Linskill brought the nun to the attention of a wider arena through this 1911 fictional story. It had an impact greater than he realised, and remains the most famous ghost story in St Andrews. It will be found on the internet when St Andrews and ghosts share the same sentence, but outside Linskill, the information I had up to 2013 was very scant. So far as published material about her is concerned, there was nothing more than a sole reliance on trying to piece together the truth behind

Linksill's fiction. So, I was never sure about her reality for this reason – now I am.

In HT 2015, p.243, I added that, 'she walks into the chapel through the south door, and is seated within the chapel itself.'

I now have a series of further confirmations for these earlier reports. A school teacher at St Leonards saw a nun standing in front of the altar. Another teacher here told me it gets extremely cold in front of the altar, like an icebox for a few seconds with no drafts or open doors. Neither were aware of the ghost, nor Linskill's legend surrounding her at St Leonards.

**Knocking noise from within the chapel**

A woman on a tour in 2019, said she was in the chapel one afternoon a few days before. She was waiting for her choir to arrive when she heard someone knocking – from the inside. Alone in the chapel, she went outside and would not go back in until others arrived.

There have also been a few other sightings of her in the grounds since the publication of GOS and HT, including once by myself and 10 students in 2017 which I record here...

**Ghost of the nun opposite the chapel**

On a 9pm tour at the end of July 2017, I was standing at the South Street entrance to the school with 10 students from the University and was talking about the history of St Leonards.

One student on the tour stopped me while I was talking and pointing down the avenue said, "Someone is standing under the light."

To the right of the large tree against the wall of the buildings under the bright halogen, we all saw the silhouette of a motionless figure. I then carried on talking as we started walking down the avenue towards the school. Everyone was looking at the figure and a few were commenting on it.

When about halfway down, the figure walked left behind the tree. Another student said, "A school pupil has just gone behind the tree. They're going to jump out at us when we get down there." Everyone started laughing and joking, then when we got to the chapel everyone went silent. I thought this unusual, then realised they wanted to sneak up on whoever it was and jump out on them rather than the other way around. When we got to the tree, there was no one behind it. The figure had disappeared. This confused them. They were looking up to see if anyone had climbed the tree and down to see if there was a trapdoor.

As with all experiences paranormal, it is only when the reports are put together that patterns emerge. There are always patterns. We had seen the nun, and there are six locations in this area where she appears. Here, the garden of Queen Mary's House, walking through the side entrance of the chapel, seated in the chapel, and standing at the altar. The last location is in the Nun's Walk, a title adopted through the town following Linskill's story about her. A plaque on the southern wall to the walk even records it as the Nun's Walk, but few in St Andrews realise its actual title is 'St Leonards Church Avenue' which Linskill records twice in his story.

**Sightings of the Nun in the Nun's Walk**

The features Henry mentions were not renovated when it was rebuilt, but it does certify the fact there was a nunnery here and makes sense of why a nun in black is seen in and around the St Leonards chapel precincts and nowhere else around St Andrews. I believe the White Lady was a Céilí Dé Pictish Royal Nun at Kirkheugh, but the Céilí Dé all wore white, not black. There is always a reason and a logic to phenomena, nothing random. There have been mistaken attributions for the nun's appearance elsewhere, including a report in a local paper of a sighting at the harbour, complete with mutilated face. I will state here, what they saw is *not* a nun and a photo they took confirms that. It is quite probable that who they saw was the visiting Augustinian monk I have seen a few times over the years out for a stroll along the Scores to the pier and very much alive!

When asked on a tour recently what the backstory was for the nun, my answer was very simple. There isn't one. We appear to like backstories, which is how Linksill's story became so popular, but unlike Linskill's ghost story, the reality is, there is no lead in, no build-up, no spooky story line in the middle and no crescendo with a gory twist at the end. Narratives of experience rarely feature any of these crowd pleasing fillers – just facts. The scary element surrounding paranormal testimony is when the penny drops and a third party either realises the experience did take place, or conversely, they still dismiss it despite the presented body of independent evidence. Although, in defence of the latter, it is often not the reports themselves that add to this conclusion, more often it is the way it has been presented that plays into the hands of sensationalism, doing its reality no favours in the process.

**The mutilated face - Linskill's fiction**

Sometimes I am asked who she is? Apart from her being a nun and there was a nunnery on the St Leonards chapel site, that is it, and as I say, there is no backstory.

The nun of St Leonards is aware of us, this is her spirit. It also appears to be the same person in five of the six locations where she is seen here. The nun in the gardens may be a Group A. impression. She is customarily illusive, and in-keeping with her former vocation, she is very shy - and she is not mutilated, as will be found shortly through the following reports.

A medium conversant in spirit communication will be able to ascertain a lot more details from her.

**Report 1.**

'A few days before Christmas 2014, I had 18 St Leonards pupils on a tour together with Dan Barlow (p.164), a teacher from the school. After dispelling the fiction of Linskill's story (I don't tend to mention Linskill or his story anymore, unless someone asks), one pupil said she saw the nun two years before in 2012 when she was 15.

She was walking along the avenue one evening when she saw a woman all in black standing next to a tree. She was near what they call the 'Half Moon' Gates leading into the complex from the Pends Lane. The mind will always try to work out the logic of what it is experiencing, so to start with she thought she was in fancy dress, but when she drew near, the woman started merging with the tree. She realised this was the ghostly nun. Terrified, she ran through the gates to the school's reception.

**Report 2.**

In April 2015, one of those on a tour was a girl, also from St Leonards School. She paid little attention to what she experienced until I spoke of the other pupils' experience the year before. That was when she realised she had seen something very similar and was almost in shock at the thought. She said she saw her in 2013 when she was 14. She was walking along the avenue and saw a woman all in black standing in front of the same tree. She thought she was in costume and a ghost tour was taking place, but there no one else around. When nearing her, she seemed to move around the back of the tree.

I asked if she could see her face. She said, yes. I then asked if her face was mutilated. She said no. This is exactly what the 17-year-old had also seen and described one year earlier.

There was no one in costume, and no ghost tours down here at that point and because she didn't defy the laws of physics, she created a comfortable scenario around the situation and thought little of it until the tour. On this occasion, she didn't appear to merge with the tree, but there is little space behind the tree, so it is possible she half merged with the tree as she moved behind it.

Walking behind the tree is exactly what we had seen at the other location July 2017, and is one of the reasons why I believe it to be the same person. To have more than one spirit sharing the same description and characteristics of behaviour in the same location is rare and unlikely, which is why it is possible to be more specific.

**Report 3.**

She was seen again standing by the same tree on the afternoon of Monday 22nd February, 2016, by two St Leonards pupils. They were not together, but they were both walking along the Nuns Walk at the same time. They both saw the Nun for a few seconds before she vanished in front of them by the tree. That caused quite a stir around the school.

**Report 4.**

The 5:30pm Halloween 2020 tour included four PhD students at St Andrews. When I mentioned about the girl seeing the nun in April 2015 and thinking she was in costume, one student, Michela, almost went white and said she was a bit "freaked out." She said, "I think I have seen her!" My mention of her being in costume jogged her memory of what she saw towards the end of 2018 one night in the early hours. She and a friend were walking along the Nun's Walk. They were going to take a quick look at the school with it being so late and no one around, and saw a nun standing by the same tree. She also thought it was someone in costume, but it was so late there was no reason for anyone to be there. Feeling something wasn't right, she became unnerved, and they double backed to the Pends Road. Again, there was no veil and she did not have a mutilated face.

# The Curious Case of the Mysterious Half Moon Girl

12 Experiences

**Introduction**

The archway through from the Nun's Walk to St Leonards School is called the Pend Arch, c.1600, from when this was the entrance to St Leonards College. The black gates of the arch are a new addition by comparison, and are known affectionately by the school as either the Half Moon Gates or the Full Moon Gates, depending perhaps your perspective.

Of all the ghosts at St Leonards, two are particularly active. We have the nun, who is one of the most famous and misunderstood ghosts in St Andrews. With her fame being generated by Linskill, she is the complete apposite to another ghost who I give mention to here, and who shares the same locality as the nun in the Nun's Walk. There are two spirits here and they are both aware of you.

What follows is an ongoing observation of an intriguing series of connected events surrounding the ghost of a young girl.

I have quite a few incidences of her, including connected poltergeist anomalies caused by her in the Nuns Walk. The majority are from 2018-2019, with only one associated experience for 2020, as most of that year was disrupted due to lockdown. I call here the 'Half Moon Girl.'

I always say on my tours, "If you are going to experience something you will," and for the most part all will observe and experience, but there are a few exceptions. Looking in the wrong direction is one; like the tour with two in the group not seeing the woman and child. There are also singular incidents involving one person through physical or emotional contact. Then there are those with a developed awareness who can perceive the generally unseen subtleties residing in the fabric of reality. Most only see what the Half Moon Girl affects here (the poltergeist activity). Whereas those who have this intuitive principle can also see the cause of the phenomena.

Before elaborating on these experiences, a few words on the nature of the latter are required with regards to present context.

**The Intuitive Principle**

Of those professing mediumistic abilities, only a select minority in any age have an awareness developed to a great enough degree where a balanced assessment of the unseen is possible.

Given the emphasis on the physical in the West, all too many make the mistake of believing they have the ability simply because they have an interest in the subject. This reliance is an ideal not a reality. Being psychic is an inherent natural quality, not a subject that can be understood or practiced by reading about it alone. Unfortunately, this is all too often the scenario for those desiring the benefits of mediumship without understanding the organic intricacies of its involvement. The 'ability', to use an inadequate word, is inherent in all from birth in varying degrees, but most choose to ignore it, so the ability soon loses its potential. As a natural manifestation through the self, if they are recognised, they have a chance to develop. They can then blossom through our lives, but they cannot be forced through simply having an interest. Once discovered, or more the point, realised within the self, they need to be nurtured as a quality if they are then to be promoted. Some who have this intuitive ability wish they didn't, and think of it as a curse, while others correctly learn how to switch it off when it arises at inopportune moments. The latter is very important for the preservation of long term sanity as you are not just dealing with one world here, and there are many in the side lines waiting to vie for your attention.

When these requisites are already intuitively developed in a few untainted by the progression of a physical bias, it is because they have retained a self-reliance for its determination. By this I mean they ignored any descent, and learnt how to trust their own thoughts and instincts. Trusting yourself is the key.

Having a state of mind free from the trappings of physical pressures is important to its promotion, so too is a neutral mind untainted by any preconceived ideas, and that is where the problem lies with the majority I spoke of earlier.

These intuitive principles are as natural as breathing for those who employ them, which is an analogy I also used in the first section for the transition to the spiritual state following death. They listen to what comes to them, and they trust their own judgement with a rare impartiality. This is objectivity without prejudice, and manifests through the nature of spirit (the hidden or higher self), and is why the analogy applies here as it does with death: The latter involves the transition to spirit, the former is its conscious employment in the physical.

Those displaying this intuitive principle tend to be realists, very precise and down to earth, with no-frills or pretence. There is no fluffy New Age terminology, and they do not rely on questions to third parties for their answers to be met. Answers that are then more often validated by historical fact and/or further testimony. This shift in perspective to a realist stance is a through 'knowing,' and as such it is not hindered by time, so a future determination can be one of its qualities.

They tend to help police forces and detectives around the world with complex or unsolved crimes. My uncle up in Kintore did this for the Grampian Police based in Aberdeen through dowsing. He was a farmer by Kintore and used his dowsing ability to find missing persons, sometimes resulting in the accurate, but sad circumstance of finding buried bodies in fields. He didn't believe in the paranormal, and never associated what he did with the paranormal, even though dowsing is one of the many aspects under its umbrella. It is only those unable to recognise or manifest these qualities within themselves who give labels so they can dismember them as readily as those who can employ them. It is just another aspect of reality for those involved. There is nothing extraordinary about any of it, or the intuitive principle. It does not follow that reality holds no surprises though. Realty holds its surprises for all, and this is a shared commonality. If anything, there are more surprises for those with the intuitive principle, as they are constantly surprising themselves. It is why the Dali Lama laughs a lot!

I have had tours where those professing such are standing in the Nun's Walk with at least two ghosts looking at them, and with palms flat and arms outstretched they say, "I'm not sure I'm picking up anything." That's when I just switch off and want to finish the tour. The commercial end of spiritual development is generally responsible for these displays. It has a lot to answer for in this regard. For all the mistaken fallacies and misunderstanding they constantly churn out for its reality, all it serves is to play on people's susceptibilities. The commercial arm in this sense rarely does the reality any favours. Nothing can aid unless there is something to aid in the first place, otherwise it is nothing more than an interest or self-deception serving to muddle potential. Any attempt at enforcing a natural ability do the ancient arts and sciences no favours in this regard. I always say those with the awareness are on the inside looking out, and for every one of them, there are hundreds of thousands attempting to look in. As I said earlier, the mistake most make is in believing an interest to be the same as an ability. This more often brings nothing but dark clouds of disillusionment or misguided conclusions for its reality, as the illusions of a fad are fragmented when expectations are not met with the abilities desired.

**Experience 1.** November 2018
An elderly couple from Glasgow were on a tour. From what they were saying as we journeyed around the older quarters of St Andrews, I knew they had more than just a passing interest in the subject of the paranormal. When the tour finished they looked at each other, and the woman said she had seen a young girl on the tour. She said she was standing in the Nuns Walk by the arched entrance to the School. The gentleman nodded in agreement then piped up and said, "She was a small girl, just standing by the pavement." His wife then nodded.

They had not spoken to each other at all during the tour, and they both saw her independently. As it turns out, they didn't want to interrupt the tour and detract from what I was saying, which unfortunately is usually the way.

**Experience 2. Collective:** December 2018 to May 2019
Day or night there is always an atmosphere in the Nun's Walk. Without knowing any of the history of the location, some pick this up more readily than others.

Until June 2019, three orange lights lined the Nuns Walk on its southern side. In December 2018, the middle light near the gates started playing up. Flickering and going off and on, as you would expect from a bulb on its way out. It was seemingly sporadic and it wasn't doing it all the time.

Apart from it evidently being faulty, I thought nothing of it until one particular 9 pm tour. We were in the school grounds and just after walking through the Half Moon gates the light went off, it then came back on and flickered intermittently. As we began walking towards the Pends it stayed on, no more flickering.

It then started doing this on every tour, and was displaying more than the random pattern of a defective bulb. It only did this when we were in this area. I never mentioned anything about it and just carried on monitoring it. Other things were also happening which I shall mention in a moment.

**Experience 3.** April 2019
I had a medium on a tour in April. I wasn't mentioning the girl in the Nun's Walk, I wanted to see if anyone else would notice her, but the light was still doing the same on every tour.

She said, "A young girl from the Nun's Walk came with us on the tour. She's gone back now. She enjoys what I do and likes what I talk about. She's been on your tours before. She was holding my finger all the way round rather than my hand."

I then told her a couple from Glasgow saw her in November. With this being the first report since then, I realised the light started playing up not long after the girl started appearing.

**Experience 4.** April 2019
Another woman in April on a tour said, "I saw a little girl standing on the other side to the nun, her name is Bella. She didn't belong to the school and doesn't think it her place to go into the grounds, so she stands by the entrance and watches the children come and go. The light flickering is the girl letting you know she is there." I had made this connection a while before, so this was a welcome confirmation.

**Experience 5.** April 2019
A few days after this, I had a large group on a tour. A woman gave out a yelp, did a sidestep jerk, and said the whole of her right side has just gone really cold. She was standing at the same

spot where the girl has been seen. Again, I had not mentioned about the girl.

**Experience 6.** April 2019 – The following week.
The following was a synchronistic anomaly. There was a lovely attentive girl with down syndrome on a tour with her grandmother. They were enjoying the tour and the girl obviously felt comfortable in my presence. When we were walking toward St Salvator's she took my finger and held it for part of the tour. That has never happened before in six years of doing the tours to that point, and it struck me, as this was the same as what the Half Moon girl did with the medium around the tour the week before. There is always a connection, in this instance, it was Group C. empathy.

There is the ghost of a small girl and a monk in Mary Kings Close in Edinburgh. I have a few people on tours who have experienced them. A woman on a tour said a small girl (the ghost) was holding her finger all the way around the tour of Mary King's Close.

**Experience 7. Collective:** December 2018 to May 2019
I would watch the light from the distance while we were walking through St Leonards School to the avenue and it would never flicker or go out, only when we were through the gates. The same when we were walking to the Pends side of the entrance to the avenue. At the Pends end of the walk, I would be speaking about the history of the school grounds (the former priory precincts) for five minutes before moving to the main Pends entrance, and again it always just stayed on.

It wasn't long before I started getting a few comments about the light flickering or going off. People thought it was the nun playing tricks as I wasn't mentioning the girl, but I knew the girl was the cause. Others would also be keeping an eye on it – especially those who got a little scared, or the sceptical ones thinking it was just a random faulty bulb issue, but as I say, it only flickered or went out when we were under it.

The incident with the light was happening so often, it got to a point in mid-April where I decided to conduct another private experiment. As we walked through the Half Moon gates I said to everyone, "It is when I start speaking about the paranormal here that light goes off," and as I pointed to the light, it did. It happened at that exact moment and did it every time. Spooking everyone out, I could feel the tone of their tour change at that point to something more tangible and serious. Some would jokingly say, "You must have a gadget in your pocket!" Maybe they thought I was plugged into the mains.

It did this on every tour right through to the middle of May when it was then not dark enough for them to be on while we were there.

To give a bit of perspective for this, I'm not talking about a few tours here. From December to mid-May, with multiple tours most days, I'm talking at about over 200 night time tours – it happened on every tour. From mid-April, with it going off the moment I pointed to it, we are looking at about 60 tours. Sure, the light was faulty, but this was far from random. We would arrive there with a five minute window either way, so it wasn't as though it was happening at precisely the same time for each tour.

Stasis spirits utilise the energy in the locality to make themselves known, which is why it can sometimes get extremely cold, as we have with 172 South Street. Sometimes with puddles of water forming where the moisture has collected. Electronics are generally the first to display odd behaviour through the associative energies inherent in electricity. Mobile phones, lights, and appliances including TV's, vacuum cleaners etc are all easily affected.

New lighting has now been introduced along the Nun's Walk replacing the orange lights. It has also been introduced in other parts of the town, but they are far too intense for their locations and detract from the historical significance of this area. I have no interest in creating atmosphere for the sake of it, but I do like aesthetics, and bright white light is not conducive to the latter. Maybe when they introduced them they didn't read the small print that they were designed as runway landing lights, or were for football stadiums, but being a school, I can see the merits for their safety aspect. It is just a shame the character of the avenue disappears at night when they are on.

**Experience 8.** May 2019

On 16th May, 2019, I had a private tour through a tour operator who informed me it was for 16 Canadian mediums. As it turned out there were two, maybe three mediums, the rest had an interest in the paranormal, barring one who was sceptical and seemed completely out of place to the others. Maybe she got on the wrong tour bus? I don't know how that happened, or if indeed she was enjoying her vacation, as the focus or 'theme' if you like for their whole trip was 'Haunted Scotland.'

I was kind of looking forward to them arriving, hoping they would be able to shed light on some of the phenomena, and fill in some of the gaps of my knowledge about what was taking place. I say kind of looking forward to them arriving, because as you know, there are mediums and there are mediums. The ones worth their salt know when and how you will die. They will never tell you because you really do not want to know. If you did know, it would ruin your life trying to alter your course, and as an understatement, messing with fate is difficult.

As it turned out, one of the Canadian mediums was of some assistance but with all best-laid plans, the tour didn't quite work the way I had hoped. It was such a warm sunny afternoon, perfect conditions in fact for a ghost tour. Whenever someone asks "when is the best time to come on a tour?" I always say "when you can get a tan rather than minus 10," as they appear just as readily during the day as at night. The 35 Americans were a testament to that. Maybe the conditions on this day were a little too perfect, as they all disappeared into Jannettas for ice cream! It reminded me of a particular tour with an elderly coach party, but that is another story.

At the end of the tour, before they all disappeared through the streets of St Andrews like cats spotting distant mice, I had a little time with them to ask what they might have picked up as they went around. There were a few inconsequential thoughts, but one of the mediums became quite serious and told me there was a young girl on the path at the entrance to the school. She was listening to me. She likes company and she is inquisitive. She said she was quite happy and didn't have the money to go to the school so she stands there looking at everyone pass.

Again, I had not mentioned anything about her on the tour and with all the experiences about the girl here, none of it was published anywhere at that time. From what she said it places her to post 1883 when the school arrived here.

I then told them I was hoping one of them would mention her. That others have also spoken about her, and we have witnessed a lot of activity caused by her on tours. She said, "You have the gift of spirit and that attracts them."

Tours do get tangibly 'busy' sometimes. There can be a 'feeling' of there being a lot more people on the tour than there are. It is not a conscious thought. Once in this groove I have to snap myself out of it. When going into the Pends Hall through the Eye of the Needle from the South Street end, I am waiting for everyone to come through, then once they are, I am still waiting for the rest. It can be as though a few spirits have brought their friends along with them.

**Experience 9.** June 2019
I always keep the tour's current, and with there being so much, I switch things about and give different information. I am always conscious of the girl when we are in the avenue, and always monitor to see if any pick anything up about her. On two tours in June they did. A woman on a tour at the same place felt something pressing against her right side. The same as the woman in April, who was shocked when the right side of her body went "icy cold".

**Experience 10.** June 2019
A man on another tour as part of a large group said something just brushed past his hand. He was again standing where the girl stands and I hadn't mentioned her.

**Experience 11.** Miscellaneous incidents – same location
Around the same time the light started playing up – December 2018, other very subtle things also started happening and still do. Individually they were the usual small seemingly inconsequential incidents, but they always attract everyone's attention. She is also attracting my attention, letting me know she is there. A small stick or a bit of bark from the tree will land near me and others. Sometimes a stone will land just by our feet. It is unusual, and there has been the odd remark when it happens. A leaf falling from the tree and landing on my head, or brushing past my cheek makes some laugh. Ordinarily these occurrences are not going to make you think you have just had a paranormal experience, they have to land somewhere right?

There are a number of trees in the avenue and on the tour, it is only by the gates where it happens. It is not random, there is no persistent bird, squirrel or cat living in the tree, there can be no wind and it is always just one leaf, stick or stone. As I say, it has never happened anywhere else. The fact it attracts everyone's attention when it happens and generates the odd comment, especially the leaf or stone, displays that it is out of the ordinary and more 'coincidental'. Remember, this is also happening at the same time the light is flickering or going off, which all adds to the general creepy ambience people feel, so in not knowing about the girl they attribute it to the nun.

**Experience 12.** The latest incident - November 2020.
Since restarting the tours for a few months following the first Covid lockdown, I started mentioning her on most (socially distanced private) tours. I was due to have a short article about her in the press, and this volume was nearing completion, so she was about to be introduced to a far greater public arena.

It was while I was speaking about her on this tour that we all heard a shuffling movement on the gravel. It was by the third tree from the gate on the north side. I glanced across and for the briefest moment saw the light shadow of a small person standing between the tree and the wall. I had seen her! She looks like the girl you may have noticed on the back cover of this volume.

I was the only one facing the tree. The others also reacted and looked round, she disappeared as they turned, so they didn't see her, but on hearing the shuffling movement, they were expecting someone to be standing there (they had sensed someone). The fact there wasn't surprised them. One of them said she felt "odd" and another nodded in agreement.

Many keep one eye over their shoulder when we continue along the avenue to the Pends, and sometimes they feel like they are being watched. Unlike the other anomalies here, the feeling of being watched is also often the nun, as that feeling has been here for years, and while it is her spirit, the nun has never caused poltergeist activity to occur. With the girl's appearance on the scene, there are now two ghosts observing you as you stroll through the Nun's Walk.

**Summing up**

Bella likes to listen to what I have to say. Like any she is inquisitive and likes watching everyone go about their business at St Leonards. Unlike many spirits she isn't tied to a specific location as such, although this is her space. She is like the spirit of the girl at Mary King's Close in Edinburgh who has free reign through the underground streets. The same with Lady Kinkell and the Fairmont Ghosts you will read about later. Energetic associations create a link. At the end of the tour she snaps back to the Nuns Walk in the same way orbs snap to different energetic locations.

I do find it interesting she doesn't think it her place to enter the St Leonards grounds. I suspect she was told not to when alive, and that prevents her from doing so in death, so she is not the same girl that has been seen by the western gable of the chapel. She picks up my tours from the Nun's Walk, so she has only been on the second half of the tour.

Aside group experiences on tours there are also personal experiences here. The girl brushing past, or an icy feeling when they stand close to her. The energies of the girl are subtle, which is why she has only been seen by a few. There are a great many subtleties involved here, and there needs to be a fair amount of energy for someone not as honed in to perceive her. This is a continual unfolding series of complexities. There are many aspects I am still missing about her. I spoke earlier about stasis spirits wanting to attract your attention, to notify they are still present, or for unfinished business especially progressed spirits). It is rarely for anything more dramatic and rarely personal.

With doing thousands of tours over nearly seven years, there was never any suggestion of poltergeist activity, or anybody mentioning Bella before November 2018. There will be a reason, or more poignantly, a trigger as to why she started appearing when she did that she has yet to present.

A problem is people waiting until the end of the tour before they mention anything to me about her, which means I only receive odd snippets of information. Had they notified me during the tour I could have obtained a lot more information, and despite some saying they will email with further details, unfortunately no one does. This is one of several unfolding mysteries. It can and often does take many years for circumstances such as this to unravel. We each have different abilities or gifts as some call them. While I see deeper into the spiritual than many, and am more what would be deemed a mystic, there are mediums worthy of their title who have spirit communication as one of their attributions. Bella is a new spirit in St Andrews and thus far she has been fairly constant in her notifications. Due to Covid-19 there has effectively been a missing year, otherwise, she would be further forward in notifying why she is here, and I would be further forward in knowing. She will present further clues as the chance arises, until then we take our leave of Bella, the Half Moon Girl.

# The Pends Hall

## Energy Centre 5. Part 1.
## **The Wishing Gate Ghosts**
(Pends public entrance)

The following is a brief historical contextual frame to give a perspective as to the main reason why there is so much paranormal activity happening in St Andrews. I have intimated some of this earlier, and a full development of the following forms a constituent part of HoS.

**Pilgrims**

St Andrews was the ecclesiastical seat of the Catholic Church in Scotland, and the Great Cathedral was the largest structure in Scotland for over seven centuries. As a mighty symbol of the power the Roman Church it commanded and emphasised the importance decreed upon the relics it contained. This was a Europe wide centre for the Cult of St Andrew, yet ironically, its ruins are the testament of an even greater power – the people.

The church encouraged pilgrims to visit holy places where the saints could intercede and bestow miracles. Reaching a peak in the fifteenth century, they would visit the sites where relics of the saints were housed, or where miraculous deeds of the saints were performed. Three of the main pilgrimage centres were Rome, Jerusalem and Santiago De Compostela. The scale of the pilgrimages was immense and the logistics difficult to imagine. To give an idea, over 250,000 pilgrims made their way to Compostela in Spain each year to the relics of St James. To put this into perspective, that is one million people every four years, and it continued for hundreds of years.

Pilgrims had been coming to St Andrews (formerly Kilrymont) following the arrival of the relics of St Andrew in the eighth century. They were brought here by Bishop Acca c.736 AD (Skene), a collector of Saints relics formerly based in Hexham. With the mainstay of pilgrims living on the continent, and the relics being on an island, the Roman Church needed something big to further drive pilgrims to these shores. From the early twelfth century, a focused marketing drive by the Roman Church would see a populist version of their arrival that steadily increased the number of pilgrims arriving through the twelfth century.

To gain an idea of the numbers arriving here, it is conceivable 20+ million made it to here over a 400 year period alone. Leighton in his History of Fife of 1840 says, 'previous to the reformation the population... [of St Andrews] has been estimated at from 12,000 to 15,000 persons.' This is comparable to Edinburgh of the time, and far larger than Glasgow. St Andrews, area wise, was considerably smaller by today's standards, so it was a lot more compact, but like today, it had a predominantly transitional residency. Present-day figures for St Andrews are approximately 7,000 residents and 10,000+ transitional students, who are replaced during the core July-September months by over 220,000 visitors alone. Post Reformation was completely different, by 1618 there was believed to be only 2,500 to 3,000 residents in St Andrews![52]

The mainstay of the pilgrims were making their way to the Augustinian priory precincts by the Cathedral and its Guest Hall, where most were looking to stay. Those of wealth stayed in the Palace which could accommodate up to 1,600 people from the 14$^{th}$ century. At its peak, the Guest Hall or hostel, could reputedly hold up to 5000 pilgrims.

'Pends' is a Scots word meaning 'covered archway', the Pends Gatehouse or Hall and dates from the 1380s, superseding an earlier structure. This was the main security gatehouse to the precincts, with horses and carts through the main gate and pedestrians through the side security gate.

Arriving here marked their near completion, and boiled down to a single file check through this narrow security entrance, known locally as 'the Eye of the Needle' for this reason. It was a bottleneck at times with the sheer numbers converging here. This was a tremendous logistical operation and relief would only come once through this entrance in knowing your accommodation for the night was assured. You then also had all the protection the church afforded once within its precincts.

Back then the plagues carried by fleas were in the process of wiping out between 30% to 60% of Europe. Believing the saints could heal them of their illnesses gave additional impetus to travel to sites with saintly associations. The problem was, they were inadvertently spreading the diseases - nothing changes.

For the millions who made it to St Andrews over the centuries, arrival was compounded by potentially millions more who died either en route or while in St Andrews, the elderly and infirm, family and friends among them. After suffering the hardships from wherever they had journeyed, the sheer emotional intensity building up through their converging here over the centuries has left its emotional scares. The energetic intensity is still very apparent.

The significance of this almost unassuming arched entrance was paramount for centuries. This was a centre of human emotion in all its forms. Anything from excitement, euphoria and relief at the near completion of their journey, to apprehension, despair and desperation from those dying, or penniless and injured after being mugged. This was raw emotion, creating a constant hysteria in all its forms over a period of centuries, and there was no shortage of it. There are old traditions here because of this. I was aware of the traditions, and on speaking with Gillian Falconer about the Pends pedestrian arch, she said her great grandmother knew of this as being the 'Wishing Gate.' Like the Roundel, this again places the tradition as far back as the late 18th, early 19th century. This is only around 50 years after the Battle of Culloden. There is no telling how old it might be beyond that time, but there hasn't been a gate on this security entrance for a very long time. Gillian said, "When passing through the gate, some stop in the archway, spin three times and make a wish before heading through." It is only from the South Street side this is done, as you pass from the chaos of the outer world, which remains a constant to this day, to the spiritual haven of the precincts, which also in part remains in situ.

There is an alternative to this tradition, or both could be done one after the other. Inside this archway on the southern wall, about 5 feet up, is a small finger sized hole. Those who know the tradition then put their finger into the hole before moving through to bring them good luck.

The flux of emotional outpouring here, like Compostela, has left an intense energetic residue that does almost overwhelm at times, so it shouldn't surprise there is an abundance of Group C. phenomena here, alongside A. and B. It is also a major reason for there being such a prevalence of activity both here and through St Andrews. With energy imprinting upon the locality like a memory, and emotion conveying a great deal of energy as an energetic residue, once the Cathedral became a quarry, the stone spread throughout the town and along with it went this residual energetic intensity, hence part of the reason for there also being a profusion of Groups A. and C. through the centre of St Andrews.

# The Phenomena

**Rashes**

The following correspondence was to myself from Lisa Fitchett, 19th July 2017.

'Thought you'd like to hear of my experience on Monday... I was in St Andrews the other day and was walking through the Pends. We walked through the wee gateway arch at the end (the one facing the street with Jannetta's on) and all of a sudden I felt like I was walking through a huge barrier of mud from my ankles to mid-calf and had this horrible sense of dread! My friends thought I was mental, going "nope nope nope nope nope" all the way through. It felt like it took me ages to get through it. When I got home my legs were itching and woke up the next day with a terrible rash on my right leg, right where the feeling was. Coming back tomorrow on my own to see if I there's anything else I can experience!'

A rash is a physical side effect of a ghost brushing past, but it is not always apparent, so there were two things occurring here.

For the Group C. feeling I know exactly how she felt walking through the arch. That feeling of walking through mud and the sense of dread is a common feature of nightmares. I experienced the same sensation a few times when I was young in a vivid reoccurring nightmare. It always resulted in being chased by something big like a wild animal. It would start with a building of fear. I would start to run, but the faster I tried to run, the slower I could, and the more dread I felt as whatever it was gained on me. I always woke up the moment it caught up with me, so never saw what it was. When I woke up I knew that what happened next was death. I describe it like trying to run through treacle or quicksand, the faster you try to move the slower you go. The force is not a pleasant experience at all.

I give a scenario for Lisa's experience in the next section on p.403. A clue to what she experienced is in this next experience about the arch from a woman on a tour a couple of years earlier.

**Something brushing past legs**

Sophie McKenna and her family came on a tour in 2015. They sent me an email about a few things that happened to them while they were on tour, and while staying in St Andrews (refer to Abbotsford Place p.492). Again, it is all to do with the attraction a few have for phenomena, like those from Saudi.

Sophie McKenna
Tuesday 4th August 2015
"When we were standing before the eye of the needle I felt something brush against my leg, then again at the Cathedral gates, then again when we were walking towards the haunted tower, I'm wondering if it was possibly the dogs?"

There is a lot taking place here. Five large black dogs are in this quarter. Each are independent of each other. Refer to Black Dogs in the next section.

**Something brushing past the hair**

On another occasion, a woman on a tour was a bit unsettled when something stroked past her hair as we went through the Eye of the Needle.

### Crying of a baby

On one of the tours in April 2017, we all walked through the Eye of the Needle to the back of Queen Mary's House facing South Street. There was no traffic and all was still. One of the ladies on the tour said to me, "Did you hear crying when we came through the archway?"
"Yes" I said, "it was a baby."
With a surprised look she said, "Yes it was!"

We both heard the same thing. It wasn't very loud. We were the first two through the archway and it seems we were the only two on the tour to hear it. I asked Ian Cantley later that night if there was a baby in Priorsgate. This was the only place the sound could have physically come from. I knew a family had moved into the first-floor apartment and they had a lot of children, but I wasn't sure the age of the youngest. He said there are no babies in the building.

There are between the world's moments here and a great many babies passed through here with pilgrims. In passing, as a historical snippet, the only defined historical reference to a baby here is King James VI when he was visiting with his mother Mary Queen of Scots, but any suggestion in that direction would be stretching the bounds of credulity beyond any kind of plausibility. It was just one of many odd moments on tours.

### Cold blast of air

There was another occasion where a man on a tour felt a cold blast of air in his face as we approached the entranceway. It was an afternoon tour in the summer, bright sunshine, very warm and completely still. It was enough for him to remark upon it, and he was puzzled by it for a while after. He said it was the only time something like that had happened to him, and that is important. It would be easy to say these things could happen anywhere, just a freak gust of wind etc. There was no wind, no traffic. It didn't happen anywhere else, it happened at a location where others have also experienced something unusual enough to react in a way uncharacteristic of normal behaviour. The same with the East Scores Path locations I recorded earlier. It was also enough for him to warrant a remark of the same. It is rarely something any have experienced before, and they are always completely unaware of others experiences.

There is nothing random about things happening at certain locations, the random factors are in not knowing when something is going to happen, what aspect of phenomena will happen, and who the recipient/s will be. Again, it is only by putting the reports together these patterns become apparent.

**Woman in white dress**

In HT pp.228-229, I wrote: 'A White Lady was seen in March 2015 at the top of the Pends Lane by a woman who came on one of my tours. She saw her only a couple of weeks before when walking up the Pends toward South Street from the harbour. When she entered the Pends Hall from the south, she saw a woman standing by the South Street arch on the pavement. The woman was wearing a long white dress. As she drew near, the woman walked through the arched entrance to South Street. Her observer was only a couple of seconds behind her and when she went through, the woman had completely vanished.'

**Woman in grey/white dress**

Before the start of a tour an American woman told me when she was young, she was vacationing in St Andrews with her parents, which would place it in the 1970s. While they were playing golf one afternoon, she took herself off to explore St Andrews. When she was walking through the ruin near the Cathedral up from the harbour [Pends Hall], she saw the ghost of a woman wearing a grey or white dress standing by the same entrance. She only saw her for a moment before she vanished. She knew nothing of the history, or that she is not alone in seeing the ghost of a woman at this same location.

**Ghost of John Knox**
**6 locations: Location 1.**

In 2014 I had a book signing in various Waterstone's stores. In St Andrews an elderly lady came in and told me when she was 8 years old she had her photo taken with a friend in the narrow pedestrian entrance of the Pends. When the photo was developed, the figure of a man was seen leaning over them, his long beard hanging down over their shoulders. She believed she still had the photo, saying she thought it was in a Quality Street sweet tin in her attic. Unfortunately, I have not heard from here since that time. Being so close to the Cathedral, she thought it was a monk, but from her description it fits that of John Knox.

Knox was a student at the University of St Andrews, he then went into the priesthood. He was a Catholic priest until 1544 when he switched and became a Protestant. He haunted this locality while he was alive as well as in death.

Halfway down the Pends Lane, a Royal Palace was built in the early sixteenth century called the Novum Hospitium (the New Inn). This was residence to Mary of Guise and James V, Mary Queen of Scots parents. The Palace was demolished very specifically in 1810 because of its ghosts. No one would stay there with its reputation of supernatural disturbances afflicting the building for over three centuries. I write extensively about its 17th century disturbances in GOS from p.102. When the Reformation struck, Mary of Guise fled to Holyrood Palace in Edinburgh and John Knox, being a humble pious man, took the Royal Palace as his residence. He spent a lot of his time in St Andrews and often wandered the grounds of the Palace of the New Inn, and the former priory buildings, including the gardens and grounds of St Leonards College in the former precincts. It was during these peaceful excursions where he would reflect and gain inspiration for his sermons.

**Location 2.**
He has been seen in the private garden of Queen Mary's House.

**Location 3.**
He has been seen standing outside Dean's Court.

**Location 4.**
He was also seen in North Street across from St Salvator's Chapel sometime after 1894. A very detailed description of the incident is in GOS p.41.

**Location 5.**
He has also been seen outside the former Double Decker building, corner of Market Street and Union Street (p.263).

**Location 6.**
There is also a report from the 1960s of a young-looking John Knox standing on the Scores Road area looking across to the Bishop's Palace. While vague, and unlikely, he did join the Protestants in the Palace during their 1546-7 occupation and preached his first sermon from within its walls. It was their subsequent capture by the French in 1547 after they spent over seven hours cannon balling the Palace that saw Knox and the others becoming galley slaves for the next few years.

# *The Pends Ghosts*

## Part 2.
## The Pends Lane

**The Dark Figure – Monk**

I had a group of 15 on a tour. We had just walked up the Pends from the Nuns Walk and were standing in the ruins of the Pends Hall. I was on the road speaking to them about the history of the structure. They were all on the pavement facing me. It was dark and very quiet with no traffic, and we were the only ones in the area. We were all alerted to the sound of someone making a singular scuffing noise on the pavement with their foot. The sound came from the pavement just the other side of the southern entrance archway where we had just come from.

It was unmistakable and we all turned to look at the same time. There was nobody there. One of the gentlemen on the tour said, "Is there a door behind there?" "No," I said, "it is just the wall." Just then we saw a dark figure appear from behind the protrusion of the arch and silently walk away from us down the pavement. There were comments from the group of, "That's impossible!" and, "Who is that?" Nobody had passed us in the Pends Hall from the South Street end, no one was following on from behind, and to be walking down the road there was nowhere they could have come from. We had just come from that direction, no one else was around. This all happened very quickly. The figure got to halfway between us and the Nun's Walk and promptly disappeared. The word dissolved is the only way of putting it.

For the rest of the tour everyone was talking about it and everyone was well confused by it. As I have mentioned a few times that is exactly what happens – every time. It fazes you, time is out of sync, and it always completely conflicts with anything you could have in your mind of what you could have expected, including your reaction. We were all very alert to our surroundings after that. It does sharpen the senses and if any had cobwebs in their mind, I guarantee it suitably blew them away. The tour party was right across the board in terms of age, nationality and vocation, which is another commonality – it doesn't matter who you are. Not everyone comes on a tour for the ghosts, but all were struck by their experience. At the end of the tour I was a bit fazed myself by it. I have experienced a lot of things, and it always catches you unawares. The situations are both unexpected and always just down right odd.

**The Pebble**

Phenomenon can be slight, like the poltergeist activity with the Half Moon Girl, with leaves, small stones, and sticks etc. Yet the potential implications are no less profound than seeing a person simply disappear into thin air in front of you. Globally it is not uncommon, but it can be the easiest to miss.

Hi Richard,

Thanks for the great tour yesterday, we (a group of 4) came along on the 9 pm tour yesterday (03/08/19) and found the tour to be both very interesting and thoroughly enjoyable.

After yesterday's tour, we walked back to Kinkell Braes where we were staying and decided to go via St Leonards school and Nuns Walk to have a look round in the dark. We didn't see or experience anything of note (apart from being a bit on edge following the tour), however, when we headed down the Pends towards the harbor, a small stone pebble was flung towards us as we walked. We were definitely alone on the street and we were sure nobody was in the graveyard area where the stone came from. The sound and feeling of the pebble being flung towards us made 3/4 of us really jump and made us exit the area really hastily! Has this type of activity or similar ever been noted on the pends?

Thanks again for the great tour.
James Drury

James also had an experience on passing Gibson House, p.285.

**The Pends Monks** (More reports in GOS)
Pete Rankin who experienced his mobile shutting down four times at the Haunted Tower, was by the War Memorial at the end of North Street with one of his friends in 1975. They were heading towards the Pends, in front of them was what they perceived to be a tall man wearing a long dark coat walking in the same direction.

**Blocked off doorway in the wall**

As they walked the man went through the ruins of the Pends Hall and walked down the left side of the road where there is no pavement. They didn't think anything unusual as he walked along in front of them. He disappeared from view at the corner opposite the entrances to the St Leonards dormitories. When they reached a spot where they could see around the corner on the Pends Lane they expected to see him in front of them, but he had completely vanished. There was nowhere for him to go.

If he crossed the road to go into the dormitory grounds of St Leonards they would have seen him. Just around the corner in the wall there is a door to the Cathedral precincts which is completely blocked off with stone. It makes sense he was heading through this sealed entrance, but the lower section is now below the level of the road (remodelled by the Victorians). He was on the level of road so this was a spirit who would have been aware of them which is in-keeping with the following:

**The Followers**

I call the monks along here 'followers' as that is generally what they do. When you see them they will follow you, always keeping the same pace, either on the other side of the road or in front of you. They get to a certain point and vanish. It was only a couple of years ago when I realised why that is. The monks were showing the pilgrims to their accommodation, which is why they are walking at the same pace. The only stretch along the Pends Lane where it happens is between the Pends Hall and the entrance to the former Guest Hall where the pilgrims stayed. Hence the stylised cover to this volume.

Important to note: Pete thought it was a black coat. They are all wearing black, they are all Augustinian monks.

**Monk – St Rule dormitory entrance**

The following is a piece I wrote in HT p.252, of something that was seen by St Leonards school pupils from St Rule dormitory. 'Early in 2015 boarding pupils of St Leonards School on looking out of the windows of St Rule dormitory, saw on more than one occasion a fairly tall slim figure standing at the entrance gate on the cobbles by the Pends Lane. Facing the dormitory, the figure is wearing a black robe, a large black hood covering the head and hiding any features. The wraith-like figure then tilts its head back and looks up at them in the window. To their horror, the black hood is empty.

They believe the figure to be a woman, but this is unlikely. We tend to think of monks as being big characters, but this is just a stereotype, the majority would have been slim, as the food was modest and fasting was frequent.'

## The Black Lady and Grey Lady

We have the famed White Lady, but this is the first time any will be aware of a Black Lady and a Grey Lady in the Pends Lane, both again so called for the colour of their attire.

I have four reports from 2014 to 2018 of the same woman in black being seen in this area of the Pends Lane, and three for a woman in grey, 1970s, 2010 and 2016.

**Pends Lane west of the Eastern Cemetery**

Black Lady seen by a man 2014
Black Lady seen by a couple 2014
Black Lady seen by a boy 2016
Black Lady seen by a student 2018
Grey Lady seen by a man 2010
Grey Lady seen by a man 2016
Grey/White Lady seen by a woman 1970s (p.382)

**Black Lady Report 1. 2014**

A man came up to me in the street not long after I started doing the tours to tell me about something he had seen a few days before. He had been keeping an eye out to tell me. One morning earlier in the week, he was walking up the Pends Lane on his way to work from the harbour. He saw a woman in a black dress standing by the high wall just up from the Eastern Cemetery gateway. He looked through the gate into the cemetery on passing, then looked up and she had vanished. He said there was no entrance through the wall where she could have disappeared to.

**Black Lady Report 2. 2014**

Another report was given to me during the summer of 2014 about the ghost of the same woman. It was a couple from Ayrshire on holiday in St Andrews. They were staying at Kinkell Caravan Site and were coming into town for lunch. With it being a nice day they walked down the cliffside path from the caravan park, along by the East Sands, over the harbour bridge and were walking up the Pends Lane into town.

They were the only ones on this stretch of road at the time apart from an elderly woman standing by the wall just past the Eastern Cemetery entrance. They said she would have been around five feet tall may be slightly shorter, wearing a long black dress that went to the ground. They were chatting with each other and when they looked again she had gone. Again, there was nowhere for her to go. They both saw her and didn't think anything odd until she disappeared. So, they came on a tour later that day to tell me what they had seen.

**Black Lady Report 3. 2016**

I had a family on a tour in April 2016. We were standing at the Pends Lane entrance to the Nuns Walk. When I began talking about the history of this stretch of road the young boy said, "I saw a ghost yesterday down there." He pointed down the Pends Lane in the direction of the harbour. He said, "It was an old woman wearing a black dress, standing by the wall, and then she just disappeared." His mother was trying to make light of his words, saying, "He is always saying he can see ghosts!" I replied, "Well no! I have two other unpublished reports of what your son saw yesterday at the same location." That certainly gave them something to think about, and this was the third report of the same woman. As we continued the tour the wee boy mentioned a few other things he has seen in their house. From what he was saying, his encounters follow the same characteristics as those I mention throughout this volume. The family live in a cottage in the borders. I think his parents started getting a little worried as it was dawning on them the things he mentioned to them in the past actually happened.

**Black Lady Report 4. 2018**

This fourth report comes from students on a tour in 2019, talking about experiences of one of their friends at Uni in St Andrews. He was walking down the Pends Lane and saw an old woman in a black dress standing by the wall near the Eastern Cemetery entrance in 2018. He thought there was something unusual about her. Before crossing the road to get a closer look at her, he glanced back along the road to make sure there was no traffic, and on looking back she had gone.

**Summing up the Black Lady**

It is rare for there to be a Hollywood style story accompanying any experience. It is rare for there to be a story at all, more matter of fact circumstantial evidence.

There was nothing outlandish about any of these experiences. Nothing sensationalistic, no one was expecting anything to occur, and characteristically they were very brief. All accounts were in the same location, and they all described the same figure of an elderly woman in a black dress who just disappeared. Also, it was only the student who thought something was out of place, the others didn't think anything unusual until she disappeared. There is no previous history or intimation of this phenomenon at this location before the first experience above in 2014. The most crucial factor, and of great importance, is that none of what you have just read has been published anywhere before now. With there being so many things to talk about on the tours, it is only after the 2016 report I started giving her an occasional mention.

**The Grey Lady**
**Report 1. 2010**

There is also a Grey Lady on the Pends. In HT p.230 I wrote: 'A local man walking down the Pends saw a woman walking up the Pends towards him. As they were approaching each other, she just disappeared. There were no entrances in the wall that she could have gone into. He described her as wearing something like a grey plastic mackintosh, the kind worn in the 1950s, but it was more to the colour and texture of the material than the styling he was referring too.'

**Report 2. 2016**

In 2016, a visitor spoke to me about his experience in the Pends. He was walking down the Pends Lane during the day and saw a woman in a grey coat in the distance walking along the path. He didn't think anything of it. He glanced down at the pavement then back up and she wasn't there. Again, there was nowhere she could have gone.

A characteristic of these reports is them glancing away and on looking back the figure had gone, and if they don't look away, the figure then just vanished in front of them.

There are more reports of Pends Lane ghosts in GOS and HT.

For the experience of the boy above in 2016, and the reaction of his parents; when they tell us about things we should neither discount nor agree for the sake of it. Remember the imagination always needs a trigger, otherwise it is not your imagination at play and being dismissive is for our benefit not theirs. We are very good at focusing on the clutter in our heads to the detriment of everything around us. The older we get the more baggage we have with a million and one things going on in there at any one time. We are always rushing around, always doing things, never stopping even to think, and never enough hours in the day to do everything we think we should be doing. The more worries and pressures this brings, the more stressed we become. Collectively this baggage serves to dull our awareness and, in the process, we miss so much in our surroundings – and we think we are aware! Activity happens around us all the time, we just have too much going on to notice. A scenario for you: You have children (that might come as a surprise!). They are late for school, you are late for an important meeting at work and you have 1% on your mobile so the world is about to disappear. When we are focused on doing something everything else is blotted out. Using the coffee cup again as an example of an object defying the laws of physics and moving from A to B in front of you. You might see it move from A to B but with so much going on it doesn't register in your mind. One of your children also sees it move from A to B and tells you what just happened. You can be dismissive, but remember this, when your child saw that coffee cup move, where was the trigger? We are very dismissive of ourselves, and even more so of others including our children, yet surely there is nothing more important for you? Perhaps if we listened to them with this trigger in mind we would be able to distinguish between what was and what was not their imagination.

Another example is from families on tours. Throughout the tour the parents are constantly being distracted, either they are thinking about everything they need to do after the tour or they are keeping an eye on their kids. By the end of the tour the kids have absorbed everything I have mentioned on the tour, whereas the parents say "there was so much information!" as they only retained bits of it. The point here is they are always completely unaware they were distracting themselves through the entire tour, and I can always see when they are doing it.

# The Doppelganger

Robert Wodrow 1679-1734. A Scottish Historian hands down to us an account posthumously published on his behalf by the Maitland Club in 1842. This is one of the earliest accounts anywhere in the world of a doppelganger and was seen in the former Royal Palace of The New Inn down the Pends:

'Upon a time, when Archbishop Sharpe was at Edinburgh, a member of the Privie Councell, and active in prosecuting criminally some men who had been at Pentland[xx], he wanted a paper which tended to a further clearing of the lybel, which was in his cabinet at St. Andrews; and so dispatches his footman in haste to bring it, giving him both the kye of his closet and cabinet, directing him to the shotle where it lye. The footman came off about ten a – cloak in the afternoon, having run very fast. When he opened the closet door and looked in, he saw the Bishop sitting at a table near the window, as if he had been reading and writing, with his black gown and tippet, his broad hat, just as he had left him at Edinburgh, which did surprise the fellow at first, though he was not much terrified; for being of a hardie frolick temper, or a little hollowed, as we called it, he spake to him myrrily thus, "Ho! My Lord! Well ridden indeed! I am sure I left you at Edinburgh at ten a – cloak, and yet yow are here before me! I wonder that I saw yow not pass by me!" The Bishop looked over his shoulder to him, with a sure and frowning countenance, but spake not a word; so that the footman runs downstairs, and tells the Secretare or Chamberlane, that the Bishop was come home. He would not believe him; he averred he saw him in his closet, and that he was very angry; and desired the Chamberlane to come up stairs; but before they were fully up, they both saw the Bishop

[xx] These were covenanters he was prosecuting.

standing upon the stair – head, stairing upon them with ane angry look, which affrighted them in earnest. Within a little, the footman came up to the closet, and there was nobody there; so he opens the cabinet, and takes out the paper, and comes away in all dispatch to Edinburgh, and was there the next morning, where he meets the Bishop and delivered to him the paper, and told him the former story. Upon which the Bishop, by threats and promises, injoyns him secrecy.'

**The Spectral Coachman and the Postilion in the New Inn**

From GOS pp.108-112: In a letter to the Rev. John Warden, and by him communicated to the Rev. Robert Wodrow in 1718 there is the account of the apparition in the New Inn. I have transcribed a more user friendly version on the left and included the original on the right for reference. My transcribed version is not meant to be definitive; it is more to grasp the detail in the story without being distracted by trying to work out some of the words in the content.

| Transcription | Original |
|---|---|
| "Alloa, 14th January 1718 "Rev. Sir, - I mind some time ago, I had the occasion to speak with you regarding something which happened in that house in St. Andrews where Bishop Ross lodged, which is as follows":- | "Alloa, 14th January 1718 "Rev. Sir, - I mind some time ago, I had the occasion to converse with you anent sume thing which fell out in that house in St. Andrews where Bishop Ross lodged, which is as followeth":- |
| ""Andrew Berrage, my wife's brother, was principle servant at the time to the bishop. He was a young man who was very apt to dispel any thought of apparitions before that time. Andrew Berrage told me and his sister, that there is a chamber in the | ""Andrew Berrage, my wife's brother, principell servant at the time to the bishop, a young man who was verie apt to crush anie surmise of aperitions befor that time. Andrew Berrage told me and his sister, that there is a chamber in that lodging |

lodging which was in possession of the bishop; that neither family nor stranger would lay in that room, because of an old superstition about apparitions frequenting that room. So many strangers arrived one day that all the rooms were taken up with them except that suspected room. My brother-in-law, endeavouring to banish such a Chimera (as he called it) out of the family, decides along with the Paige, a young lad, that they should both stay together in that room; and accordingly started a good fire in the chamber, the bed being near to the middle of the room. My brother-in-law lay down with his face towards the door, the Paige with his back to his, which allowed one to look to one end of the chamber, and the other to the other end of the chamber.

"About the middle of the night came an apparition of a coachman at the entrance of the chamber where my brother-in-law's face was pointing; at the same time, a postilion appears at the other end of the chamber. My brother-in-law and the Paige both being awake, the coachman advances towards

possest then by the bishop; that neither family nor stranger lay in that roome, by reason of ane ould suspition of aperitions that frequented that roome. It fell out, there comes so many strangers one day, that all the other rooms was taken up with the strangers except that suspected roome. My brother-in-law, indevoring too banish such a Himera (as he called it) out of the family, prevails with the paige, a young lad, that both should ly together in that roome; and accordingly set on a good fire in the chamber, the bed being neere to the middle of the roome. My brother-in-law lies down with his face towards the dore, the paige with his back to his, which obliged the one to loke to one end of the chamber, and the other to the other end of the chamber.

"About the middle of the night [comes] ane aperition of the coatchman at the entrie of the chamber where my brother's face was pointing; at the same time, the postiline appears at the other end of the chamber. My brother abd the paige being both awake the coatchman advances towards my brother in the foreside of

my brother in his bed; my brother-in-law starts scolding the coachman, calling him a drunken rascal and questioning him why he was not in bed at this time;[xxi] the apparition continues advancing towards him until it comes close to the bed, and the other apparition on the other side of the bed advances towards the Paige; the Paige all the time was smiling at what my brother-in-law was saying, he was mistaking as he thought, the coachman for the postilion that was advancing towards him. My brother-in-law rose on his elbow, swearing he will ring the devil out of the coachman, and thrusts at him with a full stroke. Until he sees his arm through the apparition, and his hand on the other side of him. After the thrust at the apparition, the coachman and the postilion each went back to either end of the room and disappeared like smoke. Then, my brother-in-law said instead of cursing, he fell praying; he then touches the Paige asking if he was awake. The Paige answered, 'Yes,' –

the bed; my brother fals a scowlding of the coatchman, calling him drunken rascall, questioning him why he was not in bed ere this time; the aperition still advances towards him till it comes close to the bed, and the other aperition in the back side of the bed advances towards the paige; the paige all the time smyling at my brother taking, as he thought, all the time, the coatchman for the postiline that advances towards him. My brother-in-law riseth on his elbow, and swears he would ding the devil out of the coatchman, and thrusts at him with a full stroake. Till he seeth his arme through the aperition, and his hand on the other side of him. After the thrust at the aperition, the coatchman and the postiline each of them went back to each end of the roome and disappeared like smoak. Then, he said, instead of cursing, he fell a praying; then tutches the paige, asking if he was waking, who answered, 'Yes,' – 'Saw you the coatchman?' said hee; who answered, 'I saw the postiline.'

[xxi] As with so many appearances of ghosts – he thought the coachman was real and this gives additional authenticity to the account.

'Did you see the coachman?' he asked; the Paige answered, 'I saw the postilion.'

"After some discussion between them, they found with their backs facing each other in the bed their faces were looking to each end of the chamber, they then relayed to each other what they had seen above. They instantly arose and sat at the fire until morning, talking to one another and swearing not to divulge what they had seen in case they frightened the rest of the servants.

"However, the secret broke out and it soon reached the ears of Bishop Ross, who in looking to persuade his servants there were no apparitions, would prove it himself by laying in that chamber alone. His servant said to him, in a joking manner, 'My Lord, allow me to be in the chamber below your Lordship.' So the fire is put on, candles placed on the table and in a little time his Lordship went to bed. My brother and the Paige sat up in the room below him. About the middle of the night the Bishop came downstairs with all speed possible and thought it convenient to bring nothing

"After some conference betwixt them, they fand that their backs being towards other in the bed, and accordingly their faces looking to each end of the chamber, declaired to each other what they saw as above. They instantly arose and sat at the fire till morning, taking wan another ingaged not to devilge what they saw, for frightening the rest of the servants.

"However, the secret breaks out, and comes to Bishop Ross his ears, who industeruslie laboured to desuad his servants, and for proof thereof he would ly in that chamber alon. His servant says to him, in a joking manner, 'My Lord, alow me to be in the chamber below your Lordship.' The fire is put on, candels placed on the table, and in a little time his Lordship goes to bed. My brother and paige sets up in the roome below him. About the middle of the night, the Bishop comes down stairs with all speed possible, and thought it convenient to bring no thing with him but his shirt, barefooted, calling for his servants; but what he saw he would reveal it to non.

with him but his shirt. Barefooted he called for his servants; but what he saw in that room he would reveal to no one.

"Sir, this is the real account my wife and I had from her brother's mouth; and next to seeing it myself I could confirm it no better.

"My dutiful service to you, your wife and family. Your Own,

"THO. HARLAW."[53]

"Sir, this is the reall account my wife and I had from her brother's mouth; and next to seeing it myself, I could confirme it no better.

"My dewtiful service to you, your wife and family. Yours ain,

"THO. HARLAW."[54]

# Black Dogs

5 Reports

## Gregory's Green

**Report 1.**

In 2014, a man walking past Deans Court one evening saw a large black dog standing on the low western wall of the Cathedral precincts. It was such an unusual sight he started crossing the road to get a closer look. As he did, the dog vanished before his eyes.

**Report 2.**

In January 2015, a young man walking along the path in front of the Cathedral saw ahead of him a large black dog walking a foot above the ground. He saw it for what seemed like a few seconds before it disappeared.

**Report 3.**

One of the more unusual experiences in St Andrews was in the lovely medieval garden through the back of Deans Court. A large black dog was moving across the grass like a large black slug with a tail, as the level of the ground has risen over the years hiding the legs.

**Report 4.**

In GOS p.123, I wrote the following about the black dog: 'Mrs Batchelor of Strathkinness related to me in 1989 that this vicinity is also said to be haunted by a black spectral dog wandering outside the confines of the court. It seems though the level of the ground has dropped over the years, or thick snow lay on the ground at the time when the dog originally roamed the area, for when seen it is pacing around a few feet above the ground!

There is also mention of this on a student internet forum which had an entry by the user name 'Princess' in late 2004 – "Has anyone heard of the ghost dog that is 'walking' above the floor in Deans Court (I think it is) because they changed the height of the rooms, but the dog is still 'walking' on the old floor... or was that just a random story I was told when I visited two years ago?"

A reply to this from 'Rae' early in 2005: '"I heard something like that when I was living in Deans Court – apparently the courtyard is haunted by a big black dog who walks a few inches off the ground because it has receded. Which doesn't make much sense, but there you go – that's it as I know it."'

**Report 5.**

In GOS p.124, I have the following brief excerpt: 'A legend across the road from Deans Court has a phantom three-legged black dog roaming around the Cathedral ruins.' GOS p.124.

The level of the ground in this area has been altered a few times. Reports 2 to 4 appear to be Group A., which is why they are observed on the level of ground present when they were alive. The odd ones out are reports 1 and 5. The dog wandering the ruins and the one standing on the western wall. Until the Edwardians remodelled the wall in the early 1900s this wall was higher. The original precinct wall was built in c.1300, which was around 10 feet high. The grounds are also at a different level, so 1 and 5 are Group B.

Therefore, Sophie on p.380 may be correct: "I felt something brush against my leg, then again at the Cathedral gates, then again when we were walking towards the haunted tower, I'm wondering if it was possibly the dogs?" Report 1. fits with Sophie's account in the Eye of the Needle, and the Cathedral Gates are just beside where it was seen. It also fits with Lisa's experience (p.379), and the rash that appeared on her leg.

When the Knights Templar were in St Andrews for a few centuries from 1160 (St John's House along with other dwellings), it would appear they imported large black dogs from Croatia to use as crowd control in this area. My thought has always been the kennels were in the courtyard of what is now Deans Court. Part of this structure was here at that time, and the stone vaults in Deans Court were built in 1100 (becoming the Archdeacon's Manse). It would also make sense of why there has never been any reports of large black dogs anywhere else in St Andrews, only here.

As a scenario for what Lisa experienced (Group A. and C.), the force could well have been the large black dog blocking the gate, which is why she found it hard to get through, and why it was only from her ankles to mid-calf. If this were the case, the dog was blocking someone's entry to the precincts. The horrible sense of dread and her saying no no no… is a mix of that person trying to get in and what would have been a very aggressive dog.

# *Ghosts*

# *North Street*

## (North Gait)

**The Mystery of the Blue Girl**

Several dwellings in North Street have ghosts, but it is the poltergeist activity that is especially prevalent in dwellings along this street. It tends to be slight and more the nature of one off incidents. Objects moving of their own accord such as a saltcellar, a mug or a pen moving across a living room table. They are not dramatic or life changing to those who witness such, they are just odd and unaccountable.

Occasionally I have visitors on tours who tell me about the ghost of a little girl wearing a blue dress in a property in North Street. It is a holiday apartment, and it is always the same thing I am told by those who see her, but there is always a reluctance to give the address. They become quite coy, or sheepish rather than defensive. It harks back to an old school mentality – pre-1993 when people thought the paranormal would detract in some way from renting properties that had a reputation of being haunted, refer to p.412.

In GOS p.190, I have the following: 'There is heard tell of a house in central St Andrews believed to be haunted by a ghostly figure known as the 'Blue Girl.' The exact locality is not stated although the ghost of a woman has been seen in Queen Mary's House wearing a blue dress.'

I also mention Linskill giving acknowledgment to a 'blue girl' but he gives no location. It appears the North Street apartment is the location as the figure in Queen Mary's House wearing a blue dress is a woman, not a girl.

**80 North Street**
**Macgregors Funeral Directors, Glass House, Innis & Gunn, The Räv**

**Innis and Gunn**

A Funeral Directors occupied this premises. A selection of available gravestones complete with gravel were displayed on the ground floor. Looking through the windows when I was young I always remember thinking how odd it was to see a graveyard indoors.

Not long after Innis & Gunn Beer Kitchen opened, an order came through to the printer behind the bar for a coffee from the ordering pad upstairs. Something they would be glad of you would suppose. Only one problem, no one upstairs. No customers, no staff, and there was nothing wrong with their systems. This wasn't a one-off incident, it was infrequent but happened a few times over the two years they had the premises. It even happened one evening when I was sitting at the bar. While we were talking about this very subject, an order came through from upstairs for a coke, much to the unsettled surprise of the bar staff and chefs. I was shown the ticket and went upstairs to have a look, no one was up there.

**Glass House**

I only found out recently that when G1 had the restaurant, before it was leased to the Edinburgh brewers, something similar was happening. A student who worked here told me when staff were getting ready to open in the morning they would have the feeling someone else was already in the property. Then when they were closing-up for the night, they would hear someone walking around upstairs, but nobody was up there. It was only before they opened or after they closed when there were no customers. Someone walking around upstairs fits with Inness and Gunn, with orders coming in through the till when no one is up there.

It was the upstairs where the funeral directors dressed the bodies. The downstairs area doesn't seem to have been affected by anything at all. I haven't heard of anything happening since it became the Räv, but then they haven't been there that long and Covid has seen it closed for quite a while. I will find it unusual if they don't.

**St Salvator's College**

Founded 1450 by Bishop Kennedy, it became the United College in 1747 following a merger with St Leonards College. The chapel was completed in c.1460. Until 2014, the clock was hand-wound every morning by the porters of St Salvator's. The University then took the plunge to stride boldly into the 21st century by giving it an electronic mechanism.

In the days when it was wound by hand, the porters on climbing the wooden stairs of the clock tower would hear footsteps on the stairs. This was often coupled by the feeling of a presence. The natural thought would be to put it down to the eeriness of the setting. However, there are other locations with a creepy atmosphere, many in fact, but not many are coupled with the feelings of a presence, or indeed the same degree of persistence with which this particular one appears to have made itself known.

A woman who came on a tour works for the University in a small office on the first floor above the right-hand door of St Salvator's College. She told me a shadow flits across the walls while she works on her computer. It is always seen out the corner of her eye and small things like pens disappear and appear the other side of the office.

**One off paranormal incident's**

Everything has a cause, and a one off anomalous incident in the comfort of your home is no different, be it a natural explanation, a psychological origin or via a spirit of the deceased. For the latter, given the pattern of causality for poltergeist activity in how spirits operate, one off instances, tend to be observed in the abstract, as we look to a localised historical association for its source. It can be years between incidents happening, if they ever do again during an occupant's tenure that is, so it can be difficult to tie them down.

Alongside the activity of a spirit with a historical association, there is also slight phenomena caused by someone close. Someone no longer with us in the physical: Partner, relation, friend. This can easily be missed in favour of the abstract spirit if an immediate connection is not made as their notification can take on many subtle forms. This immediacy tends to be when someone close has recently passed away, and they are still at the forefront of the mind through affection in thought and emotion.

The obvious indicator is sight, which we tend to think of as the most important of our five senses. It is the most complex, but the strongest and most revealing of the senses is the sense of smell. It evokes memory and emotion a lot more readily than the others. Entire scenes and circumstances can be evoked with the scent of the deceased's favourite perfume, aftershave or tobacco for instance. Personalised indicators can also be a thought of someone in particular 'coming to mind' creating an immediate association by way of impression.

These are part of what are called 'post-mortem' experiences I spoke of in the first section where a close member of the family having passed away comes back to comfort loved ones, often to notify they are ok. Longer term, it can be a reassurance in a difficult period of one's life, and that is where it become more abstract and difficult to determine.

So, unless there is something to indicate otherwise, when looking to the source, always try to determine or eliminate personal associations first before attempting to attribute the abstract or historical as the cause of the unknown in a personal environment.

**The New Picture House (NPH)**

The cinema opened its doors on the 22nd December, 1930, and was dubbed 'St Andrews Super Sound Cinema.' It was one of the most advanced cinemas in Scotland with ground breaking cinematic features. The first film to be shown here was *No! No! Nanette* (1930).

Maureen has worked here since the 1970s and was unaware of any disturbances in the building, but she did see her husband on two occasions after he passed away. He also worked there and to my knowledge there have not been any other incidences, and I am sure her brief glimpses were by way of a heartfelt reassurance for Maureen that he is still around.

# 15 St Andrews Hotels

…and their long term residential guests!

**In this section**



**In other sections**

# Ghosts

## Introduction

**Changing times**

Until 1993, many hotel establishments had a stigma about the paranormal. I used to go around the hotels in Fife asking about any paranormal experience they may be aware of in their properties. There was always a mixed reaction. Sometimes I couldn't write quick enough, while for others I had quite a job. Even in places where I knew phenomena had taken place there could be reluctance to say anything as they did not want their businesses being blacklisted through a reputation of being haunted. Oh, how things have changed! With the advent of the X-Files in 1993, the commercial value of the paranormal exponentially increased the curio value of haunted locations, especially hotels. From that year everybody wanted to stay in a haunted room in a hotel, so when interviewing some of those same proprietor's post 1993, I soon realised everyone now wanted a ghost to drum up business. I found myself being treated as if I had been sent as an emissary for the impending secret visit by a Royal couple. They were keen to open-up and tell me a lot more than they previously did or would have done before. It became commonplace to then see the legend or story of their resident ghost being written into their history, placed on a plaque outside their establishment, in menus or on handouts advertising their salient points, and all before the internet. A far cry from the reluctance of old.

Consequently, one of many universal patterns with hotels and Inns, which has become more a tradition when it comes to the paranormal, is to associate the most famous person who ever set eyes on their property as being the ghost who occupies it (p.337). There are a few ghosts I give named attributions to, but given the wealth of ghosts included in this volume, there are not many where I can give a definitive association. It takes a description adhering to that person, or a personal association in-keeping with someone specific to do so which is rare. They don't have to be historically famous, most ghosts are of everyday people, and they all have equal importance.

The turnover of staff in the hospitality industry is very high, hotels change hands and populist perception still generally adheres to it as fiction, so an enquiry to most general staff results in the same archetypal responses or expressions: a funny look, a flat denial, perhaps a mocking laugh, or a shrug of the shoulders that they are unaware of anything occurring. The former responses are symptomatic of conditioning, the latter is usually due to their not having worked in the establishment for very long. Additionally, staff rarely talk about the paranormal, or about their experiences amongst themselves. Despite the paranormal being more accepted, albeit often for the wrong reasons, people can still be reluctant to mention their experiences. The actual extent of phenomena in hotels and elsewhere will never be known for this reason, but as I have mentioned, everyone has experienced. Those who have experienced and open-up to me, are often doing so for the first time. They also want to know more about what they have experienced.

Of course, a place having paranormal associations doesn't mean everyone in that environment will experience it. A common reply of, "I've worked here for years and never experienced anything," is a fair response we could suppose, but it is all too often hijacked as a euphemism that it doesn't exist.

Unfortunately, those who deny its existence are also quick to dismiss the testimony of those who have experienced its reality, regardless of their integrity. It is called denialism, and in some ways, it can be easy to see why. You just need look at those who don't believe Covid-19 exists because they don't know anyone who has had it. This mentality of, 'if it doesn't affect me, it doesn't exist' is the same as 'I have never experienced it, so it doesn't exist.' There is no difference.

The steady flow of life passing through hotel doors brings with it a perpetual dynamic of merging energies from all quarters of human interaction. When entering a hotel or any accommodation establishment, the subconscious picks up on the general aesthetics, along with the level of hospitality, décor etc. It gives us an overall impression of a place. The same applies to any setting. These interactions of energy are shared through all life's circumstances. The difference with accommodation providers is the twofold nature of our interaction with their environment. On the one hand we have the public persona, and a decorum generally dictating a polite interaction at reception, restaurant and bar. On the other, we have life behind closed doors in the privacy of a room or suit.

These environments are the breeding ground of emotional possibilities where a full spectrum will eventually be displayed, and everything in that space will then be retained by degrees of intensity. They cover all the frailties and predictabilities of human nature, especially those involving the hidden private side of human nature in all its generally unexposed detail. Like the general ambience of a hotel, a room can be imbued with a pleasant airy feel, or the sense of something tragic, depressive or oppressive which you will now recognise as Group C. empathy.

When you stay with an accommodation provider, you are occupying a space that has recently been vacated – but only physically. It does not mean the energies of whatever took place have left that space. Remember, everything is imbued on a locality like a memory. To put it bluntly, you are sharing a bed with thousands of people and all the energies they bring to that environment. For the most part they will dissipate pretty quickly, but the residue or even re-enactment of something major that happened can be as indelible and as lucid as a set of fingerprints for those able to pick them up. No matter the public persona, there is no hiding in private from those able to perceive such depths.

# Greyfriars Inn

129 NORTH STREET

Group A.

Formerly Greyfriars Hotel, the Tudor Inn & the Tudor Café. The current name comes from the neighbouring site of Greyfriars Monastery (p.490).

Greyfriars is run by General Managers Jim and Jinty. A more personable couple you would be hard to meet.

With 20 rooms to run and an award-winning thriving bar and restaurant, they have built up their establishment to be one of the busiest in St Andrews. Aa a popular 19th hole for golfing pilgrims, this is the closest many will venture from the course to the town itself. Once they are here, they just can't leave!

This is one of many locations where I didn't think anything untoward was lurking around. I had never heard of anything taking place here when it was the Tudor Inn, but this area does have an ancient history.

This photo captures the moment when two staff members mistook me for their resident ghost. Don't give up the day job! The ghost at Greyfriars is a man dressed in black standing by the restaurant stair. He has been seen looking toward the bar area on at least two occasions by customers, and I was in the bar both times, but I was facing away from the restaurant area. It makes me wonder how many others have also seen him and either didn't think about it if others were also in the area it or just didn't tell anyone about it.

The first sighting was only for a moment. I was chatting with a visitor to the town when he said a man in the restaurant has just vanished. He was customarily confused, so we went down and had a look. It was fairly late and there was no one in the restaurant area. The fire door hadn't been opened and no one had passed us. I was wearing one of my branded tour jackets, so when he saw I did the tours, he laughed and said, "Was that you? Did you bring him in?" "Probably!" I said with a smile as he bought a couple of whiskies.

The second was more persistent before it disappeared. On this occasion it was a couple from the States. They only mentioned the figure after it disappeared. Again, they were confused, and said he was standing at the foot of the restaurant stair looking at us, then he wasn't there. He was tall, slim, dark, but not out of place. They were just visiting the town for the golf and were completely unaware of the first sighting, which fitted the same description, and the figure did the same thing - he just vanished.

There are actually two ghosts here. A medium staying in the hotel at the beginning of 2017 saw the ghost of a woman on the first floor.

So far as I am aware there is no poltergeist activity here. Both ghosts are Group A. impressions. The man was just looking in our direction rather than at us, there was no awareness.

People rarely share their experiences of this nature for the stigma it potentially attracts. If I hadn't been present, no one would have heard about their experiences, so I don't know how sporadic these ghosts are, but they are brief, and very rare to see. As far as I am aware, none of the staff have thus far seen them.

# Ogstan's Hotel

## 127 NORTH STREET

**Now Kinnettles Hotel**

In the photo is the Imperial Hotel alongside the Tudor Café long before it was remodelled with a second floor as Greyfriars Hotel.

The Imperial Hotel on the corner of North Street and Murray Park has had a few name and ownership changes over the years: The Imperial Temperance Hotel, Imperial Hotel (in the photo), Argyle House, Argyle Hotel, The Inn on North Street, Ogstan's Hotel and currently Kinnettles Hotel. There may be the odd name I cannot remember but I think I have covered it.

St Andrews architects Jesse Hall and David Henry designed this impressive Victorian building. These are names I conjure with a few times through this volume.

Building commenced in 1879 on a purpose built hotel to be called the Imperial Temperance Hotel, then in 1881 it opened its doors to a non-alcoholic orientated public. On its northern and eastern sides, it originally looked onto the parkland of Murray Park, with the sea and hills to the north in the distance. This idyllic view would only last a few years. Building work in the late nineteenth century would soon obscure the view with a tide of Victorian houses down to the Scores. The only indication of their being a park would then be the name of the street created through the middle of the former park grounds.

The first temperance hotel in Scotland was The Waverley in Edinburgh's Princes Street in 1849. Temperance was a popular Victorian trend. There were three temperance hotels in St Andrews alone. The others were Mathers Waverley Temperance Hotel in College Street and Mathers Temperance Hotel (St Regulus Hotel, St Regulus Hall of Residence) Queen's Gardens.

In 2014, when this was still Ogstan's Hotel, an intruder was spotted on the hotel's CCTV cameras in the early hours of the morning. The police were called. When they arrived, the figure disappeared downstairs toward what was then a nightclub called the Lizard Lounge. When police followed, no one was there and the bottom door to the club was locked. There was nowhere the intruder could have gone. The police saw the footage captured on the CCTV cameras of the figure going down the stairs. Then the footage of themselves going down and only them coming back up. They took the CCTV footage away with them for evidence, and like the man on the stair, it too disappeared.

# *The Russell Hotel*

26 The SCORES

**Originally called Lindisfarne, 1896**

With the majority of hotels in St Andrews having 'standardised' decor reflecting corporate ownership (admittedly some are very well done), the Russell is a bastion of fresh air as the last traditional hotel in St Andrews. Described as a Victorian themed terraced house. George Coutts Douglas, a Justice of the Peace, commissioned architect John Milne (who also designed Kinburn House) to design and build him two houses. 26 The Scores in 1896 called Lindisfarne, and Hazelbank next door at 28 The Scores in 1897.

The hotel has been run by the attentive De Vries family since 1988. A keen sporting family, especially when it comes to the game of golf. Their hotel is packed with character and charm, and an ideal base for a round or two in more ways than one.

What I always found unusual about the Russell is the complete lack of paranormal activity taking place here. There is no presence in one of the guest rooms, no wine glasses moving by themselves across the dining room tables, the gas lines to the bar don't switch off by themselves, and the eyes of the dogs in the two portraits hanging in the lounge bar above the fireplace don't follow you across the room (well not very often anyway). Nothing at all. Zilch. Or rather there wasn't until one evening when I was chatting with one of the long standing chefs.

The evening before, he was going to the restroom at 8:30pm and somebody physically grabbed his shoulder. He turned to see who it was and nobody was there. The restrooms are in the corridor between the lounge bar and the restaurant. I told him there was no history of anything unusual happening here, and his experience was the only thing I had heard. However, it is never an all or nothing scenario, nothing ever is when it comes to the paranormal. If I haven't heard of anything occurring in a location it may only be because no one has thus far come forward with their experience, not that it isn't haunted. Case in point here as a few months later it happened again. A customer was about to enter the restroom and felt the same thing. When he came back to the bar he looked somewhat puzzled and told me what had happened, so I told him about the chef experiencing the same not long before.

Since then staff have seen a man sitting in the corner by the window in the restaurant when setting up for service. It is usually out the corner of their eye, then when turning to look no one is there.

These incidences are odd, noticeable, subtle and very infrequent. There is a very pleasant air here, and while there have been theses rare incidents, I wouldn't necessarily call the hotel haunted. The same with Greyfriars and the likes of the Criterion. What I would say for here, is it appears a former resident checks into the hotel occasionally without anyone knowing and sits politely awaiting his dinner!

The Russell Hotel is a very popular establishment and famous throughout the world for the 'Du Vries' hospitality of Gordon, Fiona, Michael, and staff. I am positive others will have experienced things here, as elsewhere, and will have either dismissed them, felt them out of place, too subtle to mention, or perhaps too silly to mention. These displays of mind are unfortunately almost as characteristic as phenomena itself.

If you have the opportunity of visiting the Russell, say hi from me, and if you have the pleasure of dining in the restaurant keep an eye out for their unexpected, silent, and I may add, benign guest.

The De Vries family originally had two very successful bars in Edinburgh, The Jolly Judge and Deacon Brodies on the Royal Mile. On their father's passing, Gordon De Vries in the above photo, inherited Deacon Brodies and his brother the Jolly Judge. Gordon eventually sold the bar, which was one of the most popular in Edinburgh, and by investing in the Russell Hotel, he brought his warm hospitality to the town.

The hotel has fond memories for me. I used to come here in the 70s when I was young to see two spinster aunties who would visit us from Elgin and stay at the hotel for a week. Back then the area above the bar was a wonderful resident's lounge with great views across the bay. It is now a very sought-after guestroom in St Andrews.

My aunties would attend St James Church across the road. I always remember one Sunday when they were running late, one of my aunties was still wearing her night cap under her hairnet in the church. Not a big deal you would suppose, but they always put on their Sunday best for church and no one told her of her error until after the service. Being a highland lass of Victorian mind, going to church still partly in her night attire was one of her more embarrassing moments. The timeless feel of the Russell sometimes reminds me of their visits.

# St Andrews Golf Hotel

40 The SCORES
**Now Hotel Du Vin**

Built in 1863, a story runs that in the 1970s a man strangled his wife in room 8. The actual events were slightly different and took place some ten years later, but there was a murder.

In 1982, after a few drinks in the bar of the hotel a man did kill a woman in room 8. It gained a great deal of publicity at the time as it involved Tim Brooke Taylor of 'the Goodies' fame (if you can stretch the memory back that far). This was a long-running very popular, abstract, slapstick style British TV comedy with huge ratings. Tim was the Lord Rector of the University of St Andrews at the time and was staying in the hotel that night. He had no involvement in the gruesome events that would later transpire, but one of the reports incorrectly stated he had a few drinks in the bar with those involved beforehand. He didn't have drinks with them, but he was one of the last to see the woman alive, and also to see the murderer.

It seems though there were two couples who knew each other staying in the hotel for the night. Tim Brooke Taylor went to the reception to get a newspaper and saw a young couple. Later that night he went back to the reception to order a wakeup call and saw them again with another couple. They asked if he would join them all for a drink in their room. He obliged, but didn't have a drink and didn't stay long. He just signed autographs for them then left.

After that the woman must have gone down to the bar, as she asked if the night porter would let her into their room as her 'husband' had the keys and he couldn't be found. That was the last time she was seen alive. In the early hours of the morning there was quite a commotion coming from the room. Mrs Hughes, the proprietor of the St Andrews Golf Hotel, was staying there that night and was alerted to the commotion. A young woman was lying dead in the bed. Her name was Kay Shepherd, a student nurse from Cupar. Her boyfriend was nowhere to be seen. It emerged she had been murdered by her boyfriend John Smith of Cupar. Tim Brooke Taylor appeared in court at the trial as a witness as he was one of the last to see her alive.

The staff never liked going into the room as it can have an uneasy and creepy atmosphere. Since then there has been a presence in the room, and occupants have had the unnerving feeling of being pinned to the bed by something heavy pressing down. None who have experienced this realise there was a murder in the room, let alone she was stabbed in the chest.

The lift to the floor in which she made her last journey to her room is also believed to be haunted, but no further details.

The hotel was taken over and renamed Hotel Du Vin in 2014. Following an extensive refurbishment, none of the rooms now have numbers, just names.

Tim Brooke Taylor sadly died of Covid-19 on the 12th April 2020.

# The Scores Hotel

76 The SCORES

There is a passage that runs under the hotel. It is about four feet wide and seven feet high. I went down it in the 1980s with a member of staff. The passage started from behind a large fridge in the kitchen, but the hotel has changed quite a bit since then. We could only go as far the roots of a tree that had blocked the passage. It didn't seem to be caved in beyond this point, but it was inaccessible without cutting away the thick roots. When we went outside the hotel we found the roots were of the large tree that sits just on the other side of the pavement to the east of the main entrance in the photo. The passage is running due north. Its original purpose isn't known, indeed, not many are aware it exists and very few have been down it.

In GOS p.124, I mention the following: 'Among the many supernatural curios Linskill intimates as being in St Andrews is a phantom bloodhound,[xxii] but as with some of his other 'bogles' as he calls them, there is no further information to be found. The closest is the aforementioned accounts of black dogs at Deans Court and Cathedral grounds [reports 4 and 5], and with Linskill living in Deans Court for a time, he would have been aware of its resident phantom dog.'

Linskill's phantom bloodhound was part of a shortlist of phenomena he included at the start of his story *The Veiled Nun of St Leonards.* I knew he had added these as paranormal scraps he'd gathered over the years in St Andrews, but had nowhere to put them, as he had no further information about them. As he did also for his fictitious Lausdree Castle

Other than black dogs at the Cathedral I had no other reports that might fit Linskill's description until I received an email from a guy who had been on a tour the night before. His father had a slight physical ailment so he didn't attend the tour.

Wednesday 13th March 2019

Richard: thank you again for a great tour last night. It was greatly appreciated and very enjoyable. I'm going to get your book on amazon kindle.

This morning my father was able to golf at St Andrews and afterwards told us that there was a large ghost dog in his hotel room last night. We were staying in the Best Western Scores Hotel – top floor.

Thanks again

Dave Dottle

---

[xxii] Refer to Linskill *The Veiled Nun of St. Leonards,* GOS p.344

# *The Grand Hotel*

*(Now Hamilton Grand)*

**Hams Hame – Hamilton Grand**

Jiteen Ganesh on the following page, is a lovely gentleman who I feel fortunate to call a friend. Now working in some of the most luxurious hotels around the world, he was a member of staff for Kohler working in Hams Hame. In 2014, he had a couple of unusual experiences on the same day. He saw a champagne glass on the shelf behind the bar tilt to 45 degrees, hover there for a few seconds then fall to the ground and smash. There was nothing that could have caused it to happen and its behaviour was unlike anything Jiteen had ever seen before.

That evening he went into the kitchen, the entrance of which is a large heavy door which can only be opened by swiping the hand across an electronic sensor. After the door had closed behind him it opened again – but there was no one about who could have activated the sensor.

While Jiteen was working at Hams Hame, he was staying in staff quarters provided by Kohler up at Craigtoun, a couple of miles southwest of St Andrews. Following their evening shift, the staff are ferried up to their residence in a courtesy minibus. A few times when passing the abandoned Maternity Hospital late at night they have seen the whole top floor lit up. This was the former living quarters for nurses and general staff, but there was no electricity in the building at the time.

This building was originally the Grand Hotel, built between 1894 and 1899 by Thomas Hamilton. A successful American businessman who loved his golf. He had applied for membership with the Royal & Ancient in the early 1890s, but they refused his application. Infuriated at the decision he decided to build a hotel as close to the clubhouse as possible.

There was nothing random about his choice of location. Its size and proximity suitably overshadowed the R & A building, and from a historical perspective, it was also the site of the first golfers' club house in St Andrews, called the Union Parlour. This was created for the exclusive use of golfers by Hugh Lyon Playfair in 1835. [xxiii] The parlour facilities that included the 19th hole was shared with the R & A until 1854, when they built their own club house across the road.

The first stage of the hotel was opened in 1895, and was an immediate success. This was the grandest hotel in Scotland, the largest in Fife and the first to have hot and cold running water in all the rooms. It was also the first hotel in Scotland to have a pneumatic lift.

In the same year of its opening the New Course created by Tom Morris was opened. A shrewd move by the R &A as the hotel became so successful due to its situation and prestige it added considerably to the game's popularity.

Kohler purchased the property in December 2009, and along with Hams Hame pub and grill on the corner, Hamilton Grand, as it is now known, houses exclusive apartments. It was also Hamilton Hall of Residence for the university and had its fair share of activity from that period which I mention on p.472.

---

[xxiii] Playfair was a man I would arguably suggest did as much for the town as Hepburn before the Reformation, and Old Tom Morris for the game of golf. Refer to GOS.

# *Ghosts*

# The Golf Inn

## 1 GOLF PLACE

The hotel has changed hands and names several times in its history. This was the Golf Inn,[xxiv] the Links Hotel, McSorleys Bar, Golf Tavern, 1 Nike Place, 1 Golf Place and currently it is back to being the Golf Inn!

The area of the Golf Links now covering all the courses here was called Pilmour Links. The golf course was called the Golfers Course, then when the New Course opened, it became known as the Old Course. The name Pilmour Links was then retained for an area spanning Links Crescent, Pilmour Place, Golf Place and West Scores Walk. Charles Rogers in his *History of St Andrews* 1849, says: 'The territory now occupied by Pilmour Place and Golf Place, at the western extremity of North Street, before 1820, when sites for the houses were first feud by the Town Council, formed part of the golfing ground.'[55]

These roads were originally tracks cutting through the rough of the Links, especially Links Crescent and Pilmour Place as

---

[xxiv] There might have been another name or names between Golf Inn and the Links Hotel.

part of the early thoroughfare from Guardbridge to the Cathedral and beyond. The arrival of buildings would gradually define them as streets and the familiarity we have today. The Swilkan (Swilken, Swilkin) Bridge spanning the Swilkan Burn on the 18th fairway on the Old Course, is actually the Golfers Bridge. The Swilkan bridge, was on the main road to Guardbridge and ran over the burn at the foot of Links Crescent. The burn at this point is now subterranean.

It is believed the Inn has been here in one guise or another since 1827, certainly a stone at the corner of a gable (a skewputt) of the building has this date 1827 chiselled on it and signage in the past has reflected the same. The map of 1832, however, has no buildings marked along Golf Place and there is a reference to Mr Leslie's 'newly opened' Golf Inn in the 1860s, which would then be in-keeping with the maps. It is possible an unmarked building was here in 1827, or the skewputt stone was taken from a different building, and nearly two centuries later the skewputt gave the date added to the establishment's signage.

Dianne Lapping, daughter of the owners of this hotel when it was the popular Links Hotel and Niblick Restaurant and Bar, told me a few stories about the building. She says it was an old coaching Inn and a notorious hideout for highwaymen.

There is a secret door on the first floor adjoining the cottage to the left of the building. The hotel has seen many refurbishments so it is now concealed behind a plaster wall. It is said, highwaymen would use this as an escape route when alerted to the danger of being caught and had to make their escape from the building. One of the highwaymen was not so fortunate. He was caught trying his escape and was hung from a large tree in the area of what is now room 8, on the corner of the building overlooking the nearby Royal and Ancient Club House. He is reputed to have been seen swinging between the old cottage and the left of the hotel building. It is a great story, but there is no little romance involved here, as highwayman generally ran their course by the early 19th century, up to around 1810. It doesn't mean though that her understanding is wholly incorrect. Just substitute the word highwayman with smuggler and Dianne's suggestion retains its plausibility. As this was a great industry around the coast of Fife in the nineteenth century.

Room 8 on the first floor has a presence that has been remarked upon by guests and staff members.

Room 6 on the right of the building, also on the first floor overlooking Golf Place, has a presence that has also disturbed hotel staff over the years. Even to this day, staff entering the room feel it to be a creepy experience and try not to stay too long when cleaning the room between occupancies. So many people have stayed here over the years, there will be a percentage that will have felt or experienced something, but again it comes down to the same age-old problem I spoke of earlier with Greyfriars and the Russell, with most people keeping such experiences to themselves.

The former restaurant area on the first floor also had a very oppressive atmosphere, especially after the restaurant had closed for the night. It had a totally different atmosphere to when open and bustling with locals, visitors and celebrities. The light switches for the restaurant were some distance from its entrance and barring the light from the hallway, the room became a space filled with abject darkness. The Links Hotel was also the family residence of the Lapping's. Dianne told me entering the restaurant after it had closed would give her an unnerving feeling of not being alone. "It was the feeling someone was in the room watching you," she said.

The restaurant has played host to pretty much all the celebrities you could imagine over the years, especially when the Lapping's had the hotel, including Bing Crosby, who stayed at the Grand Hotel in its heyday.

St Andrews is known, or perhaps renowned in certain circles for maintaining the privacy of its visitors, especially its famous guests. Everyone comes to St Andrews, so not surprisingly all the hotels and bars in the area have played host to some of the most famous names in the world of golf over the years, together with Hollywood stars, sports personalities, musicians, politicians, presidents, innovators, academics and even astronauts!

Pretty much every night, Dianne's father would play host to some of the biggest names. Rarely would there be anything dramatic or scandalous, but discretion was always key for the Lapping family, and their reputation was a draw that sustained their hotel for many happy years. In-keeping with the unwritten rule of St Andrews, everything was always kept in-house. The privacy element always maintained itself in St Andrews, although admittedly not so easy now with chance meetings of the famous being met with those clamouring for their own social media attention. When Barack Obama played golf here in 2017, the course was quiet as he took his first shot on the Old Course. By the time he played into the 18$^{th}$, half of Fife was waiting for his return. Generally, though, privacy is one of the many reason's celebrities have always felt comfortable here. It was one of the factors for Prince William as his University of choice.

# Rusacks Hotel

## ANNEXE

The Rusacks Hotel overlooks Pilmour Links on the one side and the Old Course on the other. The hotel was built for Johann Wilhelm Christof Rusack by architect David Henry in 1886. It opened in 1887 as the Marine Hotel. Back then the hotel was just the middle section of the building, the north block overlooking the Old Course was added in 1893, the front south facing block in 1911. It eventually became the Rusacks Marine Hotel, so named after its founder. The three sections could clearly be seen from the car park on the western side until 2020 saw the commencement of a major extension to the west.

The first report I have in GOS p.25, for St Andrews is about poltergeist activity taking place in the annexe of the Hotel. 'In 1958 between the early hours of September 13th and 14th, a small two-storey building adjoining the hotel was the subject of poltergeist phenomenon witnessed by three members of a dance band. A thick leather belt, a book, a salt cellar and two scarves were thrown across the bedroom, and a cup, a dish and an ink-bottle were thrown off the mantelpiece. The objects mostly seemed to fly from the free end of the building towards the hotel.'

I have had plenty of people on tours staying at the hotel, but this historical report was the only one I had of anything happening there until now. The account I am about to mention also took place in the annex of the hotel, as follows:

At the beginning of 2020, I had a family on a tour from the States. They vacationed in St Andrews three years before in 2017. Loving the place so much they decided to return. At the end of the tour, the woman said they were staying in the main building of the Rusacks Hotel. She made this distinction because the last time they were here they stayed in the annexe to the hotel which is where she encountered a ghost.

Following lunch one day, her husband left with the boys for the beach. She was feeling sleepy after lunch so went back to the annexe and had a lie down rather than joining them for a walk. While having a rest, she became aware of a girl in the room. She thought it was someone her family had met but no one else was around. The girl walked across the room and disappeared through the wall. The girl never looked at her or acknowledged her and made no sound. She didn't feel scared, she was more confused and wondered who she was.

She said she can still picture her as clear as day. "If I could draw better than just stick people I could draw her for you very accurately. She was kind of Victorian looking, 4 foot high, around 8 years old, with long dark wavy hair and a greyish complexion, but very pretty. She looked like a serving girl wearing a dark brown dress that opened out at the waist, a white or cream piny tied around her waist and a light pink shawl over her shoulders."

She found her experience exciting rather than scary, and I found it refreshing to have a description so precise – believe me, it is rare. "I have seen a ghost!" is often the only morsel you will receive until you press the mind and squeeze out the details of half-forgotten memories. Far from embellishment, the resulting droplets tend to be enriched with the variety of detail only experience, or the moving picture can convey.

She was full of energy and so enthusiastic when talking about it. She wondered if the annexe could originally have been staff quarters or connected to a kitchen. The annex is by, or on the site of the former winter garden of the hotel that was here until 1921.

There is no direct association with the girl and the poltergeist activity of 1958, other than they both occurred in the annexe. Poltergeist activity is caused by the spirit of a deceased person so whoever caused it to occur, was aware of those in the vicinity. This is Group B. Whereas, the girl didn't see, acknowledge or interact with the woman. This was Group A. an impression from her own time so there was no awareness and they cannot cause poltergeist phenomena. So, there is both a spirit and an impression here.

What will the spirit make of the new extension! As I say often, they do not like change so it will be interesting to see.

A woman staying at the Rusacks spoke to me about an incident that happened in her home in England. On her mother's passing she always wore her mother's wedding ring. The only time she took it off was when having a shower. On this particular day, after her shower she dried herself and went to put the ring back on her finger but it had disappeared. She looked everywhere for it, and it was nowhere to be found.

The following year, they had a new bathroom installed. There was a shout from one of the fitters who had just been lifting the old bathroom tiles. Underneath one of them was a ring. It was her mother's wedding ring. There were no gaps or cracks in the tiles and it was impossible for the ring to have ended up directly underneath the middle of a tile.

# The Fairmont Hotel Ghosts

## KINGASK

**Clark Docherty in the grounds of his old haunt**

I have quite a lot of people on my tours who are staying at the Fairmont. Sometimes I slip in a mention of the ghosts here knowing the reaction will always be the same: A look of surprise and the comment: "But it is a relatively new hotel so how can it be haunted?" It is a reaction I also once shared until I met Clark Docherty who relayed to me an abundance of activity at the Fairmont Hotel. He worked there for 10 years from 2000 to 2010. He was there before the opening when the builders were still there. The hotel opened June 2001 as the Five Star St Andrews Bay Golf Resort & Spa and is now Fairmont St Andrews.

We got to know each other when he worked in the Dolls House Restaurant in Church Square. My ghost tours and history tours start from just in front of the restaurant, so we soon got chatting while I was waiting for tour parties to arrive and he was out for a break. I have a lot of time for Clark.

He told me there are a few ghosts up at the Fairmont (Clark is a wonderful master of the understatement). He had such an abundance of information about the unusual events here. I had no idea the extent, I don't think anyone did apart from Clark. He managed to take a note of it all during his time there, so we decided to go for lunch in the Jahangir in South Street so I could record the conversation.

Somewhere between the poppadum's, chicken korma and a garlic nan, this is what he had to say:

**Third Floor**

The front desk guy had an interest in the paranormal and had said to Clark on numerous occasions, of all the floors, the third floor is the one that gives him the creeps and puts the hairs up the back of his neck.

Before CCTV was installed in the hotel he had to do floor checks, which involved patrolling the corridors at night to make sure everything was ok, but there is something about the third floor he doesn't like.

In 2006, two housekeeping maids - Linda and Beryl were doing turndown service at night. They were on the third floor to do turndown in one of the rooms near the lift in the centre of the hotel. Linda had just entered the room and Beryl was going through the trolley in the corridor to get stuff to take into the room when she felt a tap on her shoulder. She turned around thinking it was Linda ready to ask her for some of the stuff, and nobody was there. So, she grabbed the trolley and ran!

On another occasion, Linda and Beryl were again doing turndown on the third floor. Linda was in one of the rooms, Beryl in another. Linda put a chocolate beside the bed then went into the corridor to get another chocolate to put by the other side of the bed. When she came back into the room the chocolate she had just placed was gone. She put a chocolate by the other side of the bed, then looked on the floor to see if she could see the missing chocolate. No one else was in the room and the chocolate had completely vanished.

**The Spa**

One of the girls from housekeeping who starts around 9 pm sometimes does the cleaning of the spa, and sometimes turndown in the rooms. On this particular day she was on her own and was told she was doing the spa, which involves cleaning the mirrors down, polishing, dusting, mopping the floor. She was in the lady's toilet polishing the mirror. When she looked up in the mirror there was the reflection of a little boy standing just behind her smiling. She turned around and looked at the little boy and told him he shouldn't be in there, it was staff only and she was cleaning. She recommended he goes back to where he came from, to go back to his parents because they will be worrying about him. The boy didn't speak and was just standing there with a smile on his face. She turned for a moment to lay the cloth down and take off her gloves and when she turned back the little boy had disappeared. She looked around and there was no one in the room and no door had been opened or closed. That's when she realised the little boy was a ghost. She described him later as wearing "old clothes," and from this, that he had died a long time ago. She quickly grabbed her stuff, ran up to the housekeeping office, locked herself in, and phoned the manager about what had just happened.

In 2004/5 when this was St Andrews Bay, housekeeping staff had a few weeks of traumatic experiences. There was a faint voice of a person whispering behind them in the spa, but they couldn't make out what was being said, and other occasions of something touching them.

The staff were scared to go in the spa when it was quiet. They asked security to escort them while they were cleaning in there, especially the swimming pool area. On this occasion they went through the first door, the security guy locked the door after them so no guests could come in behind them. They then went through the gym to the next door. The security guy needed his key to unlock this one. The two members of staff went through, he then followed, and before he had chance to close and lock the door, it closed by itself and locked them in. The three of them turned and started panicking, pushing the door, banging it, kicking it, and screaming, "Whose there?" There was no answer. After a few minutes the door unlocked by itself. The security guard opened the door, looked through and nobody was there. They went to the first door, checked it and it was still locked. They went straight to the office and the security guard was told to sit down. They gave him a strong coffee and a few months later he left for another job.

Between 2007 and 2013 there was also a lot of activity in the spa area. Sounds, visual phenomena, things moving, and it isn't just staff who have experienced unusual activity here. A couple of guests had an early flight and wanted to use the spa before they went, so they booked themselves in for 6am. They went into the swimming area then 10 or 15 minutes later, the receptionist got a fright when she saw two people grabbing all their stuff with shear fright on their faces. He asked if they were ok as they were running to the main door to exit the hotel. They said, "Everything is fine, but we have just seen something we can't explain, we're just going." The receptionist never found out what it was that terrified them in the spa, but we know there is the ghost of a little boy in there.

Two girls from housekeeping went down one night to polish the windows, hoover the carpet, dust, clean the mirrors, mop the floor and tidy the changing rooms etc. When they went into the main swimming pool area, they were walking through checking to make sure everything was ok. One of the small panes of glass 10 inches by 6 inches had fogged up like someone had breathed heavy on it, then a face appeared. It creeped them out and they left abruptly.

**Orbs**

Before continuing with the experiences at the Fairmont, I am going to go off base for a moment and give details of a couple of trips Clark made to Edinburgh. They serve as an important lead in to an anomaly Clark then recorded at the Fairmont.

Clark had one of the early Sony digital cameras. During a tour of Mary King's Close in Edinburgh, he was taking photos as he went around. At the end of the tour it appears customary for the staff to ask if anyone captured anything unusual whilst on the tour. When looking at what he had taken, he realised he had captured something. There was a monk in one of the photos which he then showed to the staff. Photo on p.579. One of the guides he showed it to, said when he had just started he saw exactly the same as what Clark had captured - the monk with his habit and hood up peering from around the corner. He thought it was another member of staff trying to scare him. So, at the end of the tour he went into the office and said, "Thanks guys!" thinking they were just joking around. He said, "I know it was one of you guys dressed as a monk peeking around the door, don't pretend." One of them looked at him and said, "Oh, so you've seen him as well, that's good then!" That is when he realised he had seen the ghost of the monk. It seems most, if not all the staff have seen him (p.579 and p.580).

He also had a photo from that tour of a bright blue diamond about three feet in front of him in Mary Kings Close, which the staff also thought as weird. Photo on p.579.

Clark also went to the Vaults in Edinburgh and took a lot of photos. What he saw in the photos was more of these odd diamond shaped orbs. Some of them were blue, some thick white and some of them were see through like glass, but they were all diamond shaped.

I have placed this photo here rather than in the photos section for relevancy. This is **CAI 4. No Physical Explanation.** This is where it has not been possible to attribute an image to a physical cause and has a qualification endorsed by PERL testimonial circumstance. **PERL** conclusion: **F3b.** Paranormal *origin*/no physical *cause.* I explain **CAI** on p.517 and **PERL** on p.581.

They were sent around the UK to paranormal investigators and photographers to look at them.

He also took them to a photograph specialist in Kirkcaldy. He said, "If I show you the pictures will you be able to tell me if it is light, moisture or dust that I captured?" The specialist said, "I have 25 years of experience and would be able to tell." He then looked at the photos and said, "Oh! Light comes from a source and can be reflected in glass with a focal point from the angle the light is coming from. That's not light, that is everywhere, and you told me you were in a dark building with no windows. It's not reflecting off your flash because there is nothing I can see in that picture that is reflective. No angle of light. As for damp, I have never seen diamond shapes coming from damp, and I have definitely not seen diamond shapes coming from dust. Some of them are really fogged up, other ones are just transparent. It's the strangest thing. I can honestly say I have never seen any of this before."

Clark spoke about this to fellow members of staff at Fairmont and they asked if he would bring his camera in and take photos of the swimming pool area.

This he duly did. When Clark went to the swimming pool in the spa, he took a picture from the bottom end of the pool and looked at the digital image on the back screen. There was one blue diamond at the top end of the pool, 5 to 6 feet above the tiles. Keeping the camera in the same position he then took another photo only a few seconds later, the diamond was gone. He turned the camera slightly and took another view of the pool. This time capturing all of the pool and the diamond was back, but it was now on the same side of the pool as Clark. He said, "If it were dust there wouldn't just be one bit of dust. The same if it were moisture or light, and it wasn't in the next photo taken only a few seconds later. In the third photo, the diamond was the same size and shape, but had moved position."

At quiet times in the Fairmont he would ask fellow staff members if there was anything they wanted to do. One of his friends was always saying, "The diamond at the swimming pool could have been dust," so he said, "While we are quiet, let's go up to the rooms on the lower side where things are most active. Find a couple of rooms where the occupants have checked out and housekeeping haven't yet been in. We'll shut the curtains, get pillows, shake them and disturb the air to see if we create some dust. Then I'll take a picture. The rooms are very clean anyway but I should disturb enough of the air to show up in a photo. Then we'll go into the room next door, not disturb anything and take a photo so we can compare the difference."

Armed with a plan they went to one of the rooms. Clark said, "We went into the room, battered the pillows and I took a photo." He said his friend was expecting the photo to be full of dust particles so he could prove his point, but there wasn't any at all. Dust is so fine the camera isn't picking them up, but it did pick up these same weird shapes. There were two white, slightly see through diamonds in the corner by the bedside cabinet. This left his friend somewhat dumbstruck.

They then went to the room next door and he took a photo without disturbing anything. There was this same diamond by the TV. He then took another without moving or moving the camera and the diamond was closer to him. He then took another and the diamond was even closer. In each photo the diamond was the same shape, but in each photo, it was larger, it was moving toward him. Like the photo from the other room it was white and barely see through.

**First Floor**

There was a housekeeping maid by the name of Denisa from the Czech Republic who worked in the hotel for three years. Her experience was in 2007. It was between midday and 2pm when she was in a room on the first floor doing the normal housekeeping; making the beds and tidying the room. The room was near the reception area on what they call the high side of the hotel. She went out to the trolley in the corridor, grabbed some clean sheets for the bed and went into the room and put one of the sheets on the bed. She made it nice and smooth, tightened it at the corners, then picked up the other sheet to put on top. She saw it had a mark, so put it aside and went out to the trolley to get another clean sheet to replace it. When she went back into the room there was the outline on the sheet of a body, as if somebody had been lying on the bed. She was only out of the room for a second. This has a direct relevancy later.

In 2008, a maid from Poland was checking a room on the first floor of the low side (north side) of the hotel where an occupant hadn't checked out. On entering the room there was a man in the bed. She called to him and opened the curtains. He was lying on his back and he was dead. When she saw him, she became scared stiff and ran out of the room. She had worked there for three years and had to take three weeks off work as it affected her so much. It wasn't the sight of a dead body that scared her, it was the expression on the man's face. His eyes and mouth wide open and the expression was as though he had seen something and been frightened to death.

Irene, a former supervisor of the Fairmont was in one of the rooms checking the maids had done their jobs correctly, when one of the large mirrored doors in the fitted wardrobe slid right open. She went across the room and looked to see if there was any reason how it could open on its own, but there wasn't anything. She slid the door shut and as she turned the other one did the same. These are relatively heavy doors; the room isn't slanting and it had not happened before.

A girl who had not long started working at the Fairmont was working on the front desk through the night. Sometime between midnight and 2 am she felt hungry and went through to the Kittocks kitchen to make a sandwich. When she turned into the kitchen, a man in dark oldish clothing was standing in the middle of the kitchen. He turned around and looked at her then promptly disappeared right in front of her. She ran out of the kitchen back to the front desk, told everyone what she had just seen, grabbed her bag and her coat and walked out that night. Nobody at the hotel has seen her since. This is not far from where the outline of the body was seen in the bed.

**Staff Area**

There has been the sound of kid's laughter in the back corridor of the staff area. A couple of KPs heard a couple of kids laughing and they didn't know at the time that the housekeeping girl had seen a small boy in the same area of the hotel.

In 2007, Derek and Andy, two other KPs who have worked in the hotel since it opened, were sitting in the staff canteen one evening around 10 pm having something to eat and a drink. No one else was in the canteen. Derek was facing the canteen doors down the far end and Andy was sitting with his back to them. Whilst they were chatting, Derek saw the doors open and a man in dark clothes came in through the doors. He walked behind a partitioned area to the vending machines. Derek was waiting and waiting for this person to come back. After 10 minutes he still hadn't appeared back from behind the partition. He then realised the person wasn't making any noise and there was no sound from the vending machine. So, he said to his friend, "I'm just going to have a look down there, because that person that just came in hasn't come back out from the machines. Just want to see if they're ok." He went up and looked around the partition area by the vending machines and nobody was there. That's when he realised he had just seen a ghost.

Derek also had another experience in the canteen. He was in there with another of his KP friends talking about the summer solstice which was that day. He was saying how paranormal things happen in the hotel around the time of the summer solstice. The other guy said I don't believe in the paranormal, then while they were talking, one of the lights in the canteen went off. They just put it down to coincidence and Derek wound his friend up saying, "Ah see, I told you!" After leaving the canteen they went into the kitchen where again they were talking about the summer solstice, the drain in the kitchen blew up as they were walking past. Everything in the drain just came out. They phoned the engineer thinking it was just a blockage and everything had just backed up. The engineer came, had a look, and said the drain was fine, nothing is wrong with it. Derek then put two and two together and said every time we talk about the summer solstice something happens. He was joking around to start with but when things started happening he started getting worried.

**Staff Lift**

Myself and Charles (Chaz), one of my colleagues of the time were talking about ghosts, and how the hotel was haunted. Charles was saying how he doesn't believe in that kind of thing, but the staff lift freaks him out because it is always moving on its own. I said to him jokingly, "It's just spirits playing around with you. They like to play around with things now and again."

The staff lift at the high side of the hotel starts below the ground and goes up the three guest room floors with trolleys for the maids and maid service areas. The engineers have been out numerous times to fix faults with the lift, but on checking they don't find anything wrong. Yet for some reason, it still goes up and down on its own. On lots of occasions, eh, every day, the lift moves on its own. The lifts are activated either by pressing the button on the outside to call the lift to the floor you're on, in which case the light on the button illuminates outside the lift door, or by someone in the lift pressing the button for the floor they want to go to. So, you will be working away and on occasion the lift doors will just open. There is no one in the lift, and the light on the outside hasn't lit up, so it hasn't been called by anyone, and no one else is around. No one goes into the lift and pushes the button and runs out again because no one is really interested in doing that kind of thing, and not every day! There have been times when people have been down waiting on the lift and the people on the third floor have actually had the lift door opening on its own before it has been called. Then, when they get in and go down, they have asked the people on the lower floor who sent the lift to the third floor, or was anybody going to get in it? The answer is always nobody has been near it. So there has been verification on both sides that nobody has requested the lift.

On this occasion we were working in the laundry on the ground floor, it was on a night shift, 8 pm start to 4 am. I said to my friend Chaz, "What we'll do Chaz, when we go on our next break we have to go past the lift to get out the back. We'll go up to the lift and I'll ask a question and see if I get a response." So, Chaz says, "Ok, yeh yeh this will be interesting." So, we went down during our break and I stopped at the lift. Chaz was quite a bit away from the lift in the corridor and was watching me. I said to Chaz, "Ok I will ask a question and see what the response is." I was about three feet away and I said clearly and precisely, "If there is anybody here and you wish to communicate, please open the lift door," - the lift door opened. My friend Chaz proceeded to run down the corridor and out the hotel. Needless to say, the hairs on the back of my neck were standing up. Chaz never walked past that lift at night again. He would always walk up to the first floor along the corridor and down the fire stairs to the laundry.

**Laundry Room**

Clark was working with Ian one night in the laundry room. It was common for them to find cutlery etc., in the table cloths that had got mixed up with the linen when they were being cleared away. So, they would always shake the sheets first to make sure nothing was mixed in and damage the washing machines. They would then put the cutlery on top of a machine that was out of order so they were out of the way. The top of the machines are about 6 feet high. On one of their nightshifts the cutlery they found was put together on top of this machine. They then carried on working and 20 minutes later they heard a clatter. They stopped what they were doing and had a look to where it came from. There was a fork on the ground several feet away from the machine. The machine was broken so it wasn't on, and there was no vibration from the other machines. They went back to work, and a few minutes later they heard the same again. They looked and there was another piece of cutlery on the floor, again a few feet from the machine. The rest of the cutlery was still bunched together from when they had put it all together. That was the only incident in the laundry room that he can remember as the cutlery had never done that before or since. They were the only ones in the laundry room and nightshift at the Fairmont is a skeleton staff.

**Approach Pathway to Fairmont**

Derek, mentioned earlier, has had a third experience. He was walking up the path from the Fairmont to the bus stop at the top of the road. As he was walking, he got to the gravel path and heard footsteps in the gravel of someone coming up behind him. When he turned around the footsteps stopped. It was quite a mild humid night, with no wind so you could hear everything. He carried on and something started following him again, making the same noise in the gravel behind him. It followed him up towards the Fairmont entrance and the main road by Kingask House before it stopped.

**The Clubhouse/Restaurant Poltergeist**

An Irish guy who worked behind the bar in the clubhouse knew there were odd things taking place in the building. He had never experienced anything himself, but like many staff members he felt it had an eerie feeling at night time (Group C.), especially when alone in the building. At the end of one particular night he was alone in the building doing the cashing up. In the restaurant area there is a flat-screen TV at either end of the room. One was switched off and the other was on a radio channel playing background music. As he was counting the money the TV playing the radio switched itself off. He thought this was strange, grabbed the remote and put it back on so the place wasn't in complete silence. As he carried on counting the money it switched itself off again, and the other TV switched itself on. He grabbed all the money and legged it out of the building to the hotel.

There is a well-known activity that happens at the clubhouse. There is a fire door that seems to open and close on its own. Being a fire door, it can only be opened by using the push bar from within the building. They hear the door slamming shut when it was already closed as there is never anybody going out at the time. The door is very heavy and makes a loud bang when it closes. It has been heard by numerous people and especially by staff members.

One of the engineers at night when no one else was in the building was down that part of the building and heard the fire door slam shut. Along with the loud bang, the push bar always rattles. He was a bit freaked out. He went back to the hotel and told his boss he wasn't going to do the clubhouse at night ever again. So, he had to go back and finish his job in the morning.

The reports from Clark of his experiences, and those of his colleagues at Fairmont over the years are far from sensationalistic and follow the classic patterns of phenomena.

**A trip to Fairmont**

I went up to Fairmont with Clark to get a better idea of the locations he had mentioned.

The day before we went up to Fairmont I had a party of around 50 people on a tour, including the tour director for the group who said they were all staying at Fairmont for a few days. When I met up with Clark, I said, "I wonder if we'll bump into any of them while we are here? Mind you, there are so many of them, they'd all recognise me, but I'd only really recognise the tour director, and being late-morning they're probably all away sightseeing or golfing."

When we arrived at the hotel we were greeted by one of the concierges at the main entrance that Clark knew. He introduced me and we went in for a tour of the hotel. It made a pleasant change to be taken on a tour. Clark took me right through the hotel, visiting the locations he spoke about above. Being a five-star hotel there is full access to all areas of the building, including behind the scenes with its network of staff corridors leading to the restaurant kitchens, laundry and staff rooms etc.

The first location we went to was a guest room on the same level as the main entrance near the reception area. This is what Clark called the high side of the hotel. The room was the one Denisa, the housekeeping maid had an experience in 2007, where there was the imprint of a body in the bed only a few seconds after she had fitted the sheet.

I was taking a couple of photos of the door to the room with the corridor stretching in the distance when the door opened. Standing in the door was the tour director from the previous day's tour! We looked at each other and after a momentary pause, we recognised each other and had a brief chat. We were both struck by the sheer coincidence of our chance meeting. Although he had been on my ghost tour the day before I didn't want to spook him about their being a ghost in his room, so I told him I was just taking a few photos of the hotel for my website.

There are 211 bedrooms at the Fairmont. What are the chances of me standing outside the only room I was going to take a photo of, out of all the rooms in the hotel. Then for the door to open at that same moment, and for it to be the tour director, the only person from a group of 50 people I would recognise from a tour the day before!

I still think about that moment. The odds must surely be massive, well for starters 211 to 1 for the room alone. Then there is the door opening at that exact same moment I was taking a photo. We were in the hotel for about an hour, so 3600 seconds x 211 = 759,600 to 1 for that door to open at that moment. Add in the fact this was the only person I would recognise out of an occupancy averaging 422, so adding in another 211 and the odds increase to 160,275,599 to 1 against. Add say another 11 hours for the door opening anyway in that period = 1.76 billion to 1 against.

We made no noise and he was just going to get a newspaper from reception. The fact also that I mentioned the tour director to Clark before we arrived at the hotel, not thinking there would be a chance of bumping into him, and there he was. This was like Maia randomly finding the only relevant newspaper cutting out of 13 kilometres of archive, p.65. The odds of her doing that are unfathomable.

There is nothing random in these events. If there was ever a word to describe our chance meeting, synchronicity would suffice more than adequately, and it wasn't the only odd thing to happen while we were there. Following our visit, when we started driving out of the clubhouse car park I felt something sweep past the top of my head - front to back, like a hand brushing past my hair. There was nothing in the car that could have done that, and it has never happened before or since while in a car anywhere. The sensation was the same as the light brushing past the head or body experienced by those on my tours at specific locations. It is possible something knew the reason we were there and was saying goodbye. After all, at one time they were as alive as you and I. It would make sense that it was the little boy who seems more tactile. Sitting in the car my head was the right height for him to brush his hand past my hair as we left, although the fire door slamming is more forceful and points to the man. For it to be the boy brushing his hand past my head is also suggestive from the following:

I had a woman on a tour September 2020 from Germany who said she was sensitive to phenomena. I knew this to be true when she said she didn't need to put her hand into the lower chamber of the Haunted Tower. Saying, "A lot of things happen to me, I don't need to prove to myself their existence." These were the exact same words I say to people if they ask if I have ever experienced anything in the lower chamber.

She was telling me while she was in bed in her hotel room the night before, she felt what seemed like four light fingers brushing past her neck. It was quite gentle and her impression was of someone wanting to give her a hug. She thought it was a child. I asked her where this was. It was the third floor of the Fairmont Hotel. The same floor where, amongst other incidences, the chocolate had disappeared.

**Why are their ghosts at Fairmont?**

The activity is fairly-widespread throughout the whole hotel, covering different floors, locations, and types of activity, from the figure of a man, a little boy, the sound of two children laughing, to widespread poltergeist activity affecting objects and electrical equipment. The man and boy are intelligent spirits, Group B. They are aware of us, they are not malevolent, and there doesn't appear to be any Group A.

Hotels can certainly have their ghosts, and even though the Fairmont only opened its doors in 2001, a place doesn't have to have a long history to be haunted, there is a council house in St Andrews for example where someone died six months ago and they are still in the kitchen.

It is also not just localised to the hotel, the clubhouse/restaurant by the cliffs also has poltergeist activity, so again, an intelligent spirit or spirits are causing the phenomena. There is always a reason for a place being haunted and the Fairmont is no exception, but there is no obvious reason as to why they are there, and why at both locations?

The presence of ghosts suggests either something happened in this vicinity: Murdered travellers or pilgrims en route to or from Kinkell Chapel and St Andrews, or the misfortune of being mauled by a wild boar etc. Could there have been a dwelling or dwellings here where something happened? The popular premise of the Fairmont site is that it was just fields before its arrival. So, as a starting point, to find out who the man and the two children are, it is a matter of finding out, what, if anything could have been here, for them to be here. Fairmont occupies the former lands of Kingask farming estate, so what is the history of Kingask?

I could have published this volume in 2019. The search for an answer to explain the phenomena was the reason for its delay, and what I have found, I really did not expect on several levels. Certainly, what I found is not something many will be familiar with, as it took me down some surprising avenues of research.

My starting point was to explore this area by sifting through all the historical OS maps for the Kingask area. I found a map from 1775 by John Ainslie for Major General John Scott. It marks a collection of cottages west of the clubhouse / restaurant building called Gingask. No *visible* evidence now remains.

Of much older origin, there was also a fort on a promontory about 400 feet to the northeast of the clubhouse/restaurant, so there have been inhabitants in this area before.

The map is around 75 years before the present Kingask Manor House was built just to the west of Fairmont, which, from the architectural records was c.1850, by architect George Rae. It replaced a much older dwelling called Newbiggin which Canmore archaeology relays as having a possible medieval association.

I found in the early nineteenth century the family of Anderson and Lindsay had both Kingask Estate and Newbigging Estate in the parish of Burntisland by the south coast of Fife, which they sold, hence the name here with a slight spelling variant. Spinkstown is now Kinkell farm, and Spinkstown Farm is now a different dwelling located across the road from the present Kingask Manor House – they switched the names around.

This area is also volcanic. Just to the west of Fairmont, on the shore below what was Kinkell Castle, are three volcanic vents. Each are denoted by large rock structures or volcanic plugs. The most prominent and well known is the Rock and Spindle, standing some 6 metres in height as a volcanic sea stack plug. There is also a vent at Craigduff, a little further along the shore to the west by Kinkell Ness.

These vents were caused by water heating to boiling point by the molten magma at the earth's core. The steam or gas forcing its way to the surface cracked and fragmented the rock above. On breaking through, the tremendous pressure caused a great eruption of molten lava to shower the localised area. It then collapsed in on itself. On cooling down it then left either stacks of stone as we have at Kinkell, or plugs more uniform with the landscape blocking further eruptions.

The molten lava spewing out of these volcanic vents hit the air at speeds of between 200 and 300 metres a second, equivalent to 1,080 kilometres an hour, quickly cooling into shapes they solidified on the ground as rock known as agglomerate or bombs as they are known. The lava was accompanied by volcanic ash that cooled as pyroclastic rock known as tuff. The preserved town of Herculaneum in Italy was covered by 80 feet of pyroclastic rock when Vesuvius erupted. Walking through a large manmade tunnel through the rock from the town to present ground level was quite an experience.

Deposits of this mix convey a degree of energy. The deeper and more widespread these rock formations are, the more energy they convey. They are only found in three small locations in this area, and intriguingly each deposit has a dwelling directly on top of them. Fairmont clubhouse/restaurant, Kingask Manor House (Newbiggin), and Pitmullen House (Thornbank). These are energy centres. It is not present under the Fairmont Hotel, but there is something of far greater energetic significance here. I found that Fairmont Hotel is built by the site of Kingask Quarry, confirmed on the OS 6" map of 1893.[56] I have overlaid Fairmont on google earth with the 1893 map showing the extent and placement of the quarry at that time. Marked by the smaller oval and notches.

**Location of the volcanic vent and former quarry**

The rock they were quarrying was Picroteschenite olivine-rich dolerite. The extent of the olivine dolerite presence underground can be seen in the British Geology Survey of the area which I have marked with the larger oval line.

The stone is a fine grained intrusive igneous rock similar to basalt. This is very different to the ash and molten rock mix that rained down following a volcanic explosion. This was the molten rock still pushing up to the surface by volcanic action. As the surface lava cooled it solidified and plugged the vent. The quarry is still marked on the OS 1:10,560, 1949-1969.

Looking at the British Geology Survey there are three areas in this locality where olivine-rich dolerite is found. One is between the rough and the road to the Castle Course Clubhouse, halfway along the western side of the 14th fairway of the Castle Course, called the Kinkell Vent. One occupies a small area only yards to the north of the clubhouse/restaurant. The third is under the Fairmont Hotel, so the Fairmont Hotel is built on top of a volcano. It is far from active so it is not likely to erupt any time soon. In the absence of any formal name I have named it the Kingask Vent.

Olivine dolerite is a very hard stone and used as facing stone on buildings, counter surfaces, ornamental stone and headstones. Olivine itself has an extremely high melting point, so quarried olivine stone was used in foundries to protect floors, and in more recent times the area around burner tips on boilers etc., – but that is not all.

The Fairmont site is olivine rich. Olivine is also known as chrysolite and magnesium olivine, so-called for its olive green colour. It also has a more familiar name, olivine is peridot. These names are interchangeable for the semi-precious gemstone that was once considered more valuable than diamond, and like diamonds, these are the only two gems not formed in the earth's crust. They are formed at a much greater depth in the earth's mantle still pushing up to the surface by the volcanic action, which is what we have here. It is why they are so hard and have an extremely high melting point.

Peridot, was also called an 'evening emerald' by the Romans and the 'gem of the sun' by the Egyptians for its golden quality depending on the level of iron content. It was believed to be one of the favourite gems of Cleopatra.

There are a lot of beneficial properties associated with this gem. Physical and spiritual healing powers. It wards off negativity and cures depression by balancing the emotions. It gives restful sleep (which is appropriate for Fairmont), enhances confidence and inspiration, aids in visualisation and slows the ageing process. It is one of the ancient gems, venerated widely, and used profusely in jewellery. It is also the birth stone for the month of August. These are also all descriptive of the natural qualities inherent at energy centres.

Another function for peridot is its religious significance. Mentioned in the bible, and occasionally mistranslated as topaz, it was a protection against evil spirits. As a sought after gem, it was set into shrines and treasures of medieval European churches. In its purest form it is bright emerald green in colour and has been mistaken for emerald, especially in a lot of ancient caches of treasure. It will most certainly have been a feature of the Cathedral treasures, including the reliquary housing the bones of St Andrew, which was said to have been heavily jewelled. The olivine for the medieval treasures would probably have come from Europe, but the possibility of them coming from here cannot be ruled out as the church did have quarries.

The quarry is not marked on earlier maps but it does not mean there was no quarry here. The further back we go, the less detail we generally find marked on maps, whole villages disappear from history in this way let alone quarries.

G.E. Allan D.Sc writing in 1904 says: 'The magnesium of rocks has an important bearing not only from the geological but also from the physical standpoint, viz. in its relations to regional magnetic disturbances.'[57]

The olivine crystals at Fairmont are magnesium-rich and low in silica having accumulated in melts by the magmatic process. This generates strong magnetic fields with a high electromagnetic energy inclusion. Meaning Fairmont is also a great energy centre and along with the clubhouse/restaurant they have a more intensified degree of natural energy than those of Kingask Manor House (Newbiggin), and Pitmullen House (Thornbank) which do not have this olivine-rich dolerite deposit. This has a direct bearing on the level of phenomena at those two locations, especially at the Fairmont.

Ghosts are amongst us all the time, and phenomena can happen anywhere, however, through the fact that everything is energy, given the nature of energetic attraction, a heightened energetic inclusion means we perceive more readily, and Group B. utilise it more readily. That is how it works. Energy centres are often marked by stone circles or large menhir stones for this reason. They are employed to concentrate and harness the energy above ground. The enhanced spiritual nature of energy is the reason the locality of Kirkheugh was the first religious settlement in what became St Andrews and the reason why there are 16 ghosts in its immediate vicinity.

There was mention of disturbances being heightened at the time of the summer solstice at Fairmont. This is traditionally a time of regeneration, a recharging of the spiritual batteries as it were. In the solar calendar it is a time when the magnetic fields reach their peak. It is, and always has been the most significant pagan festival for this reason. The fact it physically marks the longest day is proportional as a secondary factor. This isn't speculation, presumption, or conjecture, it is a fact, it is the reason, and it has held its own since our arrival. It is why there may be a more noticeable increase in disturbances during this time at Fairmont.

Energy is not fixed. Localised energy centres link up forming corridors of energy or ley lines.

I have marked them above. There is one running SSW through the Clubhouse/Restaurant, Fairmont and Pitmullen House. The lines are not set to the width of what I have drawn, the energy along ley lines splays out, but they do weaken the further they are from the source. The energy centres of Kirkheugh 1., Haunted Tower 3. and North Gate 4. link together, as they do with St Rules Tower 2. and the Pends 5. with North Gate 4. and etc.

It is why something can happen in one location and they appear in another. One of the locations for Lady Kinkell is on the coastal footpath by Kinkell Caravan Park, another near Kinkell Castle which is nearly half a mile away (p.505) – the key is the prevalence of energy in the locality coupled with these laws of attraction I stated earlier.

I also mentioned earlier I had delayed the release of this book by nearly two years. As it turned out I am glad I did as a lot more has happened in that time in St Andrews (synchronicities again). The reasoning was to try and find out more about why

Fairmont would be so haunted. It is something that has been niggling me since my first meeting with Clark in 2017 about the phenomena. Before then for this area it was only Lady Kinkell I had heard about on the neighbouring estate. During the latter researches for this volume I found my answer.

I have established above there is a high degree of energy here which is conducive to the manifestation and accentuation of phenomena. The following potentially reveals the identity of the ghosts at Fairmont and why they are here.

I heard that in the 1950s a multiple murder took place in Kingask House which is not far from the Fairmont on the same former estate of Kingask. That a family of four had lived there and the woman on believing she had cancer had some sort of breakdown. She murdered her husband and two children and then committed suicide. As it turned out, apparently, she did not have cancer.

There is also said to be a large indelible bloodstain engrained in the floorboards in one of the rooms at Kingask (upper bedroom) that none have been able to remove. If true, it is the same as at Holyrood Palace, where there is the blood stain you can see on the floorboards from the murder of Mary Queen of Scots private secretary Rizzio. I spoke earlier how he was murdered by Lord Darnley, Mary Queen of Scots second husband in 1566 in front of a pregnant Queen. Stabbed to death, the blood where he lay ran in a large puddle across the floorboards and is still there.

When researching such story's, I often find the truth is more often less dramatic than what we hear, with the rich pickings of embellishment and rumour finding its way of recreating a story out of conjecture. So, for Kingask I began by going through the births, deaths and marriage records for St Andrews from 1950 to 1959, to find out the truth, but an exhaustive general search came back with 419 pages of deaths for the St Andrews district alone. To narrow it down I changed my search to deaths for ages 1 to 15 for those years and looked for a surname where two children had died in the same year. Only 1 page came up, and on that page, were two names for the same year:

John Samuel Weir, aged 4, 1958
Marjorie Blair Weir, aged 1, 1958

The records did not give any detail as to where. I then changed the search to Surname: Weir, 1958, St Andrews deaths. Four names came up. The names were of the above two children and:

James Wallace Weir aged 30, 1958
Nancy Blair Weir aged 28, 1958

Which led me to the grave on the next page.

The family grave is in the Western Cemetery in St Andrews. As can be seen it gives the date of their deaths and confirmed they were at Kingask. Samuel Weir who died two years later had Kingask Farm, his son James Weir lived in Kingasak House with his family. They were both farmers for Kingask Estate.

I then searched all the local and national newspaper archives and only found one article about the incident at the foot of the front page of the Herald Express, September 1958.

Herald Express

'Let U.N. take over Formosa and the people decide their own destiny later on'

# GAITSKELL VOICES A WARNING ON QUEMOY

## Get rid of Chiang, he tells conference

DRIBERG CALLS FOR DRIVE

Shots at police: man is detained

# Chiang warns: We go it alone if necessary

LATE NEWS

2 MORE BRITONS WOUNDED BY CYPRUS TERRORISTS

LIFEBOAT TOWING YACHT TO BRIXHAM

REMANDED ON MURDER BID ALLEGATION

Search widens for two escaped prisoners

Man with bombs gets 6 years

The eagle and its prey

Baby among crash dead

Flooding at Teignmouth

FAMILY OF FOUR FOUND DEAD

Princess prepares for Brussels trip

Starlite

The BEAVE BOAT

# FAMILY OF FOUR FOUND DEAD

A FARMER, his wife and two children were found shot dead to-day in their farmhouse at Kingask, near St. Andrews, Fife. They were James Weir, aged about 30, his wife, Nancy, four-years-old son, John, and 18-months-old daughter, Marjorie.

All had wounds believed to have been caused by a .22 rifle.

All four were occupying the same bedroom.

The discovery was made by the farm foreman, Mr. David Lee.

He said: "Mr. Weir did not turn up as he usually does at 7 o'clock to see the men started. When he still had not arrived at 8.30 a.m., I went to the house and found it locked.

"I got a ladder and looked through the bedroom window. I saw a face on a pillow on the bed and a body lying on the floor.

"I did not go into the house and I do not know whose body was on the floor."

Mr. Lee said that when he last saw Mr. Weir at 7.30 last night, "he seemed to be in his usual spirits."

St. Andrews police said in a statement: "At this stage there is no reason to believe that death was due to any outside cause."

**Herald Express**
Monday 29th September 1958

**FAMILY OF FOUR FOUND DEAD**
A FARMER, his wife and two children were found shot dead today in their farmhouse at Kingask, near St Andrews, Fife. They were James Weir, aged about 30, his wife, Nancy, four-years-old son, John, and 18-month-old daughter, Marjorie.

All had wounds believed to have been caused by a .22 rifle. All four were occupying the same bedroom.

The discovery was made by the farm foreman, Mr. David Lee.

He said: "Mr. Weir did not turn up as he usually does at 7 o'clock to see the men started. When he still had not arrived at 8.30 a.m., I went to the house and found it locked.

"I got a ladder and looked through the bedroom window. I saw a face on a pillow on the bed and a body lying on the floor.

I did not go into the house and I do not know whose body was on the floor."

Mr Lee said that when he last saw Mr. Weir at 7.30pm last night, "he seemed to be in his usual spirits."

St. Andrews police said in a statement: "At this stage there is no reason to believe that death was due to any outside cause."

Looking at the Met office records, it was a very windy 13 degrees with heavy rain that day. On looking at their death certificates they were last seen alive on the evening of 28th September at 7:30pm and were all shot in the head. James Weir had gunshots to the head rather than 'gunshot' that was stated for the others, so she shot him in the head more than once, then shot her children with single shots also to their heads, then shot herself in the head. I have not been able to find any other intimation in the local or national newspapers of the incident. With it being a triple murder, two of those being young children and the fourth a suicide, and being so close to St

Andrews, I can only think the nature of the incident warranted it being hushed up. However, it seems the Herald had slipped through the net as they published the details only hours after the gruesome and tragic discovery.

The only other reference I have found barring general farming entries for the Weir's is the following from three years earlier, which, given the context, I found fairly creepy in itself:

**St. Andrews Citizen**
Saturday 15 October 1955
'**WANTED**, someone to baby-sit one evening weekly and willing to stay the night on odd occasions. Apply by letter to Mrs Weir, Kingask, St Andrews.'

This was to babysit John Samuel Weir who was only 1 year old at the time and who Mrs Weir would go on to murder three years later.

Sudden death, especially when accompanied by violence is far from the only reason why spirits may remain, but of all the variables, they are in one sense the most obvious to make sense of when looking for the reason as to why they may remain. Sudden violent death can jolt the spiritual energetic fabric causing them to remain as in life. They often don't realise they are dead. They can interact and observe us, they have an awareness, and an intelligence. There functions of thought are more automatic and acute than we are accustomed to. It is the same sharp process of clarity achieved through the meditative state, which you will only understand if meditation is one of your disciplines. Their sense of time, as with the meditative state is also different. Their functioning is not dependent on time in the same way we are in the physical. Their reality will be impossible to comprehend when we live an eternal present with only the past as our reference. Their own time is no time and all time. Years appear as timeless moments.

The Fairmont ghosts are of this nature, and the only two ghosts to have been seen here are of a man in dark oldish clothing and a small boy wearing old clothes. Both have acknowledged those who see them. They are aware, Group B. and they are the cause of the poltergeist activity in the hotel, the clubhouse/restaurant and along the path between Fairmont and Kingask House.

There is the sound of a couple of children laughing, whispering, chocolate disappearing, a child's fingers brushing past a woman's neck and also my hair when leaving Fairmont that day, plus the impression of someone lying in a bed just along from Kittocks Kitchen where the man has been seen. These are all telling signs, in fact, all the activity fits with those murdered with unnerving accuracy. I do not believe in coincidence and no other ghosts have ever been seen at Fairmont to suggest otherwise.

One could suppose a more sombre circumstance for the father, reflected by those who see him, but there is no malicious intent inherent in any of them. If anything, it is the opposite, laughter, the boy smiling and no one has heard any crying.

None have tried to communicate, meaning there is no unfinished business, so no heavy atmosphere.

I have spoken how there can be a greater sense of disturbance following alterations, and Fairmont is quite a complex that has seen the whole Kingask area being quite dramatically redeveloped and landscaped. The new buildings at these energy centres along these corridors of energy or ley lines have attracted and focused them, and so too have the dynamics of their living counterparts.

For this situation, the heightened energies of Fairmont and the clubhouse/restaurant are the dominating factors – not the location where they died. A violent sudden death gives the reason for them to still be here, and the ley lines linking between Kingask, Fairmont and the clubhouse/restaurant is how they can flit or energetically snap from one to another.

It is not a case of them taking what we call 'time' to go from A to B for example. Time is relative, energy is instantaneous, spirits can snap between these locations like an image snapping to a grid in photoshop. The same with the orbs I spoke of earlier, they just appear and disappear from one energetic location to the another.

The diamond shapes Clark took with his camera are of orbs. The energetic encapsulation of the essence of spirits. They can be circular, oval, triangular, square or diamond shaped. In the first room where Clark took a photo: "There were two white, slightly see through diamonds in the corner by the bedside cabinet." I believe these were the two children, and being in the corner by the bedside cabinet, may correspond with where they lay on the floor beside the bed at Kingask after being shot. It is why the farm foreman, Mr. Lee, only saw two bodies when looking through the window. "A face on a pillow on the bed [father] and a body lying on the floor [mother]." The children were hidden from view on the floor down the other side of the bed. With this, I would suggest the single orb moving toward him in the other room was the father.

I have heard from people having stayed at Kingask who felt there was something not quite right about the place (Group C.), but I haven't heard of any disturbances taking place there, nor at Pitmullen House, although I would be very surprised if nothing has. Nothing happening would go against the grain of the constituent laws governing the dynamics of these energetic principles. They are as inquisitive as we are and they have free reign across this entire area. The child in the Cathedral grounds, the Half Moon Girl, and the unexpected, yet most welcome guests who collect on my tours are other examples. For the children here, this is their playground, they are aware and they are watching. One of the two main areas is the third floor with its poltergeist activity. This is the highest point where energies gravitate. Remember, energies spiral clockwise upwards from the earth, as with standing stones and graves etc. It does the same with buildings. The energies weaken as they spiral upwards, so poltergeist activity is displayed throughout the hotel including the third floor, but they have only been physically seen on the low levels - the spa, canteen and kitchen.

The spa is closest to the former volcanic vent and quarry where the energies are more intense, and more conducive to manifestation. It is why the activity is more physically pronounced at that location. It is also pronounced at the clubhouse/restaurant, but thus far, I do not have any reported sightings. When somebody does come forward it will be either a little boy or a man. Again, the youngest child has thus far been heard, but no current reports of her being seen.

Between the energies of the environment and the energies of the self, the heightened level in one can supplement a lower level in the other. So, those with an acute energetic awareness will be able to perceive them in these other areas more readily through their own energies than those without.

The importance though is for the final progression of their journey in spirit, not our curiosity. A spiritualist/medium with genuine experience in spirit communication, and a fundamental first hand understanding of spirit nature, may be able to assist in this. On the other hand, a jet set 'spiritualist/medium' tinkering with their own intuition, after being suckered into the more populist ideals, will only waste everyone's time - not least their own when there is more focus on guessing what spirits are present. It is certainly not enough to say the spirits are quite happy and leave it at that. Tragically, that is all too often the case, as was noted earlier. The former is blagging it, the latter only gives a reassurance for the occupants, not the spirit. Neither do anything to address the issue at hand. Progression is important, and not something the spirits are aware of. They need to be educated and released from the burdens of their physical stasis, and that takes the professional spiritual experience of a mediumistic counsellor, not the whims of misguided spiritual aspiration.

# *6 St Andrews University*
# *Halls of Residence*

❖

Hamilton Hall of Residence
*former – now Hamilton Grand*

St Regulus Hall of Residence
(St Regs or Regs)

David Russell Apartments
DRA, (was DRH – David Russell Hall)

University Hall

Southgait Hall of Residence
*former (refer to p.269)*

McIntosh Hall of Residence
(Chattan)

# Hamilton Hall of Residence

(Former)
Now Hamilton Grand

The University bought the property in 1949 and opened it as Hamilton Hall, a residence for 110 students. There was always talk amongst them of a bearded figure being seen in the building.

On the University forum there was a message from Skytom who says: 'Hamilton Hall has lots of stories about strange goings on. Most tales seem to involve rooms on the 4th floor. The manageress has a file of all the stories from the last 15 years or so and they are really interesting. Quite a few students have drawn diagrams of the things they saw and many accounts are scary because they are so similar.'

Hamilton Hall closed in 2006, and unfortunately, I have not been able to track down the manageress to see if she still has the file. Refer also to GOS p.30.

Hamilton Hall was purchased by Kohler in December 2009. Most of the external structure remains the same, but it was gutted internally with the floors being rebuilt on the same levels as the windows. Kohler also added two top floors. Converting it to excusive apartments he changed the name to Hamilton Grand.

The cleaners see the ghost of an elderly man with a beard fitting that of Old Tom Morris in the apartment on the second floor overlooking the Old Course. He stands motionless looking out one of the large corner windows. A presence is also felt when the apparition is not physically seen.

There was an irony when the students were here. While they had the best views in the game of golf, for them this was a hall of residence with a view. Golf at best was a curiosity with few having an interest in the game and most wouldn't have been aware of Old Tom Morris, or what he looked like.

I know one of the families who have an apartment here. A lovely family from Florida. They have my books and come on my tours when they have overseas visitors. Thus far they haven't experienced anything themselves, but I am sure they would love to.

There is another location only a stone's throw from here where a figure has been seen, who, by association of where he is seen, could certainly be Old Tom Morris, refer to p.489.

*Hams Hame*

There have also been things happening in Hams Hame. This is the bar and restaurant on the lower corner of the building I spoke of above in the section on hotels, p.427.

# St Regulus Hall of Residence
## (St Regs or Regs)

The initial phase was built in 1868 by George Rae who built Kingask Manor House. This was only three years after the completion of the Queen Street (Queen's Gardens) town houses along here. In 1877, this was leased to the St Andrews School for Girls Company, the first girl's school in St Andrews (St Regulus North). Shortly followed by the block across the road of 2, 3 and 4 Queen's Terrace (St Regulus South), which by 1890, were part of seven boarding houses for the girls at St Leonards School through the centre of St Andrews. Each with their own housemistress and housekeeper – including St John's House and Priorsgate.

In 1882, they bought a property at St Leonards, and on converting it to a school, they moved there in 1883, becoming St Leonards School for Girls.

This was the school house of St Regulus, it then become St Regulus' Hotel, owned by Mr Rusack, who you will know as the person who built the Marine Hotel in 1887 that would become the Rusacks Marine Hotel, then the Rusacks Hotel.

Margaret, the 14 year old daughter of The Third Marquess of Bute, went to St Leonards Girl School in May 1890. She was a day girl and stayed in St Regulus' Hotel with her governess Miss Cuthbert. She liked the school but the curricula didn't agree with her, so she only stayed for one term.

Certainly by 1903, it had become the Mathers Temperance Hotel with regular demonstrations and sales of cosmetic products. In the 1920s it was a retirement home of sorts for former school officials provided for by Mrs Annie Younger of Mount Melville. The University then bought it in the 1950s, and in-keeping with the original structure they extended it along Queen's Terrace to what we have today. Unlike one of its former vocations it opened as a male only hall of residence.

**The Ghost**

A room is kept locked because of the ghost of a man who was causing too many disturbances and upsetting the students occupying the room. The report is short, but the phenomenon is impacting. He is very persistent, and despite the room being locked, I often get comments about him from students at St Regs on my tours – they hear him from neighbouring rooms.

## David Russell Apartments

(DRA)

Formerly known as David Russell Hall (DRH), the ghost of a man is seen flitting around inside one of the blocks. A number of students have come forward on tours to tell me they have seen him, so a period spanning 2014-2020.

This isn't a prowler or the likes. The sightings are always fairly shadowy but distinctly male. He vanishes while being observed, and does so in ways not physically possible. There is no information as to who it might be, but I always remember the student's residences of Fife Park having the same in the grounds in the 1980s. In the same way as DRA, students would mention to me almost in passing if I knew of anything about Fife Park. They would then mention what they saw. The reports were always customarily brief and again consistent. The phenomenon was sporadic, it was always the same observance, and the location was always in the grounds, never in any residence. A similar observance has been made in Kennedy Gardens by students as follows...

## University Hall

### Wardlaw

There is the ghost of a man in Kennedy Gardens, near the entrance to the hall of residence. He was seen a few times at night through the winter of 1997/1998 by students making their way to or from University Hall. This went around the hall pretty quickly and students stopped walking along here at night. One could easily suppose on hearing this that it has all the hall marks of someone loitering around. However, there is one important detail. He always vanished in front of those who saw him.

Built in 1896, this was the first University 'hall of residence' in St Andrews, and Wardlaw was the first exclusively female residence in Scotland. It is still a female only residence. The first warden was Miss Lumsden, who you may recognise as the first headmistress of the St Andrews School for Girls Company that would become St Leonards School.

Two rooms on the 3rd floor of Wardlaw have a presence. The ghost of a girl has been seen in a mirror on the corridor. Plus, the handprint of a child has clearly been seen on the window evaporating the condensation that forms in the mornings.

## Southgait Hall of Residence

*former*

Refer to p.269

# McIntosh Hall of Residence

(Chattan Hotel - *former*)

The building was leased to the University in 1921, the students call it 'Chattan.' It is easy to take reports of ghosts and poltergeist activity as an abstract through horror film creations and the likes, or from 'paranormal investigations' masking brief moments of escapism from mundane lives. Dubbed as entertainment for many, they each forget these were once people of this earth, with lives to lead, with aspirations and families. Some cruelly cut from this realm before they can fulfil their dreams. They leave behind those who loved them and can only dream on their behalf the potential of what could have been achieved for a brighter future.

One of the reports for here was from a female student who was aware of the hall being haunted. She believed it was a student who fell to his death out of a window, but she had no further details and was never sure if his death was just a rumour.

14th June 1993, The Herald

**Student falls to his death from University hall**

A STUDENT fell about 70ft to his death from the bedroom of his third-floor flat in a St Andrews University hall of residence on Saturday, the final day of term. It was then that Mr and Mrs Shedden, of Hillside Street, Stevenson, were told of the death.

The third-year science student had been taking photographs from the window of his flat when he slipped and fell into the garden at the rear of the residence.

No-one saw his fall and he lay unnoticed for a short time until his body was seen by another student. An ambulance was called but he was found to have died from serious head injuries.

A post mortem examination is likely to be held today and a report submitted to the procurator-fiscal at Cupar. A Fife Police spokesman said at the weekend: "It appears to have been a tragic accident."

Another report stated: 'Mr Derek Shedden, 21, a chemistry student, overbalanced while taking photographs of the town from his room. His parents had just arrived in St Andrews from their Ayrshire home to collect their son. When he failed to meet them as arranged they began a search of the McIntosh Hall of residence in Abbotsford Crescent.'

There are a few ghosts in McIntosh Hall. Whether one of these is of the unfortunate student losing his life in such a sudden and tragic way is not conclusive, but the location is specific to the third floor, and it is the ghost of a young man in one of the rooms who stands by the window. Verified independently by two students staying here in different years, both are post 1993.

There have also been many reports over many years in nonspecific locations around the building. There are a few ghosts at McIntosh. Reports of a presence being felt in some of its rooms, cold spots, lights turning themselves on in vacated rooms, toilets flushing with no assistance, and books and papers being moved around in rooms by unseen hands.

In 2005, a student internet notice board carried similar stories and accounts to some of the above.

A student I met in the mid 1980s saw the ghost of a male figure dressed in dark clothing move across her room. Another report is of a male figure dressed in black, so there is a history here of phenomena also occurring pre-1993 as well as post.

Refer to GOS pp.170-171, for further details and historical associations of the building.

# *St Andrews Town West*

## Hallow Hill

Situated some two miles to the west of Kirkheugh, just along from Canongate Primary School is Hallow Hill. 'It became Hallow Hill or Hallowhill [Haly Hill or Holy Hill], following the discovery of stone cists in 1861,[xxv] when it was concluded the hill should be designated Hallow Hill as the burials were of 'the present, or Christian period'' (Anon 1861).

They had discovered a Celtic long cist cemetery. After this, the records of the excavation location seem to have disappeared. It wasn't until 1975, following the discovery of human bones in the garden of a newly built house at 12 Hallow Hill that archaeologists realised this was the 1861 site.

The area around the top of the hill was about to be further developed for housing, so archaeologists wanted to do what they could before this happened. In exactly the same way as Kirkheugh in 1980, little did they know when they commenced the digs here the extent of what they would find. Or that Hallow Hill would develop into an archaeological site for the next two years.

The site is of the same period as the arrival of Christianity to St Andrews at Kirkheugh. The graves here dating from the 6th

---

[xxv] I mistakenly report it as 1867 in GOS.

to 9th centuries. At Kirkheugh, the Christian graves date from the 6th to the 8th century (earliest graves 500 BC). They had found the site of a Celtic Christian community founded shortly after Kirkheugh - the two settlements are connected.

The archaeologists discovered 145 burial sites, and with it they unearthed a mystery. A high proportion of the bodies found here were of 'children and immatures' (Walker 1861). At Kirkheugh they were adults.

Also discovered was a cobbled road, signs of buildings and a church dating before the 12th century, so before what eventually became St Mary on the Rock which was in the 12th century.

The steep embankment of Hallow Hill is still a popular place for sledging, a tradition that has continued for many years.

I always remember when the archaeologists realised it was going to be a big project and needed 'a regular workforce' as it was stated in 1975. I wanted to volunteer to help with excavations, but I was too young. It was those on the dole they used for the job (the local unemployed) through the Manpower Services Commission as it was then called. I'm sure many have memories good and bad of the Manpower Services in 70s, I know I did during Maggie's recession in 1980s St Andrews.

The following extract is from the Archaeology Data Service and gives a comprehensive report of the initial finds at Hallow Hill which then spurned the two-year dig.

**Excavations at the long cist cemetery on the Hallow Hill, St Andrews, Fife. 1975-77 by Edwina Proudfoot with contributors.**

'Pressure for housing in St Andrews was intense in the late 1960s, at which period considerable development to the south of the burgh took place, while in the early 1970s, as part of this expansion, a large housing estate was planned for the whole of the Hallow Hill, then in agricultural use. Public interest in the possible significance of the name was so great that the development site was reduced and the north of the area became a public park adjacent to the Lade Braes Walk. The summit of the Hallow Hill remained part of the development, although the site of the 19th century discovery of long cists is clearly recorded on the Ordnance Survey map (1966) at NGR: NO 4940 1565, albeit that the precise site was not known (NMRS NO 41 NE8). The importance of the Hallow Hill was widely known locally because of the published reports of the long cists discovered in 1861. However, no provision was made by the various authorities for potential archaeological excavation or for recording discoveries that might be made during house-building. Extensive terracing and landscaping of 12 Hallow Hill had been required as a planning condition prior to construction in order to reduce the overall height of the house on the hill summit. During the course of these works many lorry loads of soil were removed entirely from the site, while a substantial amount of soil was bulldozed to form a garden terrace on the north-west and build up sloping ground on the east and south of the plot. An unknown number of long cists and other features was destroyed (JCB driver, pers comm,[xxvi] 1975). Later, during excavation of a trench in the east part of the garden, quantities of redeposited, broken human bones were found, and have been interpreted as coming from the terraced area, where only one cist (Cist 14) was afterwards recovered, deeply compressed by the bulldozer into the subsoil.

However, it was only when Mr Fullerton, then owner of no 12, was preparing a path across the north-east part of the garden that he discovered stones and bones, which he immediately reported to Professor W. Frend of the University of Glasgow, who contacted the University of St Andrews. It was agreed that an excavation was desirable while part of the site was still accessible, because this provided an opportunity to investigate and perhaps to confirm at least some of the details recorded in

[xxvi] Personal communication

1861. In due course the author was asked to organize a small excavation in the garden, in October 1975, and was assisted by local volunteers.' Refer also to HoS.

They had found Pandora's box, and over the next two years they would start to lift its lid. All it took to fully open the box was to then build housing around the top of the hill for the ghosts to appear, and appear they did.

## The Hallow Hill Ghosts

In GOS p.183, I wrote: 'This grassland hill just off Law Park Wood is haunted by shadowy figures and an ominous presence which sweeps over any when walking this way by night as a short cut through to the Lade Braes below. In fact, few walk this way by night for this reason.'

When I published that book, I had no information of anything happening in any of the houses built in the vicinity of Hallow Hill or neighbouring area in the 60s or 70s, but since then I have managed to obtain a few details. There will be a lot more…

**Hallow Hill Residence**

The occupants have always been aware the house is haunted by a woman. She was seen by one of the occupants of the dwelling a number of years ago, and as recently as January 2014 when a 12-year-old girl went up to the bathroom. When she came downstairs she said, "Mummy there is a woman in the hall."

**17 Hallowhill**

This property is believed to be haunted by "ghosts," but I have not thus far been able to ascertain any details.

## 6 Morton Crescent by Hallow Hill

Hi Richard
About my experience, it took place probably between 1972 and 1974, in fact, it was only months before they carried out an archaeological dig in the area [1975]. The address was at 6 Morton Crescent. I was sleeping in the front upstairs bedroom and woke at some point during the night to see two men with swords and shields fighting each other. They both had beards and helmets and one had a nose shield on his helmet. The floor level was at their waist level. As I was only 6 or 7 at the time from what I remember I only watched it for about 30 seconds or so then shut my eyes hoping they would go away, which they did once I opened my eyes not long after. I remember hearing shouting and screaming. I think that was what woke me in the first place and after I had shut my eyes the noise stopped soon after.

Hope this is useful to you and it would be interesting to find out when they carried out the archaeological dig so I could put a closer date on it.

Regards
Kevin Gatherum

There is a strange feeling of abandonment about Hallow Hill. That whoever was last here left in a hurry, which is why I find Kevin's encounter so interesting. An odd feeling that it should be busy, that something should be happening here, and it appears it still is. If a medium worthy of their status came here, what marvels would they uncover?

**New Park School**

98 Hepburn Gardens is the location of the former New Park School. Built as an independent school in 1933 by Cuthbert Dixon, the main house has now been turned into flats.

This was originally an all boy's school for day pupils, then expanded with borders c.1938 to the 1990s. In the 1970s it started admitting girls, and closed in 2005, when a downward trend in attendance of independent schools saw a merger with St Leonards, becoming St Leonards - New Park.

The main school building is a Victorian Villa. Ian Cantley, the former janitor of the school, who you may recognise as a porter at St Leonards, told me there is the ghost of a man in the building, the sound of footsteps, and the sense of a presence. He said a man died in the building. There doesn't appear to be a history of poltergeist activity, while footsteps could be Group A, with a presence being felt it points to Group B.

**Kinburn House**

Now St Andrews Museum, the house is featured in GOS. Built in 1856 by architect John Milne, this was a former residence of David Hay Fleming, a Victorian historian of St Andrews I have referenced a few times throughout this volume. This is where his book collection was housed before it moved to a purpose-built library in the centre of town from the 1930s to 2000.

Greta Boyd, who also features a few times throughout this volume and in GOS, had a few odd experiences at Kinburn, and so too has her daughter. As a background, the following is from GOS, followed by an interesting update.

'In 1975 whilst working in Kinburn House she heard heavy footsteps in the corridors at times when nobody else was in the building. Occasionally this was accompanied by the feeling of a presence standing behind her. It got so bad that on one occasion she rapidly left the building because of the awful feeling she had of a "fearful presence."

Her daughter saw the ghostly figure of a woman one evening in one of the upper stories of the building. They had just finished work and were the last to leave. After locking the door of Kinburn they began making their way along one of the gravel paths spreading its way through the grounds, when her daughter turned and saw a woman staring down at them from a window in the building.' Refer to GOS p.184.

In 2014, Greta and her daughter came to a book signing I had in Waterstone's, St Andrews. It was the first time I had seen Greta since the 1980s whilst conducting researching for GOS, so it was a real pleasure to see her again, and to meet her daughter. Her daughter said she also heard footsteps in the corridors of Kinburn House and they both had uneasy feelings.

In very similar circumstances to Greta and her daughter's experience, a few ladies came on a tour in 2019, they said they were cleaning Kinburn House. When leaving the building and locking up, something attracted their attention. Some of the windows have large draped banners, but a man was looking down at them out of the first floor window near the entrance.

## Jigger Inn
(The Jigger)

There have been feelings of being watched and the sense of not being alone when the bar is closed to the public. There are occasional cold spots, glasses have flown off the bar or moved of their own accord, and an indistinct figure has been seen standing next to the fireplace. These incidences span many years and are customarily sporadic.

The Jigger Inn is a very famous watering hole, and only yards from the 17th fairway of the Old Course. The cottage was built in the 1850s (1852?) as the Stationmasters lodge for the first railway station to serve St Andrews in 1852. In 1887 the station for the town moved to behind the present bus station and this became the goods junction.

Just in case you wondered why there is now no train station in St Andrews, it was closed in 1969 as part of Beeching's short-sighted merciless cuts of the UK's railway network. A move that mirrors centuries of British governmental incompetence. Fortunately, everything appears to function despite their intervention, not because of them - but they don't make it easy!

Over the years, the Old Course Hotel has been extended and the Inn is now joined as an extension of the hotel. It had a different feel when it stood on its own and doesn't really feel like a cottage anymore. In the same way the Isle of Skye doesn't really feel like an island since they built the bridge.

**17th Hole of the Old Course** Burial ground
This doesn't currently involve ghosts, but I mention it here as it is by the 17th hole and holds its own interest. The Rev. C. J. Lyon in his *History of St Andrews* of 1838, remarks in a footnote referring to before 1826, when they then began clearing the Cathedral rubble of centuries to make way for a town burial ground that, 'where the cemetery was formerly situated cannot now be known*; but in various parts of the town and suburbs, human bones have been found in great quantities; and in particular, near "the first hole" in the Links, a vast number of human skeletons were recently discovered, when digging the foundations of some houses.'[58]

This is where we need to take some care. There were never any buildings where the current 1st hole is located. The period in question was when the 1st hole was still the current 17th hole, as they played the course clockwise until c.1870. The burial ground is under the redundant patch of land on the southern side of what is now the Old Station Road, by the 'Road Hole' – the present 17th. The houses and burial ground Lyon were referring to is along this stretch of now redundant land.

*I believe he was taking about the pre-Roman Church, in which case he is quite correct. He would have been completely unaware of the Kirkheugh or Hallow Hill burials at that time, but even with this, there is a gap from the 8th century Kirkheugh, and 9th century Hallow Hill, to those in the grounds of Holy Trinity Church, north of St Rule's from c.1141.[xxvii] There are also the missing burial sites for the town from the late 16th century to 1826, and where were the early pilgrims buried who succumbed to their fate whilst here? Could this be a site of pilgrim burials or a plague?

**Alleyne House,** 8 Gibson Place
This was the residence of the famed Andrew Lang (b.1844, d.1912). An avid collector of folk and fairy tales. As an authority on fairy lore he is the famous author of 20 sought after books on fairies. He was president of the Society for Psychical Research in London and wrote extensively about the subject. He was nominated for the Nobel Prize for Literature, and records when he saw a ghost in his home whose costume

---

[xxvii] There was also a quarry behind the present 1st tee of the links. Part of it is still exposed and is where the bandstand sits. Another part is now under the area of the Martyrs Monument. It became a plague pit and contains 503 bodies from a plague sweeping through the town in 1605. Occasionally, bones from the plague have been exposed by great storms having caused landslides along the cliff face by the Step Rock (now the St Andrews Aquarium). A mythology attributes the bones to witches burnt at the stake along this hill, and their remnants being tossed into the sea, but these were plague victims and Witch Hill is the land between St James Church to the Palace. The 'witches' referred to, were initially Catholics who refused to adhere to the Protestant faith and were burnt at the stake along here. So, they were not 'witches' in either the horror film sense, or the earth religion promoting its own form of witchcraft from the early half of the twentieth century. There was also no 'ducking' in St Andrews at what is known as 'Witch Lake' by the Step Rock, as, uniquely, their appears to have been no 'witch trials' in St Andrews. The Protestants knew who the Catholics were so there was no need for a trial. If they hadn't already fled, or been converted to the Protestant movement, burning was a way of ridding them from St Andrews. They were heretics in Protestant eyes, so by virtue, they were devil worshippers, hence the 'witches.' Protestants were heretics in Catholic eyes and Presbyterians were heretics in the eyes of Episcopalians and vice versa, and both were heretics in the eyes of the Roman Church! It was quite a time.

was 100 years out of date, placing it to the 18th century. This must have excited him greatly.

**St Regulus Ladies Golf Club,** 9 Pilmour Links

Situated a few doors along Pilmour Links from the Rusacks Hotel is St Regulus Ladies Golf Club. Established in its current premises in 1949, its formative origins began through former Madras College pupils and associates in 1913.

A member of staff started working in the basement offices here in 2014. Working the early morning shift she finishes at 10am, so it is generally quiet. Not long after she started, she would hear the main door above on the ground floor closing, and footsteps of someone walking across the floor. On going up to see who it was, there was never anyone around. She mentioned it to other staff who said, "That is the ghost!" The staff have heard it on a regular basis for years and she has now been hearing it herself for over six years.

**Tom Morris Shop,** 7-8 The Links

The oldest golf shop in the world *was* the Tom Morris Shop on the Links overlooking the 18th green of the Old Course. Trading since 1866, in 2010, the St Andrews Links Trust took charge of the property. In 2018, far from being a successful PR exercise on par with the genius of 1 Nike Place, they rocked the golfing world by permanently changing its name to 'The Open' as a branding exercise in collaboration with the R & A. This wasn't there first marketing faux pas. In this same year, their appeal to trademark the name 'St Andrews' was rejected by the EU General Court because it is a town!

From the outside, this small historic golf shop overlooking the 18th now lacks its former prestige. Internally, this is partially counterbalanced by more of its original character being exposed due to work carried out by the trust. All credit to them for that, however, this has been overshadowed I would suggest, by costly marketing strategies out of touch with its grassroots.

Tom Morris opened his golf shop here in 1866, and lived in a house to the back facing Pilmour Links.

Like most retail premises, it is fitted with CCTV motion cameras. One morning when the staff arrived for work (when it was the Tom Morris Shop) they saw one of the cameras had been activated during the night. They reviewed the footage and a figure is seen on the screen walking across the shop floor in the early hours of the morning. The shop was closed and alarmed. There were no signs of a break-in and nothing was touched or missing. Being at night, it wasn't possible to distinguish any features. Could this also be Old Tom?

**Greyfriars Monastery Grounds**

The following is a brief background to haunted locations now occupying the former expansive grounds of Greyfriars Monastery. It was founded by Bishop Kennedy c.1458, one year after King James II banned the game of golf through an act of parliament.

It stood on what was then the far western side of St Andrews and was the monastery for Franciscan Friars or Grey Friars, appropriately named after their greyish brown attire. There pious Order in St Andrews was relatively short lived, only surviving some 101 years before the Reformation took hold.

Following the commencement of the Reformation in St Andrews, 1559, it fell into ruin and decay. In 1567, Mary Queen of Scots granted the grounds to the Burgh of St Andrews.

The adjoining land to the west of the monastery had been the crofts of George Allan. On John Wood's map of 1820, most of the lands west of what is now Greyfriars Garden were the property of a Mr Armit. East of this was owned by the town. Certainly, on the plan of St Andrews for 1849 this had all been turned into parkland called Sir John Gladstone's Park. The boundary being marked by the roads of North Street (north), North Bell Street (east - Greyfriars Garden), Market Street (South), now St Mary's Place/Alexandra Place, and the Windmill Path (City Road, west).

This was still very much on the fringes of the town. A few ruined remnants of the past including wells and some of the monastery precinct boundary walls still survive. The roads of Hope Street/Howard Place, and the eastern part of Abbotsford Crescent were created on the land in the mid to late 19th century as a thoroughfare between Alexandra Place and North Street.

**Howard Place**

Four female students were sharing a ground floor flat in Howard Place. There is a large patio off the living room to the garden. Each night, the last one to bed would make sure the doors were locked. They would then take the key out of the patio door and put it in a drawer. Every morning the key was back in the door. They thought it was odd and began wondering if one of them was playing a trick, but as Clark mentioned with the lift at Fairmont, why would anyone bother?

Three of them went away for the break leaving one in the flat. The following morning, the girl remaining in the flat knew there was something more going on - the key was in the door. As far as I am aware this is still taking place.

**The Abbotsford Place Ghost**

I received an email from Sophie McKenna following a tour with her family in 2015. She and her family had several experiences during the tour (p.380), and at the house where they were staying in Abbotsford Place. Some are attracted to phenomena through their natural energetic ambience as we have here:

Tuesday 4th August 2015

Hi Richard,
We are just back from the tour and would like to send our thanks to you once again. We found the tour fascinating! In regards to what my grandmother said about Abbotsford place at the start of the tour, we have been coming here for many years. I slept down in the living room as there was a bedroom just off the lounge. I always felt really uneasy as if a presence or someone was watching me. Several times the door handle would shake. I now sleep up the stairs and there is the same heavy feeling in the room, the whole house, in general, is like this. I know these are very old buildings. The first night we were here I was awoken by a loud laughing and shot up in bed. I asked my mum if she heard it too which she said yes. Then we

couldn't get back to sleep. We then asked my auntie about it and she said she heard me asking my mum and saw me standing beside her bed, the thing is, I wasn't standing and I certainly wasn't out of bed. Spooky.'

Thanks again,
Sophie McKenna

I have since received another email from Sophie:

Friday 12th June 2020

Hi Richard,
In regards to Abbotsford Place it was number five we stayed in that year. I'm glad that was our last time staying there as whatever was going on made us feel very uncomfortable. I've always felt a presence in the house if I'm honest and the same for number 4 Abbotsford Place, we occasionally stayed there too.

Kind regards
Sophie

Built in the second half of the 19th century, they occupy part of the grounds of the former monastery site.

The large building by the entrance to Abbotsford Place was the Cottage Hospital (formerly Greenhill Villa) from 1880 to 1902 (p.502). It is all part of the former Greyfriars land and adjoins that of the Students Union.

**Students Union**

In GOS p.169, I have the following: 'The grounds are haunted by the fleeting spectre or shadow of a male figure in dark clothing. [Similar to the figure of Fife Park and DRA, p.475.] Within the building, an unaccountable oppressive atmosphere or force has been felt. Electrical equipment placed within the eastern area has a tendency to malfunction with uncanny regularity, and the customary bouts of extreme cold associated with a haunting have also been experienced. The origin of the presence is unknown, but it is likely to be one of the Franciscan monks who inhabited the nearby Monastery.'

Everything is still taking place. The figure is of a monk. Seen in the grounds and the building along with poltergeist phenomenon, especially in the north eastern part of the building, which is the site of the former church of Greyfriars. The grounds were occupied by West Park Hotel, built in 1838 and extended in 1861. Described as an elegant building it was architecturally full of character and charm. Set back from St Mary's Place it closed in 1967, and was demolished in 1970. There will be some who are aware of what took place in the hotel, as it will have shared the same disturbances taking place in the building that then superseded it.

The new Students Union opened on the grounds in 1973 as the new hub of student life in St Andrews. Keeping the social life busy for many thousands of students over the years, this is a building filled with grand memories. When I left school in 1981, Mr McCruden, my history teacher at Madras College lent me one pound so I could go for a beer at the union. A few weeks later, I went back to school and repaid his pound.

In 2013, the union moved into a new phase. With the University planning for the future, they spent around 12 million on an extensive internal and external remodelling project of the building. Opening in 2015, the glass-fronted building looks quite impressive, and with major structural changes come the ghosts. The work carried out seems to have increased the activity here.

I saw the monk in 2014 while work was well underway. The building was in a constant flux of transformation, yet cleverly, it always remained open throughout. Once a section was finished, everything would transfer to that section. They then closed the part that had been open and worked on that. Each time you went in, you were never quite sure where you were!

I was standing at the back bar at the beginning of summer in 2014. The students were away for the summer holidays, so the bar was quiet. I was there for about 10 minutes and became aware of someone standing behind me. There had been no sound. I turned to see who had come into the bar and saw who it was. The figure of a large man was standing only a couple of feet away from me looking at me. He had the size and build of a rugby player. A large bald head, clean-shaven and a neck nearly as thick as his head, a deadpan expression, broad shoulders and wearing a dark brown habit with a hood that was down and widening around his neck. He was standing motionless. It was almost as if he had been looking over my shoulder. I'm 6' 2," he was taller, I would say around 6' 7" or more. It was only for a brief moment that I saw him, then he just disappeared. The majority of ghosts are as real as you and I. He fitted that category well. He is aware of us and appears to be the cause of the poltergeist activity.

I had heard about him, I had written about him, but I had never met him until now. It is not the first time he has been seen in the back bar. When he appears, it is always under similar circumstances, and the bar was directly on the site of the monastery.

I went to the reception and told Mandy (Amanda Barnes) the night porter what had just happened. She was both excited and scared, as she had to lock up at night on her own. A couple of weeks later I received a text message from Mandy at around 2 am on Saturday 14th June, 2014. 'I've seen him!' was all she said. It was all she needed to say. I knew exactly what she was referring to. I went in the next evening and she told me she was locking down the building and he was standing by the Porter's cabin, just to the left of where Mandy is in the photo. She got quite a scare and didn't hang around in locking up. The next day she told the staff and management, and apologised as she didn't have time to fill in her timesheet!

On Friday 27th June 2014, Mandy closed the building for the night and pulled down the shutter to the new reception before locking up the building. When she arrived the next morning and opened the building, the shutter was up. Nobody had been in before this and being a big heavy shutter, it couldn't do this by itself.

The next night, Tim, another porter at the Union, was on duty. He closed-up the building for the night and on opening the building the next morning he found the door to the gent's toilet was locked. He had locked the building down the night before but he hadn't locked the toilet door as he didn't have a key, so he had to phone around other members of staff to find one who may have a key to come in and unlock the toilet door.

Staff have felt a presence within the building and lights have been switched on and off in the Rectors Café at the front of the building and in some of the upper rooms.

On the 26 July at 9 pm, 2014, Susan Anderson a member of staff at the Students Union experienced something which questioned her surroundings. 9 pm was quite early in relative terms for the union bar, so with it being quiet, she was cleaning and stacking glasses behind the bar with her back to the public area. She heard voices behind her and on turning to serve them, no one there. It was her first experience of something happening. She also saw figures out the corner of her eye, and again on turning for a better look to see who was in the bar there was no one around.

I was speaking with Sandy Mackenzie, the long-term bastion of the bars in the Students Union for a great many years. He wasn't overly surprised when she spoke to him about what she was experiencing. So many things have happened over the years in the Union it was simply more confirmation for Sandy that things do occur here.

Since writing up this piece, Sandy sadly passed away towards the end of 2015. With 20 years of service at the Students Union, Sandy and his colourful ties are sadly missed by all who knew him, including me. His funeral service in Holy Trinity Church was completely packed full to the back western wall. There was standing room only as town and gown paid their respects. No matter how busy Sandy was, he always had a smile and time for everyone. He loved seeing everyone enjoying themselves.

One of the bars of the Union has been named 'Sandy's Bar' in his honour, and branded with one of his famed colourful ties as a heartfelt tribute and thanks to a man who loved everybody and who everybody loved.

**Inchcape House and Hostel**

Directly across the road from the union is Inchcape House at 4 St Mary's Place. It was built in 1861 for S. Grace. Before this in 1835, a hotel called Inchcape Private Hotel stood here.

The present building also served as Inchcape Boarding House. The first floor and attic floor of this sizeable Victorian house is known as Inchcape House Hostel (St Andrews Tourist Hostel). The building was occupied by Cantley & Caithness, a firm of Solicitors and Notaries.[xxviii] The ground floor was then the Grill House Restaurant from 1999, owned by G1. Then changing to Mammacita through its tenure.

The hostel has the ghost of a man. Described as being tall and wearing dark clothing, he has been seen numerous times, always standing in the foyer at the top of the stairs on the first floor. He has also been seen by the hostel's reception area and at the reception counter. Described as being faint but distinct he vanishes in a moment.

**Greyfriars Monastery Chapel** (Site of)

Corner of Market Street and Greyfriars Garden

In 1991, a graduate of Glasgow University was on a visit to St Andrews. After a night with friends, he was on his way to his residence at around 2 am and decided to rest awhile in the garden on the corner of Greyfriars Garden and Market Street.

He sat on a bench and became aware of someone else in the garden. In the shadows, he saw a man across the other side of the garden. He was walking sluggishly and slightly hunched. He thought he might have been disabled but could have been injured.

---

[xxviii] The firm became Murray Donald & Caithness 1999, then Thorntons, 2014.

The graduate knew something wasn't right with what he was seeing. The figure appeared to be aware of him sitting on the bench, and keeping his distance walked round the garden skirting its edge. He got up and started walking to the entrance, the figure moving at the same pace kept his distance then just disappeared. The graduate ran out of the garden to his residence. He was unaware of the history in this locality and the significance of where he was. The ghostly figure he saw was a monk, but not the same one as the other reports in the grounds, and different to what myself, Mandy and others have seen.

**Corner of Greyfriars Gardens and Market Street**

151 Market Street – The Nationwide Building

This was W. R. Kermath, Registered Chemist and Druggist, then for years as Lloyds Pharmacy. It was then the Halifax and now the Nationwide. In the late 1970s, a couple of pharmacists were in the cellar of the property one evening when bottles started flying off the shelves across the room.

All the buildings along here, including 12-16 Greyfriars Garden on the corner of Greyfriars and North Street, were owned by Captain Campbell in 1844 and date from 1836.

**10 Greyfriars Garden**

I have four separate accounts for this flat. Three different residents who lived in the property over a five decade period all reported the same thing. There is the ghost of a monk who wanders the rooms of the flat and when he hasn't been seen he has often been felt.

More recently in 2017, a group of students staying in the flat have heard the attic door banging up and down continuously and fairly rapidly around 10 to 15 times when there has been no wind. They believe the place is haunted and came on a tour to find out if I knew anything about it. They didn't know about the monk, but believe there is someone in the attic.

**9 Greyfriars Garden**

In 2016, this was the residence of five students who came on a tour to tell me every once in a while they hear the sound of a doorbell playing what sounds like a nursery rhyme that none could place. No doorbell around there plays a tune. They have all heard it and the can never pinpoint the source.

I had other students on a tour that have also stayed here. They said objects and personal items are disappearing. When they know something is missing they spend a long time searching and end up pilling everything out of drawers but to no avail. Then the object/s reappear in obvious places. There is also the sense of a presence. Sometimes they talk to the ghost and call it Archibald. When they don't, more things happen.

Unknown to them, that was the best thing they can do. They were unaware there is a connection between acknowledgement and the disturbance ceasing. There are so many examples of this being the case through St Andrews. John Marini at the New Inn, the manageress at Little Italy, the same at the Cancer Research Shop, and etc. The students were also unaware of any previous activity here and what is still taking place next door.

# St Andrews Town – Southeast

We move our attention now to a few locations in the southern quarter of the town.

**No.6 Kinness Burn Terrace**

A student on a tour asked if I had anything for 6 Kinness Burn Terrace, which until her mention of this residence I hadn't. She said it was a student flat. She was staying there and told me at the end of the tour there are sounds of footsteps from the attic and things are moving around. She was a little unnerved about it, but nothing had harmed her and she was moving out soon after.

**Nelson Street**

A few students came on a tour and told me they were staying in a student house in Nelson Street. They said, "There is the feeling of a presence in the house. It isn't so much a feeling of being watched, more that we are sharing the house with someone else. Someone is in the house with us!"

Unfortunately, I didn't get their address so have always wondered if it was one of the properties hit by a stray German bomb dropped by a plane flying out to sea during the Second World War.

It is believed St Andrews was never a place the Germans looked to intentionally bomb, although there were rumours about the Bute and connections with anthrax development. Following their raids, if they had any bombs left they would offload them before heading out to sea to conserve fuel. Although I have been told the flight path of any inland bombing raids would not pass over St Andrews on their way to Europe, unless they were dramatically off course, which could be the case here.

The bomb landed on the 6th August, 1942. It was a direct hit on one house, and neighbouring houses were extensively damaged. It killed 12 people and severely injured others.

**Cottage Hospital, Abbey Walk**

The Cottage Hospital on Abbey Walk (Abbey Park), was also known as St Andrews Memorial Hospital. A few have come forward to say they used to hear a child crying in the hospital. It was especially prevalent in the late 1980s and early 1990s in the woman's ward, formerly a children's ward. No explanations were ever found for the sound. This was reminiscent of Mount Melville House up at Craigtoun (GOS p.194), following its conversion to a maternity hospital. There were the sounds of a baby crying, but despite it being a maternity hospital, they could never pin point the source of the crying.

The Cottage Hospital was built in 1902 as a replacement for two earlier Cottage hospitals. The first was St Andrews Cottage Hospital which opened with 6 beds in 1865 along the road at at 33 Abbey Street, and demolished in the 1960s. Founded by Dr John Adamson (p.272), and his surgery partner, it was dedicated as a memorial for Lady (Elizabeth) William Douglas of Grangemuir.

Proving inadequate, a building called Greenhill Villa was purchased in Abbotsford Place in 1880 and turned into the Cottage Hospital with two wards. With limited space, the hospital closed in 1902 when the purpose-built hospital then opened its doors on Abbey Walk.[xxix] This closed in 2009 when the new St Andrews Community Hospital opened on Largo Road. Five years later, in February 2014 the Cottage hospital on Abbey Walk was demolished to make way for Ayton House. Private student accommodation called 'Hello,' to ease some of the burdens in the town. While more accommodation was

[xxix] There was also a hospital on St Mary Street called St Andrews Fever Hospital (Scarlet Fever). Opposite the New Inn.

more than welcome, there is always a caveat in St Andrews, it is certainly not cheap!

**Kinness Burn Monks**

Shore Bridge spans the fresh waters of the Kinness Burn marking the boundary between St Mary Street and Abbey Walk. East of the bridge there are a series of stepping stones which are clearly visible in the summer when the burn is low. Marked on the St Andrews OS map of 1893, it is here that monks have been seen crossing the burn in procession.

**Woodburn Terrace**

Pete Rankin and his partner were in the living room of their home watching TV. The baby was upstairs and a baby monitor was beside them in case of any problems. It was just the three of them in the house. The silence from upstairs was broken by a voice coming through the baby monitor. It sounded like someone being killed, a man's voice trying to shout, "Help me!" The voice was deep, gargled and very menacing to the point of being demonic. Pete had lived there for around 30 years. He is not easily spooked, but after hearing this they moved house after all that time. Refer also to p.182, p.311 and p.388.

**St Nicholas Farmhouse Bed and Breakfast**

With its idyllic setting only yards from the East Sands, the B&B has been owned and run for over 40 years by Ann and Bill Pressegh. While they have not experienced anything themselves, the ghost of a man has been seen by those visiting and staying in the house.

The building is on the site of St Nicholas Hospital, a medieval leper colony and hospital (pilgrim hostel) founded in the 12th century by the Céilí Dé. It was a leper colony until 1438 run by monks who also had the disease. The stigma of leprosy changed through time, but there was a period when none of them were allowed entry to St Andrews itself, and if they were heading further north they had to circumnavigate the town and they were not allowed to stop until the town was behind them. They were beggars in alms and their survival was solely dependent on the goodwill of those heading in or out of St Andrews. It was part of Kinkell Estate, owned by the Céilí Dé that extended eastward from here around the coast.

The current building was the farmhouse for St Nicolas farm until 1975. Many years ago, when a silo was being installed near to the farmhouse, three skeletons were found, one on top of the other. It is believed they are still there. They were dated to the fifth to seventh century so of Celtic/Pictish origin, and certainly earlier than the leper colony here. There is also believed to be a crypt still underneath the house and a boulder with an equal-armed cross was found here in the early 1990s.

The ghost of the man here is believed to be that of a farmworker who was dragged into the silo and killed.

**The Grange**

A large house just before the Grange Inn when leaving St Andrews was haunted by the ghost of a woman among other paranormal disturbances. The building was demolished October 2016.

# *The Ghost of Lady Kinkell*

## 4 Reports

Kinkell Castle stood to the south east of the Castle Course Clubhouse carpark. There was also a chapel here that goes all the way back to c.875 AD. Only 300 years after the foundation of Kilrymont, give or take literally one or two years.

The chapel at Kinkell was dedicated to St Anna, the mother of the Virgin Mary, grandmother of Jesus. It was built by Kellach, the Céile Dé Bishop (Abbot) of Kilrymont at that time. The name means ceann coille or head of the wood. Sibbald wrote, 'Kellach, Kilkell [Cella, Kellach,] corrupted into Kinkell.'[59] A great many pilgrims stopped here en route to and from St Andrews. Many arriving by sea into Kinkell Bay.

**Report 1. Kinkell Castle**

Before his death in 1929, Linskill said of Kinkell Castle, that it 'was believed to be haunted by the apparition of Lady Kinkell who silently roamed the area of the chapel.'[60]

**Report 2. Kinkell Caravan Park**

A family on a tour said they have a caravan by the coastal path up at Kinkell to the west of the former castle. She told me her husband was sitting in the living room watching TV late at night in 2017. It was summer and very hot, so the door at the end of the caravan was wide open overlooking the sea. He saw the figure of a woman in white walk past the window on the footpath near the caravan. It was dark outside so he noticed the figure in white all the more. Being the early hours of the morning this struck him as odd, so he went to have a look. Nobody was to be seen walking along the pavement in either direction. His wife timidly asked me if there were any ghosts up at Kinkell. I told her about the ghost of Lady Kinkell who roams her former estate along this stretch of coastal path to what is now the Castle Course Clubhouse. That she has been seen along the coastal path of Kinkell Braes between the caravan park and Kinkell wearing white. She became quite concerned and said, "He's up there on his own at the moment. Once he hears this, he may not want to be on his own as often!"

I have many people from Kinkell on my tours. It is rare for Lady Kinkell to be seen. Apart from her ghost, I have not heard of anything else happening up at the caravan park itself. However, it doesn't mean there isn't anything else happening up there, so if you do see her or experience anything, you must let me know!

**Report 3. Kinkell Coastal Path**

Another report comes to us from Alexa, a waitress at the Fairmont Hotel. The report was passed to me by some guests staying at the Fairmont who came on a tour early 2020. She was telling them she saw a small woman wearing a white dress at about 1 am sitting on a bench on the coastal path along from the Fairmont. She thought it was a girl but as she drew closer it was a small woman with white hair – who then just disappeared.

**Report 4**
**Kinkell Coastal Path by the Castle Course**

The following is from Mike D. He sent me a few reports of his experiences in this area that I recorded earlier, including something brushing past his head along the East Scores Path, and an experience at Ninewells. This following account is his experience at the Castle Course, which he kindly enclosed along with information and references about Kinkell Castle and Estate that assisted in my researches for that area.

# *The Ghost of Lady Kinkell*

Fri, 04 Aug 2017

Hi Richard,

Good to see that your ghost tours are getting great ratings. I must go along on one soon. I'm moving back to St Andrews in September.

I was in email conversation last night and this morning with a friend who was also born and brought up in Fife when we got on to the subject of ghosts. I had not realised that he too had seen people that appeared then disappeared. In fact, he may have had more sightings than I have. I found your article in the Courier last January.

Indeed. I was sceptical but not closed to the possibility of what are known as ghosts. They seem to defy physics, given current understandings of physics. However...

You may recall you were talking with my mother at Kinburn Museum. She introduced us and I told you about the young lady I saw in unusual (in retrospect medieval or earlier) attire near the Castle Course, formerly the area of Muckross and Kinkell Castle?

Someone I recounted this to remarked at the amount of detail I was able to describe. I had a camera with me during the encounter but thought it rude to take a picture without asking first. In retrospect, this may seem frustrating but it illustrates how solid and real the presence appeared to be i.e. a normal human, just oddly attired and may be slightly off colour in her face, slightly green/grey hue if I recall correctly but the rest of her was very normal. I have yet to find any accounts of genuine attire from those periods to match what I saw.

Her hair was completely covered if I can presume she had any by a white scarf or covering. She wore a transparent veil so I could see that she had almond coloured eyes and a chemise that didn't hide much in the bright sunshine. There was something odd about her shorts. In retrospect, I realised these were a cotton wrap, fashioned in the manner of shorts.

I don't recall whether she had bare feet or sandals, odd because I stepped aside for her which was appreciated. She responded to "Hi" with an intake of breath, which might have been meant to sound similar. When I looked back to do a double-take on the odd attire she had gone and there was a smiling middle-aged man in the distance, enjoying the walk in the warm weather I expect and oblivious to what had occurred.

I have been on that walk many times but cannot point to exactly where this occurred. Admittedly, the path has changed in places since then, somewhere between 2003 and 2006 I think. I estimated her age, as she appeared, as between 17 and 23. My feeling about the period, based on the outfit is 1200s–1400s, but could easily be earlier. There must be a clue in the quality of the material though? Surely, a veil and chemise that fine would not have been common to ordinary folk? My guess is that she succumbed to illness evidenced by the slight hue to her facial skin (as I recall it). She was slim but not visibly starved.

If that really had been a student prank, I would be astonished.

Regards
Mike

Mike later emailed again with further details:

Hi Richard,
The lady's facial skin seemed a little off colour but the rest of her skin appeared normal. Note that her skin was not the white colour associated with a typical anaemic these days. She was not suffering a fever and appeared to walk perfectly well.

Regards
Mike

There are several possibilities here, but firstly, Mike has had an encounter with both Lady Kinkell and Lady Buchan, which as an observation I find interesting. The head scarf was probably made of silk which would have the transparency. This was imported mainly from Italy. Originating from China it came through the ancient Silk Road to the merchants of Venice who controlled the bulk of the trade to Northern Europe. It was rare, so it was costly, accessible to the upper classes and the church.

The cotton wrap, or chemise sounds like a very fine cloth. It could also have been made of silk but is more likely to be made of very fine linen which does have a transparency in strong sunlight. The chemise was the most popular undergarment for over 500 years, developing through to the late 18th century, which unfortunately doesn't narrow it down in terms of a time period for when she was alive. They generally went down to their knees and were white or off white.

She sounds like a wispy character and her attire, or the lack of, would have attracted a degree of attention – unless she were in her night attire, hence the undergarment. Her being off colour, could have been an illness, and confinement to bed would then explain her scantily clad appearance. Illness or not, she appears to be wearing what she was wore when she died.

The feint complexion was also the fashion of the day. White skin was fashionable to the point where the surgeon would cut a vein in their arm and allow enough blood to leave the body until their complexion went the colour they were desiring. Not a service I imagine they offer in Boots, or maybe they do? They would also use lead based powder mixed with water to whiten their skin. Many died of lead poisoning as a result!

Through the Middle Ages, married women were not considered to be fully dressed without a head covering.

Whatever period she is from, her attire was certainly expensive. For her to acknowledge Mike with an audible air is rare, and unlike the reply by a supposed ghostly 'nun' I read about at the harbour, her response was what he perceived as being an "intake of breath."

Between the acknowledgement and the factor of her not always being seen in the same location, means this is her spirit, she is aware of her surroundings and those who see her. Characteristically, she is always seen on the former Kinkell Estate, where it would appear her energies have free reign.

There is a selection of noted families over the centuries holding the Kinkell title. With many generations within each there is nobody obvious at this time to furnish a suggestion as to her identity. Sibbald writing about Kinkell Castle and Estate in 1710, says:

'A few illustrious Fifeshire families have been resident here over the years; amongst them were the Moubrays, then by marriage the Hepburns, the Monipennies of Pitmilly [of Pitmilly House fame], the Hamiltons and John Ramsay Esq.'[xxx61]

I have written a history of Kinkell Castle for HoS, focusing on the Hamilton family. They were the last occupants of the castle, and their little known association with the murder of Archbishop Sharpe, lead to the abrupt end of Kinkell Castle as a noted family seat in Fife for many centuries. It follows on from what I wrote in GOS with another angle from build-up to aftermath, and is primarily from a Kinkell perspective.

Maybe at some point I will delve into the other families, here, especially the Monipennies. If I do, it will be with the aim of furthering existing research into Pitmilly House a few miles east. It remains the only insurance pay-out for arson/poltergeist activity. In GOF, I have previously unpublished experiences, along with some of Lorn Macintyre's extensive research, and a very informative article by Tom Ruffles of the SPR, as a review of Lorn's research with additional material, GOF pp.208-223.

[xxx] By the time General Ramsay had the estate in the late 18th century the castle was a roofless ruin.

# Photos

## Introduction

**How valid can photographs really be?**
While photos have the potential to strengthen the integrity of the paranormal it will never happen. Photos will never constitute as proof regardless of what they purport to display. There are too many variables. Not least the factor that those who are already dismissive of the huge wealth of corroborated

testimony available to us are not going to be convinced of its reality by an image in a photograph. The pre-judgmental approach of the sceptical mind precludes anything other than a physical, psychological or doctored origin. Especially when, with a little knowhow and advanced technology at our fingertips, we can easily slip in an overlay to an image in software like photoshop and leave social media to do the rest.

It may surprise however, that doctored photos of this nature are rare. It may also surprise that we don't need any of that when the most common photos purporting anomalous activity are through illusions created by our own perceptions. So, when it comes down to it, we needn't worry ourselves about fake photographs when we are perfectly good at seeing things that aren't there ourselves.

We are the master of our own illusions, and the interaction of the lens with its surroundings cause all manner of problems for our perception to deal with. Lighting and weather conditions, a trick of light on glass or stone creating vague, often blurry, yet recognizable images.

Seeing familiar images or patterns in objects is the most common form, and faces are the most common images we humans see in objects. Facial recognition is called Pareidolia, and is believed to be one of the first self-preservation mechanisms imprinted upon us when we appear in this particular time, on this particular planet. It comes to us from the Greek with German usage for the same in 1866/7.

The immediacy of what we see provides irresistible proof to those eager to believe, but eagerness and the paranormal rarely mix.

There is an adage: 'We see what we want to see' and we take our leave accordingly. There are variations to this, Goethe writing in *Faust* says 'each one sees what he carries in his heart.' Robertson Davies in his 1951 novel *Tempest-Tost* says: 'The eye sees only what the mind is prepared to comprehend.' It is important to note these apply in equal measure to the believer as they do the sceptic – there is no difference. My own one is 'we see what we expect to see' – and that also works for both.

Most fall into either the believer or sceptic camp, and each can be quick in jumping to conclusions to the negation of the overall body of evidence surrounding their production. This is called top-down processing. The importance is the analysis not the assumption. Empirical Science live by the former, but when applied to purported anomalous images, sceptics are quick to adopt the latter, and neither factor in all components of CAI following this introduction or PERL (Appendix 2).

In evaluating a photo, it should always be conducted with a neutrality of mind as its starting point, if that is, we are to make a reasoned judgement without bias. However, given the potential complexities of perception and an eternity of conflicting viewpoints this is not so easy.

From its invention, photography has always involved the manipulation of images to develop and refine techniques, and along with it comes the inevitable controversy. Sir David Brewster, an early pioneer of photography was Principal of St Andrews University 1837-1859. Amongst his many inventions was the kaleidoscope in 1816, which in modern times has been comparable in popularity to the mobile phone. He also invented the first portable stereoscope producing 3D images. In his book *The Stereoscope: Its History, Theory, and Construction,* published in 1856, he wrote: 'For the purpose of amusement, the photographer might carry us even into the regions of the supernatural. His art... enables him to give a spiritual appearance to one or more of his figures, and to exhibit them as 'thin air' amid the solid realities of the stereoscopic picture. While a party is engaged with their whist or their gossip, a female figure appears in the midst of them with all the attributes of the supernatural. Her form is transparent, every object or person beyond her being seen in shadowy but distinct outline.'[62] Brewster then explains one of the methods of introducing a ghost in this way: 'The parties which are to compose the group must have their portraits nearly finished in the binocular camera... When the party have nearly sat the proper length of time, the female figure, suitably attired, walks quickly into the place assigned to her, and after standing a few seconds in the proper attitude, retires quickly. If this operation has been well performed, all the objects immediately behind the female figure, having been, previous to her introduction, impressed upon the negative surface, will be seen through her, and she will have the appearance of an aerial personage, unlike the other figures in the picture.'[63]

There were many techniques, and they were designed for amusement, but the first image publicised as a genuine spirit appeared five years following Brewster's book in the 1861, by William H. Mumler in the States. The image was a self-portrait he took himself and when developed, his cousin who died some 12 years earlier appears in the photograph. What you are looking at is the first selfie ever taken with a ghost.

Mumler called himself a medium and spirit photographer and went on to produce hundreds of portrait photos of deceased relatives appearing with the living.

He reached his peak during and after the American Civil War of 1861-65, where some 620,000 souls lost their lives. All was coupled with a dramatic rise in the popularity of spiritualism as there was an endless supply of grieving relatives looking to gain reassurance that their dearly departed had survived death.

Spirit photographs gained such recognition that Mary Todd Lincoln, Abraham Lincoln's wife, went to Mumler in a bid to have her portrait taken with her assassinated husband – Abraham Lincoln. The ensuing spirit photo of them both moved the popularity of Mumler and spirit photography to a new level. It also became a favourite with the spiritualist mediums of the day, as they appeared to offer proof of life after death and strengthened their movement. Unfortunately, it did little to strengthen its reality outside those grieving loved ones.

Mumler was taken to trial for fraud by P.T. Barnum of Barnum's circus fame, but was acquitted as they could not prove his photos were fake, however the suggestion had been enough to tarnish his reputation – but, I must add, only with the sceptics. For the believers, and those who knew the reality of the spiritual, his photos were still causing a sensation, and still do to this day. Not least because Mumler always maintained the genuineness of his photographs despite all the odds of there being a number of ways they could be fabricated, including double exposure. The thing is, the chances of him having a photo of the deceased is slim, and if the deceased appearing in a photo was not recognised by the grieving relatives he wouldn't have lasted two minutes.

Move forward 160 years and the bereaved are no longer queueing to have their portrait taken with their lost loved ones yet the fascination for photographs of ghosts remains as strong today as the controversy surrounding them.

# *Ghosts*

# Categories for Anomalous Images

(CAI)

## CAI

1. Natural Anomaly - with no paranormal suggestion
2. Natural Anomaly - suggestive of a paranormal origin
3. Borderline image - between natural and paranormal
4. No physical explanation
5. A Simulacrum or fake/doctored image

**Introduction**

As fascinating as they can be, anomalous images provide us with no shortage of conjecture to uphold the viewpoint of the sceptic and the believer alike, but they do little of themselves to further anyone's understanding of this rare and elusive phenomenon.

Things are not always what they seem, and this is especially true of the paranormal. It is subtle, and even the suggestion of it being a reality beyond fiction is an uncomfortable premise for many. So, photos are the easiest to simply dismiss regardless of the imagery they contain.

The substance of some images are more obvious to determine than others, but in some ways, this is why care must be taken in their evaluation, and that is where 'Categories for Anomalous Images' or CAI come in. I created CAI to give an additional way of making a more informed decision about an anomalous image.

Most anomalous photos will initially fall into either CAI Categories 1. or 2. If there is any background information for an image's production, be it contextual, testimonial, circumstantial etc., the image might then be more suited to one of the subcategories of CAI category 3. or even category 4. no physical explanation.

If background information for its production is available, this can then be reinforced through PERL (Paranormal Experience Reference List), Appendix 1, p.597. When using PERL with a photo, add in all the PERL categories that apply.

I have included CAI category examples using a selection of anomalous photos taken in St Andrews, and have used the photo on p.546 and p.559 as examples of CAI and PERL to give an idea. The second of the two also has an explanation of the PERL breakdown giving a PERL conclusion.

# CAI Categories

## Photo Category 1.

**Natural Anomaly - with no paranormal suggestion**

**1.** Rare anomalous images produced by physical means.

CAI categories 2. to 4. can be used in conjunction with PERL if background details are known about an image.

## Photo Category 2.

**Natural Anomaly - suggestive of a paranormal origin**
with PERL involvement

2a, 2b, 3 and 4 can be employed in conjunction with each other.

**Sub 2a. Natural/man-made/electronic means**
Anomalous images suggestive of a paranormal origin that are produced by natural/man-made/electronic means. Something physical moving across a photo when it is being taken, double exposure, blurred images, motion blur causing streaks of light etc.

**Sub 2b. Vortex or breath factor**

Breathing out when taking a photo in damp/cold conditions can create a fine mist that is not seen at the time an image is taken. The phenomenon is called 'vortex' or the 'breath factor' and the sceptic will happily attribute *all* photos displaying this as being created by either breath, cigarette smoke or mist.

**Sub 3. Pareidolia**

Pareidolia is known as an 'incorrect perception' in seeing familiar patterns or shapes; especially faces and bodies formed by colour, light, shadows, reflections, gradients on surfaces such as stone, glass, wood, patterns in mist or clouds for example, and interpreted as being anomalous with possible paranormal origin.

One of the most famous being in 2004, when a slice of toast with the image of the Virgin Mary was sold to an internet casino on an eBay auction for $28,000.

This photograph is one of the earliest and most famous for displaying pareidolia as the eye adjusts between two familiar images. One is the popular portrayal of Jesus or Rasputin (being from the location it was taken). Can you see the other?

**Sub 4. Illusions**

Optical illusions produced by natural or manmade means causing the same effects on the mind as pareidolia but embodying a wider scope for its creation and effect.

# Photo Category 3.
## Borderline Images
with PERL involvement

**Sub 3a. Borderline Image 1**
Where it is not possible to be 100% sure an anomaly is attributable to a physical cause, but something isn't quite right with either the image properties and / or PERL involvement (especially **PERL – C1d, C1e**).

While hoaxes cannot be ruled out, these revolve more around the pattern of phenomenon not fitting with the characteristics of how phenomena operate. Pointing to the observer experiencing physical phenomena and mistaking it as being paranormal in origin due to their knowledge of the paranormal coming from a fabrication of fiction. This applies to a number of circumstances throughout this volume.

**Sub 3b. Borderline Image 2**
While an image can appear to have a physical *cause*, it is not possible to be 100% sure an image is attributable to a physical *origin,* when taking into account image properties / surrounding circumstances / testimonial circumstance of PERL.

**For PERL analysis with 3b:**
PERL analysis **3b.** is especially poignant with **C2d.** if resulting from poltergeist activity and the image captured part of what was happening. PERL - **D1.** strengthens the integrity of phenomenon, especially when **D2** is also present. In these instance's it takes away the random factor and points to the *cause* being physical, the *origin* of the *cause* being paranormal - switching CAI - **2a.** or **b.** and **3.** to this category Sub **3b.** The same applies to general anomalies, refer to PERL - **D.**

**Sub 3c. Borderline Image 3**
Where it is not possible to be 100% positive an image is attributable to a **physical *cause or origin*** given the image properties and / or testimonial circumstance / PERL involvement.

**Sub 3d. Borderline Image 4**
Elements of doubt for **CAI 3a.** through **3c.** are is still present, so with **3d.** a physical cause cannot be ruled out, but is unlikely given the strength of image / testimonial / PERL circumstance / involvement. The image fringes on the border of **CAI 4. No Physical Explanation.**

## Photo Category 4.
### No physical explanation
with PERL involvement

This is where it has not been possible to attribute an image to a physical cause and has a qualification endorsed by testimonial / PERL circumstance / involvement.

## Photo Category 5.
### A Simulacrum or fake/doctored image

I have put fake photographs last because regardless of the motivation, of these five categories, there are far fewer fake photos than there are photos creating their own illusions and being interpreted as having a paranormal origin. This applies also to testimony – very few people make up testimony, and it is generally recognised when they do. By comparison to physical explanations, the contrivance of photos or testimony are extremely rare, which as I stated earlier is an interesting observation when populist belief would have these as being the most common.

# *CAI Example Photos and analysis*

❖

The following is a visual and analytical journey through some of the quarks of reality found in the photographic image around St Andrews and a few from Edinburgh.

99% of photos portraying purported anomalous images have a physical and/or psychological explanation. Very rarely an image will present itself that is not so easy to explain away or dismiss. I have enclosed a few images below that are representative of four of the five CAI categories. I have not included an example of **CAI 5. A Simulacrum or fake/doctored image** as they are rare by comparison to **CAI 2. Physical/psychological cause 2a., 2b., 3. and** 4.

None of the photographs have been published before barring Marysia's photo, which she posted on a forum to find if she could glean any explanation. A move popularly associated with the opening of the portal of Hades in the south-western region of Turkey.

I have included 22 photos, 5 taken by myself and 17 submitted to me by those who took them. I have photos submitted to me all the time so these are snapshot examples. There is never any ulterior motivation in their submissions, and a commonality is their wanting to find out more about what they have taken. I have published them along with their accompanying testimony where provided and my analysis of the same based on CAI and PERL.

Some of the following reproductions do not capture the detail of the original images which are all in colour and can further highlight the anomaly. So, for the benefit of colour observation, I have put most of the images onto a private webpage as an extension of this volume to give a clearer indication. Note: There is NO link on the website to the page. You need to type this into your browser: standrewsghosttours.com/mgos

When viewing these images, it is important to bear in mind what I have written earlier about photos and CAI. More importantly, consider what you have read through this volume. If you do, your mind will be more open to evaluating what you are looking at before making any predictable conclusions in either direction.

The photos range from natural unusual phenomena, illusions and borderline images through to seven images comprising a mix of ghosts and orbs in St Andrews and Edinburgh where there is no physical explanation.

Borderline images form the mainstay of what I have included. Once you have read the accompanying testimony, background data and my analysis of the same, it is then up to your own determination.

*CAI Example Photos*

# PHOTO CATEGORY 1

## Natural anomaly with no paranormal suggestion

❖

Two Examples

**CAI 1. Natural Anomaly**
Rare anomalous images produced by physical means

**CAI Natural Anomaly 1,** Example 1

## Cathedral Precinct Wall

Sunset Light

Photo by Louis Kenna 2018

# CAI Example Photos

October 2018
I start here with a photo taken by Louis Kenna who was on one of my tours with his family. The anomaly is the way the light was shining through the loop hole in the north wall of the Cathedral precincts. I was present at the time and saw the natural phenomenon myself. It only lasted a few seconds as the sun set in the west the moment we were walking past the loop hole. Louis had his mobile in his hand and was quick to capture this very rare and unusual moment. By the time I produced my mobile it was gone. I have never seen anything like this before that day or since along here, or anywhere for that matter.

It was like a flame of gold coming through the opening and really highlighted the sandstone in its true colours. He took a few photos in quick succession so I have included two on my website. His children were amazed. Black and white unfortunately does not do it justice, in colour it looks incredible, and just as it was when we saw it.

This was a rare natural anomaly, there was no suggestion of a paranormal nature.

### **CAI Natural Anomaly 1**, Example 2
## Martyrs Monument
With the R & A building in the background

Photo by Richard Falconer 2016

**CAI 1. Natural anomaly**
Rare anomalous images produced by physical means

I am sure we have all seen examples of this phenomenon, especially in films. I took this back in 2016. Like Louis's photo it captures the light of the sunset, this time the sun is setting directly behind the monument and the R & A Clubhouse. It is rare to capture the setting sun in this position, there are only a few days in the year when it is possible, and it only lasted a few seconds. Again, black and white does not do it justice – original on the website.

# PHOTO CATEGORY 2

Sub categories 2a, 2b, 3 and 4

## Natural anomaly suggestive of a paranormal origin

❖

CATEGORY 2, sub category 2a

## Natural/man-made/electronic means

1 Example

**CAI 2. Sub 2a. Natural/man-made/electronic means**
Anomalous images suggestive of a paranormal origin that are produced by natural/man-made/electronic means. Something physical moving across a photo when it is being taken, double exposure, blurred images, motion blur causing streaks of light etc.

## **View over St Andrews Bay**
## from the Scores Road by the Palace

Steaks of light and figures

Photo by Lorraine Irvine, 9th September 2014

Motion blur is a common natural phenomenon. In this image the mobile picking out the bright light of the moon caused

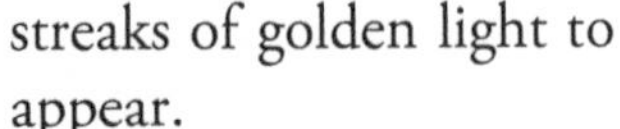

streaks of golden light to appear.

Lorraine took this digital photo on a tour when we were outside the Palace. A large golden moon was rising above the North Sea almost like a hazy sunrise.

When looking at this photo on the website you may notice what looks like the feint image of a group of people standing across the upper half of the photo. It is like a double exposure. However, it is easy to forget the whole image is subject to motion blur which distorts everything in the image, not just the streaks of light. Subconsciously we pick and choose to try and make sense of what we ae observing.

Even with no motion blur, the image is so feint it would be equally suggestive of straining the imagination to make out anything more than the natural haze of pixelated clouds.

# PHOTO CATEGORY 2

Sub categories 2a, 2b, **3** and 4

## Natural anomaly suggestive of a paranormal origin

❖

CATEGORY 2, sub category 3

## Pareidolia

3 Examples

**CAI 2. Sub 3. Pareidolia**

Familiar patterns or shapes such as faces and bodies formed by colour, light, shadows, reflections, gradients on surfaces such as stone, glass, wood, patterns in mist or clouds for example, and interpreted as being anomalous with possible paranormal origin.

**CAI Natural Anomaly 2, sub 3. Pareidolia.** Example 1

## Window of Queen Mary's House

Face in window?

Photos taken by Thomas Bremner, 15th August 2019

The first is with no flash, the second is with a flash and what looks like a face, probably caused by the flash on the window.

**CAI Natural Anomaly 2, sub 3. Pareidolia.** Example 2

## Window at St Leonards

Face at the window?

Photo by Jackie Wilson, 17 November 2019

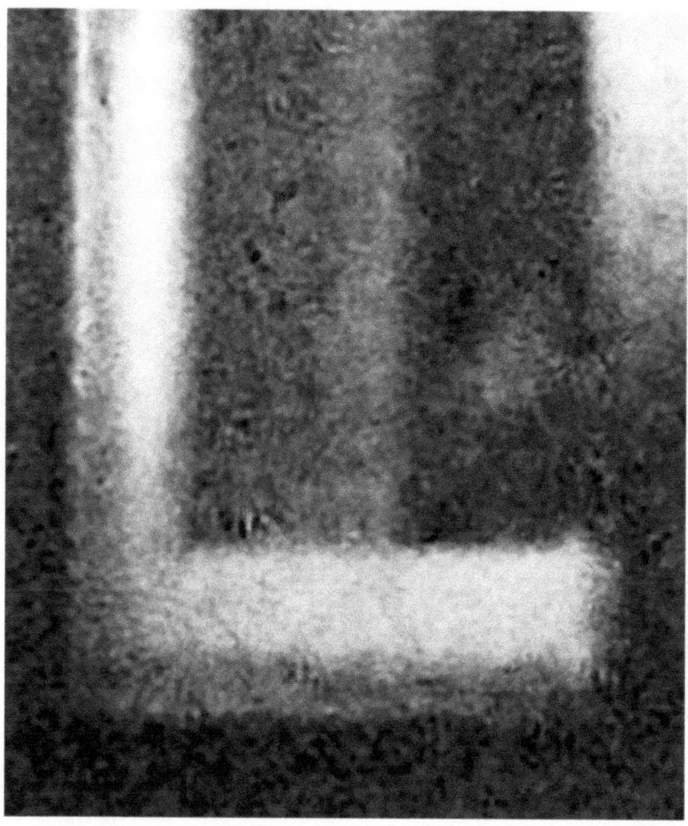

Is there a face in the lower right pane of the photo? The mind in looking for familiarity is making a familiar image out of the pixels, so this is pareidolia. It takes a while to see it, and like many optical illusions it depends how you look at the image as to what you see. In terms of perspective, if it were a face it would be between 2 and 3 inches in diameter.

**CAI Natural Anomaly 2, sub 3. Pareidolia.** Example 3

## Bishop's Palace, Siege Tunnel

Man with sword?

Photo by Phyllis Cameron, 7th September 2015

"Hi Richard this photo was taken of my daughter Hannah in the tunnel under the castle, I can def see an image of a man to the left of her elbow and I think he looks like he is holding a sword, what do you think?"

I went there and made a comparison. The face and sword etc., is caused by the light highlighting the formation of rock.

# PHOTO CATEGORY 2

Sub categories 2a, 2b, 3 and 4

## Natural anomaly suggestive of a paranormal origin

Sub category 4

## Illusions

3 Examples

**CAI 2. Sub 4. Illusions**

Optical illusions produced by natural or manmade means causing the same effects on the mind as pareidolia but embodying a wider scope for its creation.

Example 1.

### Bishop's Palace

Figure in white

Photo by Richard Falconer 2014

**The White Lady illusion in the grounds of the Bishop's Palace**

In October 2014, myself and a party of 12 I had on a tour, all saw a figure standing in the courtyard of the Palace grounds. It was very bright and motionless. It was dark, the time being around 8pm, and the moon was rising over the horizon of the sea. We all looked at the figure in disbelief, trying to make sense of what we were looking at.

One of the group went down the track of Castlecliffe to have a look side on into the Palace. When he came back he said it "looked like a reflection in a window from either the moon rising or perhaps students in the castle with a light?" The latter didn't fit with what we were looking at. The next day I went to the Palace to see the staff. On explaining what we had seen, a curator and myself went to the spot where we believed we had seen the figure. There are no windows in the Kitchen Tower so it wasn't a reflection. The figure was standing by the vaults of the Kitchen Tower.

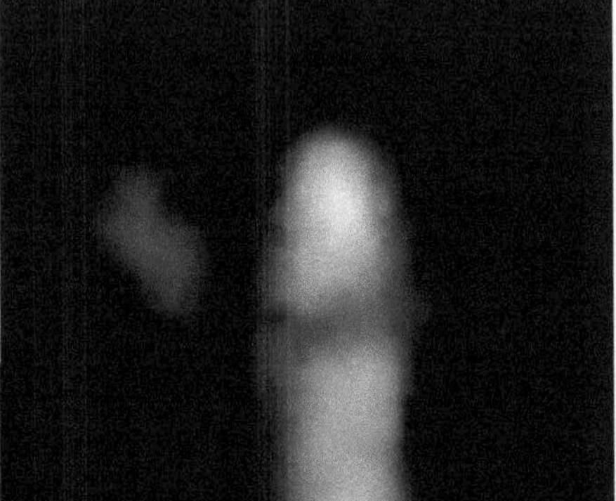

A few days later, I was also in the Palace talking to members of staff about it. One of them had been on duty the day we saw it. She said, "that evening they had accidentally left some of the lights on in the Castle overnight."

A few days later, a party of us saw the same thing in the same position. We all took photos. The next day I went to the Palace and found the lights had again been on. This explained the mystery. The bright light we had seen which looked like a figure in white, was actually the back of the stone arched entranceway to a vault of the Kitchen Tower lit by the dim light within. It shows how easy it is to mistake a physical explanation for a supernatural one.

**CAI 2. Natural Anomaly – 4. Illusions.** Example 2.

## St Rule's Tower

Figure in right hand window

Photo by Richard Falconer 2015

I used to have this on my website. It looks as though it could be a monk standing in the window. Then I realised it is created by the stone wall of the internal newel stair running up the back southeastern corner of the tower. The internal wall is highlighted by the sun shining through the window and only happens at certain times of the year when the sun is in the right position.

**CAI 2. Natural Anomaly – 4. Illusions.** Example 3.

## St Andrews Cathedral

Figure in white

Photo by Richard Falconer 2020

The mind is quick to trick the unwary. A common illusion during day tours is in the top right-hand eastern gable window of the Cathedral. When looking from the west it appears to be the shape of a person. People have spooked themselves into believing it to be the White Lady and mention it often on the tours. I then point out the light colour is the sky behind, and if it were a person it would be some ten feet high and three feet wide. The shape is the same as what we have seen in the Cloister arch, but what we see is a lot brighter with no physical cause.

❖

Another example in passing, is a photo someone took of the eastern gable of the Cathedral side on. It did it's rounds on a few local websites and probably Facebook sites etc., and eventually found its way to a national newspaper for Halloween. I was contacted as to what I thought about it but never had chance to reply. It is purported to show a face in the former north window at the top of the north tower of the eastern gable. You have to search within the photo to try and make anything out, which is always one of the first signs that it isn't anything to do with the paranormal. It would easily fit with **CAI Natural Anomaly 2, sub 3. Pareidolia.** and was as vague as Example 1 to 3 above.

When I eventually saw what it was supposed to be, I went down to the same location and took a look for comparison. The face was just the way the light highlighted the stone in the tower, and as indistinct as it was, it still managed to hit the national press.

Most of the photos included here would have done the rounds in the press had I submitted them over the years, which I didn't, and neither did the copyright holders to the photos. This is especially true of the example I have for **Sub 3d. Borderline Image** 4, p.559. If I had submitted that one it would have gone viral big time. It is very similar to a photo taken at Hampton Court Palace taken in 2015 that did go viral and was featured in all the major tabloids.

# PHOTO CATEGORY 3

Sub categories 3a, 3b, **3c**, and 3d

# Borderline Images 3

4 Examples

**CAI 3. Sub 3c. Borderline Image 3**
Where it is not possible to be 100% positive an image is attributable to a **physical** ***cause or origin*** given the image properties and / or testimonial circumstance / PERL involvement.

Example 1.

## Palace Siege Tunnel Photo

Faces in the mist

Photo by Joe Chapman 2003

The next two image examples appear to display vortex and pareidolia. This combination is normally reserved for category 2. sub 2b **Vortex or breath factor** and category 3. **Pareidolia.** However, I have placed these two images in this category as they both have PERL, indicating the ultimate origin of the cause is not necessarily as clear cut as may be determined at first sight.

This photo was taken by Joe Chapman from Texas at the foot of the ladder. There was no mist seen with the naked eye when it was taken.

The following is his correspondence:

Sunday 13th July 2014

Richard......thank you for the e-mail follow-up and the information you sent regarding experiences similar to what we encountered in the 'mine' area of St Andrews back in 2003. My son-Scotty Chapman-who was recently over there made the contact with the lady at St Andrews and I do appreciate your searching us out. I am enclosing the photo of which Scotty spoke. It was taken as my wife Sandy and I along with two friends were about to depart the mine area....and the person's feet on the ladder are my friend Steve. As Sandy started up the ladder I told her to stop and look back so I could at least have a picture of some of us down in that area.

There was no appearance of the fog or mist or whatever as I snapped the shot. That evening at a bed and breakfast as we were downloading the day's photos to my laptop computer we noted the appearance of the 'ghosts'----the little man in the upper right hand corner with the white beard and his arms at his sides was instantly visible to all of us. Not as visible were the 1-2 photos of faces in the lower left side of the picture and they really became apparent later that same year when we had projected the shot onto a screen of some 4 feet by 5 feet....and then we and several others made out the faces.

I had intended long before now to try and contact someone about the photo and actually sent an e-mail to St Andrews within the last year. But, I never heard back from anyone.

So... if this is of use to you please feel free to use it and I would appreciate the shot you are referring to that is somewhat similar if you can e-mail to me.[xxxi]

Best regards,
Joe Chapman

**Analysis**

Mist is present in the photo and there are images of faces, especially on the left formed in the mist, and as Joe mentioned, what appears to be a seated figure on the right.

Taking the image at face value it would be easy to dismiss the mist as vortex, and the faces to Pareidolia, given the cold damp conditions in the passage, but there are several reasons why I have placed this in a borderline category.

While there will be photos and experiences in the passage I am unaware of, not many will fall through the net. If something unusual occurs here, the Visitor Center staff are amongst the first to be notified of the details, they then contact me. The contact for this particular photo and report found its way to me

[xxxi] The photo Joe refers to is the photo in the next example.

through Alison Sullivan a custodian at the Palace Visitor Centre at the time. She told me about the photo, and gave me the details of the person who took it. I contacted them in the States which resulted in the enclosed reply from Joe and the photo.

To date, this is the only one of this nature the staff were aware of. To put this into perspective, the Palace had over 91,000 visitors through its doors in 2018 alone. Many of those would have gone down the passage, and given the nature of tourism, hundreds of thousands of photos have been taken down here over the years. So, while vortex is a recognised physical phenomenon, it is not a common feature, far from it, and it is certainly not a common feature in the passage.

Easiest way to understand is to go down there with a view to reproducing the above image yourself. To do this though you need to place yourself in the position of someone casually taking a photo, not someone trying to unnaturally generate a fine mist, and you will see how difficult it is to recreate. The same when people try to recreate orbs they dismiss as specs of dust (Clark, Fairmont, for example). Let alone to then see faces.

Along with this, there are additional factors here which reduce the odds of it simply being vortex even further. I have another report for this location in the passage which gives an additional perspective to this image:

A gentleman on one of my tours in May 2015, had been down the siege tunnel and took a few photos at the point where the ladder goes down to the Catholic end of the passage. He said, "With the naked eye I saw nothing unusual, but when I went to take a photo I could see a lot of mist through the viewfinder. When I took a photo there was no mist. It was only at this part of the passage where the mist appeared in the viewfinder, everywhere else in the passage was fine."

There are several important factors in his statement that has a bearing on Joe's photo. He was in the same part of the passage. It didn't happen anywhere else in the passage, so the mist wasn't caused by his breath, and this is not the dampest part of the passage.

I recorded earlier in the section about the Palace of three separate incidences in the passage. A party of 12 ladies I had on a tour in May 2015 had gone down in 2013. When they were at the ladder the area became extremely cold and all the lights went out. They all screamed and, in their panic, scrambled their way to the entrance which wasn't easy; the roof is low, ground uneven and they were in near pitch black conditions. When they neared the entrance, the lights came back on. There is no switch for the lights in the passage and the Visitor's Centre staff had not been near the light switches.

There are also the two separate parties of women from the States in 2014, who independently heard the chanting of monks in the passage on different days.

The faces and figure in the photo are in-keeping with the history of the location. As a brief recap, the Protestants laid siege of the Catholic Palace in 1546. The Catholics set to work digging a tunnel to blow up part of their own residence to get them out. The Protestants found where the passage was heading and dug a counter tunnel. Fourth time lucky the opening with the ladder is where the Protestants and Catholics met underground in 1547. The result was an unknown number of fatalities, especially in the lower section of the passage with the Catholics at the foot of the ladder where this photo was taken.

It is these other factors that makes the photo more compelling, and lends credence to the anomaly being something more than just our trying to make physical sense of what we are seeing, because of our understanding of vortex and our fallibility to pareidolia. This again is coupled with our lacking in understanding for the nature of how paranormal phenomena operates, which I give more details for in context of this image, with the next anomalous image sharing similar associations.

**CAI 3. Sub 3c. Borderline Image 3.** Example 2.

**PERL example: B3, B4, D1b, D1c, D2a, D2b, E2c. F2b.** Borderline: Physical *cause* and paranormal *origin*

# The All Saints Church Photo

Phantom Figures in Armed Conflict

Photo by Marysia Denyer 2012

Marysia took this photo of four of her friends on the evening of 30th November 2012 in the courtyard of All Saints Church.

Dear Richard,
It was lovely to meet you today and chat with you. Please find the attached puzzling photo taken on 31/11/12 outside All Saints Church.

Best wishes
Marysia

A former member of the Royal Burgh of St Andrews Community Council, Marysia is an enthusiastic longstanding member of the St Andrews Preservation Trust, Museum Volunteer Guide and Garden Co-ordinator!

There was no mist in the courtyard that night. It was dry and clear, and those present were unaware of anything untoward, including Marysia, who said the scene looked normal when taking the photo.

If you look closely at the mist you may see there are many faces around her friends. Although it is difficult to count them all, there are at least 10. Marysia described the faces as being "really quite sinister-looking and menacing," which is perhaps not altogether unfounded, as there is more to this scene then it appears to portray.

As with the previous photo, Marysia's photo at first sight appears to display vortex and pareidolia, so I could also have placed it in **Photo Category 2**. *Natural anomaly - suggestive of a paranormal origin*, however, it too has additional background circumstances that cannot be known from the photo alone that cannot be ignored.

The mist producing the faces is in-keeping with an incident having taken place in the same locality that Marysia was unaware of.

I reported the following in GOS p.67, 2013:

**Phantom Figures in Armed Conflict**

From James Wilkie 1931: 'In a somewhat narrow way that emerges near the castle and probably once ended at a port,[xxxii] there are (or were) houses which tales are told. A dwelling which need not be more closely identified was sometimes disturbed by the sounds of armed conflict, and shadowy figures of Highland clansman and Hanoverian troopers were seen crossing swords. The tradition is that after the Battle of Culloden some of the fugitives succeeded in reaching the east coast not far from Inverness and escaped by sea. They arrived at St. Andrews, but were tracked to this house where they had found shelter, and were slain or taken prisoner after a fierce fight.'[64]

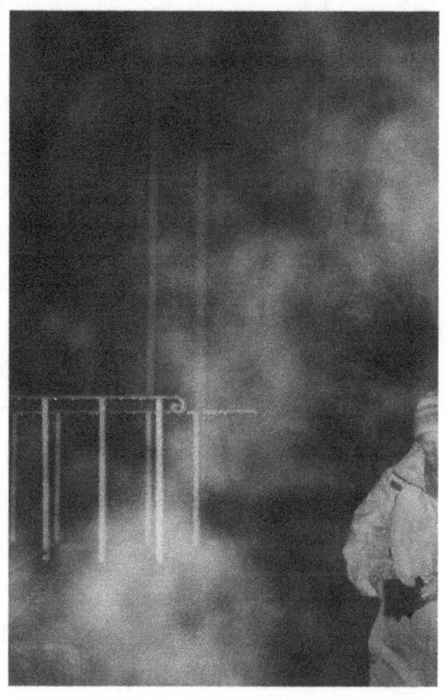

Linskill wrote an article called *A few notes about Castle Wynd*, the date is unknown but appears to be from around 1918. 'About the middle and at the west side of Castle Street there stands in an old garden a house of great antiquity, whose walls are said to be in places twelve feet thick. An article about this old building, from the pen of Mr J. H. Crawford, appeared in the Scottish Field of July 1916, entitled "Vale! O Vale." This house is now the property of All Saints Church, and must in by-gone days have belonged either to St Salvator's College or to the Castle. The gardens of the former probably extended as far east as Castle Street. This old house in later days was a great meeting

[xxxii] This was the Castle Gate situated at the foot of North Castle Street to the western side of the Palace.

place of the Jacobite's [18th c.], the noble followers of the Stuart race; and from some old books found in the attic, it is clear that Episcopal services were held there. In the south portion of the garden of this house now stands All Saints' Church.'

I have two reports of people walking along North Castle Street who have heard what they described as a "commotion." The clashing of swords, shouts and screams. Both incidents only lasted for a few seconds, and on both occasions, it was followed by complete silence. There was nothing to make the noise and no one else was around. One is from a visitor (2015), the other a student (2018). On both occasions they came on a tour to tell me what they heard.

Linskill mentions the grounds of the Jacobean house is now All Saints Church. The battle took place at the location where Marysia took the photo in the garden. Next to this at the southern end of All Saints Church and garden is Castle Wynd House. There has been poltergeist activity here certainly since 1975. Due to its proximity to the Church courtyard and garden it is possible the phenomena are related.

For this particular photo, we can still go down the vortex and pareidolia route and attribute any attempt to link the faces and a Jacobean battle as coincidence, and anything else to wishful thinking. It is though all too easy to be dismissive without understanding the nature of how phenomena operate and paranormal exploration is eternally hampered for this reason. The energies causing paranormal phenomena utilise *everything* in the physical at their disposal in the locality, which on the surface makes it easy to attribute anomalies to a physical cause, but that cause may not then be reflective of its origin, which in the abstract of the physical would remain undetected. Far from grasping at straws here to make sense of our observations, while a physical cause and origin could well be the same, this abstract does not consider any circumstance that may switch it all to a paranormal origin, or to a borderline physical cause for its production, and paranormal origin for the faces.

The premise being that the faces produced in the mist may actually be present and not just as a feature of pareidolia, PERL.

If we were to add in there had been previous experiences at this same location of the sounds of battle with shouts and the clashing of swords, would that phenomenon make sense with the battle taking place here, and would its association then give more plausibility for the faces also being connected, or would we still put it down to coincidence? If we were then told those experiencing the sounds were unaware of this obscure battle taking place at this location, and that Marysia and her friends that night were equally unaware of both the sounds being previously heard here, and the battle taking place, would it then make any more sense? Or if we were then informed that the only two locations where there has been experiences of the sounds of a battle in the history of St Andrews are the figures fighting with sword and armor up at Hallow Hill, and here. And that two known locations of a battle or skirmish taking place, both have a mix of mist and a display of faces in-keeping with these past violent episodes. Will we still be as dismissive or does this strengthen their potential?

There is also something else. I mentioned for the last image, 'while vortex is a recognised physical phenomenon, it is not a common feature in the passage.' The same applies to this image in the courtyard, and also for that matter to St Andrews in general. It can be a very damp city, and for all the photos taken here each year through the damp cold months of autumn through spring, aside these two photos there will be very few, if any with apparent displays of vortex and pareidolia phenomenon, especially at localities with a history in-keeping with the images displayed. It is only because pareidolia cannot be ruled out, despite the additional historical circumstances of the location, and the interconnectivity of previous experiences here that I have put it in a borderline category and not **CAI 4**.

CAI 3. Sub 3c. **Borderline Image 3.** Example 3.

## Madras College South Street Campus

Figure at the back

Photo by Arlene Brown, St Andrews, 2016

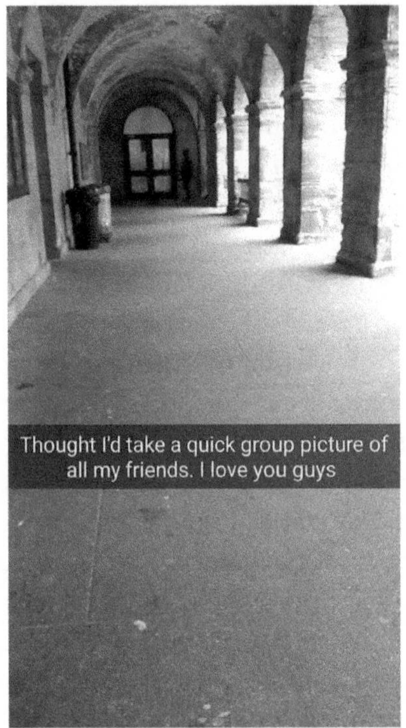


Arlene was in the quad waiting for her school mates to arrive off the buses. It was 8:30 am and the place was deserted, so she took this photo to send to her friends while she was waiting for them to all arrive.

It was only later when looking at it that she spotted the figure at the back, but there was no one around.

I have put this in **CAI borderline image 3.** because while it could be a physical person just walking through the shot, Arlene saw no one, so applying logic untainted by presupposition, unless we are to override our neutrality of judgement, how can we be sure?

**CAI 3. Sub 3c. Borderline Image 3.** Example 4.

## East partition wall, near top of the Pends

Bright figure on the wall?

Photo by a visitor on a tour 2017

Submitted by a visitor on a tour. This is the same part of the wall where the figure in white was described as being "as bright as a light," and only yards from where the bright orb was seen in the Pends Hall.

It was my mention of the figure being seen here that prompted her to take the photo. It was a misty night with the haar closing in, and there was nothing at the time to attract our attention.

This is reminiscent of the experience shared by Michael Alexander and his sister on the wall by the Haunted Tower. Of that experience Michael said it was a "strange white smudged / ill-defined light towards the left-hand top corner of the tower." There is street lighting along the Pends Lane opposite, but it wouldn't highlight the mist in this way, there was no moon and she didn't use a flash. Refer also to Orbs p.134.

# PHOTO CATEGORY 3

Sub categories 3a, 3b, 3c, and **3d**

# Borderline Images 4

2 Examples

**CAI 3. Sub 3d. Borderline Image 4**

Elements of doubt for **CAI 3a.** through **3c.** are is still present, so with **3d.** a physical cause cannot be ruled out, but is unlikely given the strength of image / testimonial / PERL circumstance / involvement. The image fringes on the border of **CAI 4. No Physical Explanation.**

Example 1.

## Cathedral Precincts

Ghostly figure

Photo by Francis Quinn 2019

***What the haar brought in…***

On the 28th of February 2019, I was in the Cathedral grounds investigating a photo sent to me by a couple on a tour a few days before. They were on the 7:30 pm tour Saturday 23rd February 2019. On the morning of Sunday 24th, they went to the Cathedral for a wander around. The haar was present and very thick through the grounds and the town. It was a cold day which is also a characteristic of the haar blocking the sun and bringing the cold air from the North Sea. Being a cold February

Sunday morning, they had the grounds to themselves, or so they thought…

Francis took a photo from the right-hand Cloister archway of the graveyard looking toward the Square Tower and North Wall. In the photo is what looks like a figure standing looking at the cross-shaped grave on the right.

**Photo I took of the same location a few days later**

She sent me the image, and on telling me about the above circumstance she wanted to see what I made of it.

I went to the Cathedral to see if I could reproduce the photo. Her photo has part of the upper arch where she took the photo from, so I was able to stand in exactly the same place and take a few photos. I was looking to see if there was anything in the grounds that could be mistaken for being a person. It is common for shadows highlighting stone for example to give the illusion of something being present.

I found there was nothing at all behind the grave where the figure is standing that could in any way cause this anomaly. Also, when looking at the photo, the north wall has all but disappeared with the haar, so the figure wasn't caused by light hitting a configuration of stone on the back wall for example.

In the photo I took, there is nothing that could be mistaken for a figure. You will note also there is no haar when I visited, so it gives an idea of what the north wall looks like from this angle, and again there is nothing that could produce the illusion of a person standing where it was. I took several photos and it wasn't possible to reproduce anything like that in the photo.

There is a very dark grave to the right of the cross-shaped grave the figure appears to be looking at, because of where the figure is standing only the top left corner can be seen.

I read the inscription of the grave it was standing behind and those in the area to see if there were any clues as to who the figure might be, but there was nothing obvious.

I have again put this in **CAI sub 3d. borderline image 4.** because there will always be those who say there had to be someone there, despite they being the only ones in the grounds at the time. It is why photos can never constitute as proof, so I can only leave it to you to decide.

If you have read everything thus far in this present volume, maybe the question to ask is not whether it is a ghost or a physical person, it is whether you are ready to believe the testimony you are given. If you are going to be selective in the testimony you choose to believe, would that not say more about you than the nature of the testimony itself?

Personally, I have no reason to doubt the integrity of something they didn't expect to see in the photo. After having experienced so much myself of a similar nature, I find it quite logical that Francis Quinn unknowingly captured something the haar brought in from St Andrews past. With PERL involvement, it is why sub 3d fringes on the border of **CAI 4. No Physical Explanation.**

**CAI 3. Sub 3d. Borderline Image 4.** Example 2.

**PERL A. B4. C2c. C2d. D1b. D1c. D2a. D2b. E1.**

**PERL** inclusion:
**F3a.** Borderline: Paranormal *origin* with no physical *cause*
Refer to Appendix 2 for PERL terminology

## The Old Course

Bodach-Glas

Photo by Elsa Botha, 1 July 2019

This borderline example is in two parts. The first part is an explanation and examination of the photo. The second, concerns an obscure legend of the Old Course that uncannily fits with the image it portrays.

## *CAI Example Photos*

In 2019, I received this photo and the following from South Africa:

Saturday 14th September 2019

My brother and sister in law recently visited St Andrews and having taken the above photo saw the figure just to the left of center. They swore no one was there when they took the photo and can't really explain who or what it is. Can you pass on to any interested parties and maybe they can offer an explanation. Perhaps an apparition?

Regards
Phil Weston

The photo has been taken on a clear overcast day, the figure is slightly blurry, and there is an odd distortion in the clouds above the figure. It hasn't attracted the attention of the others in the photograph so it is either just a person walking through the shot and they didn't see the figure, or there was no figure as Phil stated for when it was taken.

I showed the curious photo to Bruce MacIntosh, an old friend of mine in the town and one keen on photography to see what he made of it. He said it was a stitched photo, which means it is a photo comprising multiple photos stitched together to make the panoramic shot. The distortion or repartition of the cloud segments above the figure is the camera trying to compensate for the figure in the shot. It is trying to keep up with something moving through the frame while the camera on the mobile is being panned. So, logically he believed it was just a person moving through the frame and there was nothing supernatural about it.

I emailed Phil hoping to gain more specific details. Correspondence can often go cold, but I gratefully I received a swift reply from the person who took the photo. He had contacted his sister in law and this is what she had to say:

Tuesday 17th September 2019

Hi Richard,
My name is Elsa Botha (Maria Elizabeth) I am Phil Weston's sister in law and took the photo of the strange image. A very interesting photo, and makes one think.

My husband, Chris and I were on a month-long holiday visiting different countries in Europe and the UK. My husband is a keen golfer and St Andrews golf course was one of his preferred places to visit. During our Scotland visit, we stayed in Edinburgh and needless to say, took a road trip to St Andrews on 1st July 2019, walked around the golf course and took some pics and bought souvenirs, to show friends and family.

I took the photo with the strange image and didn't spot this apparition in the photo immediately. I only became aware of it when we were back in South Africa. I jokingly referred to it as the St Andrews ghost.

Regarding your request for more information, the photo was taken on 1 July 2019 at 13h15 on an overcast day. I didn't see anything that I can remember that could have caused this.

Our primary reason to visit St Andrews was for the golf. Really, St Andrews is after all the heart of golf!

I personally took the photo on pano, with my iPhone XR. No fancy lenses or anything. I stay in Zimbali coastal resort, KwaZulu Natal, South Africa. I am a bit sceptical about the paranormal. I won't say the paranormal doesn't exist though and have read some books, like e.g. the ghosts of England. Never knew anything about ghosts at St Andrews. Phil only told me after sending the photos to you, that he will let me have your answer.

You are correct, we haven't been on any of your tours, my husband does not believe in any ghosts or paranormal activity.

Best Regards,
Elsa Botha

**An Enquiry into the Photo**

In general terms, analysis by a third party looking at anomalous imagery, will, in the first instance, be an abstract evaluation before further circumstances for its production are known or considered.

For Elsa's photo, if we take out the blank dismissive of it being anything other than a physical person distorted by stitching, and equally take out the first impression of it being a ghost, the way to give a more balanced appraisal is to look closer at the photo itself and take into account the background detail/ circumstance for its production which is so often ignored. To then compare with other photos displaying similar idiosyncrasies or anomalies. These can then potentially give an insight contrary to our initial thoughts in either direction.

Bruce's explanation is a logical conclusion. Being a panoramic shot, the figure moving through the frame makes sense of the odd replication of the clouds caused by the stitching. It also dismisses the factor of it being a photoshop overlay. If it were, there wouldn't be any sign of stitching above the figure.

If you take a look at google images and what can go wrong when taking panoramic shots (with often humorous consequences), you will see how people, dogs or cats, (the latter two being the most popular examples) when moving through a panoramic frame can appear distorted, exaggerated, diminished, elongated or fragmented. Dogs and cats with stretched bodies and six legs or squashed bodies with two legs. Importantly, for all of these there is no suggestion of a paranormal origin.

A similar photo to Elsa's was taken at Hampton Court Palace by Holly Hampsheir, a 12 year old girl of her cousin Brook. The photo has the back of Brook as she walked through the room. Behind her is the dramatic image of a tall female figure with long hair standing behind her. It was posted on twitter, then hit the national newspapers in February 2015. It was dubbed 'the ghost of the Grey Lady,' which I might add was a generous connection to one of the many ghosts frequenting the Palace.

It was suggested the photo was due to what is called image aliasing. Whereby the digital camera on the phone, in trying to take a photo in fairly dark conditions, merges moving objects and distorts them as it scans and stitches together the location, as Bruce had also suggested for Elsa's photo. In this instance a person moving through the frame. So, we have established quite conclusively how the distortion in both photos occurred. From this you might wonder why I have still placed this photo in **Sub 3d. Borderline Image** 4, when it would be easy to assume **CAI 2. Sub 2a. Natural/man-made/electronic means** or **CAI 2. Sub 4. Illusions** as being more appropriate. Taking the nature of the physical distortion into account, this is not the end of the enquiry. There are additional circumstances. Add in PERL involvement, including a legend fitting the same description, and we have **PERL F3a. Borderline: Paranormal *origin* with no physical *cause*,** placing it as **CAI 3d. Borderline Image. 4.** which is also borderline with **CAI 4. No Physical Explanation.**

Holly said Brook was the only one wandering through the room. The figure is on the other side of the security ropes which are alarmed. She is also wearing a period dress which would certainly have attracted their attention. She took another photo few seconds later, there is no one else in the second photo, let alone someone resembling what she had captured, only Brook.

A link to the photo will be found on the webpage and has all the hallmarks of this current curious photo with the stitching. [xxxiii]

Elsa has a cursory interest in the paranormal and her husband doesn't believe in it at all. No matter how unusual it appeared to be, a ghost is not the first thought that would come to mind. For there to be a suggestion means they were sure there was no one around who could have been in the way at the time. Phil Weston mentions in his email: 'They swore no one was there when they took the photo and can't really explain who or what it is.' Elsa in her email says 'I didn't see anything that I can remember that could have caused this.'

Both locations were quiet so they would have been more aware of anyone being in the vicinity, especially someone walking through their shot. Unless a spontaneous photo is taken of something catching the eye, photos are generally taken with more composure. When we are about to take a shot, we look to make sure there is a clear window where no one is going

---

[xxxiii] Alternatively, do an internet search for: Hampton Court Palace Grey Lady photo, Holly Hampsheir for good measure. Once you see it you will see what I mean. It is not reproduced here as the license fee for commercial reproduction through major newsgroups is unfortunately too prohibitive.

to be walking through the frame. Easier when it is quiet, pot luck of course when it is busy. If someone does then walk across our shot we may then curse them, and if they realise we may receive an apology. We may then just wait a few seconds and take another, and if we didn't notice at the time we can retrospectively curse whoever it was, or ourselves for not noticing. We have all taken photos where this has happened, and had the almanac: *The Modern Victorians Guide to Popular Photographic Hazards* been published, it would have saved many a ruined photographic plate.

I could have done with that almanac myself on the day the Scottish Parliament opened at the top of the Mound in Edinburgh. It was a great day with a procession walking down the mound with the new proud MSP's, Alex Salmond, Donald Dewer etc. The Queen was opening the parliament and was in her open carriage. I took a photo as they came down the mound and through the viewfinder, I will never forget her expression. She was looking directly at me and was not that far away. Rather than smiling there was an almost concerned look on her face. I was using an old camera and didn't realise until the moment had passed, I had forgotten to take the lens cap off. Hence her concerned expression! but I detract.

This is a golf course, while not everyone visiting this area wears golfing apparel, those in the photo are wearing light jackets, it was never going to rain, and whatever the figure is wearing appears somewhat out of place for the conditions. I have checked the Met office records, and for this day and time in St Andrews, the temperature was 66 degrees Fahrenheit or 19 degrees Celsius. We were in the middle of the 2019 heatwave across Europe with countries and cities smashing all records. It wasn't a blustery day. The wind was a moderate north westerly breeze, nothing that would create the hair of the figure to be blown so dramatically that the long grey hair was up in the air above their head, and the figure appears to be wearing something more suited to winter conditions. The figure in Holly's photo is wearing period costume. Both would make them hard to miss, both somewhat out of place and both were right in front of them.

While the stitching/image aliasing explains the distortion of these two images being caused by someone walking through the frame, it doesn't explain how the figures came to be in the frame. Where did they come from and where did they disappear to after the photos were taken? Ghosts generally appear as real as you and I, and digital photography is able to pick up images we are unable to detect with the naked eye.

Both photos share the same phenomenon through very similar circumstances of production and testimony, and only the stitching is physically accountable. As with Holly's photo, we could think Elsa's photo was just a passer-by they didn't see, and the stitching gives the impression of something it is not.

Whether coming from the stance of believing in the paranormal, or believing it doesn't exist, we are quite happy to stretch the boundary of plausibility to fit with our preconceived ideas in either direction, even to the point of physical or paranormal impossibility.

On balance however, the fact is, if Elsa's and Holly's photos were to be summed up on the basis of the photos alone, it would not be possible to determine whether they have captured a physical person or the ghost of a person - such is the nature of ghosts, and such is the nature of the photographic image. It is why Mumler was acquitted, they could not prove his photos were fake. From the testimony of there not being anyone else present when the photos were taken, and no one in costume present in Holly's second photo, points to their not having a physical origin. This conclusion is not based on belief for its dependency. Knowing of their existence, belief is not a term I use for the paranormal. It is based on fact through their testimony, and for those not involved this should be important. As a variation of what I stated on p.108, to negate or ignore testimony, reveals a lot more about the belief of the individual than it does the phenomena any could look to frivolously decry.

So, for purposes of this analysis with PERL involvement, paraphrased for CAI, we thus far have PERL:

A. Testimony

**C2c.** When an anomaly is not recognised as being nonphysical in origin as it doesn't appear to defy the laws of physics. The physical impossibility of its nature is only revealed through information pertaining to surrounding circumstances the recipient [CAI: third party] was unaware of at the time. In this instance: Physically impossible circumstances.

**C2d.** Unable to explain the nature of the image, but the experience [of not seeing anyone it could have been] cannot be denied.

There is also another aspect to Elsa's photo - its location. By way of example, the reports of the sound of coach and horses in St Andrews could easily have been from anywhere around the town, but there is nothing random taking place. They are focused on the same locations, they share in the same characteristics, and most have no idea there is even a suggestion of this phenomena here. Those experiencing are not diehard believers or wishful thinkers. These are residents, students and visitors spanning a great many years and from across the world, including: the family from Saudi, New York lawyers, US Senate staff, and high flyers of US/European corporations amongst them. As I stated, they are here for golf not ghosts. The latter is just not on their radar - that is St Andrews.

Like **Borderline Images 3c.** examples **2.** and **3.** Elsa's photo could have been taken anywhere: East Sands, South Street, the Cathedral grounds or anywhere across Scotland. For that matter it could have been taken anywhere around the world, but it wasn't, it was taken at the Old Course, and the image in the photo fits perfectly with something else here, which has its own involvement through the nature of synchronistic attraction:

**The Bodach-Glas**

In 2013, I wrote this in GOS: A legend of the Old Course 'has it that a nobleman playing golf on the Old Course stopped mid-game, claiming to have seen the *Bodach-Glas,*[xxxiv] or grey-haired man, which warned of impending death in his family. He died later that night. Now, to see the grey haired man when playing on the course is said to be a dark omen.'[65]

The original piece comes from Savile in 1874, when he wrote: 'Of the Bodach-Glas, or "dark grey man," whose appearance is said to herald the approach of death to certain clans in Scotland, and of which Sir Walter Scott has made such effective use in *Waverley.* When relating the end of his hero, Fergus mac Ivor, we have the following well authenticated instance of its having been seen in our own day.

The late excellent and justly popular Earl of Eglington[xxxv], whose sudden death was truly felt as a national loss in Scotland, and who is famed for an attempt to revive an ancient custom of mediaeval times by the tournament held at Eglington Castle in 1839 [it was a duel with swords], was engaged on the 4th of October, 1861, in playing on the links of St Andrews, at the national game of golf. Suddenly he stopped in the middle of a game, exclaiming, "I can play no longer, there is the *Bodach-glas.* I have seen it for the third time; something fearful is going to befall me." Within a few hours, Lord Eglington was a corpse; he died the same night, and with such sadness, that he was engaged in handling a candlestick to a lady who was retiring to her room when he expired. Henderson, in *Folk Lore,* mentions

---

[xxxiv] Grey spectre, or dark grey man

[xxxv] The Earl of Eglington was Archibold William Montgomerie, a keen sportsman, member of the Royal and Ancient Club House in St Andrews and a member of the House of Lords.

that he received this account of Lord Eglington's death from a Scotch clergyman, who endorses every particular as authentic and perfectly true.'[66]

Eglington had said to 'bystanders on more than one occasion, "There's my little old man again?" as if he had become more or less familiar with the object.'[67]

George Barker's Dictionary of National Biography 1885-1900 states: 'He died of apoplexy at Mount Melville House, near St. Andrews, the residence of J. Whyte Melville[xxxvi], on 4 Oct. 1861, aged 49, and was buried in the family vault at Kilwinning, Ayrshire, on the 11th of the same month.'[68]

In the nineteenth century, apoplexy was any sudden death generally occurring a few seconds following loss of consciousness. We now know it to be a fatal stroke.

Gardiner MD in 1874 records 'Lord Eglington was taken suddenly ill on Monday, the 30th of September 1861, which was the day he had been playing golf on the Old Course. He [actually] survived for five days and died on Friday, the 4th of October.'[69] He was Eglington's physician and goes on to dismiss the *Bodach-glas*, but admits he was not privy to the conversations Eglington had amongst his friends, on or off the course.

**Portents and Omens**

This is a slight distraction, but portents and omens are more common in ancient family environments as they can be monitored over long periods of time and associations can be observed more readily. Especially with the prior notification of

---

[xxxvi] You may recognise the name J. Whyte Melville. He laid the foundation stone for the R & A Clubhouse. His memorial fountain sits in Market Street. He owned a great deal of land around St Andrews including his namesake the Mount Melville Estate (Craigtoun) and Bogward.

a family tradition. The mere suggestion is then enough to always keep one eye open for anything resembling the same.

Warnings of an impending death are personal associations relating to something symbolic to that particular family or area, and anything can be representative as being a portent of death once an association has been made: A Raven, or the sighting of a particular ghost or banshee appearing just before the death in a family etc.

In the circumstance of the Earl, the meaning he gave to what he saw foretold his own death, but they do not give the same associations to all who may experience such things. For most there will be no meaningful association and their appearance is unusual but not premonitory. The coach being heard or seen is an example. It has the same legend of ill omen to any who hears or sees it, but that was an association recorded by Linskill with Sharpe or Beaton's coach after their murders. It will have come from an older tradition through the town, and from this, we could infer, for there to be a connection, which came first, the sightings of the coach or the death of these archbishops? Either way I don't hold any importance to it.

It is true the woman who heard it above Hoggs on two occasions fell ill following both instances, but the majority are fine afterwards, including myself and Ronnie Howe.

**Who is the *Bodach-glas* of the Old Course?**

If we were to consider the *Bodach-glas* as a possibility, aside the legend of the curse which I give mention to by way of explanation, rather than giving way to any connection with present circumstance, it doesn't explain who the *Bodach-Glas* is, or why it is here.

In 1866, Henderson gives an interesting comment: 'The more common passage of death is for the Elleree (a seer, one gifted in second-sight) to see the man (the *Bodach-glas*) wrapped in his shroud, and according as the shroud covers more or less of the figure, will the death be near or remote.'[70] Being written only a few years after the Earls death. With it pressing heavily on his mind he would no doubt have been aware of these factors.

During my years of research, I have collected a thousand and one titbits of information about a great many aspects of St Andrews as well as elsewhere. They just sit there waiting for a context with which to give them life, like jigsaw pieces waiting for the right picture to come along for them to fit into place. Until then, of themselves, they hold little value. The following is one of those titbits.

The hair of the figure in Elsa's photo is grey/white and the cloak is a dark blue. You will see it on the webpage. This area was part of the *early* 'Pilgrims Way' from Guardbridge to St Andrews. Their attire was always distinctive so everyone knew who they were. I found an interesting piece about them. They often travelled in long, often dark blue robes which served as coats and sleeping bags while they were on their journey.

Of the many photos they will have taken on their holiday in Scotland and elsewhere, it happens at the Old Course, and happens to fit the description of the *Bodach-Glas*, who, in turn fits with that of a pilgrim visiting the relics here when the Cult of St Andrew held its importance, and gives a reason for the *Bodach-Glas* being seen where it has.

**PERL involvement for this photo adapted for CAI now also has:**
**B4.** Historical associations of the locality in-keeping with the anomaly/and or having a bearing on the nature of the anomaly.
**D1b.** Additional anomalous incidences occurring independently in the same location.

**D1c.** Two or more anomalies occurring independently in the same location, with at least one independent anomaly involving the **same description**/circumstance.

**D2a.** Recipient/s having no prior knowledge of physical historical associations (if present) in-keeping with the nature of the portrayed anomaly.

**D2b. Strengthens the factors in D1.**
Recipient/s having no prior knowledge of anomalous associations in the locality.

**E1.** Anomaly/ies with a purported physical cause and physical origin. If **D.** is present it can switch **E1.** from **F1.** conclusion to **F2.** or **F3.**

With four of the five **D.** categories applying here, the image switches from **E1.** to an **F2.** or **F3.** sub category for the conclusion. In this instance it is:

**F3a. Borderline: Paranormal *origin* with no physical *cause***

If it were a physical experience and not an image, it would be:
**F3b. Paranormal *origin* with no physical *cause***

An unsuspecting visitor from South Africa inadvertently revitalised an old legend through capturing something she was unaware of at the time. Something that will certainly appeal and excite those who have an interest in the *Bodach-Glas* mystery. For the rest, well, now you are in possession of the photo and all the surrounding information including PERL, I leave what I have written to your own judgement.

PHOTO CATEGORY 4

# No Physical Explanation

7 Examples

**CAI 4. No Physical Explanation**

This is where it has not been possible to attribute an image to a physical cause and has a qualification endorsed by PERL testimonial circumstance.

**PERL** conclusion:

**F3b.** Paranormal *origin* with no physical *cause*

Example 1

## Haunted Tower

ORBS

Photo by Richard Falconer 2015

I In 2015, I was granted permission by Historic Scotland to enter the Haunted Tower. This was a rare privilege and one otherwise reserved for HS staff. I took a series of photos in the lower and middle chambers from different angles.

The photo on the following page has a number of orbs and was taken just after the photo on p.146. This is the only one with orbs. If it were dust particles, light spots, lens spots etc., which are easy to dismiss anyway, they would not just appear in one photo out of a few taken in quick succession.

It is very rare for anyone to see what it actually looks like in the middle chamber. In this photo I am inside the chamber facing west. The entrance gate is out of shot to the left. The chamber you are looking at is part of the internal chamber configuration but it is not actually in the tower, it is hidden in the precinct wall itself extending west from the tower. It is 8 feet high, 3 feet 3 inches wide and 7 feet long.

This is where some of the bodies, including that of the White Lady were concealed. The whole chamber itself is a reversed L shape. This is the long part of the L. The short part forms the space in the tower that can be seen through the gate. When added to this long part of the L, the entire chamber length running east west is 10 feet 8 inches.

**A series of orbs.**
**Middle Chamber of the Haunted Tower**
Can you see something else in the photo?

The Catholic Church are masters when it comes to creating visual illusions and red herrings. The photo illustrates how wide Hepburn's perimeter wall is at that point, which you would never realise from the outside. Just along from here is a loophole and the wall at that point is only around three feet thick at the most. I move into the architectural configuration of the Haunted Tower through David Henry in HT and HoS.

A common fallacy is to dismiss orbs as either fine specs of dust on the camera lens, or the camera is picking up the general level of dust in the area. This has been disproved countless times and as with most aspects of the paranormal, the casual dismissal says more than the circumstance surrounding their production. Go into a dusty environment and kick up as much dust as you like. Take as many photos as you like, as Clark did at Fairmont, and you won't get any orbs, and certainly not just appearing in one photo out of a series of photos as we have here.

It is rare for them to appear. The setting will more often have a history of activity and there is nothing random about anything occurring in the vicinity of this chamber of secrets.

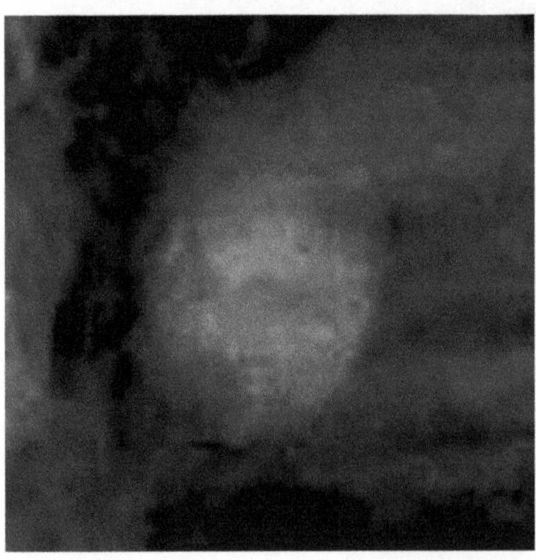

Zooming in on the second orb up on the left, and bearing in mind that orbs are the energetic essence of spirits, not specs of dust, is this orb Classic pareidolia or something else?

Back in 2003, I was working in Edinburgh and was invited by Jason, one of my friends, to visit the flat he was staying in. He was a medical student training to be a naval surgeon. He had been there for around six months as the guest of a friend of his who bought the flat around ten years previously. He said there had been a sense they were not alone in the flat for quite a while, but things had stepped up a gear.

They were disturbed by poltergeist activity, especially in the living room come kitchen area. They both heard a large bang late one night coming from that area. They went through and all the drawers and cupboard doors in the kitchen area were wide open. All the pots and pans were stacked up on top of one another in the middle of the living room floor.

The area would also go extremely cold for no reason and Jason had felt a presence a few times. Things were also going missing then turning up when least expected, which brought paranoid suspicions between them. The tension added to what amounted to be an already unfortunate uneasy atmosphere in the flat.

I went around one afternoon with Jason when his flatmate was at work. I got Jason to take as many photos as he could of the living room/kitchen area with an early digital camera he had purchased. We then went through to another room where he downloaded them onto his flatmates computer so we could take a look. Straight away we were struck by what we saw. We saw or felt nothing out of the ordinary when in the living room while Jason was taking photos, but what we were now looking at were massive orbs. Some were round, some were oval shaped, and all were filled with differing colours – none of which corresponded to the setting or background of the environment. The scene was like when bubbles are blown in the air, not just the customary golf ball or tennis ball size. Although perspective is difficult, one of the oval orbs appeared to be around four feet or more in height. We had never seen anything like it.

The most remarkable photo though was one of the last he took. It was of myself sitting on the settee. This photo had no orbs at all, instead sitting next to me, as close as she could be, was a young slim woman wearing a large purple dress with a bonnet on her head. She was leaning into me slightly on my left side with her head resting almost horizontally on my shoulder. She was very slightly transparent, so the settee could just be seen behind her. She was as clear as day and as recognisable as a person as I was. We looked at each other completely dumfounded. It appeared we had found part of the cause for the disturbances as there were many orbs in the room, so she was only one of several spirits here.

I left the flat, and when I saw Jason the next day, I asked if I could get a copy of the photos. He said when his flatmate arrived back that evening and saw the images, he was so scared he didn't delete the photos, he took his computer to bits and wouldn't let Jason go near it. To this day I don't know if his flatmate still has the photos, but by all accounts, he was completely spooked out, and in denial of what he had seen, which is an unfortunate common side effect.

Jason was only there as a temporary lodger. He had to live their longer than he would have wished but his medical studies took precedence.

The result is the most remarkable set of photos nobody other than Jason, myself and his flatmate will probably ever see. I can still visualise them all, but the woman, I will never forget her.

Personally, for myself, of all the paranormal incidents I have experienced, the fact she was sitting next to me with her head resting on my shoulder, remains for me one of the most extraordinary things I have ever seen.

It doesn't surprise at all that something happened to prevent the photos from being made available. This happens a lot when it comes to the paranormal. There is a mechanism through circumstance often preventing the capture of genuine images from being made available to a wider audience. Then when they are, they can be so clear they will easily be rejected anyway.

The photos Clark took of diamond orbs were on a floppy disc and he had tried a few method to try and retrieve them. He then passed the task to myself. Three months, four laptops, a floppy drive and disc drive later and I managed to retrieve them. You will see four of those photos on the following pages.

PHOTO CATEGORY 4

# No Physical Explanation

Example 2

**CAI 4. No Physical Explanation**

This is where it has not been possible to attribute an image to a physical cause and has a qualification endorsed by PERL testimonial circumstance.

**PERL** conclusion: **F3b.** Paranormal *origin*/no physical *cause*

## The Vaults - Edinburgh

ORBS

Photo by Clark Docherty 2007

Three diamond shaped orbs. One of a series of photos taken by Clark on a visit to Edinburgh which I also reproduced on p.443.

PHOTO CATEGORY 4

# No Physical Explanation

Examples 3 to 5

## Mary King's Close - Edinburgh

Monk and diamond orbs

Three photos by Clark Docherty 2007

Photo explanations on p.442

First photo taken with a few diamond orbs and a vague shape in door.
Second photo is once in room with a monk and many diamond orbs.

Large blue double diamond orb and small diamond orbs

## Mary King's Close - Edinburgh

Example 6: Face of a man

This is a photo I received a few years ago. It was also taken in Mary King's Close. It is not light hitting stone causing pareidolia.

Face of the monk or the face of the figure in Fil's photo?

PHOTO CATEGORY 4

## No Physical Explanation

Example 7

## Mary King's Close - Edinburgh

Figure of a man

Fil Dearie with Joe Salugabaite.

The photo is an automatic one that can be taken as a souvenir. They were the last ones in the close, so there was no one behind them – or so they thought!

I was aware of the ghost of a monk and a young girl, but this is different. It is a man standing in the doorway dressed in armour, thick padding or a large overcoat with what could be big long boots.

# *Appendix 1.*

## PERL

### Paranormal Experience Reference List

Looking at the bigger picture

For both PERL, and PERL in conjunction with CAI, add all the PERL categories that apply.

As I wrote in the first section, the testimony of every experience has a duality where the experience itself is coupled with the mind trying to work out the logic of its experience.

There is nothing random about how the paranormal operates, it is quantifiable. The determination of an experience can be enhanced through PERL, and so too an image purporting anomalous imagery which are rarely as obvious as they appear at first sight.

The paranormal and logic match completely. The caveat being the general Western mind having little understanding of how the paranormal operates, carries a distortion of logic driven by the physical and misses valuable insight.

PERL adds circumstantial data alongside any testimony to understand the nature of psychology and the paranormal dynamic as a whole. For the paranormal spectrum it gives insight into the governance of paranormal law as patterns of experience.

When PERL is applied to CAI to further determine the nature of photographic images it can switch an anomaly from physical to paranormal and vice versa through cause and origin.

# PERL

## Category and sub category details

For photographic images use CAI pp.517-522 first.

Add everything that applies.

**Categories:**
**A. Testimony**
**B. Physical locality**
**C1. C2. C3. Psychological considerations**
**D1. D2. Reinforcement: Negation of the random factor**
**E. Physical intervention/nonphysical involvement**
**F. Conclusion: The root *cause* and *origin* of an anomaly**

## A.

**Testimony**
The nature of the anomaly to be determined in conjunction with all other PERL considerations.

## B.

**Physical locality**
**B1.** Geographical, geological, structural, and climatic information of the locality at the time of the anomaly/ies.

**B2.** Energetic considerations of the locality

**B3.** General historical associations

**B4.** Historical associations of the locality in-keeping with the anomaly/and or having a bearing on the nature of the anomaly.

# C1. C2. C3.

**Psychological considerations - Perceptive variations**

These can lead into far deeper and complex areas of psychology, involving perception-based conclusions through belief-based opinions. Applies to physical and nonphysical.

## C1. Physical

**C1a.** Psychological inclusions and factors underlying physical or physiological factors. The latter includes anything from ill health/poor constitution/medication and etc.

**C1b.** Whether the recipients were looking to experience anything consciously or suggestively (with hindsight).

**C1c.** Physical visual/audible phenomena being given a paranormal attribution. Elements of these can apply in any setting, but **C.** can be negated if any sub factors of **E.** or **F.** are present.

**C1d.** Reading paranormal phenomenon into physical anomalies:

Wishful thinking/eagerness to believe despite the premise of an 'open mind' and etc. Looking for paranormal explanations where there are none.

An incident can be attributed to visual, including pareidolia, similar to **CAI 2 - sub 3**, and the optical illusions of **CAI 2 - sub 4.**, together with physical visual/audible effects caused by rodents, wind, faulty electrics, traffic, earth tremors, people and animals etc., and audible via cooling pipes and settling houses, central heating, branches brushing against a window, and etc. The only limitation for a list of physical causes is the imagination.

**C1e.** Playing on suggestive expectations:
Once a paranormal association has been made, the placebo effect can suitably put us on edge. Feeling spooked, we then look for, and attribute anything to a paranormal origin, which is why we jump when the phone rings for example.

There is also **suggestion**: Reading physical anomalies as paranormal occurrences through atmospheric conditions/setting again causing placebo effect/wishful thinking/desperation or eagerness to believe despite the premise of an 'open mind' and etc., resulting in false positive explanations. Similar to **CAI 2 - sub 2a** and **sub 4.** Those who call themselves 'believers' often fall into this category.

**C1f.** It works both ways. Eagerness not to believe despite the premise of an 'open mind' and etc.

## C2. Nonphysical

**C2a. Misattributing a paranormal event for a physical cause:**
There is simply no thought or suggestion of another possibility other than a physical one. This is a common factor of paranormal experience, generally through its subtlety, where we are not expecting it, so we just don't think of the paranormal as being the cause of our experience. It is the direct opposite of placebo **C1e.** and dynamically contrary to **C3b.**

**C2b. Delayed realisation:**
When an anomaly only becomes apparent after it has occurred. A niggling feeling that something wasn't right. Then realising it wasn't physically possible for it to have happened, or that whatever occurred was out of place: No physical contact or defying the laws of physics for example.

**C2c. Phenomena not appearing to defy the laws of physics:**
C2b. Variant: When an anomaly is not recognised as being nonphysical in origin as it doesn't appear to defy the laws of physics. The physical impossibility of its nature is only revealed through information pertaining to surrounding circumstances the recipient [CAI: third party] was unaware of.

Physically impossible circumstances, or describing mannerisms or characteristics they were unaware of. Seeing a figure in the window of the Square Tower when there is no floor, a child describing the mannerisms of a stranger in the house who turns out to be a grandfather who died before they were born, etc.

**C2d. Seeing is believing:**
Anomalous activity that cannot be explained in physical terms. While the recipient/s are unable to explain the nature of what has been experienced, the experience cannot be denied.

## C3. Nonphysical

### Psychological considerations

### Variations of a theme to the negation of experienced phenomena

These are variations of a theme where the recipient of paranormal phenomena is either in denial of their experience, or attributes their experience to a physical cause, however tenuous. Associations that have more to do with the psychological temperament of the individual than to the experience itself and is the direct opposite of **C1**. Involvement.

**C3a. Dismissing the paranormal as a possibility:**
No matter what happens there will always be those who refuse to accept the nature of what they have experienced. Unable to comprehend, denial of the experience (often through deep

rooted subconscious fear), putting the experience down to imagination etc. Conditioned responses involving culture, media etc. The list is long, involved, and is more often caused by peer influence through misinformation from an early age.

**C3b. Invincible ignorance fallacy:**
A recipient who experiences phenomenon and looks for a physical cause – however tenuous, despite a physical cause not being known. Known as invincible ignorance fallacy, it is a psychology term that applies more than adequately here.

# D1. D2.

### Reinforcement:
### Negation of the random factor

Strengthens the idea that neither the incident/anomaly nor the location was random, regardless of origin. Applies to visual or audible anomalies including ghosts and poltergeist activity. This then negates **C.** and reinforces **A., D1.**, and the integrity of the incident/anomaly, especially if a few of the following are present:

# D1.

**D1a.** Anomalous incident/s witnessed by more than one person.

**Additional determining factors**
Anomalous incidents are further reinforced if one or more of the following components are present, regardless the plausibility of their being a physical or psychological cause for the occurrence. If present they strengthen the integrity of phenomenon in general, so these are of great value. This is very important, the paranormal is far more wide reaching and subtle than the obvious displays retained by our consciousness. It is

not always what we see, it is what we miss. For present purposes these will suffice:

**D1b.** Additional anomalous incidences occurring independently in the same location.

**D1c.** Two or more anomalies occurring independently in the same location, with at least one independent anomaly involving the same description/circumstance.

# D2.

**D2a.** Recipient/s having no prior knowledge of physical historical associations (if present) in-keeping with the nature of the portrayed anomaly.

**Strengthens the factors in D1.**

**D2b.** Recipient/s having no prior knowledge of anomalous associations in the locality.

# E1. E2.

For images: **E1.** and **E2.** can be employed in conjunction with 'Categories for Anomalous Images' (CAI) using CAI first.

# E1.

**Physical involvement**

**E1.** Anomaly/ies with a purported physical cause and physical origin. If **D.** is present it can switch **E1.** from **F1.** conclusion to **F2.** or **F3.**

## E2.

### Non-physical involvement

**E2a.** Anomaly/ies where a physical cause cannot be ruled out, but appears to have a non-physical origin.

**E2b.** Anomaly/ies with a physical cause and non-physical origin. Also, recognised in **CAI 2. Sub 3b. Borderline Image 2.**

**E2c.** Anomaly/ies where a physical cause features in its production including poltergeist activity and electronics.

**E2d.** Anomaly/ies where a physical cause is not possible.

## F.

### PERL Analysis – Testimonial Conclusion

The root *cause* and *origin* of an anomaly

**Physical/Non-physical (paranormal) involvement:**
For non-physical (paranormal) involvement, PERL only requires **D2.**, which can be further reinforced by **E.** However, the more weight carried by **D.** and **E.**, the more pronounced the involvement becomes, and when **D2.** is present, the harder it becomes for temptation to then negate the facts.

The *cause* and *origin* of an anomaly are not necessarily the same. It does not always follow that a physical *cause* will have a physical *origin.* When the testimony is not so clean cut, based on factors within **D.**, the determination of the nature of the *cause* and *origin* of an anomaly can change from a physical *cause* and physical *origin* to having a physical *cause* and a paranormal *origin,* or to a paranormal *origin* with no physical cause.

**F1a.** Physical *cause* and physical *origin*

**F1b.** Physical *cause* and borderline paranormal *origin*

**F2a.** Physical *cause* and a paranormal *origin*

**F2b.** Borderline: Physical *cause* and paranormal *origin*

**F3a.** Borderline: Paranormal *origin* with no physical *cause*

**F3b.** Paranormal *origin* with no physical *cause*

An example of **F.** is the photo utilising PERL with CAI on p.559: **PERL A. B4. C2c. C2d. D1b. D1c. D2a. D2b. E1.** With conclusion: **F3a.** Borderline paranormal *origin* with no physical *cause.*

The first categories to watch out for when determining the nature of purported phenomenon are considerations **A.** and **C.** If **D.** is present, especially **D2.** they negate any seemingly random factor of the anomalous incident and override **C.** Delving deeper, look out for **B4.** reinforced by **D1b.**, **D1c.** and **D2.** These then give a greater insight for **E.** involvement, and the accentuation of phenomena through a pattern of incidences in a location are a good indicator of **B2.**

The list is not exhaustive, individual circumstance will generate further insight.

# *Ghosts*

The following is a quote from a commentary by Chinese philosopher Mo Tzu (470–391 BC), making a judgement on a legend about the ghost of Tu Po, who had killed his king before an assembly of feudal lords in retribution for being executed by the king under false charges. It is a legend, but his commentary upon it is not. I have reproduced it here as it serves to typify how an ancient culture developing into one of the world's foremost countries for scientific research, operates in harmony with their spiritual understanding and embraces the paranormal as an inherent aspect in their way of life.

"If from antiquity to the present, and since the beginning of humankind there are those who have seen the bodies of ghosts and spirits and heard their voices, how can we say that they do not exist? If none have heard them and none have seen them, then how can we say they do? But those who deny the existence of the spirits say: "Many in the world have heard and seen something of ghosts and spirits. Since they vary in testimony, who are to be accepted as really having heard and seen them? Mo Tzu said: As we are to rely on what many have jointly seen and what many have jointly heard, the case of Tu Po is to be accepted."

I always say spiritual reality is more real than real.
We *are* the ghosts to other realms.

# *Appendix 2.*

## Reality beyond belief – A deeper insight

### The Apocryphal Sciences

Expanding the brief introduction to this volume with something more substantive, to understand how and why the mindset of the populist West has been conditioned into believing the paranormal to be fiction, and by extension, the spiritual to be a belief divorced from reality, we must move to an earlier age, to Christianity, especially through the Roman Church, to the sciences of the day, and to the main protagonists through the natural philosophers and magicians. I shall be exploring their public influence and their unified relationship with magic and spirituality as encompassing the subtle realms of spirit where the paranormal has its base. Of the involvements extending to spirits of the deceased, and their correlation with the nature of angels and demons. I shall explore acceptance and persecution, and how these early magicians as mediums operated in relation to both the church and the surrounding paranoia generated through the common people caught in witch hunt hysteria. All then leads through the development of the western physical sciences with a switch in the 19th century populist mindset to its currently accepted form.

❖

**Early western research and understanding**

The supernatural has always been associated with the spiritual and the art and science of magic. Plato in Greece created 'the Academy' in c.387 BC, or the 'University of Athens' as it became known just outside the city of Akademeia, which gives an idea of where that name came from. This was the world's first university and would have continued had the Romans not laid siege and destroyed it.

In the early middle ages through the Roman Church, the quest by scholars for an enlightened understanding of reality encompassed intellectual and spiritual knowledge. They promoted an embodiment of the physical, the philosophical, the spiritual and the supernatural. This was directly reflected through the ancient sciences coming to us primarily through Greece, Egypt and Babylon around the 2nd or 3rd century AD.

The oldest science is astrology/astronomy, originating in Mesopotamia nearly 5000 years ago. Although the terminologies did not exist at that time, the principles did. They were exploring the heavens and the patterns of their configurations as correlating with events on earth. From this, crucial factors could be gathered to ascertain underlying physical and spiritual factors, including the ability to know what would otherwise be hidden, and this included the determination of the future. Everything had its base in the spiritual. The physical was viewed as its outward expression. In this manner, scholars were recognising how everything is related, and through a greater exploration of the ancient sciences, a greater understanding could be gleaned between the relationship of the self and the universe, one being reflected in the other.

The scope of study for the ancient scholars and their Catholic counterparts can be summed up by the Christian axiom, 'On earth as it is in heaven,' borrowed from the ancient Greek Hermetic axiom, from the Emerald Tablet and often paraphrased as: As above so below; "That which is above is as that which is below, and that which is below is as that which is above". This being the unification of man with the universe. The Microcosm with the Macrocosm.

From the 13th century in what was the High Middle Ages, the Church created universities across Europe for the priesthood. They borrowed their formula from the Greeks which they turned into Christianised teaching. The curricula incorporated the study of the seven liberal arts including astronomy and later the three Aristotelian philosophies of physics, metaphysics and moral philosophy. Their acceptance and incorporation of both a spiritual discipline and a physical nature was part of a golden age of perception.

However, all was not quite as it seemed. Research through the church had boundaries. The Church had a cautious air of celebration for the ancient sciences as they exercised condemnation for those elements deemed contrary to public church doctrine, so large elements of knowledge and perceived understanding were excluded or supressed from a wider Europe and ultimately a global audience at different periods. For example, biblical interpretation gave rise to theological arguments for and against whether astrology and indeed all the divinatory sciences including geomancy, were even acceptable subjects of study.

In the *early* Middle Ages, astrology had been outlawed altogether as they had a fear of predictions not being met with their favour. 'The church has set her face sternly against any attempt, on the part of the laity, to inquire into the future. The code of Justinian had made divination a crime.'[71] Despite this, it then found favour with the church during the Renaissance Period through from the 14th century when it was deemed appropriate. Referring to this in 1889, Legge says, 'In France, if we may believe Pierre I'Estoile, there were, in the reign of Charles IX [1560s-70s], no fewer than 30,000 persons openly engaged in the practice of divination.'

Even with this, it was still marked by high level debate as to what was practicable given their doctrine, and this was a dilemma they would either face or try to publicly avoid, not just with astrology but with exploration in general. With doctrine and teaching not keeping up with progression, this would prove to be their Achilles heel from their formation to present day.

The history of astrology through the church often mirrored that of other subjects, philosophies and ideas. The boundaries to research, or more the point, the public disclosure of discoveries, was not always clear as to what might constitute as being heretical. The pros and cons for their merits were often micromanaged levels of interpretation. This was partially driven by the ever-shifting social and political leadership influencing thought and viewpoint. It came down to the favourability or otherwise of successive Pope's, and was based on their understanding and preference of the time. Both had far-reaching life and death consequences that appear alien to us today, but whatever they decided through their whims could see you praised in one breath and condemned in the next. They could also be blurred by public interpretation and misunderstanding when not up to speed with the latest doctrinal thought of the church. Individual or mob hysteria through ill-informed fanaticism had been an ever present concern for centuries. It was then up to the church if they chose to explain their merits to the laity within the framework of doctrine or just uphold the public opinion of heresy.

**Hypocrisy and Heresy**

The sciences were flourishing but they were being closely watched in more ways than one. Although astrology is a prime example of a science the church has never found any hard and fast resolution for since its arrival in Europe, the church was closer to private scholars than any of the time and most since would ever suppose. The Vatican were involved in a great many fields of study that went far beyond their own doctrine, including the study of texts they had banned, plus many more besides that none outside the Vatican, both then or since, will ever be aware exists. Accordingly, in private the Vatican could meet new discoveries with no little excitement through private agreement, but public perception could place both the Vatican and the natural philosopher in a very difficult position. The church could not compromise their outward appearance. Scientific discoveries created a dilemma, a secret hypocrisy where every discovery had the potential to shine an inner light on their own morality while exposing the flaws of their doctrine. Europe was a very dangerous place to find your expression for these reasons. Going against the public persona of Church doctrine was never a light undertaking. It was often resolved through internal complex political compromises as they looked at the nature of the charges being brought against those publishing their findings and those in possession of the same. To retain their morality, a charge of being in possession of banned texts or holding heretical views could replace the initial charge of heresy through their discoveries, it was a slight deflection and could still see you burn, but it was enough of a distinction for them to maintain their private morality whilst still appeasing public discontent. A classic example of this is was Bruno, burnt alive in 1600 which I shall speak of later. Another, from a slightly earlier period though not as dramatic, was Nicolaus Copernicus, a canon of the church. He published his initial heliocentric theories about the earth's rotation and its revolution around the sun in 1514. He wouldn't publish his developed theories concerning this until 1543 in his De revolutionibus orbium coelestium (On the Revolutions of the Heavenly Spheres), but his wasn't a new idea. He had read the ancient texts and took his idea from the Egyptians who knew about these thousands of years before. 'In the foreword to the fifth volume of *Harmonices Mundi* (1619) it was written; 'Yes, I have stolen the golden vessels of the Egyptians to build a shrine to my God ...'

With a life's work complete, it would be easy to assume Copernicus was promptly burnt at the stake for his published suggestions, but he died only two months later in favour with the church. They had accepted his theories and even promoted them through some of their European universities. This is important to note on two counts. It marked the start of the Scientific Revolution and the popular misconception widespread through the Catholic faith was that the earth through the scriptures was *the* centre of the universe, not that it was *at* the centre of the universe. This is why the church had privately agreed with Copernicus and held him and his astronomical undertakings in high regard. Outwardly it became a different story. While this was taking place there was increasing pressure for the church from the laity, who, in not understanding this distinction, opposed the theories of Copernicus, believing they went against the church and its teachings. So, it is a common misconception that the church opposed his theories. Bowing to public pressure they eventually did ban it, but not until 1616 - some 123 years following both its initial publication and his death. A full repeal of its prohibition wouldn't then come for another two centuries.

Copernicus: De revolutionibus orbium coelestium, has been described as the most popular book nobody read, as philosophers went straight to his section on heliocentricity and ignored the rest. An accolade not recreated for another four centuries with the publishing of Steven Hawkins - *A Brief History of Time*. A book everyone wanted to be seen to have on their shelves but few will ever know what the pages look like inside. His publishers could have saved a fortune by just printing a book cover on a cardboard box!

**The Witch Hunts**

Heresy as a reality applied to any opposing doctrine to the church in power at the time of wherever you happened to be, and like the Catholics, the Protestants were quick to denounce any veering from their own brand of Christian doctrine. Their logic dictated that if you were against their particular church you were in consort with the devil. Within this, the line was very thin, but like today it was thick with ignorance. The layman believed the lay magician (especially the early physician) wielded great power and could cure them of all manner of ills that would befall them. They would be sought out for these reasons, but by this same respect, when they were struck by a spell of bad luck, or their ailments got worse, they easily became scapegoats for their misfortune and could be accused as practicing black magic and witchcraft.

In the 15th century, this all gave rise to the witch hunts across Britain and Europe as a legitimate excuse to rid themselves of both undesirables and ill fortune. The trials involved volatile practices that would sustain itself across Europe for over 200 years and affect thousands of people. In Spain this included Jews, and in France 15,000 Knights Templar were tortured. Paranoia was paramount. If you didn't die of the many plagues sweeping across Europe, it was wise to decry others of witchcraft before being accused of the same and finding yourself being tortured or suffering at the stake. There are countless extreme examples of the frivolous manner with which accusations could arise with fatal consequences. Contrivances through the inquisitors and the witchfinders were wholly born out of superstition and fear. Doing anything deemed as being uncharacteristic to normal behaviour was more than enough, like walking along the side of the road you wouldn't normally do, being left handed, or not attending church. In 1544, Cardinal David Beaton of St Andrews, had a woman in Perth, Scotland, drowned in a pool for not praying to the Virgin Mary while in childbirth.

The contrivances were partly fuelled by the Malleus Maleficarum (the Hammer of Witches) that appeared in Germany in 1486. This was a manual for witchfinders and inquisitors written by Heinrich Kramer, a Catholic priest.

Within this volume he gave details in how to find, torture and kill suspected witches. It had everything they needed and each copy would see a great many suffer in ways the torturers could not previously have imagined possible.

Through accusations of devilish scenarios and demonic pacts by the inquisitors, all the innocents could do to make the pain stop was agree with their fantasies and give names of fellow innocents. Their fabrication and embellishment under extreme duress exemplified the fears, the paranoia and the imagination of the Christian mindset as the cause of their misfortunes; of death and of sorrow. Salem being a classic example of how hysteria, once unleashed, could see events spiralling out of control and lead to self-prophesying conclusions.

The last embers of the witch trials would burn out in the 18th century when the belief in witchcraft as a perversion of Christian doctrine through heresy subsided. They no longer believed witchcraft existed, which in essence it never did! There has always been plenty of hysteria and imagination for its existence, but there was no direct religious antithesis in the form of 'Devil worship' and for that matter black magic only exists through the instability of misguided attempts to practice it.

The fabrication has been revitalised in more recent times as a potential through fictional stories, horror films, ill-informed documentaries and the tabloid press looking for sensationalistic headlines to sell more newspapers.

## Magic

### & the Mechanics of Existence

Like the paranormal, magic is another highly complex and completely misunderstood field of study and practice utilising the spiritual through an adherence of the spirit and an understanding of the mechanics of existence through experience. The two forms are high magic, or ceremonial magic for the divine advancement of the spiritual self, and mundane magic primarily for physical gain, but if used wisely, the latter will enhance the former. The Egyptian culture was inextricably linked with magic, and spirits of the deceased were integral to their system as an aspect of reality for thousands of years. Indeed, the same through various cultures in the East and West.

I have paraphrased the following from Giovanni Pico della Mirandola, an Italian catholic philosopher writing in his 'Oration on the Dignity of Man' as an introduction to his '900 Theses' in 1486. This became the first book to be banned by the Catholic Church.

Giovanni Pico della Mirandola was brought in front of the inquisition which gave him a real scare. Most copies of this book were burnt and he was forced to retract what he had written, including the following, which succinctly and accurately sums up the profession of the magician, both historically and currently:

'The magician is the minister of nature and not merely its artful imitator. This very wise man approves and maintains this magic… when he was invited to take part in rites of evil spirits, he said that they ought rather to come to him, than he to go to them… making him their lord and master. As an art or a science, magic is filled as it is with mysteries, it embraces the most profound contemplation of the deepest secrets of things and finally the knowledge of the whole of nature. This beneficent magic, in calling forth, as it were, from their hiding places into the light, the powers which the largess [generosity] of God has sown and planted in the world, does not itself work miracles, so much as sedulously serving nature as she works her wonders. Scrutinising, with greater penetration, that harmony of the universe which the Greeks with greater aptness of terms called *sympatheia* and grasping the mutual affinity of things, she applies to each thing those inducements, most suited to its nature. Thus, it draws forth into public notice the miracles which lie hidden in the recesses of the world, in the womb of nature, in the storehouses and secret vaults of God, as though she herself were their artificer. As the farmer weds his elms to the vines, so the "magus'" unites earth to heaven, that is, the lower orders to the endowments and powers of the higher. Hence magic appears divine and salutary. Beneficent magic, excites in him an admiration for the works of God which flowers naturally into charity, faith, and hope. For nothing so surely impels us to the worship of God than the assiduous contemplation of His miracles and when, by means of this natural magic, we shall have examined these wonders more deeply, we shall more ardently be moved to love and worship Him in his works, until finally we shall be compelled to burst into song: "The heavens, all of the earth, is filled with the majesty of your glory." I have been led to say even this much because I know that there are many persons who condemn and hate it, because they do not understand it, just as dogs always bay at strangers.'

These wise words of the high magician ring true through any age. For the most part, high magic or ceremonial magic was not necessarily out of step with the Vatican. There was always an understanding that magic worked. By correlation, as examples with the church we have the three wise mages as practitioners and the miracles of Christ and the saints as a testimony of its operations. So, not all practices were viewed as a threat to the church. When circumstance led to a beneficial outcome the church believed it was the work of angels and saints and lavished praise on them accordingly. Public perception for elements of magic were more often removed from the church and the reality of its practice. To the laity everything was and to a degree still is black or white, with the only grey areas being their understanding on such matters, so magicians involved in the high magical arts kept their involvements completely secret from the outer world partly for this reason. Partly also that misunderstanding inevitably serves to also debase the sacred sciences and the divine principles therein contained (all knowledge is not for all). This secrecy also applied within the Vatican yet within this, and as I mentioned, if the intimation of high magical undertakings rose to the surface in a public manner such as those we have with Giovanni Pico della Mirandola, the Vatican would be poised to publicly decry and privately deal with what they were privately researching or agreeing with. One of the great mysteries associated with this was in 1494, when at the age of 31, Giovanni and a friend were found dead under suspicious circumstances at his home in Florence. It wasn't until 2007 when their bodies were exhumed to find the cause - they had been poisoned by arsenic.

**MAGIC and Necromancy**

Ghosts in medieval times were not widely promoted in literature as 'ghosts' but there is a mountain of literature where they speak of spirits, angels and demons. They also speak of the effects of poltergeist activity and of seeing departed relatives.

Magicians/natural philosophers comprised some of the greatest minds. They were the scientists of the day. As esoteric scholars they were part of what is now known as the 'Western Mystery Tradition', a term popularised by the influential French Catholic priest and magician Eliphas Levi in the 19th century. To connect with the spiritual energies, ceremonial operations were constructed with a ritualistic air borrowed primarily from the Roman Church, who employed the ceremonial for the same reasons as a focus and vessel for the directing of intent. Like the church, they were also more than aware of the supernatural and ghosts. The miracles and the resurrection of Christ notifying of survival being primary examples of acceptance and promotion. With this they were aware of the effects the deceased could have on the living, and how the attributes of saints could be of benefit for example. The adherence to the existence of spirits is as old as mankind and communicating with spirits was another form of divination.

Part of the reconciliation of the universe for the magician is a harmonising of their understanding of the spiritual. With the physical being a manifestation of the spiritual, spirts of the deceased could hold keys to aspects of reality hidden within the physical and thus give guidance.

There appears to have been a difference in church acceptance between communicating with spirits who appear to you and summoning spirits to communicate with them. The first is acceptable within the church as the bible is full of such communications. Whereas, summoning spirits are considered as disturbing or tampering with the dead through black magic or sorcery. Although it could be argued the act of prayer is the drawing or gathering of higher principles, powers, influences and spirits often denoted by the magician through association and simile as angels for example. The result is often indistinguishable. They both involve communion and communication for a beneficial outcome.

In its simplistic form, the name necromancy comes from the ancient Greek nekrós meaning dead body and manteia meaning divination. Go deeper and to paraphrase the etymology dictionary, manteia came from manteusthai – to prophesy, and mantis – one who divines, a seer prophet or one touched by divine madness. There is also mainesthai - be inspired, which is related to menos - passion, spirit. Its purity changed to late Latin as necromantia and from this it became necromancy. In the old French there is nigromancie which is black magic, necromancy, witchcraft and sorcery. So, the variations in spelling and alterations of meaning would give slightly different connotations for how the name is perceived, and how it would then be publicly received. A seemingly accepted and innocuous act could be interpreted as being contrary to doctrine depending on perspective or interpretation, and that is where it could easy turn against the practitioner, especially during the witch hunt period. At its most divine we have one gaining insights through communing with spirits that could be construed through a base representation as raising the dead for hidden information of the same, be it about the future or something concealed. So, within this, understanding could see an accepted outcome, while the process to obtain that outcome could again see you burn.

## Angelology and Demonology

The mechanics of reality and the secrets hidden behind the veil of nature have always been of prime consideration to the magician, with a focus on perfection in all things within the sphere of universal involvement. They understood that the keys for understanding the mechanics of reality and paranormal phenomena is to understand energy as being the underlying principle of existence. It is also the governing principle behind the nature of time. The energy I speak of is spiritual energy, physical energy is just its physical aspect or element. Everything is energy, it is ubiquitous. We are energy, which is why it has been called 'the life force,' or Prana in Hindu. More appropriately in Prana, energy also translates as the 'vital principle'. It is intelligent and dynamic. It is very real and very often tangible. Mankind has harnessed it for thousands of years and without it nothing would exist. Energy conveys the full spectrum of spiritual dynamics as aspects of a greater whole, with each aspect commanding a very defined and very real energetic attribution. The magician's familiarity with energy was and is exhaustive, and not as an abstract academic exercise or philosophical construct. Energy influences each one of us through the forces they both singularly and collectively represent and portray. As symbolic personifications of very real universal forces prevalent through reality and comprising the energetic dynamics of the universe, they were quantified and personified into type, scope and remit. Employed accordingly, each are representative of their own hierarchical structure of energetic intensity and attribution. You will know them as angels and demons and by necessity there are choirs and legions of them respectively, but do not be fooled by any preconditioned supposition as to their nature from religious doctrine or Hollywood film alone. Their quantification as a structural representation for what they convey holds true regardless of belief. The unification of the magician through esotericism requires them to be understood and harmonised by assimilating their energies within the self. To command is to overcome, and to assimilate is to know. To negate anything is to negate a potential within the self as a reflection of the 'all' through spirit, so any preference or persuasion towards any one attribution to the negation of any other could be dangerous. Great care has always been advocated for all spiritual undertakings. When the energies they represent are assimilated, they must be done with impartiality, otherwise they can overwhelm and obsess the mind and influence behaviour. With safeguards representative of this very real potential, it is why humility in all endeavours is also very important that they do not tip the balance of the natural equilibrium and inflate the ego as a sure sign of an obsessive nature. Assimilation has always been one of recognising truth in every quarter. Everything by necessity was and is at their disposal, so there was no adherence to any one doctrine or religion above another. It is why they also employed Babylonian, Egyptian, Greek and Roman Gods for example. Like the hierarchies of angels and demons, they too are personifications of vast universal energetic principles and govern all forces within the scope of their remit.

The majority in magical and esoteric arcane circles look to attain what I speak of, but few in any lifetime ever make it beyond the theoretical stage. Its complexities attract intellectuals, but it is a trap to treat it all as an academic exercise. It can and does take many years if not lifetimes to achieve the necessary level of knowing required through experience for it to be a natural vocation integral to and within the self, academia alone will always miss it through perceiving it as an abstract.

**MAGIC - So who were involved in magic?**

The late 16th, early 17th century saw new peaks in scientific/ magical learning and exploration, concurrent with peaks marking its destructive apposite 'the Witches Hammer', which was now coming down hard in certain quarters for elements pf these disciplines. The high magic of the magicians continued through the middle ages with a relative safe passage. Their pass of immunity from suspicion by the layman and thugs seeking out heretics was through this inherent secrecy, it was also maintained through respectability. With status, who would ever suspect? A connecting link at this time was through Tubingën University, Baden-Württemberg, in Germany. This is where a close circle of natural philosophers/magicians of note created an invisible college. An Esoteric Order known as the Rosicrucian's. They promoted an understanding of the ancient sciences and spiritual philosophies under a Christian allegorical framework, operating concurrently with the more conventional sciences as taught in the universities. Those of learning were versed in all the disciplines of the day, remember they negated nothing and furthered their knowledge accordingly.

The core of their Rosicrucian Order is embodied by Christian Rosenkreuz or Christian Rosy Cross. An allegorical German knight/philosopher and magician whose symbolic journey through the Middle East in the early 15th century mirrored the journey of man and his quest for the perfected enlightened state by the uniting of the self with the higher self. His journey is recorded in the Fama Fraternitatis, the first of three short coded Rosicrucian manifestos written anonymously and widely distributed between 1614 and 1617. Their mission was to prepare the whole wide world for a new phase which includes awareness of the inner worlds and the subtle bodies, and to provide safe guidance in the gradual awakening of man's latent spiritual faculties during the next six centuries toward the coming Age of Aquarius.

Of course, their order through the publication of these manifestos clashed with the public doctrine of both the Roman and Protestant Church who each banned them accordingly as heretical treatise. However, unlike their publications, which were spread far and wide across the continent and carried their own popularity, the identity of who wrote them and those involved, like their undertakings, were well hidden from both public and church gaze. With all the natural hallmarks of magicians, their eye for detail, perfection, and for invisibility in their undertakings, gave them a freedom conducive to profound personal insights, albeit one carrying cautionary caveats. Their magical discoveries would either kept in-house so to speak, or were marked by individual spiritual progression.

Comprising some of the greatest minds within the learned and scientific community of Europe, members included Christoph Besold, seven time University Chancellor at Tubingën. He was a Qabalist, learned in Arabic, Hebrew and Islamic culture and astronomy. He studied astronomy with Johannes Kepler at the university. Another of their number at the university was Georg Rodolf Weckherlin. Among his many vocations he became assistant to the British poet Milton who wrote Paradise Lost. It can only be surmised the degree of influence Weckherlin exerted in the promotion of that famous and epic poem. Another at the university during this period was Johann Valentine Andrea. He concerned himself with the conveyance of ancient esoteric spiritual wisdom and would become noted for his depth of Rosicrucian understanding.

You may know Johannes Kepler as the Father of modern astronomy. He was also a noted astrologer as well as a Christian esotericist/magician. His three laws of planetary motion changed the face of how the universe is viewed and became a major influence on Newtonian law. Other members during this period, but not at Tubingën, and whose influence through their physical discoveries had equally profound effects on western thought were: Dr John Dee (1527-1608), Isaac Casaubon (1559-1614), Sir Francis Bacon (1561-1626), Sir Henry Wotton (1568-1639) and Robert Fludd (1574-1637). Then coming at a slightly later period we have Elias Ashmole (1617-1692) and Thomas Vaughan (1622-1666). Queen Christina of Sweden (1626-1654), Robert Boyle (1627-1691) and another surprise for you - Sir Isaac Newton (1643-1727). They were all magicians and they were all conversing with spirits.

Beginning with Dr John Dee, he was a close advisor to Queen Elizabeth I. Isaac Casaubon was a philologist (studied the history of languages) and a classical and Hebrew scholar. Sir Francis Bacon was a candidate for Shakespeare, he is also a candidate as founder of Rosicrucianism. A premise endorsed by AMORC (Ancient Mystical Order Rosae Crucis) and one I would not dispute. Sir Henry Wotton was also a politician who warned King James VI in Scotland of a murder plot against him. In return he spent three months in the King's Court, then when James became King James I of England and Ireland he was knighted and given the embassy in Venice. Robert Fludd was a Paracelcian physician, qabalist, cosmologist, astrologer and noted alchemist, and while Kepler was the father of astronomy, Fludd was the father of Freemasonry. It was through him that Elias Ashmole became one of its early members. Ashmole was a Royalist Politician, astrologer, alchemist, and antiquarian. Thomas Vaughan was a philosopher of magic and mysticism and a Rector of a parish in Wales. He translated the Rosicrucian texts the Fama and the Confessio into English in 1652. A 'Braid Scots' version had already been published around 1633. Although not certain, it is believed he wrote a number of tracts under the pseudonym of Eugenius Philalethes. He was also a Paracelcian alchemist and died through inhaling mercury vapour following a failed alchemical experiment. *All* were proponents of Hermetic and Kabbalistic teaching incorporating Christian and Jewish mysticism, eastern philosophy and emerging western thought involving magical, philosophical, spiritual and ceremonial studies, in unison with disciplines and practices that included the employment of magical, astrological and alchemical texts. As I say, nothing was negated.

Their Rosicrucian movement is based on Paracelcian principles. Paracelsus, also known as Philippus Theophrastus Aureolus Bombastus von Hohenheim was an alchemist, kabbalist, physician, botanist and Hermetic philosopher. Developing the ideas of the four elements and the three alchemical principles of Mercury, Sulphur and Salt, the Hermetic approach to his work related to the 'as above so below' principle I spoke of earlier. The Macrocosm with the Microcosm and how man was united with the universe through particular principles and building blocks of nature, thus uniting with God who pervades all things through the spirit as denoted by the higher self, and the journey represented by the Chemical Wedding, which was the third of the Rosicrucian Manifestos.

During the same period when these natural philosophers/magicians were at Tubingën University in Germany marking the foundation of their Rosicrucian Order, Rudolph II of Bohemia (the Czech Republic) was seeking the philosopher's stone – the elixir of life of the alchemists that also had the functionality to turn base metals into gold. This was Rudolph II von Habsburg (1552 - 1612). Holy Roman Emperor, King of Bohemia, King of Hungary and Archduke of Austria amongst his impressive array of titles. He had a vast fortune and a life-long passion for the arts and sciences, especially for the occult/esoteric sciences of astrology/astronomy and alchemy which he had a particular fascination for. He amassed the largest collection of art in Europe and drew together the greatest artists and natural philosophers/magicians of the day. His seat was in the castle of Prague and sparing no expense, he drew upon this collection of unique esoteric, magical and scientific minds in his quest for the Philosopher's Stone. As Holy Roman Emperor, Rudolf was Roman Catholic and many of those early Rosicrucian minds holding court in Prague were Protestant, but Bohemia, headed by Rudolph was enjoying a religious freedom where ideas could be freely discussed and shared without church interference or influence, and they did not allow their religion to interfere with their work. They included Johannes Kepler and Christoph Besold of Tubingën. Heinrich Khunrath and Count Michael Maier. Maier was a philosopher, alchemist, esotericist, and Rudolph's physician and imperial counsellor. Known for his occult knowledge and medical ability, he was granted the title Imperial Count Palatine. They all knew each other, they all served prominently within his court at around the same time, and all, including Rudolph benefitted greatly. There are also two other names to conjure with for this same period. Dr John Dee I mentioned earlier and one Edward Kelley.

**MAGIC - Dr John Dee**

Dee was one of the most trusted and closest advisors in the court of Elizabeth I during the Renaissance Period. She called him 'my philosopher'. He was an astrologer, astronomer, philosopher, alchemist, mathematician, geographer, cartographer, navigator, cryptographer, magician and as I intimated earlier, a fellow Rosicrucian. It was Dee who coined the term 'British Empire'. Some of his work survives as a unique magical system of Enochian Magic, employed to this day by high ceremonial magicians as a highly potent workable system of Angel Magic. This is a complete system and there are beginner's guides, but do not be fooled, this is a system rooted within the magical arts. It is not a system for the beginner with no or little theory or practical understanding of magic. It is full of traps for the impetuous and foolhardy, and it will burn you if you are not prepared. It is not related to the Angel Magic of the 'New Age' movement in any way, shape or form. The Enochian System is a difficult and demanding path to tread and is as far removed from the fluffy commercial perception of angels as you are ever likely to find.

Dee employed the services of a scryer (an early medium) called Edward Kelley as a conduit or vessel for the transmission of information of these powerful forces personified by these angels. Some so powerful the mere intimation of their presence could signify the immediate exhaustion of life. At the very least, the intensity of their energies appears so overwhelming they would be mistaken for demons of a high ranking nature. Dee was their attraction as he would understand the highly complex coded allegorical system they were about to give him the instructions for, along with the keys to its employment through Kelley.

Some of Dee's magical equipment is displayed on the ground floor of the British Museum. He was also possibly thee foremost cryptographer of his day, which stood him in good stead, as he was also a successful spy for Elizabeth I, especially in Europe. Although he was one of the closest advisors to the Queen, his name is usually conspicuous by its absence when 'historians' speak of her spies. Academics in general tend to shun or decry anything to do with magic as they don't have the first idea about what it is, and what they don't dismiss bears no resemblance to its reality. If this sounds familiar with the paranormal it is because anything fringing the ignorance of populist acceptance tends to be ignored or decried.

His code name was 007. Adopted centuries later by British spy and author Ian Fleming for his James Bond series of novels. Fleming and Dee were both famous British spies. Fleming being the initial brains behind the acquiring of an enigma machine from the Germans. There is a suggestion that Dee was the founder of the British Secret Service. If it were not Dee, he was certainly one of its early exponents. 007 was also the last three digits of the phone number of Fleming's agent. A connection that has been attributed as his source. However, the associations of Dee will have suited Fleming's creativity far more readily than plucking three meaningless random digits of his agent's number, which he would have observed more as a humorous coincidence than a moment of abstract inspiration.

Dee employed Electional Astrology to ascertain the most propitious time for the Queen's coronation which would then favour her reign. However, his most noted success with astrology for Elizabeth came in 1588. She received word the Spanish fleet was on its way to invade England. She consulted Dee for advice on what to do. Dee created an astrological chart. He told Elizabeth there would be a great storm and advised her to do absolutely nothing. She took his advice. If he were wrong of course, it wouldn't just be his head on the block. A great storm did indeed destroy most of the Spanish fleet that day, much to the relief of Dee, the queen, and the country I am sure. In the right hands, astrology works, period, and Dee was her trusted advisor for a reason. The consequences were too great for either to doubt the integrity of the system. That is the level with which astrology was being employed and the level of trust the queen had in Dee.

**MAGIC – Edward Kelley, the medium, the alchemist**

Kelley was also talented, as there is no denying has scrying abilities. What he relayed for Dee to record over a seven year period was coded, highly technical and complex by the standards of any age. The structure is so deep, it is not a system any could have made up. It would be like saying to a layman his life depended on completely rewiring a major telephone exchange with all the connections in the right place. Neither understood the deep technicalities of what was coming through the angels, yet what they ended up with was very clever, coherent and powerful, as the intelligences involved operate and motivate the core of existence. It is a system that has profound ramifications for any able to adhere to the strict conditions required for its employment.

Rudolph II invited Dr John Dee and Edward Kelley to Prague. Kelley's motivation in life seemed to be driven by a lust for the high life. I am probably being generous here when I say he did whatever it took to get what he wanted by doing the least amount possible for it. Sounds familiar with the mindset of many in present day society, for example, desiring the results of fame without any creative merit to back it up.

Kelley was held in high regard for his alchemical abilities but gained a reputation for his successes through highly dubious means, namely deception. Rudolph had unlimited funds for anyone who could produce the philosopher's stone – the elixir of life. He already had a kingdom but kings were always looking for more, and it wasn't just gold Rudolph was looking for, it was eternal youth. For Kelley, the riches Rudolf would bestow proved irresistible and so he made promises none of the other natural philosophers were able to commit to. For all the great work Kelley had done for Dee, the promises he foolhardily made to the king would prove to be his ultimate downfall.

While he was in Rudolph's court word soon spread that Kelley could produce the philosopher's stone. To give an idea, Lord Burghley, the chief adviser to Elizabeth I, wrote to Kelley saying, 'perhaps you might send her a small quantity of your gold-making powder, 'in some secret box', just enough 'as might be to her a sum reasonable to defer her charges for this summer for her navy.' So, no pressure then!

Could he produce the elixir of life… eh, no. Did Rudolph and indeed Elizabeth I and her court believe he could… oh yes! Kelley was dazzled by the king's lavish payments of money, land and titles in return for the production of the philosopher's stone. He also had an overt love of wine, and was spending a king's ransom on that particular elixir alone. He was living the life he had always dreamt of being accustomed to, but it was a charade. A bit like never having picked up an artist's brush and spending the money given to you by an oligarch after promising you could create an indistinguishable forgery of a Picasso. The trouble that could get you into is where Kelley now found himself. Following two failed attempts at making the philosophers stone, the king imprisoned Kelley in a tower. This sobered him up very quickly in several ways. In trying his escape from the harsh conditions, he fell from this said tower and died shortly after of his injuries in 1597. There are a lot more twists and turns, but if you thought all this would make a great movie you would be right.

**MAGIC - Giordano Bruno**

This was all taking place during the period in the Renaissance when these foremost scientific minds were applauded or decried by the church for their discoveries. It was only three years after Kelley's death that Giordano Bruno (Filippo Bruno), a protagonist of Copernicus, furthered his own theories. He was an Italian Philosopher, magician, mathematician, astronomer, hermeticist and Dominican Friar. You may have gathered they all had very similar interests and more often a lengthy string of academic titles. They were also all Rosicrucian's and of the same period, Bruno had also spent time with the others I have mentioned at Tubingën University. It is not clear whether Bruno met Dee, but they were certainly aware of each others work, and it appears they were more than adept at narrowly missing each other. While Dee was at the court of Rudolph II in Prague, Bruno was in England, then not long after Dee returned to England, Bruno was in the court of Rudolph II!

Bruno's research led him to publicly record that the stars were also suns surrounded by planets, and the universe was infinite with no centre. His research soon attracted the attention of the Catholic Church. He had been staying in Venice and finding himself at the blunt end of the Venetian Inquisition asked to be transferred to Rome where he would be able to communicate with greater authorities. He then suffered at the hands of the Roman Inquisition for seven long years. Bruno was correct, the church was reticent to prosecute him. In those seven long years there will have been a great deal of discourse, with the church learning as much from him as they could. Like Copernicus, the Vatican privately agreed with him and his findings, but through public pressure they had to be seen to be upholding the official line to prosecute any opposing their religious doctrine. Bruno's sentence was finally passed in 1600. At his trial he said, "Perhaps your fear in passing judgment on me is greater than mine in receiving it." A direct reference to their private morality. He was condemned to be burnt alive at the stake for heresy, but it wasn't for his astronomical views, being a political scapegoat for public approval, numerous charges were brought against him including dealings in magic and divination. He was taken to Campo de' Fiori, a large market square in Rome, hung upside down naked on the stake and either gagged with a leather bridle or an iron spike driven through his tongue to stop him speaking before being burnt alive. He has since become a symbol for freedom of speech and the most imposing and powerful statue of this hooded figure now stands dominating the square where he met his end. It is complete with bronze engravings of his trial and subsequent execution around the base. When I first encountered his statue, it was purely by accident whilst wandering through the narrow streets of Rome on my way to the Vatican. When I found who it was, it had a lasting impression.

Unlike Copernicus, for Bruno there has never been any retraction by the Church. The closest was exactly 400 years after his murder when Pope John Paul II in the year 2000 gave a general apology for "the use of violence that some have committed in the service of truth". The moral dilemma and private hypocrisy of the Catholic Church, even after so many years is still intact and upheld.

It was during the ban of Copernicus' book that Galileo was also tried for heresy in upholding amongst many other observations that the Earth revolves around the Sun. They were all adhering to the same precepts, and privately the church agreed with all of them, the problem again was their public presentation, so in 1633 Galileo was forced to recount his statement. This he did, and in return he would spend the rest of his life under house arrest rather than being burnt alive which again played to their morality.

In most of Europe, the Catholic religion held together the fabric or fable of reality for the laity and their place within it for many centuries. Bruno, Galileo and Copernicus (posthumously) were amongst the most famous protagonists to suffer at the hands of the Vatican for the sake of appearances. And there resides one of the many problems with doctrine. It is fixed as much in interpretation as it is in word, otherwise there would not be at least 40 divisions in Christian denomination ranging from slight variances in belief to major variations in biblical interpretation that sets each of them wholly apart from each other, the Catholic and Protestant faiths being prime examples. Doctrine works until observational understanding displaying a greater truth has the potential to expose any frailty. This is universal, generally doctrine is fixed to the period and level of understanding at the time of writing and if it doesn't evolve with discovery, hypocrisy through deflection of the truth is then the only avenue open if it is to maintain its integrity.

**Vatican involvement and Queen Christina of Sweden**

The Rosicrucian Order were operating secretly within the heart of the scientific community. The Vatican were the same, they had scholars working for the promotion of an understanding of the esoteric, the magical, and alchemical processes beyond their walls. Both were operating under the same lines without compromising their respective outer appearances or the integrity of the ancient systems they were studying and employing. If there could be any doubt in this, the following will put Vatican involvement into more perspective.

Queen Christina of Sweden was one of the most extraordinary figures in history few will have heard of. She was a Rosicrucian and magician but of a slightly later period than those I have mentioned. Born in 1626, she was one of those rare individuals whose life was characterized by unimaginable opulence and colour. Like those before her, she specialized in philosophy, mathematics, religion, alchemy and magic, and like her Rosicrucian brethren, she kept her studies secret from all not of the Order. She had amassed around 6,000 books and manuscripts, and like Rudolf II, she was a great collector and patron of the arts. Books have always been one of the hallmarks of the magician, Dr John Dee held the largest library outside the universities and the largest in England.

Like Rudolf II, Christina received all the main scholars and scientific practitioners involved in the ancient sciences, and it would be through these meetings her Rosicrucian involvement would blossom. Like attracting like, as the mysteries (out with the odd bad apple tainted by ego) have always tended to do.

To the public gaze, she was seen as an arbitrary figure, the epitome of extravagance and woefully wasteful. Given such public attributions none would suspect her arcane involvement. Such is the key of a magician. She was respected and of great standing, so she posed no threat to anyone, while privately she was silent, studious and spiritually advancing.

Several scholars have written about Christina at length with varying degrees of objective success invariably mixed with misplaced fantasy as they attempt to fill in the gaps of a life they knew nothing about. Christina's life, especially in Sweden was extraordinary enough without the need for any embellishment but not many then or since were aware of her underlying motivation which is easy to misinterpret. Much in the same way as Aleister Crowley in more recent times. As one of the greatest magicians of any age Crowley wrote extensively. Everything was profoundly profuse, deeply spiritual and conveyed the same directives of the magician for the divine promotion of the higher self as his predecessors. But the common man saw no inclination to read any of his published work to find out what he or his teachings were about. They were quite happy to dwell on him being the devil incarnate when he was the closest any would come to meeting a divine being incarnate.

One of the best and highly recommended papers about Christina I have found is by Nathan Alan Popp for his detailed thesis at the University of Iowa in 2015, which took him to Sweden to conduct his research. Like many, he doesn't appear to be aware of her Rosicrucian involvement, or at the least to have held any importance for her associations in this direction to give any mention, but his extensive research for the first part of her outer life typifies the opulence she enjoyed, although the potential for opulence would never leave her side.

Her coronation in 1650 was the most extravagant Sweden had seen. In fact, it was probably the most extravagant celebration anyone in Europe had seen since Titus and the 100 day games of Rome in 80 AD.

It took place at Ulriksdal Palace, then known as Jakobsdal, 6 kilometres north of Stockholm. Popp writes extensively about this, so the following is just a very brief snippet to give a mere flavour of a very detailed lengthy account of extraordinary opulence and is well worth reading. He says: 'Traditional precedent set a period of celebratory spectacles to be held for one week after the coronation ceremony, but Christina's lasted the entire fall season.

Feasting and merriment began the evening of the coronation and was celebrated across the city. A whole ox stuffed with chickens, geese, turkey, etc. was served to the public in Stortorget Square, outside the castle. A fountain with a sculpture of the goddess of fertility spouted red and white wine for all to enjoy for three days. Fireworks were launched to the northeast side of the city, as the feast ended.'[72]

Christina explains in a pamphlet she authored 'called *Pronostiques de la reine Christine* (the Predictions of Queen

Christina) that she was blessed with the power of divination.'[73] It has been suggested she was immortal - which comes from her alchemical associations. Christina kept her purity and would not marry. From this, one of her more recent academic biographers found her 'eccentric and incapable of finding solace in her life.'[74] As I say, her real life was completely hidden. To mainstream perception unaware of her secretive involvements she was eccentric, she was also young and immensely rich. I would argue, because of her involvements, and contrary to her onlookers and her recent biographers, that she found more solace than any could profess in their lifetime, and most could equally profess to meet.

Interestingly a wholly inaccurate film was made in 1933 by MGM about her life up to her abdication. It was called Queen Christina or *La Reine Christine.* The starring role went to Greta Garbo. It is a fanciful tale about romance, something Christina had no physical interest in. In the film she falls in love with a Spanish envoy, abdicates and journeys with him to Spain.

In realty, it was her reluctance to marry that resulted in her abdicating her throne in favour of her cousin to continue the male air to the throne in 1654. She commanded great respect, and given the patriarchal nature in Sweden, this arrangement was met with acceptance.

Following her abdication, far from journeying to Spain she promptly set out for Rome where she was greeted as a Queen by Pope, Cardinals and the whole of Rome itself. She converted to Catholicism and was revered by the Vatican. Christina was now working for the church as an ambassador. She was a prize resource to have within their city walls and had her own apartment in the Vatican not far from the Papal quarters. Being away from the public gaze and with no royal responsibilities she could continue her work without unnecessary distraction. Unlike the relationship between Rudolph and Kelley, this was the chemical wedding. For the Vatican and the Catholic

Church, it was a perfect marriage and both were exemplary in their Papal obligations to secrecy.

They plied her with riches and luxuries otherwise only afforded to the Pope. As a patron of the arts, she continued, or rather increased her alchemical labours and researches until she died in the Vatican in 1689.

There has been a revelatory suggestion that at least two Pope's had an interest in the occult. That is incorrect. She had been the guest of five consecutive Pope's alone and would not have survived long had any one of them expressed an interest against the occult. The exploration of the universe was a merger, a union of the physical and the spiritual and everything was God's work. The alchemical secrets both she and the Vatican gained have never been published. Could the Vatican church have the philosopher's stone? she certainly did something within Vatican walls that appeased them greatly, something miraculous you might say. Venerated as a saint, she is one of only three women to be buried in the Papal Crypt in the Vatican.

**Down to earth with a bump**

With the advent of the Scientific Revolution through Copernicus in the 16th century another conversation had also been taking place outside the walls of the Vatican. The natural laws and spiritual laws extending through existence were recognised by the universities right up until the 17th century as incorporating physical, spiritual and esoteric principles, but the Renaissance period had seen a very gradual movement of streamlining in the scientific study of the physical away from the spiritual and esoteric sciences.

Physical technological breakthroughs had been on the rise across Europe. The Scientific Revolution saw systematic experimentation as their prime method of research. Scientific instruments were becoming very popular and held a particular fascination for both scholars and all who could appreciate their purpose. Importantly, there was an immediate tangibility to their inventions and discoveries, so they could see the results of their labours more readily than the often laborious and almost imperceptible processes of spiritual attainment through a refinement of the self. There was an elaborate pocket sundial owned by Cardinal Wolsey in England. Gerardus Mercator in Belgium with satellite navigation, Zacharias Janssen in the Netherlands with the first compound microscope, and further into the 17th century, Galileo invented the basic thermometer and despite being forced to recount his statement that ran concurrent with Copernicus and Bruno, he was the first to view the stars through a telescope.

There were as many complexities of thought associated with the sciences developing through the natural philosophers as there were different perspectives. With these physical breakthroughs came change. It had partly been engineered by Sir Francis Bacon I mentioned earlier, who is also known as one of the fathers of empirical science. In 1620 he published a work called The *Novum Organum* or *New organon, or true directions concerning the interpretation of nature.* It became known as the Baconian method and formulated empiricism through inductive methodology of facts as a means of studying and interpreting *natural* (physical) phenomena. It became a system where evidence for truth comes from a synthesis of people's experiences and observations displaying the same. This can then give an argument for determining probability rather than through ideas or traditions alone. It became the foundation of empirical science, but of itself, his method equally applies to the quantification of paranormal experience through testimony. It is the testability of paranormal phenomena through repeated observation and experimentation under a 'controlled' environment that is not possible.

This was not necessarily a new idea for Rosicrucian's or magicians, nor for that matter many natural philosophers of the day who had been employing this model for a long time.

Indeed, the concept of empiricism (as opposed to rationalism) is of a much older origin through Aristotle in 350 BC and ancient Greek teachers known as the sophists c.5$^{th}$ century BC. Bacon brought empiricism to the forefront as a mode of western scientific research that narrowed down these often opposing processes and perspectives.

Sir Francis Bacon, and Paracelsus before him, were more than aware of the different dynamics of thought taking place, after all, let us not forget, proponents like Paracelsus were amongst the leading exponents of the discoveries of their day. However, natural philosophers were finding themselves as involved in debate over the merits of the ancient sacred sciences in relation to physical exploration as they were in just getting on with it all. Nothing changes!

So why would the potential head of an esoteric secret order promote ideas for a physical quantification when it surely contradicts the principles of their spiritual mission? It was partly about deflecting public and church focus away from their door and partly that physical exploration was an important branch of science the main players of the day were all involved in – but, it must be remembered not exclusively. With the volatility of the witch hunts there was no telling how it was all going to play out. For those involved in the ancient sciences, their outward appearance was always opposite to their ultimate focus, some of which could be counted as heretical. Their hidden life was part of a different world. For all tense and purpose's, the world they were exploring is the one that motivates this one, and they had to safeguard themselves from the 'mob' by whatever outward guise they could.

There is another name worth mentioning at this point, Robert Boyle. Natural philosopher, theologian, alchemist, physicist and again a Rosicrucian. He was a founder of the Royal Society. He sat on its council and is known as the first modern chemist. As time progressed, to even mention the ancient sciences was becoming apocryphal in certain academic circles involved in the physical sciences, with many in corresponding about Boyle then as now refusing to acknowledge his alchemical roots and insisting on recording him as a chemist.

**The double lives of Sir Isaac Newton and Elias Ashmole**

Another to conjure with at this period is Sir Isaac Newton (1642 – 1726). He was possibly the greatest mathematician of any age. Born the same year Galileo died, he was also a physicist, theologian, alchemist, and occultist. Again, studies of the ancient sciences held more importance for Newton than his studies of a physical scientific nature, although it is the scientific breakthrough's he will always be remembered for. In-keeping with the magician he was very reclusive, which again was misinterpreted as hiding away from critics when all the while, like the others, including Queen Christina, he was just getting on with serious research and enquiry that demanded a particular brand of separation from the outer world. This was succinctly summed up by John Maynard Keynes in a lecture he wrote for the Royal Society titled *Newton, the Man.* It was delivered by his brother on his behalf in 1946. 'Until the second phase of his life, he was a wrapped, consecrated solitary, pursuing his studies by intense introspection with a mental endurance perhaps never equalled.'[75]

Newton not only changed how the physical universe was viewed, he was pivotal in changing how academics would view science which is crucial to my present enquiry. Newton was in possession of a large library with some 1,700 books. Elias Ashmole had a similar collection of 1,758 books (again in-keeping with the magician), along with a large and varied antiquarian collection which he donated to the University of Oxford, who formed the Ashmolean Museum.

Ashmole remember was one of the early Freemasons. He was also a Rosicrucian and knew Newton. They both shared in very similar interests including alchemy and the intelligence of nature extending to angels. Ashmole was in possession of John Dee's original papers and became a proponent of his system of Enochian Magic. Crucial papers of how Dee's system worked were discovered purely by accident in '1662 or 1663 [when] a Mr. and Mrs. Jones of Lombard Street in London had occasion to move a chest, which they had bought shortly after their marriage, from its customary place in their house. Hearing something rattle they looked closely at the chest and Mr. Jones discovered a secret drawer [hidden compartment] containing various manuscript papers and a rosary and cross of olive wood. Being unable to understand the contents of these papers, they paid no great attention to them and many were eventually lost through being used by their maid to line pie dishes [!!!]. Two years later Mr. Jones died and although the chest perished in the Fire of London [1666], the manuscripts, such as were left, were preserved. Mrs. Jones married again, this time to Thomas Wale who was a warder at the Tower of London and was acquainted with Elias Ashmole. Learning the story of the discovery of the manuscripts and that the chest had once belonged to John Dee, Wale sent them to Ashmole on 20 August 1672 for his perusal.

Ashmole had in his hands four magical books written by Dee [and dictated by Kelley] and also the diaries of his magical experiments between 22 December 1581 and 23 May 1583.'[76] The record of this is from Ashmole writing about how the manuscripts were discovered. They could so easily have been lost and indeed it is incredible that pages were being used to line pie dishes. These then made sense of the Enochian system.

Ashmole was now looking at the 'Action of Spirits' which together with a document that had already been published with the title '*A True and Faithful Relation of what passed for many years between Dr. John Dee and some Spirits*'. 'These Actions are the records of visions of angels and other spirits and the messages delivered by them as seen and heard by the scryer

[Kelley] with the aid of a crystal ball, and then immediately related to Dee, who though present saw and heard nothing.'[77]

'Newton asked himself whether it was possible to discern different intelligences, perhaps even distinct principles with distinct centres of consciousness behind the material surface of things. This is not to say that he ever saw these principles as angels sitting on clouds or visualized them in any naively anthropomorphic way - but neither did he see them as being completely impersonal, let alone as pure abstractions. He called them 'Intelligencers' to imply volition.'[78]

Elias Ashmole was also one of the founders of the Royal Society in London, becoming formalised as a Fellow of the Society weeks after its formation at the beginning of January 1661. Newton would then become a Fellows of the Society some eleven years later in 1672.

For Newton to have been introduced to Freemasonry and Rosicrucianism through Ashmole is highly likely. Those in both of these organizations were involved in the exploration of the same esoteric disciplines as Newton. Newton wrote over one million words on the subject of alchemy alone and never published any of it, yet they were widely read, which sounds like a riddle. It was his fellow likeminded fraters who read some of his material, but there is so much of it, to this day most of it has still not been read, let alone studied.

Keynes in his lecture also says: 'He parted with and published nothing except under the extreme pressure of friends.'[79]

He also wrote volumes about theology and the nature of God. Rob Iliffe in his *Priest of Nature: The Religious Worlds of Isaac Newton,* 2017 says:

'A number of factors conspired against the publication of Newton's private theological writings. In the eighteenth century Newton had become an icon of Enlightenment *philosophers* and his scientific achievements were regarded by them as emblematic of scientific rationality. Newton's deep personal piety and preoccupation with matters of biblical chronology and prophecy, had they become widely known, would have challenged Enlightenment assumptions about a necessary opposition between religion and science. Subsequently, his religious views (or at least what was known of them) came to be regarded as an embarrassment or, at best, irrelevant to his reputation and achievements.

On the other side, those who wished to perpetuate the image of Newton as a godly scientist had to reckon with the fact that his unpublished writings exhibited unmistakable evidence of deeply heretical views. Newton was never able to reconcile himself to the idea that Christ was truly divine and part of the triune godhead. On the basis of his methodical biblical and historical researches he had arrived at the view that the doctrine of the Trinity was a corruption of true Christianity. Newton had been careful to conceal his position from his contemporaries, and with good reason. Public knowledge of his private beliefs would have had catastrophic consequences for his career and maybe his life. The first custodians of his literary estate, Newton's half-niece and housekeeper Catherine, and her husband John Conduitt, who succeeded Newton as Master of the Mint, were understandably concerned to preserve Newton's reputation, not just as a man of science, but as an exemplary Christian. Accordingly, they were disinclined to see his heterodox views made public.

Newton's scientific papers eventually found their way into the Cambridge University Library in the late nineteenth century. The bulk of the alchemical and theological writings, however, did not make a public appearance until 1936, when, for financial reasons, their owner put them up for auction at Sotheby's.'[80]

The bulk were purchased through two main individual's who donated them to libraries in Cambridge and Jerusalem. Many of the documents are now online.

Few academics have delved into Newton's vast writing on alchemy and theology, and if they did, without a level of understanding to appreciate their worth, who is any to suppose that what they contain doesn't mirror the same degree of spiritual depth venerated by his physical insights into the universe.

Not all natural philosophers were Rosicrucian or magically minded, far from it, but they were of a Christian mind and their observations of existence were nonetheless entwined with the spiritual. Over time though, rather than continuing the ancient disciplines and complexities for long term spiritual reward, many academics were now excluding the ancient sciences from their field of study and concentrating on the physical alone as a disparate science. This would all have a long and lasting impression upon western thought to present day. Apart from a few select members, the Royal Society was becoming elitist and arrogant in their scientific outlook. When it came to the ancient sciences, far from seeing their merits they gradually viewed them as a movement whose purpose was to lead them to where they now were. Nothing more.

**A shift in scientific expectation**

Historian Michael Hunter in 2015, writing in his *Boyle Studies: Aspects of the Life and Thought of Robert Boyle (1627-91)*[81] wrote: 'Boyle was the victim of a crucial shift in expectations concerning the proper nature of science, with a new paradigm emerging in the image of Newton which discredited the entire style of science that had preceded him and which Boyle had exemplified so fully.' Hunter's observation is an important one, if not a little bitter. but he was quite correct in remarking about a shift in science by those who saw Newton as their saviour. Boyle, Wren, Newton, and others were all Rosicrucian's and were heavily involved in the esoteric sciences.

Practising magicians had always been a minority, but in comprising some of the most influential scientific minds it was the magicians, who, in being at the forefront of understanding also represented the cutting edge of physical science. They were geniuses in their own fields and each had to keep their arcane undertakings hidden from all barring those of their own circle who shared like minds in perspective, understanding and practice. They were each progressing the sciences in all their forms and each became unwitting victims of their own success when it came to emerging minds solely focusing on the physical sciences. Boyle was far from exempt in this himself, which is why Hunter's remark is a little harsh as it was Boyle's contribution that saw alchemy move to chemistry.

This new brand of science had found its niche and was developing its own physical identity out with the church or the scholars of old. Where there was once conflict in church doctrine through the perceived union between the physical and spiritual, many of those now involved in science were developing a rationale where externalised understanding about the universe were divorced from any form of inner exploration.

There was no opposition from the church for this departure in thought, as their physical model had effectively taken spirituality out of their new found science. With it being separate from the church, the laity could still deem their discoveries as heretical but the church was no longer directly involved. In the main however, their discoveries were immediate, practical and beneficial for the laity, so it was more in the way of a mutual shift of sorts in perception.

The discoveries they were making were groundbreaking, fresh, and furthering their depths of physical understanding. In 1661 Robert Boyle published *The Sceptical Chymist.* His work was one of these groundbreaking moments that would see the spiritual qualities of alchemy being dropped in favour of its physical composition - chemistry. In 1655 the first peer-reviewed scientific journal was published by the Royal Society. In St Andrews, mathematician and astronomer Sir James Gregory created the first meridian line in 1673, some 211 years before Greenwich, and Sir Isaac Newton's description of the fundamental force of universal gravitation was published in his *Principia* in 1687. His grand synthesis or Newtonian Synthesis from the same held that physical laws applied equally to terrestrial and celestial realms. That the influences of gravitational force on earth might also apply to the moon as a satellite for example. This was science fit for a scientific revolution and it had the backing of the people as well as academics who were fascinated by the discoveries being made.

Marking a pivotal switch in the way science would now be represented and studied, in 1687, Newtonianism would mark the end of the scientific revolution as contributions for physical scientific breakthroughs had eclipsed spiritual or esoteric disciplines in popularity. Newton's application for the physical processes of celestial bodies would then overshadow astrology which would see it dropped in favour of astronomy and a purely physical makeup of the universe. Kind of ironic that astronomy had now become the standard mode of enquiry into the universe when it was originally seen as a way of making astrology more accurate! Their science completely bypassed the enquiring element of this relationship, and ironically it was Newton, who, through his deep understanding and foresight, stumbled into a trap by inadvertently instigating exactly what he was looking to avoid. Discovering the gravitational forces determining the motion of planets for example in no way negates a greater operation at work, whereby their position at a given moment can determine present and future events as the physical expression or as a manifestation of a spiritual dynamic.

Scholars did not break away from the spiritual/esoteric sciences or disciplines because of any lacking in their integrity, noted scientists and academics including Paracelsus, Isaac Newton, Johannes Kepler and Robert Fludd were employing both. As a model, the physical sciences were running concurrently with these other scholarly disciplines.

Christian morality and academic understanding were now co-existing as two separate bodies without necessarily conflicting with each other. For the church, they were carrying on as before in welcoming new physical breakthroughs in their exploration of God's creation, but more so now as a public display than before.

A shift in emphasis through this evolving process of succession would see the Scientific Revolution eclipsed in the 18$^{th}$ century by what became known as the Age of Enlightenment. A title carrying no little irony when enlightenment had previously been reserved for high spiritually minded pursuits. With many natural philosophers now focusing on this emerging methodological science they would soon become known as scientists. They would lose sight of the true worth and merit of everything having gone before, and the interconnected relationship between 'self' and reality would become a spiritual abstract connected solely with belief through the church as mediator.

The result led to the methods of the once learned natural philosopher being deemed as primitive by comparison and would come to be associated as nothing more than early forerunners of an evolving process, with little extending worth or merit beyond this. It was both an evolution of the physical as well as a revolution of new thought in how the mechanics of the universe operated, and importantly it was an emerging western science that had no spiritual involvement. There was also another appeal to all this, one the ancient sciences couldn't compete with – it was new, which made it all the more appealing and well suited to these new generations of enquiring minds, including Immanuel Kant for example. He was an 18$^{th}$ century pioneer of Western philosophy and it doesn't surprise that he struggled with the faith of his Protestant background in the light of (physical) science.

**Diluting the foundation of reality**

By the 19th century, these concepts were becoming more defined and cemented in the minds of scientists and layman alike. With the mainstay of the academic community focusing their attention in this direction, they were looking to make it known that this was a *new* science and they did not want the old tainting the new.

As a simile to the apocrypha and the sometimes turbulent misinterpretations for aspects of the magical arts and sciences including the divinatory sciences with the Catholic Church through the centuries, they denounced it all and looked to discredit their value to promote their own. This included the supernatural which was still adhered to by many, but it was all misinterpreted, misrepresented and diluted as the imagination or nothing more than a superstition or a belief system through religion. Becoming completely lost to future academics, the spiritual sciences had in essence become apocryphal sciences which naturally drove these sciences still further underground.

It has been repeatedly recorded by those looking to decry the merits of these sciences that astrology for example was increasingly found unreliable and wanting. As it turns out, this was because the intricacies of operation to accurately determine a chart and the mysteries they contained were increasingly far more profound, complex and distant for the majority to now understand. Their inexperience in constructing and interpreting charts led to an impatience of how the system worked that goes way beyond the integrity of the system itself. Their inability to take the time necessary to involve themselves and employ the ancient sciences in the ways they were designed would eventually see them become labelled as 'inexact science's'. They reinforced their concerns quite forcibly by authoritatively stating astrology and any natural science was a pseudoscience and not within their remit. This is all crucial to our present understanding. The likes of their forcible tone had not been seen since an initial outward perception of radicalisation and suppression of the natural sciences by a Catholic Church shaping its own remit in the Roman period.

**Radicalisation**

Empirical science now excluded those elements no longer fitting its new remit and Darwin was also about to shake things up through the publication of his theory of evolution in 1859. The church absorbed his findings and realising its potential gravity left creation for the laity to decide.

The change in emphasis and the reliance on the esoteric disciplines all but gone, thousands of years of study and wisdom were now relegated to superstition and conjecture. However, it never disappeared. While the mainstay of the academic community was committed in focusing all their attention on the physical quantification of the physical universe, the church and esoteric organisations retained a unification of the spiritual and esoteric sciences in their universal enquiry of reality. It must also be realised that most of Europe were still religious. Likewise, even though this scientific model was now firmly rooted as the only science the West would come to recognise and trust, it would create a void in human understanding when it came to the nature of self and of nature of life and death. The public came to have many questions this populist science was never created to answer, and its antithesis through Christian doctrine with its binary heaven and hell ethos was increasingly found to be wanting in many areas it appeared only the church hierarchy were deemed as being privy to. There was no middle ground. This void led to the creation of another movement which offered a partial and important resolution as a variation to what magicians had been preoccupying themselves with for thousands of years…

## Spiritualism

Eleven years before Darwin's theory in 1848, spiritualism came to us through the Fox sisters in New York. It rapidly spread across America and before long the popularity of what they were doing found itself on the shores of Britain and Europe.

As with anything new, spiritualism carried with it a mix of acceptance and rejection at the time, and invited more extreme out of touch factions of the church in the States to decry it as witchcraft and talking with the dead as Necromancy. A popular notion extending through horror films.

The popularity of spiritualism reached a height during the American Civil War and again with the Great War of 1914-18, which coincided with Spanish Flu and killed more than those killed during the war itself. With so many losing their lives mediumship had entered the commercial mainstream, and anything popular will always attract elements of fraudulence to cash in on the success of the fashion or trend of the day, no matter its involvement. Mediumship was hijacked by those looking to exploit its initial integrity and would become a feeding ground for those looking to cash in on the grief of widows.

There were approximately one million mediums/fraudsters in the State alone during this period. One of the fraudulent mediums is someone you will be familiar with - Harry Houdini. His career began as a stage medium, communicating messages from beyond the grave to unsuspecting audiences as part of his early 'medicine shows'. His partner and wife would be in the audience during the shows relaying information to him through a code they worked out between them. He then switched to escapology.

He always believed in the paranormal and went onto regret his early exploits. An unlikely partnership was then forged between Harry Houdini and Sir Arthur Conan Doyle, creator of Sherlock Holmes. Doyle was a firm partisan of the paranormal and spiritualism. He was also a member of the SPR. This is the Society for Psychical Research in London, created to investigate and correlate global paranormal phenomena in 1882.

Both Houdini and Doyle devoted a large part of their lives to its investigation. Their motivation was to preserve the integrity of genuine mediums while protecting the public from would be charlatans. Houdini knew all the tricks charlatans got up to, after all he had been one himself, and exposed as many as he could while travelling across America on his escapology tours. With him decrying mediums, to the physical scientific community he was their witch finder general. As it turned out, he was also considered the same for the spiritualist movement as they too looked to expose the seemingly never ending supply of fraudulent mediums looking to exploit those grieving.

Houdini and Doyle were hardly ever out of the press in their respective countries for this reason, as well as for their own public engagements through their respective fields. The publicity gained by the exposé of fraudsters, especially through Houdini, saw a high profile that would both taint the profession in the eyes of those who didn't believe, and intrigue those who did. With science believing it was all a hoax, they not surprisingly relished what Houdini was doing. He gained a huge amount coverage in his task and it all depended on how it was reported. In one sense he inadvertently accelerated the misconceived perception for some that mediumship was a complete hoax. This led to further mistrust for the validity of the paranormal in general, but only in certain quarters as the publicity also had the opposite effect. The popularity of mediumship just grew through the publicity it gained as there was an understanding that not every medium was fraudulent, it just took a while to work out which was which.

Houdini and Doyle met each other and worked together in the States and England. They visited homes and spiritual parlours and exposed many fraudulent mediums of their day. Their exposés did nothing to quall the open minds they had of its reality, and following the death of Houdini's mother, he had paranormal experiences which he would never reveal.

Houdini famously said his greatest escape would be to come back after he died and communicate from the afterlife. There was a secret code I mentioned which only he and his wife Bess knew. This is the code they had employed in their early days to gather details of those in the audience when he was a stage medium, and no one else ever knew it. Following his death, Bess offered $10,000 to anyone who could help her contact her husband. This was the same amount Houdini had offered for anyone to come forward with proof of mediumship while he was still alive. That was a great deal of money at the time and probably comparable to James Randi, a stage magician who would follow suit later in the 20th century by offering $1 million for the same.

A medium called Arthur Ford contacted Bess in 1928 that his spiritualist group had made contact with Houdini's mother and Houdini himself through his spirit guide called Fletcher. He said that his mother had given information in code relating to Bess and Houdini. The message from Houdini's mother read:

ROSABELLE ** ANSWER TELL ** PRAY ** ANSWER ** LOOK ** TELL ANSWER ** ANSWER ** TELL

Ford then recorded what Houdini had said to them: "He wants this message signed in ink by each one present. He says the code [to break the above coded message] is known only to him and to his wife, and that no one on earth but those two know it. He says there is no danger on that score, and that she must make it public. Announcement must come from her. You are nothing more than agents. He says that when this comes through there will be a veritable storm, that many will seek to destroy her and she will be accused of everything that is not good, but she is honest enough to keep the pact which they repeated over and over before his death. He says, 'I know that she will be happy, because neither of us believed it would be possible.'"

**This is the cypher for the code known only to Houdini and Bess and given to Ford through his spirit guide Fletcher:**

| 1. Pray = | A | | 6. Please = | F |
|---|---|---|---|---|
| 2. Answer = | B | | 7. Speak = | G |
| 3. Say = | C | | 8. Quickly = | H |
| 4. Now = | D | | 9. Look = | I |
| 5. Tell = | E | | 10. Be quick = | J |

**K** is then Pray, **L** is then Answer and so forth.

The message was passed to Bess. She affirmed it as genuine.

**The message from Houdini to Bess by the same method:**
**– Houdini - Fletcher – Ford – Bess:**

| Answer = | **B** |
|---|---|
| Tell = | **E** |
| Pray, answer (1 and 2) = | **L** |
| Look = | **I** |
| Tell = | **E** |
| Answer, answer (2 and 3) = | **V** |
| Tell = | **E** |

The code when deciphered read:

**B E L I E V E**

The 'veritable storm' Houdini in spirit had communicated to the mediums of what would happen – did happen. Sceptics from all quarters were furious and spat more feathers than found on a flock of birds. They used everything at their disposal to try and discredit Ford and Bess – Houdini had proven survival in the afterlife, yet the sceptics could not come to terms with this at all. Maintaining the validity of what had transpired, both Bess and Ford would eventually die stronger for their convictions.

Sir Arthur Conan Doyle met Ford when he came to Britain. The conclusion of Doyle and other prominent members of the SPR was that he was genuine. Ford for his part never took the $10,000 offered by Bess even though it was now his and it was a great deal of money. The $1 million offered by James Randi was never claimed. Those who did come forward were far from the calibre and integrity of Ford and a great many other mediums who would rarely charge for their services.

### The Switch

Physical science had now become the dominant science of the West. Being created as a model to quantify the physical universe alone, it was never designed in any shape, way or form to encroach on the spiritual, the esoteric or the paranormal. It completely broke away from these areas of study and exploration, not because of what these other sciences represented, but because of the potential imposition by the church on physical discoveries when met with public gaze. So logically, within the empirical scientific model the spiritual and the paranormal does not exist. This premise had now evolved. During the industrial and scientific revolution from the

Victorian age through to the 1920s discoveries were being made in scientific and technological circles that were improving people's physical lives. Major breakthroughs were running concurrently with a thirst for the spiritual, but with the popularity of mediumship being overshadowed by fraudulent mediums taking the stage it gave the scientific community plenty of ammunition to decry the whole movement. It then became easier for the layman to assume that if science says it does not exist, then it does not exist full stop, not that it just does not exist within the remit of the empirical scientific model. Academics should have clarified this misunderstanding, but with new generations believing their science to be the only science, they were equally unaware of their own fabrication. They believed themselves, then, as they do now that the paranormal was and is fiction.

With this premise being encouraged through fiction as fiction, it is the reason why the populist Western assumption for it not existing has stuck as a conditioned misconception, a misguided belief or knee jerk opinion to this day. That is how and why from our earliest days, like the girl who left the review, we have been weaned and conditioned into *believing* the paranormal is the stuff of fiction, make-believe, the product of an overactive imagination or there has to be a physical cause. You get the picture, but the reality again is the opposite. It is a belief to think it is fiction, which has been reinforced through the fraudulent element, the mountain of fictional books, horror films, dramas and sensationalised documentaries having grown out of a fallacy, all endorsed and reinforced by both the media and empirical science over recent years.

Science conveys important research in a great many fields, the questioning and long overdue disclosure here is not to the legitimacy, integrity or value of the scientific system itself, it is the boundaries set by its remit that dictates its methodology then translating to public opinion that is the issue or stagnating force here when it comes to the spiritual or paranormal.

Our desire for change or for something new is often translated as progress, but not in the present context. Their physical adherence has blinkered and dulled the mindset of the West by negating and excluding great chunks of reality that everyone once took for granted as valid aspects of reality and predominantly still do in the East. You see, there are vast areas of exploration to be had, but when exploration is restricted, decried or negated through its own model, it denies the enquiring mind a chance to develop an understanding beyond the doctrine of its own controlled parameters. Empirical science currently looks to decry over 200 topics concerning different aspects of reality alone as 'pseudoscience's', including the paranormal and alternative medicine having developed over thousands of years in the East because they do not fit the remit of their model.

I saw a cartoon a few years ago that sums it all up. A doctor is seated at his desk scratching his head, a man stands in front of him. The doctor says "We have tried everything we can and I'm afraid there is nothing more science can do for you, so we are going to have to refer you to an alternative medical practitioner who has a 98% success rate".

Is there any wonder that for everything empirical science has created and achieved it has left many unanswered questions about the nature of reality, of existence and of the self? How many subjects dealing with aspects of reality do they need to reject before they realise their model is completely inadequate if they are looking to determine *everything* in the universe? And that the physical only forms part of the universal equation. How far does it all have to go when there are still scientific factions out there who do not acknowledge psychology as a science for example? They use their distain to discredit these subjects, but why should the paranormal, psychology or for that matter any field of study be dependent on an empirical scientific model created to specifically quantify the physical aspects of reality for their acceptance, or for them to be known, that they even exist or that they work?

We have been brought up to trust in physical science, but it is not the only scientific model, it is however, the only bully in the room. An accolade once reserved for the church. Science has now taken over this mantle as its own religion in its role of what is and what is and what is not accepted or permissible as valid exploration by discrediting the same. These were the very reasons physical science broke away from the church in the first place. History always repeats itself and hypocrisy never dies.

**The promotion of a fallacy through perpetual conditioning**

Taking on board the scientific stance, there is no shortage of those looking to qualify paranormal phenomena as not existing outside a fictional frame. Add in a whole plethora of potential psychological factors representative of exceptions to the rule and we have quite a collection of surrogates for its dismissal. Not least the power of suggestion in its many forms and various media avenues feeding the populist elements of opinion as their own stereotypical endorsements. These cannot be ruled out of course, but to use these as qualifications for a blanket dismissal is surely at best naïve.

When it comes to the subject of the paranormal, the power of suggestion is the most powerful tool in our armoury for distorting our understanding of reality. For the paranormal it connects with two opposing forces. One is suggestion producing expectation, excitement, placebo, and fear which I mentioned earlier in this volume with regards to Enfield and elaborated upon further through p.154. The other is through the unwitting perpetuation of conditioned misinformation about the paranormal to an endless supply of emerging generations. The cycle begins in our formative years when we naturally accept what we are told by our peers and teachers. No matter the validity there is a blind acceptance and believing the first thing we are told soon becomes second nature to us. It all becomes the foundation stones for our opinions to manifest as guiding lights shaping our understanding. It is all then qualified by others in our sphere of involvement also adhering to the same values, thoughts and opinions. It is where the herd mentality comes in, and by extension, when it is then reinforced through media influences it becomes all the more engrained and its acceptance normalised through particular spheres of influence. It is why fake news is so popular.

Truth has no dependency on how many people either adhere to truth or reject it. We live in our heads and our thirst for truth is an ideal we like to think we uphold, but we are hypocrites. Our thirst for truth is a wholly superficial one. As we get older our acceptance of facts is always dependent on what is comfortable for us to believe that fits with our existing ethos, not what is true. We believe what we want to believe and we hear what we want to hear, and like when we were young, if it comes from a source we trust, it comes with the same caveat of blind acceptance, regardless of where it resides in the increasing melee of fact and fiction. This selective acceptance of what we believe to be facts produces an insular outlook. It causes further distortions to successive generations as we pass it all on and tell them to accept what we are giving them. It once again brings us back to the power of suggestion from an early age and completes another cycle as they then grow up and do the same.

With no thought to question, we are quick to reject or ignore anything that goes against the grain of these pre-existing conditions. In defending a stance that has no more qualification than "my "parents told me, so it must be true", anything conflicting must then justify itself, no matter its validity or source, and that is only if we were open to listening to information contrary to our initial understanding.

Given all this, with us switching off to anything conflicting with our current understanding, it is easy to see why sceptics could not come to terms with Houdini and his mother communicating through Ford to Bess, despite Bess being the only living soul who knew the code, Through our lives we do the same and we will defend our stance in the face of opposition, no matter the logic of any counterargument being presented. We are what we think we know, and as we get older, to contradict our understanding of the paranormal for example that it is not fiction would be to challenge and question our existing beliefs and the statements of our peers, teachers, science, and the media. "They can't all be wrong!" we laughingly cry. Well, when it comes to the paranormal, now you know how and why they are all wrong. There are inherent dangers of course in this statement, the realisation of this has the potential to shake the very foundations of who you think you are to the core, and the majority are insecure enough as it is. It would mean having to challenge your opinions and your beliefs that form and shape your understanding, to then rethink and rebuild your understanding and so yourself from the ground up. This rarely happens as the mind can be as stubborn as it is hypocritical, but imagine for a moment what would happen if you did. The danger I mentioned is very real but the potential rewards are far greater. Its composure is one of personal liberation as it opens the door to us becoming free of the burdens of a mindset passed to us when we were young. This is coupled with a realisation that the mindset of who you think you are came to you from those around you – that your thoughts and beliefs were never your own, that you just inherited them and innocently accepted them accordingly. They then became your own thoughts, and you then pass them on to others. All the while reinforcing the viewpoint of a fallacy I spoke of, coming to us initially through what ironically became known as the age of enlightenment.

Conditioning operates on many levels, and takes on many forms. It can also come to us through propaganda, an idea, a movement, an adherence to a particular religion, a belief or belief system, or simply as an understanding that whatever you believe is beyond anything else of the same genre.

**MAGIC versus a movement for the lost**

Taking a literal stance with the teachings of the esoteric mysteries has always been a big mistake. This has also been apparent since the late 19th century when literature becoming more freely available partially opened the doors of wisdom to the curious with no inherent natural understanding of these underlying principles. It opened the floodgates of imaginative interpretation to the layman, filling the gaps of allegorical magical code as recorded within mystical treatise with misinterpretation that developed a literal stance through western society and pseudo spiritual factions overlaying their own beliefs.

The magician still exists, but everything that was traditionally under the umbrella of magic and the many practices of the magician have fragmented into individual elements of study and practices you will be familiar with: Communicating with the dead through necromancy is commonly known as mediumship and spiritualism; healing is commonly portrayed through Reiki and faith healing. Astrology is still thriving, although its usage is often stripped of its original depth and focuses more on pandering to the whims of the layman as a medium for fortune telling. One of the modern umbrellas for these subjects is the New Age movement, which I would call commercial spirituality. It incorporates many beliefs and faiths of a 'spiritual' nature, and a dumbed down version of mundane magic called 'results magic'. Where the background training of the magician, including the study, spiritual understanding, disciplines and necessary experience are bypassed in favour of an escapism from reality – not as a movement towards it. Without understanding the mechanics, spells are cast as quick placebo fixes to psychological problems and a movement towards a material improvement rather than affecting internal dynamics for spiritual advancement. They will never work. If they are perceived as working it is through suggestion and wanton misattribution, nothing more.

# Appendix 3.

## Paranormal Acknowledgement

"How can people hold such weird beliefs in phenomena that have repeatedly been thoroughly debunked by mainstream science? Especially the scientist - how can he be unaware of the mountains of research invalidating the claims for the existence of such phenomena? Apparently, he is also unaware that the postulated existence of such paranormal phenomena is utterly incompatible with all the known laws of physics. He must surely be unaware of all this, for if he were aware, he would be deeply embarrassed to be associated with such potentially reputation-damaging research and would fear no longer being taken seriously intellectually by his colleagues."

Ralph Lewis M.D.

**Mimicking paranormal behaviour**

There are those in empirical science who make it their mission to replicate phenomena in a bid to prove it all has a physical origin. Grants are given and academic papers are endlessly written on a multitude of theories. All are attributed through the mould of various analytical, psychological, neurological or chemical disciplines. 'Controlled' scientific tests are conducted, behavioural studies and psychological qualifications are included, and all as an attempt to find physical solutions for paranormal observations and experiences.

Sure, they are able to recreate the feeling of a presence for example in the confines of a laboratory setting using electromagnetism through electrodes on the head, or to demonstrate various replicative techniques through psychological/chemical means, but they do so in a very clinical and isolated manner. It seems what they are able to replicate is more suited to activity generated through everything I mention in PERL C1.

Because phenomena are observed in the physical does not necessitate a physical origin. In determining the cause, the mistake is looking to the recipient as the origin, but being a physical science, there is nothing else they have to go on.

Abstract attempts at mirroring paranormal behaviour through physical scientific replication does not mean the cause is the same as that recreated by its replication. While the replicative causes cannot be discounted, they will only be attributable to a minority of cases. For example, no amount of physical replication will recreate 16 people including myself hearing a scuffing noise and as we all look to its source a figure in black appears silently walking away from us down the path then just vanishes about 15 feet later. I made no suggestion of such phenomena being there, so no placebo, and everyone observed it, adults and children alike. The same with myself and the 10 students when we saw the nun, or the White Lady witnessed by myself and the 9 Austrians who didn't believe in ghosts. If they had gone into St Rule's Tower the day after spending 10 minutes trying to take a photo of a person in the top window to show it was not a ghost, it would have changed their lives when they looked up and realised the tower is hollow.

Scientific replication only covers part of the paranormal spectrum and their experiments are conducted with complete disregard for the nature of individual and collective circumstance surrounding the experience. For instance, it in no way follows that it can then be equally replicated given the scope and conditions on the ground under the circumstances with which phenomena is actually experienced. Also, the setting and the phenomena they look to replicate may include a few different aspects occurring at the same location at the same time. The odds against their replicative methods all being present at the same time also puts pay to their endeavours. Add in isolated independent corroborative testimony of the same through experiential replication forming localised and global patterns of phenomena that the recipient/s were totally unaware of and we have circumstances that wholly contravene any attempt at replication by physical, chemical and/or psychological means, not least its random adage.

Their approach is selective and restricted. Choosing to ignore anything they are unable to physically analyse and quantify is to completely ignore the body of overwhelming independent testimony and the shared understanding for its reality being presented at every turn. Yet their findings are used as a blanket qualification to decry all instances of that particular phenomenon. Their conclusions hold as much weight as a fraudulent medium being proof that mediumship does not exist. Yet it all serves is to both reinforce the belief of sceptics and frustrate those who know it does through experiencing its reality first-hand.

Paul Bloom wrote that most scientists as individuals 'prefer to be proven right, and are highly biased to see the evidence in whatever light most favours their preferred theory.' The term grasping at straws in desperation for anything other than what the paranormal is comes to mind. Science in its present form will never nail down anything that does not have its feet firmly planted in the physical universe. They were flawed from the outset in this regard. How can they look to disprove that which they don't believe exists in the first place by using a model created specifically for a physical only quantification to quantify a nonphysical source? Science has dispelled many myths and accelerated our understanding in a great many fields of research, but trying to fit everything into the inadequacies of their existing model is like trying to hammer square pegs into round holes. They will always be destined to abject failure. All they have demonstrated to themselves is how a few singular elements of physically perceived aspects of paranormal phenomenon can be physically replicated within their own remit. Despite the flawed premise of their enquiry and these obvious, if not selective omissions from their seemingly desperate endeavours, replicative success is nonetheless met with academic acclaim and praise from likeminded academic circles. This is nothing more than a continual and conditioned self-serving exercise to reinforce what they believe they already knew, and so strengthen their argument for its dismissal. It has more the hallmarks of techniques in tactical analysis you would learn if you were looking to become a politician than a serious and genuine enquirer into the nature of reality.

**Occam's Razor**

Those not willing to listen or comprehend anything associated with the paranormal reminds me of something Dr David Hay Fleming wrote in 1897. He was a St Andrews Victorian historian and antiquarian. The greatest historian the town has known. He wrote a piece concerning the widespread belief that the Cathedral in St Andrews was demolished at the Reformation. He said: 'There is not a single scrap of contemporary evidence to prove that the cathedral was demolished at the Reformation. The ablest historians now acknowledge this, yet the old fable is repeated and perpetuated by the tongues and pens of those who are either too prejudiced to receive the truth, or too indolent to inquire into it.'[xxxvii]

Interestingly, empirical science uses Occam's razor to explain away the paranormal; 'the simplest solution is most likely the right one no matter how implausible.' This disclosure masks the hypocrisy. It is only after eliminating the ill-fitting

---

[xxxviixxxvii] Fleming, Dr. Hay LL.D: Handbook to St. Andrews and Neighbourhood. St. Andrews Citizen Office, 1897. p.53

theories of the plausible that the implausible becomes the only possible outcome, and the implausible is surely to a paranormal origin, but many are unwilling to acknowledge this one thought sitting at the back of their mind that would make complete sense of an experience. It doesn't explain the how or why to them, and neither it will given the stricture of their parameters, but it would give them a starting point as to the cause. A variation of this was penned by Sir Arthur Conan Doyle for Sherlock Holmes: 'When you have eliminated the impossible, whatever remains, however improbable, must be the truth.' Doyle knew the truth of this with regards to the paranormal. There is a logic associated with it that some scientists also agree with but will rarely publicly state or will be decried if they do.

**Mindset and Methodology**

I find it interesting as an observation that with having different groups on the same tours, rarely the twain appears to meet. It is rare for a sceptical group slipping through the net on a tour at the same time as another group eager to tell me their own personal experiences. When I mention nonfiction and the paranormal in the same breath a group can look at me like they have just lost their winning syndicate lottery ticket. Then on the next tour they are full of smiles like they have just found a winning ticket and want to tell me how they are going to spend it.

People often tell me their experiences before the start of a tour, and sometimes I ask those present if they can remember experiencing anything of a paranormal nature, or if they can remember anything they have put down to their imagination. The result is always a mixed bag, but one very recent tour stands out as a snapshot. One woman said "Definitely not!" which made me chuckle as I knew it was a kneejerk response rather than a qualified thoughtful statement. One of the women said the night before she had the bottom of her coat tugged on a tour of the Edinburgh Vaults when no one else was around.

While another said she heard a voice in her home, again when one was around. A gentleman said scratches appeared on his back. I jogged the memory of one on the tour when I spoke of imaginary friends. She said she had an imaginary friend called Peter when she was about four years old, and a gentleman who didn't think he had experienced anything later said he saw a ghost when young but put it down to his imagination. With these responses, the woman who denied experiencing anything became very attentive to what I had to say and really enjoyed it. Had everyone reflected her initial response, it would easily have set the tone of the tour to one of negativity and scepticism in what I was saying. Another example of this could be someone having a bad day, and if they display a deadpan reaction to my humour it gradually rubs off on others present until it feels like I am giving a tour to a collection of zombies fresh out of the morgue. It shows how much of an influence those around you can have on a subliminal level as a contagious attitude.

Those looking to decry the reality of the paranormal are unable to pass the stage of eternally debating the reality of anything beyond the physical, physiological or psychological through theory, speculation or dismissal. As I mentioned earlier, we like to think we want to know the truth. We like to think want to know facts. The truth is we live a hypocrisy. We will only accept as true what is comfortable for us to accept, anything else will be rejected, no matter the truth it contains. With this in mind, I always say on my tours, "I have never met anyone who thinks they have a closed mind, but I have met many who don't have an open mind." One woman on a tour replied "that is how it works is it!"

"Oh yes" I said. She then switched off whenever I explained aspects of phenomena and gave me a bad review.

From the days of Paracelsus, Johannes Kepler, Dr John Dee, Sir Francis Bacon, Robert Fludd, Giordano Bruno, Elias Ashmole and Sir Isaac Newton to present, there are prominent members of the scientific community who know and accept the reality of the paranormal and the spiritual. In the same way many in the hierarchies of the church share far more liberal theological and scientific views than the official line as perceived by the laity, and far more than what physical science will acknowledge. Don't forget, the predominance of the spiritual and esoteric studies of the church and esotericists come from far older sources not born out of religion or belief for their dependency to be met with understanding. Following on from what I mentioned earlier, modern science has forgotten this, and they have forgotten they are not the only science open to us. To ignore the merits of hundreds of subjects dealing with aspects of reality because they do not fit with the remit of their physical stance is to ignore the premise of what science originally set out to achieve and the real reasons they broke away from these other sciences in the first place.

They need to remember their past, and take a fresh look at the ancient sciences, and those seemingly apocryphal subjects they discarded as nothing more than forerunners of their 'modern science'. They will then realise what they discarded was more advanced in particular ways than they ever gave credit for. To do this in no way involves belief, faith or religion, and it never did, but it does require a mental framework open to greater possibilities away from this conditioned stance. This is the only way the populist western ideal will have a chance to evolve rather than stagnate through a blanket of conditioned responses, and replication negating the natural laws of universal operation. This is all especially important for future generations. Otherwise progression through a true understanding for a great many aspects of reality that could otherwise enhance our lives and give insight for deeper exploration will forever be missed.

As a starting point I would suggest physicists study Newton's alchemical and theological writings, and do so with an open mind. By doing so, there is a chance what they are looking for will come to them. The race is on!

**How many currently accept the paranormal as a reality?**

One of the keys before interviewing anyone about their thoughts on the paranormal is to take them out of the herd mentality of a group. The majority then become a lot more amenable and open in their own spiritual views and equally with the paranormal. Far more so than they would otherwise reveal, as many feel awkward in a group mentality and will not share their true thoughts on the matter for fear of ridicule, so the herd mentality is never reflective of what people really think, which in turn is also reflective of the generalities of western society as a whole. If anything, the herd mentality is only reflective of the alpha amongst them with the loudest voice reflecting a closed sceptical mind that often mirrors deep rooted insecurities. A common cause is experiencing something when young that terrified them, so they shut out any suggestion and switch off by putting up a wall or barrier to anything alluding to its existence. When I get them on their own, that is generally the case, but it often takes a degree of reflection for them to remember or indeed to admit and talk about it.

**Statistical analysis**

For statistical analysis on the subject, in China there is an acceptance of the co-existence of both the living and the deceased with at least 80% adhering to a spiritual understanding with only a small percentage having any dependency on religion or belief for the same to be met with acceptance. In China its reality is just a given. For religion, Pew Research Centre statistics, 2015 place the global figure of those who believe in God at 84%. This also complies with an article for The Guardian in 2018 which stated: 'In the US, a survey of scientists in 2009 found they were roughly half as likely as the general public to believe in God or a higher power. One in three scientists said they believed in God [so around 33% in-house] compared with 83% of the general population. Just under half the scientists polled said they had no religious affiliation, compared with only 17% of the public.

Jennifer Wiseman, a Christian astrophysicist and director of Dialogue on Science, Ethics and Religion, a programme of the American Association for the Advancement of Science, told ABC News that science was a "wonderful tool for understanding the physical universe" but religious belief provides answers to bigger philosophical questions in life. "We are physically connected to the universe and I think we have a deeper connection as well." ' She was refreshingly on the right track, but it is bigger and deeper than that confined by the parameters of religious belief.

The figure of 80% is also reflected in the UK. For the paranormal, a study by VoucherCodesPro in 2015 found 82% believe in the paranormal, with 31% having seen a ghost or felt a presence. Other poles put this figure in the UK between 68% and 80% believing they have had a paranormal experience, and in 2018, OnePoll in the US on behalf of Groupon found 60% of Americans believe they have seen a ghost.

I did like Mark Suster's bid for statistical irony when he said as a light hearted quip that "73.6% of statistics are made up" as a slant on Disraeli's comment of 'lies, damned lies and statistics', so I thought I would take a look at poles with the lowest statistics for those believing in the paranormal and found YouGov in the UK gave 39% for those believing a house can be haunted by some kind of supernatural being and 34% believing in ghosts, so, while there can be a differentiated distinction between 'some kind of supernatural being' and a ghost? The potential distinction is far from being common knowledge, so I don't know why they would make a distinction, other than maybe some believing a supernatural being to be real and 5% believing the specific terminology 'ghost' as being fiction, which is more than possible, but their figure is a lot lower than the global averages. Another YouGov pole for the UK says 43% believe in God or a higher power, but when it comes to spiritual beliefs not necessarily adhering to an organised religion the figure by Christian think tank Theos had '77% in the UK as believing some things could not be explained by science or any other means.' The "any other means" is where I come in as I hope you have found I can explain it all. It should be obvious by now why science can't explain it, and hopefully why once again populist perception would dictate the same.

As you can see there is quite a variation in statistics which is dependent on the poll being taken with variables through demographics and how the polls are taken. YouGov say: "Our incentive system is designed to attract people who are not interested in the subject in question, as well as those who are passionate about it." The thing is, I am not quite sure how they can determine how many are or are not interested in a subject before they conduct a survey? and if this were the case surely the result would be 50/50 when it came to the paranormal.

I used to think the ratio for the UK and the US averaged at an even split of 40/40 for and against the realty of the paranormal with the remaining 20% not sure. It is very clean cut and easy to remember, but given the various poles it is incorrect. The actual figure does seem to reflect the global stance of 80% adhering to some form of spiritual understanding with this same figure being reflected in those believing in the paranormal, which is what you would expect. The 20% either being not sure or sceptical, is the figure I mentioned on the tour where the girl gave her review.

None of this weakens the merits of science, far from it, a survey by The British Social Attitudes in 2019 had 85% in the UK 'trusting university scientists "to do their work with the intention of benefitting the public". However, when it comes to the spiritual and the paranormal it is a different matter, with only a percentage of that 20% agreeing with science in their dismissal of its reality. This again is reflective of the 80% adhering to some form of spiritual understanding. As I demonstrated earlier, their model was never designed to incorporate its reality. Their dismissive stance was never qualified for anything more than in trying to discredit the spiritual/esoteric sciences and ergo the paranormal to bolster the value of their own 'new science'.

**The Conclusion**

The word paranormal comes from 'para' meaning in this instance 'apart from', and 'normal' meaning 'conforming to a typical or expected standard', so paranormal means 'set apart from the normal'. The word normal carries with it many variables. Here in the UK we could think traveling abroad as being normal by any standard of measure, but according to the US State Department only 42% of Americans have passports. In 1990 it was only 4%. So, what is accepted or perceived as normal can have different geographical connotations. The same with governmental laws and morality. What is accepted as 'normal' in one culture is often alien to another.

When looking at the overall global poles, the conclusion for the belief in the spiritual at 80% means it is an accepted or normal part of our reality, and the paranormal, far from being set apart from 'normal', turns out to be a normal aspects of our reality we just don't tend to experience very often. Asia has always been where we also were also for thousands of years, which is again contrary to populist assumptions on the matter, which you will have gathered comes to us from an academic minority whose authority we are expected to trust when we are looking to understand the reality around us.

**Summing up**

Both spirituality and the paranormal are widespread across the world, and there is a general acceptance that science is trusted for its physical research, but given these poles, neither the spiritual nor the paranormal require religious or scientific sanction for them to be accepted aspects of our reality. It shows how the integrity of either the beliefs or understanding of the majority differs from populist perception in believing it to be fiction, a premise driven through media and science etc. It also shows how despite all the odds of the dismissive tone by particular scientists, peers and teachers following this populist 'authoritative' mantra that 'ghosts do not exist', that the general public have successfully ignored them all, which will come as an unexpected surprise, not least because far from it being a minority who accept its reality, it is they who form the minority in this regard in their blanket conditions and more often scientific, atheistic, and/or humanist dismissal.

For the rest of us, well, we have more in common with each other than we realise or I imagine would ever have suspected. Sweep aside clinical indoctrination and you find the physical façade masks something a lot deeper. We are a spiritual species and we are all part of a reality beyond belief.

[1] Photo courtesy of D. C. Thomson & Co. Ltd, Dundee.

[2] *52 Weeks of Historical How-To's, Week 1: Special Collections Ghost tour*, https://special-collections.wp.st-andrews.ac.uk/2013/10/31/special-collections-ghost-tour/

[3] Jung, C. G. *On Synchronicity*, 1951

[4] Spottiswood, John, Archbishop of St Andrews, from *The History of the Church of Scotland*, 1855, published by the Bannatyne Club, p.44

[5] Fleming, Dr Hay, *St Andrews Standard Guide*, J & G. Innes., St Andrews Citizen Office. This edition reprinted 1949, p.66

[6] Underwood, Peter: *Gazetteer of Scottish Ghosts,* Harper Collins, 1973, p.169

[7] Lamont, Stewart, *Is Anybody There,* Mainstream Publishing, 1980, pp.38-39

[8] Lucas, Steven, *Counselling. Psychology Definition Of The Week: Selective Perception.* 2009

[9] Griffin, Ricky.W, *Fundamentals of Management*, Cengage Learning, 2013, p. 259.

[10] Underwood, Peter: *Gazetteer of Scottish Ghosts,* Fontana/Collin, 1973, p.169

[11] Stevenson, Katie, Brown, Michael, Ed. *Medieval St Andrews: Church, Cult, City*, Boydell and Brewer, 2017, p.129

[12] Photo courtesy of the University of St Andrews Libraries and Museums, Scrapbook of W T Linskill 1926-1928, section 2, p.17, ms38078/1.

[13] Underwood, Peter: *Gazetteer of Scottish Ghosts,* Fontana/Collin, 1973, p.169

[14] Green, Andrew, M.: *Ghosts of Today,* Kaye & Ward, 1980

[15] *thehazeltree.co.uk/2014/10/17/ghosts-of-st-andrews/*

[16] Wordsworth, J, *St Mary of the Rock, St Andrews, Fife, in* Youngs, S M & Clark, J (eds) 'Medieval Britain in 1982,' *Medieval Archaeology* (1982), p.219

[17] Ibid
[18] Lunt, Wiley and Sons, 2011
[19] Alexander, Michael, *The Courier*, D.C.Thompson, 15th April, 2017
[20] Lyon, The Rev, Charles Jobson, *History of St. Andrews.* Vol. 2, William Tait; Edinburgh, 1843, pp.155-156 and Fleming, Dr. Hay, *Handbook to St. Andrews and Neighbourhood*, New Edition, St. Andrews Citizen Office; St. Andrews, 1902. p.60
[21] Linskill, W. T, *St. Andrews Citizen*, 29th Jan 1927. p.3
[22] University of St Andrews Library, ID JHW-C-195, Wilson, Dr, John, Hardie, (1858 - 1920), Cellardyke, Scotland, University of St Andrews (photographer)
[23] Leighton, John, M, *History of the County of Fife*, 1811
[24] Stevenson, Katie, Brown, Michael, Ed. *Medieval St Andrews: Church, Cult, City*, Boydell and Brewer, 2017, pp. 129-130,
[25] Linskill, William, Letter of correspondence to Bailie Hall, 1887, University of St Andrews, Special Collections, Scrapbook of St Andrews Antiuarian Society 1884-1905, ms38078/2, p.40
[26] http://www.orkneyjar.com/folklore/ghosts/skaillhouse.htm
[27] Green, Andrew, Website - Mystical World Wide Web – Article: *The unexplained explained.*
[28] Cook, Helen: *Scots Magazine. Haunted St. Andrews*, Nov 1978
[29] Wilkie, James, *Bygone Fife: From Culross to St. Andrews*, Blackwood; Edinburgh, 1931, pp.360-361
[30] Fleming, Dr Hay, *St Andrews Standard Guide*, J & G. Innes., St Andrews Citizen Office. This edition reprinted 1949, p.6
[31] Mackenzie, J, Moloney, C. J., *Medieval Development and the Cemetery of the Church of the Holy Trinity, Logies Lane, St Andrews*, TFA/3, 1991, pp.143-160
[32] Ibid
[33] Rees, T, Gordon, D, Matthews, A, *Excavations within the Graveyard of the Holy Trinity St Andrews*, TFJ 14, 2008, pp.56-68
[34] Lang, Theo, *The Kingdom of Fife*, 1951, Hodder & Stroughton; London, pp.200-201
[35] Kirk, Russell, *St. Andrews*, B. T. Batsford Ltd, 1954, pp.121-122
[36] Reid, Norman, *The StAndard*, Issue 13, March 2008, pp.38-39, https://news.st-andrews.ac.uk/wp-content/uploads/standard/StAndard_issue13.pdf
[37] Ibid, pp.38-39
[38] *A Royal Foundation: 400 Years of the King James Library*, https://arts.st-andrews.ac.uk/digitalhumanities/exhibitions/king-james/artefactsandcuriosities.shtml
[39] Reid, Norman, *The StAndard*, Issue 13, March 2008, pp.38-39

[40] Ibid, pp.38-39
[41] Lewis, Roy Harley, *Theatre Ghosts,* David & Charles, 1988
[42] St Andrews University School of Divinity website
[43] Kirk, Russell, *St. Andrews*, B. T. Batsford Ltd, 1954, p.88
[44] Wilkie, James, *Bygone Fife, From Culross to St. Andrews*, Blackwood; Edinburgh, 1931, pp.354-355
[45] Ibid
[46] Ibid
[47] Ibid
[48] Cant, Ronald, *The University of St Andrews: A short history* (3rd edition, Dundee, 1992), pp.35-36
[49] Henry, David, F.S.A. Scot: *Knights of St. John with other Mediaeval Institutions and their Buildings in St Andrews.* W. C. Henderson. K. Son, University Press, 1912, p.183
[50] Ibid
[51] Ibid
[52] Parker, Geoffrey, *The Kirk by Law Established*, Aberdeen, 1988, p.24
[53] Lyon, The Rev, Charles Jobson, *History of St. Andrews.* Vol. II, William Tait; Edinburgh, 1843, pp.398-9 (From private letters addressed to Mr Wodrow)
[54] Ibid
[55] Roger, Charles, *History of St Andrews*, Adam & Charles Black, 1849, p.69
[56] Fife and Kinross Sheet IX.SE (includes: St Andrews and St Leonards) Publication date: 1895. Date revised: 1893.
[57] Allan, G.E. D.Sc. (1904) VI. *On the magnetism of basalt and the magnetic behaviour of basaltic bars when heated in air*, The London, Edinburgh, and Dublin Philosophical Magazine and Journal of Science, 7:37, p.45, p.61
[58] Lyon, Rev, C. J: *History of St Andrews*, 1838, p.194. The Edinburgh Printing and Publishing Co.
[59] Sibbald, Robert, *History of Fife and Kinross*, 1710, pp. 348-349
[60] Lyon, Rev, C. J: *History of St Andrews*, 1838, p.194. The Edinburgh Printing and Publishing Co.
[61] Sibbald, Robert, *History of Fife and Kinross*, 1710, pp. 348-349
[62] Brewster, Sir David, *The stereoscope; its history, theory, and construction, with its application to the fine and useful arts and to education.* London, J. Murray, 1856, p.205
[63] Ibid
[64] Wilkie, James, *Bygone Fife, From Culross to St. Andrews,* Blackwood; Edinburgh, 1931, pp.359-360

[65] *The StAndard*, University of St. Andrews Staff Magazine, Issue 17, Philippa Dunn, November 2009. pp.18-19. Also available as a PDF online:https://www.st-andrews.ac.uk/media/press-office/standard/StAndard-Issue17.pdf

[66] Savile, Rev. Bourchier Wrey, *Apparitions: A Narrative of Facts*, Longmans and Co, London, 1874, pp. 146-148

[67] Ibid: Gardiner MD, W.T, *A note on spectral illusions and other warnings in a case of Apoplexy; with reference to the fatal illness of the of Eglington*, p.336

[68] Barker, George Fisher Russell, *Dictionary of National Biography, 1885-1900, Volume 38*, p.303

[69] Savile, Rev. Bourchier Wrey, *Apparitions: A Narrative of Facts*, Longmans and Co, London, 1874: Gardiner MD, W.T, *A note on spectral illusions and other warnings in a case of Apoplexy; with reference to the fatal illness of the of Eglington*, p.334

[70] Henderson, William, *Notes on the Folklore of the Northern counties of England and the Borders*, Longmans, Green and Co, 1866, London, p.294

[71] Legge, F, The National Review, Divination in the Seventeenth Century, Vol. 13, Iss. 73, London, 1889, p.92

[72] Popp, Nathan Alan, *Expressions of power: Queen Christina of Sweden and patronage in Baroque Europe*, PhD (Doctor of Philosophy) thesis, University of Iowa, 2015. https://doi.org/10.17077/etd.l17f2yt2
, pp.181-5

[73] Popp, Nathan Alan, *Expressions of power: Queen Christina of Sweden and patronage in Baroque Europe*, PhD (Doctor of Philosophy) thesis, University of Iowa, 2015. https://doi.org/10.17077/etd.l17f2yt2
, pp.110

[74] Buckley, Veronica, *Christina Queen of Sweden: The Restless Life of a European Eccentric*, New York and London: Harper Collins Publishers, 2004

[75] Keynes, John Maynard, *Newton, the Man,* **1946,** https://mathshistory.st-andrews.ac.uk/Extras/Keynes_Newton/

[76] John Dee's Actions with Spirits, 22 December 1581 to 23 May 1583 by Christopher Lionel in partial fulfilment for the degree of Doctor of Philosophy at the University of Birmingham, October 1981.

[77] Ibid.

[78] Ibid

[79] Keynes, John Maynard, *Newton, the Man,* **1946,** https://mathshistory.st-andrews.ac.uk/Extras/Keynes_Newton/

[80] Iliffe, Rob, *Priest of Nature: The Religious Worlds of Isaac Newton,* Oxford University Press, 2017

[81] Hunter, Michael, *Boyle Studies: Aspects of the Life and Thought of Robert Boyle (1627-91),* Ashgate Publishing, 2015, p.24

# References

Lightning Source UK Ltd.
Milton Keynes UK
UKHW011545270921
391258UK00003B/73